INTRODUCTION.

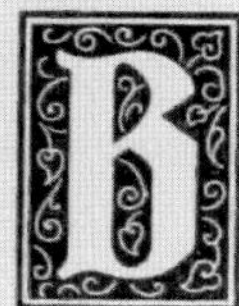Y way of introduction the writer desires to state that "Seattle and the Orient" is published to act as an opening wedge into a country up to this time very little known to people residing upon Puget Sound. It is for the purpose of introducing ourselves to the people doing business in Siberia, China, Japan, the China Archipelago, the Philippines and Hawaii, and to eventually open a way by which closer trade relations may be promoted, that this book has been published. The subjects treated are in no instance overdrawn, but are secured by direct contact with the people interested, and are plain matter of fact statements of affairs as they exist in Seattle and in Western Washington. The illustrations shown are the best procurable, and will afford the reader a fair idea of what can be found in the metropolis of America's great Mediterranean. Such a showing as the following pages make cannot help but impress even the most casual observer that Seattle has a future before it of very great magnitude. Unquestionably it is destined to become the largest city upon the Pacific Coast. It has every material advantage to make it so; it has almost every imaginable resource upon which to draw for support; it is the center of one of the greatest lumbering sections in the world; it has inexhaustible coal mines; it is the central point from which the gold fields of Alaska and the British Northwest Territory are reached; it is practically the center of all the mineral wealth of the Northwest; and it is moreover the natural geographical entrepot for the great Oriental markets, a fact which in time will make it the greatest shipping port in the United States. An attempt has been made to enumerate its varied resources in succeeding pages, and a story has been told which will prove both interesting and instructive. It has been the aim of the writer to take up the industrial side of Seattle and portray a condition as near the actual as possible. The information in all cases has been received from direct interviews by those actively engaged. The same thing can be said of its wholesale and jobbing houses, and of its banking interests and financial affairs. Very great care has been exercised in all cases to avoid anything which

would look like exaggeration, and it is hoped that whoever may peruse this volume may form a pleasing opinion of it.

In handling the matter which goes to make up this book, the various subjects have been sub-divided and classed under appropriate headings, and the aim has been to make each article as pointed and as terse as possible. The pictures from which illustrations have been made have, in most instances, been taken expressly for this publication and are from subjects selected by the publisher. The Seattle Daily Times takes no little pride in being able to present to the public a volume of so much general merit as is possessed in this one. Were it not for the general enterprise of the people who make up its inhabitants, it would be impossible to make such a showing as has been made, but the Seattle spirit naturally predominates and the result shows for itself.

At no time in its history has Seattle grown so rapidly as it is growing now. New packing houses, new sawmills, machinery houses, planing mills, and other establishments that employ a greater or less number of men, are being built, and a general air of improvement prevails on all sides. The city as a municipality is not behind in the general march of improvement, for it has commenced on a very extensive scale very considerable street improvements and work of this character, all of which adds to the steadily advancing progress.

There can be no doubt but that Seattle will continue its steady growth for a great many years.

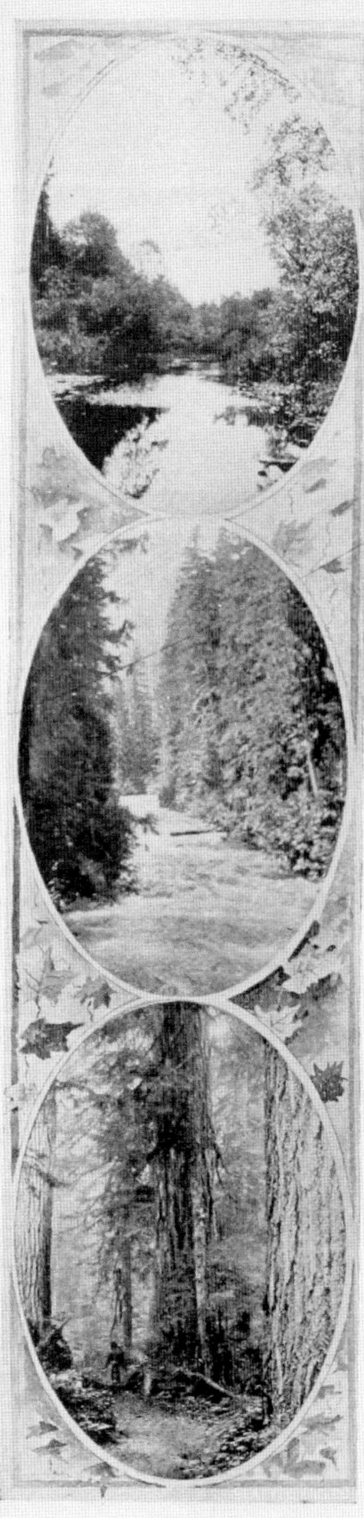

Seattle
...and the...
Orient.

Souvenir Edition.

The Seattle Daily Times

CONTAINING the past and present of Seattle, showing how very considerable its many manufacturing interests have become and the importance and standing of its wholesale trade. The range of subjects taken up embrace everything in relation to Seattle, from its location on Elliott Bay to its desirability as a residence city. Its Illustrations show its harbor, its shipping, its principal manufacturing concerns, wholesale houses, street scenes; also its parks, lakes and suburban lines.

The lumbering as carried on in Western Washington is given very particular attention and in addition to showing the large mills, many scenes of logging camps are presented. The contents include Seattle's varied resources, from the virgin gold of Alaska to its coal mines near at home, from its fish supply to its farm products.

EDITED AND COMPILED BY

ALFRED D. BOWEN.

Published by
THE TIMES PRINTING CO.
Seattle, Wash., U. S. A.
1900.

PRICE 25 CENTS.

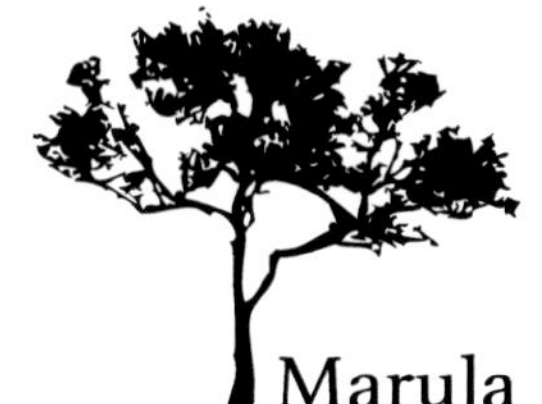

An imprint of Arcadia Publishing

Seattle and the Orient
Edited and compiled by Alfred D. Brown

A Marula Historical Reprint
Originally published in 1900

Published by Arcadia Publishing
Charleston SC

ISBN 978-0-7385-9483-5

Printed in the United States of America

For all general information contact Arcadia Publishing at:
Telephone 843-853-2070
Fax 843-853-0044
E-mail sales@arcadiapublishing.com
For customer service and orders:
Toll-Free 1-888-313-2665

Visit us on the Internet at www.arcadiapublishing.com

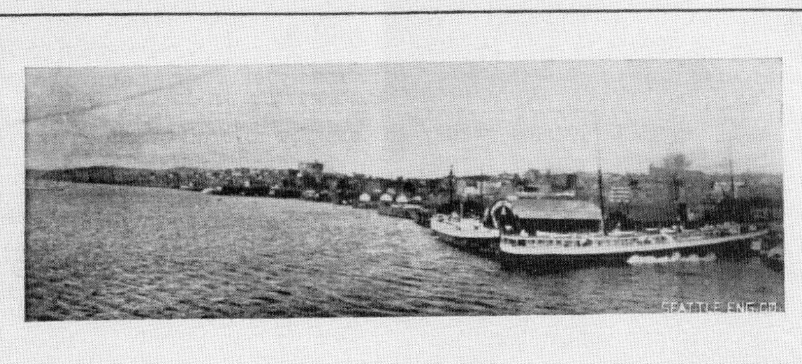

SEATTLE

ITS PAST, PRESENT AND FUTURE.

By ALDEN J. BLETHEN
Editor in Chief, Seattle Daily Times.

WHEN William Henry Seward, as Secretary of State for the United States of America, purchased Alaska in 1867—a territory containing nearly six hundred thousand square miles and extending from the Arctic Ocean to Dixon's Entrance, at 54 degrees and 40 minutes north latitude, where the boundary line between the United States and Canada should have been established—there was scarcely a hamlet on Elliott Bay, where now sits enthroned a magnificent young Giantess—the "Queen City of the Mediterranean" of the Pacific—"Seattle," with her one hundred thousand energetic, pushing, rushing, throbbing and enthusiastic people!

In 1869, when this same great statesman determined to visit the southern portion of the mighty domain wherein his prophetic vision had discovered untold wealth in mineral deposits, and had passed through Seattle on his way, there were not a dozen houses, only a few shops, and a very common "landing" to be found at "the port" named after the leader of a great Indian tribe.

But in spite of the insignificance of the "hamlet," the obscurity of the "port," the paucity of population and the absence of all railway facilities, the former great Secretary went to Alaska—not by way of the Golden Gate, as many foolish men have since done, but by the way of Seattle—and the great American people as well as many foreigners are following suit today, for more than one hundred thousand gold miners have passed and repassed its gates since the discovery of gold in the Northwest Territory, and later in Southern Alaska, in the lower valleys of the Yukon and along the Bering Sea shore—especially at Cape Nome, Cape York and Cape Prince of Wales.

Even after Henry Villard had succeeded in driving the "golden spike" that completed a transcontinental railway line to the Pacific Coast—Seattle had but ten thousand people—but even then she had shipyards, foundries, machine shops, sawmills, lumber yards, breweries and manufactories of furniture, carriages, crackers, barrels, boxes, cigars and medicines.

The Seattle of 1900, however, not only has all those industries, multiplied and intensified a thousandfold, but she has increased her population "ten times" in the seventeen years which have intervened. To demonstrate the former point we need only point out the fact that there are four thousand firms engaged in business in this city, representing two hundred and fifty different lines of business—and that in many lines there is absolutely no competition, while in other lines competitors multiply and increase into the hundreds.

The Seattle of today is the commercial metropolis of Puget Sound—a great arm of the ocean, which extends up from Cape Flattery, through the Straits of Juan de Fuca to Olympia, the capital of the commonwealth, for a distance of three hundred miles—and has no rival either along this magnificent body of inland water, nor along the entire Coast—and with no possibility of any rival north of San Francisco, a thousand miles away to the South, in the next hundred years.

To understand what it means to be the metropolis of a commonwealth like Washington—both from the standpoint of commerce and population—one needs only to remember the immense possibilities of this great state when the products of the mines, the soil, the forests and the sea be taken into consideration.

The area of Washington represents sixty-nine thousand square miles—with a population of six hundred thousand souls. The state is divided into three great climatic belts and really has but two seasons—the "rainy" and the "dry"—wherein the thermometer rarely exceeds 70 above in summer nor 28 above in winter. On the Pacific Coast the rainfall frequently reaches one hundred and twenty-five inches per annum, while a fall of sixty-five inches occurs in the Puget Sound country and about fifteen inches in the great plateau lying between the Cascade Mountains and the Rockies, and known as "Eastern Washington."

When one considers that the mineral deposits of Northern and Eastern Washington—consisting of gold, silver, copper,lead and coal,are to be found in greater quantities and in richer veins than in any other state of the nation, he may begin to calculate the vastness of the wealth from these sources alone. In the judgment of experts, there are copper mines in the Cascades that will exceed the famous Anaconda mine of Montana, and gold and silver deposits to be found in the great counties of New Whatcom and Okanogan, which will eclipse the famous mines of Cripple Creek in Colorado.

In the matter of coal, in quantity the deposit is almost inexhaustible, and the quality is not equaled west of the coal fields of Pennsylvania. When one considers that Southern California has an excess of iron ore and no coal, while Washington has an abundance of coal, but little iron yet discovered, the opportunities for the opening up of great steel and iron manufactories in Seattle, by exchanging Washington coal for California iron ore, will be apparent, and one would scarcely dare to place a limit thereto.

Taking up the item of lumber—let the world gaze on these figures: The State of Washington has thirty-five counties—and in every one there is a great growth of timber yet uncut.

While some counties contain less than a "billion feet," these counties tell their own tales: Clallam, Snohomish and Whatcom over 25,000,000,000 each—Lewis 30,000,000,000—Jefferson 32,000,000,000, and Chehalis alone 39,000,000,000—making one grand aggregate in the entire thirty-five counties of the Commonwealth of "five hundred billion feet" of merchantable lumber! Who dares put a value to the timber interests of Washington? Lumber today may be worth $12 a thousand, but who will say what it will be worth in twenty-five years from today, when the timber interests of this great Commonwealth will be in full flow of commercial demand?

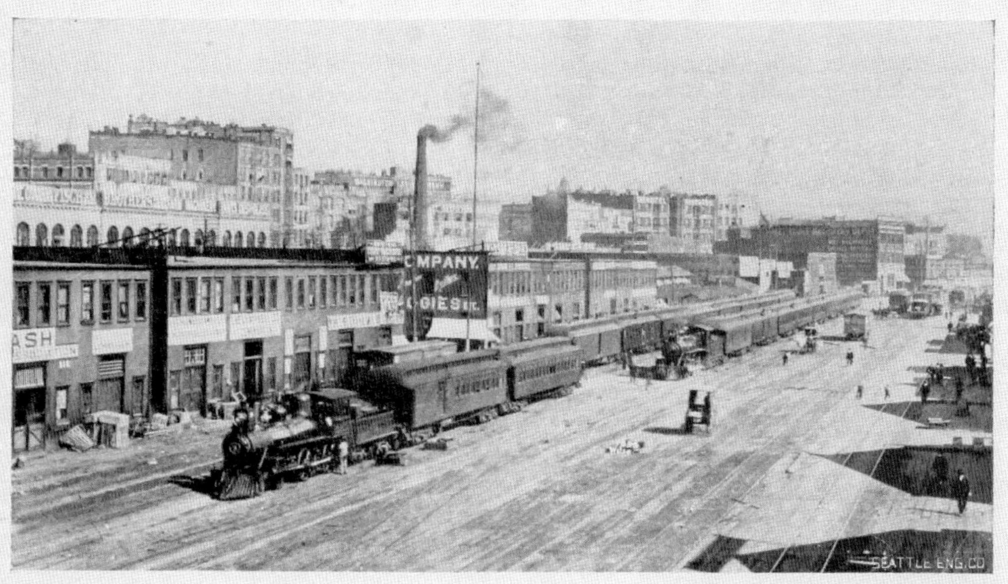

RAILROAD AVENUE.

It will not be out of place to say here briefly that a vast number of lumber mills have been erected and are in active operation throughout the Puget Sound country, and that the cut for 1899 reached the enormous figures of nearly "five billion" feet, in which were included more than 212,000,000 feet of timber and over 3,451,000,000 shingles.

Coming to the product of the soil of the great Commonwealth of Washington, there is probably no other state in the Union that touches it in diversification and quality when the fruit product be added to the agricultural. No such potatoes, squashes, melons, New England pumpkins, to say nothing of carrots, turnips and beets, were ever turned out of any soil—and when one comes to the farm gardening, involving strawberries, currants, gooseberries, raspberries, cherries, pears, plums and peaches, one may travel a million miles and never see the "quantities" nor taste "flavor" like that of the products of Washington.

Strawberries that grow as large as tomatoes in Eastern States, have the flavor of the field strawberry of New England. The peaches of the North

Yakima district, which is only a typical belt, lying between the great mountain ranges of the Cascades and the Rockies, have never been qualed upon the Pacific Coast. Michigan nor Massachusetts never exceeded Washington in the quality of her apples, nor came within a gunshot of her pears and plums.

We believe it to be no exaggeration to say that Washington furnishes opportunities for a population of ten millions of people—every one of whom could be actively employed, before her vast resources would be covered, and that it would take a thousand years to exhaust them all.

But it is not alone in the mines, where men dig for the precious metals—and that mineral which helps heat and light our homes and becomes a part of the power which makes our industries possible—but out of Puget Sound, the greatest inland sea of salt water bounded by any portion of the American continent, and along the shores of the Pacific Ocean, which forms the western boundary of the commonwealth, is to be found a never ending source of wealth—the "fishing industries" that have made both Sound and Coast famous throughout the world.

And it will be proper to state here that, because of the extraordinary temperature of the Pacific Ocean and the mountain streams in this latitude, the finest quality of fish which the oceans of the earth produce, are caught out of the fresh water streams and lakes of Washington and taken from Puget Sound and the Pacific Coast, lying within the limits and boundaries of this state.

In the fresh water streams may be found abundance of the speckled salmon trout—and from the salt water is obtained the halibut, the salmon, the cod, the mackerel, as well as a crab of great size and most delicious flavor, to say nothing of oysters which even rival the blue points of the Atlantic,—and from this great variety there was packed in the canneries of Washington alone last year, more than a "million cases" of salmon—and all were gathered within the short season of July, August and September, which represent the months in which these fishes "run."

Of the future of Seattle we consider ourselves wholly unable to speak. To an optimistic mind there opens up a vision of the future, ladened with a wealth of natural and artificial products, a golden harvest of metals, and a commercial trade with five hundred million people, who inhabit nations whose boundaries touch the other side of the Pacific waters, that are so startling in the commercial values which will represent them in the next fifty years, that to state what the probabilities really are would be to use sucb terms as would lead the ordinary reader to believe that the author had really "gone mad" on the future growth of this commonwealth, and the possibilities of its metropolitan city.

Therefore, suffice it to say, that if in the period intervening between 1848—when gold was first discovered in California—and its semi-centennial anniversary in 1898, there were taken from the bowels of the earth in that state more than a "thousand million of dollars," the indications are that more than three times that amount of the shining metal will be taken from Alaska and the State of Washington in the period of time that will elapse between 1900 and 1950.

Gold, to any considerable extent, was not really discovered in the Northwest Pacific country, bordering on the Arctic Ocean, until 1897—yet since that time more than "one hundred millions" of gold have been dug out of the earth in Southern Alaska and the Northwest Territory, whose center is

Dawson city, the valleys of the Yukon and along the Alaskan shores of Bering Sea—of which more than nineteen millions have been brought to the Government Assay Office in Seattle alone, within a period of eighteen months prior to September 1, 1899!

From all these evidences we do not believe that we shall prove to be a false prophet when we predict that before the year 1925 shall have been reached the population of Seattle will have passed the half millionth point, the Commonwealth as a whole the three millionth mark—and that the commercial trade from every point of the vast Pacific, including the Hawaiian Islands, the Philippine possessions, the mighty trade of the Alaskan Coast—combined with the trade of China, Japan, Korea and Russia—will all have aggregated a tonnage and a value that will place Seattle among all the cities of America next to New York as a commercial seaport.

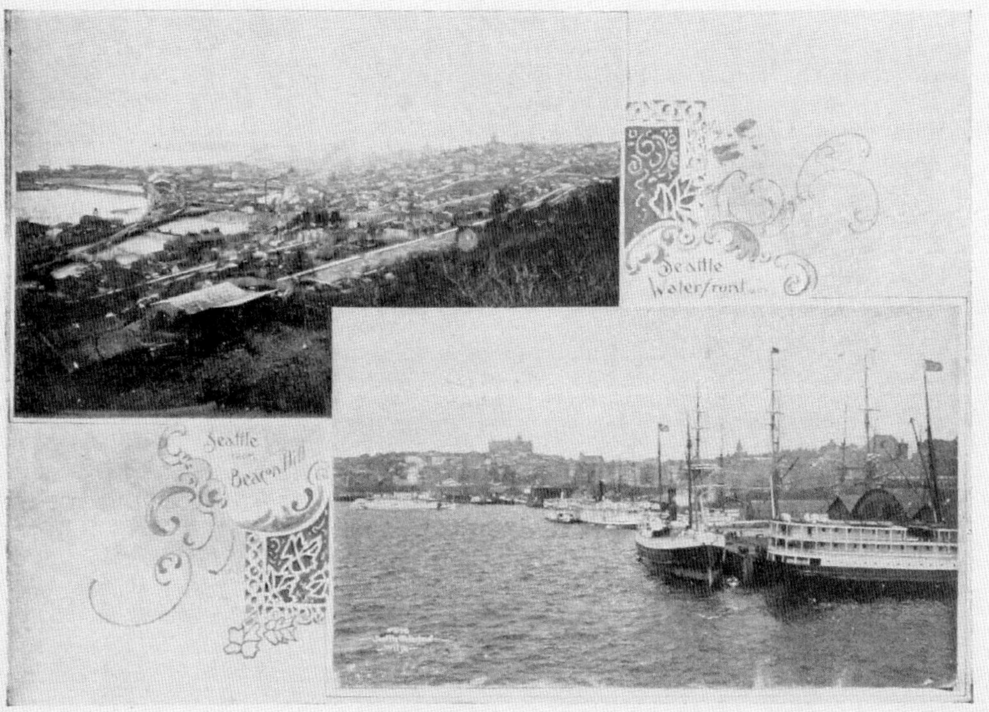

SOME VIEWS OF SEATTLE.

A BIT OF HISTORY.

Seattle is not an old town; in fact, in writing a bit of history regarding this phenomenally prosperous and flourishing city of the year 1900, one has only to look back fifty years to see an absolute wilderness on the spot where this city now stands. The first settlement made on Elliott Bay was in 1851. The first white man who settled here was D. T. Denny, who in September of that year located a claim on the east side of the bay, and in the spring of 1852 built a cabin and moved his family here. Among other pioneers who first buildt cabins and started a settlement in what is now Seattle were W. N. Bell, C. D. Boren, A. A. Denny and D. S. Maynard. W. N. Bell built a cabin on the site of Bell Town, now North Seattle; C. D. Boren built on the eminence afterwards known as Fort Decatur at the foot of Cherry Street; D. S. Maynard built his cabin near the site of the New England Hotel; while that of D. T. Denny was a mile and a half north of that occupied by the Bell family, or near where Kinnear Park is located today. Later in the same year H. L. Yesler and other settlers found their way here. These cabins were built after the usual fashion and consisted of fir logs covered with cedar shakes, and usually contained but one room. They were primitive in the extreme; but although primitive and rudely fashioned, they were none the less picturesque and afforded habitable homes for those hardy pioneers who had ventured much in opening up a new territory. In looking over the magnificent city that has since risen upon the site of those early homes, one can scarcely conceive of Seattle having been densely covered with an almost impenetrable forest less than fifty years ago. From 1852 until 1857 very little change occurred to give Seattle much importance as a coming metropolis, but beginning about 1857 it began to attract to itself quite a few settlers, and the next few years, following in quick succession, very considerable progress was made, until Seattle began to be spoken of as a village of some importance. However, 't was not until along in the latter part of the seventies that the town had reached over three thousand inhabitants. When Jay Cook began to point his great railroad enterprise to the West, the people of Seattle began to realize that their position on Puget Sound would eventually become one of importance. The people who cast their lot here in those and succeeding days have been well repaid for their perspicacity, and the faith which dominated every early citizen on Elliott Bay (and which took root at this period) has never wavered from that day to this, and the Seattle spirit, which stands for progress, and for united effort, is as thoroughly embedded today as at any time in its history. Because of its permeation in every strata of its business life Seattle has unaided and entirely free from all corporate influence, successfully forged to the front, until today it has absolutely no rival, and the day is not far distant when it will become the chief city on the Pacific Coast. Can any one question its great future when tney stop to think that this city of 90,000 inhabitants was a wilderness but forty-nine years ago? If such great progress has been made during that period, what will the next forty-nine years bring forth?

It might not be out of place in briefly speaking of the history of Seattle to state that the name originates from the name given to an Indian chief who lived in this vicinity. It can also be remarked by way of preface that Chief Seattle and his squaw Evangeline were well-known characters up to within a very few years past, but they have since been gathered to their fathers.

In 1855 the Indians and whites had an open rupture, and most of the surrounding country settlements were disturbed and a number of people killed. On the 26th of January, 1856, the Indians attacked Seattle, but owing to timely warnings (perhaps from Chief Seattle himself) Fort Decatur was thrown up, and with this defense and the assistance of a government vessel which happened to be lying in the bay, the Indians were repulsed and the Indian war was at an end.

In 1863 the first newspaper was published; in 1864 the Territorial Court was established; in 1869 a Town Government. In 1870 the inhabitants of Seattle numbered 1100, but after that time the population as hereinbefore stated grew quite steadily. Beginning with 1870 steamships began to make frequent visits; the coal mines at Renton were opened up by a short line of railroad; the merchants began to do a considerable wholesale trade; streets were graded; schools, churches

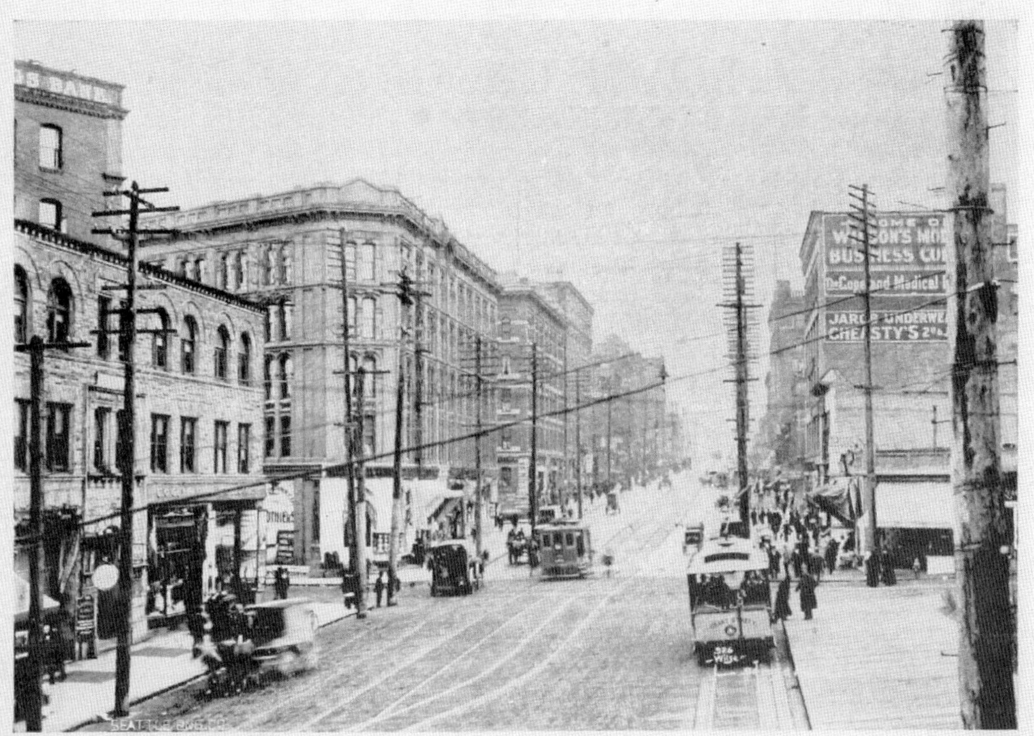

Second Avenue Looking North.

and hospitals were erected; and in the latter seventies a daily newspaper was started. The growth of Seattle since 1880 is of too recent a date to need any extended remarks; and the fire of 1889, which destroyed property having an aggregate value of from ten to twelve millions of dollars is also recent history. The fact that within a year from the fire the burned district was rebuilt on a larger and finer scale than before, and that it today stands as one of the best laid out, best built and best conducted cities on the Coast, shows the indomitable spirit which has prevailed at all times, particularly since it became a city of any importance.

A BIT OF GEOGRAPHY.

Where is Seattle?

No doubt this question may be asked by some into whose hands this book may fall; and in the event that any one can be found, who is in ignorance of the location of Seattle, on Puget Sound, the following condensed information is printed: Seattle is located upon the eastern shore of Elliott Bay, something like 125 miles from the Pacific Ocean by way of Puget Sound and the Strait of Juan de Fuca. Elliott Bay is one among the larger indentures on Puget Sound, and probably forms the most advantageous harbor upon this inland sea. Puget Sound itself is practically an arm of the sea, having a shore line in American territory, and wholly within the State of Washington, of nearly two thousand miles. The Strait of Juan de Fuca, which forms the northern boundary between the United States and British Columbia, a body of water some fifteen or twenty miles wide, affords an inlet to Puget Sound, which is absolutely free of the dangers which usually beset harbor entrances the world over. It is practically like sailing a ship into an open sea, and where the waters form Puget Sound it is land-locked, and not only secure from storm, but affords a uniform depth of water, which gives adsolute safety, and room for the combined shipping of the world should it all seek to enter here at one time. Puget Sound is approximately two hundred miles in length, with an average width of possibly ten miles. It is made up of a succession of little bays and indentures, and is quite irregular in shape, although forming a comparatively straight course from the straits to Seattle or Elliott Bay. If one will take occasion to look upon the map he will notice that Puget Sound occupies about the central portion of Western Washington. The State of Washington lies between the 46th and 49th parallels of north latitude and the 117th and 125th meridians of longitude west from Greenwich. British Columbia forms its boundary on the north, the State of Idaho on the east, Oregon and the Columbia River on the south and the Pacific Ocean on the west. Its greatest width north and south is two hundred and forty miles, and its greatest length east and west is three hundred and sixty miles, constituting an area in round numbers of nearly seventy thousand square miles, or about forty-five million acres. About twenty thousand square miles or thirteen mil-

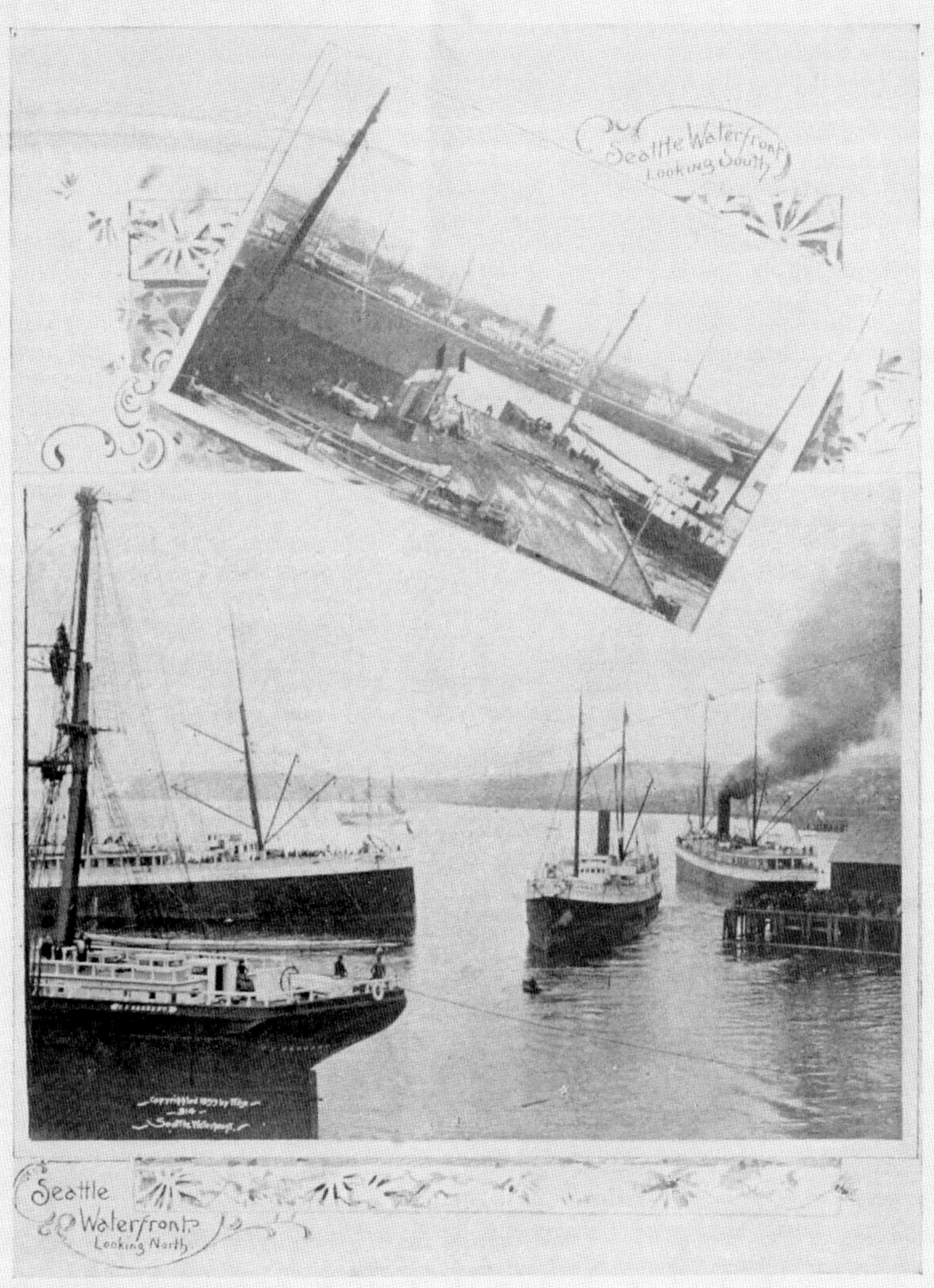

HARBOR SCENES OF SEATTLE.
The upper picture shows one of the big Oriental Liner taking on her cargo.

lion acres are west of the Cascade Mountains; fifty thousand square miles or about thirty-two million acres are east of the mountains. The mountains herein referred to are what are known as the Cascade range, running north and south, and extending far into British Columbia territory. Comparatively speaking, the eastern slope, or what is known as Eastern Washington, is free of timber, and forms one of the richest sections of wheat-producing lands known in the United States. The mountains themselves are full of minerals, consisting of gold, silver, copper, lead, iron and coal, together with building stone and many other products not now particularly known to commerce. In the western part of the state, using the Cascade range as a dividing line, the land for the most part is heavily timbered with fir, cedar, hemlock, tamarack and other merchantable timber. An estimate placed upon a fairly conservative basis, places the timber lands at twenty million acres; grain producing and grazing lands, ten million acres; and bottom lands, which are covered with a rich alluvial deposit such as is found in Western Washington, bordering the streams and indentures of Puget Sound, at something like five million acres. The mountainous region, comprising the mineral belt, and which is also timbered, is estimated at about ten million acres. The present population of the state is probably close to seven hundred thousand people. The total valuation of all property, according to a late census, is placed at $229,-137,539.

Seattle is the chief city of Western Washington, and as before stated, is situated upon Elliott Bay on Puget Sound, and is now a city of not far from ninety thousand inhabitants. Its chief industries in the way of manufactures, and its large jobbing trade and other resources are spoken of in greater detail upon pages farther advanced in this book. It is the purpose more particularly in this article to render a brief description of Seattle's location, not only in a geographical way, as relates to the balance of the State of Washington, but also its geographical position as compared with the rest of the world. When it is taken into consideration that Seattle is but two weeks' sail from Vladivostock in Siberia, it can easily be seen that Seattle, indeed, is very close to the threshold of the Orient; and it is not a matter of exaggeration to state that Seattle is in a position to maintain trade relations with all the countries lying to the west of us better than any other city of the United States; in fact there is but one logical outcome, and that will be that all shipments to and from that country (and by "that country" is meant not only Siberia, but China, Japan, Korea, the Philippine Islands and Hawaii) will eventually make this Puget Sound their entrepot. When one takes into consideration the fact that Vladivostok is the eastern terminus of the great Siberian Transcontinental Railroad, eight thousand miles in length, with the vast empire yet lying in a state of wilderness, and Seattle but two weeks' journey from it, some little idea can be formed of the future of the Queen City of the Pacific Mediterranean. The commerce of the United States with Russia now goes through the Atlantic cities to Liverpool and St. Petersburg. The completion of the Rusian railroad will naturally change this, and this vast traffic will flow westward through Seattle.

THE SIZE OF SEATTLE AND OTHER INFORMATION.

The City of Seattle, which now contains a population approximately estimated at 90,000 inhabitants, has an area of twenty-eight square miles. Its longest distance north and south is eight and one-half miles, and its longest distance east and west is seven and one-half miles; its shortest distance east and west is two miles. In 1880 it contained a population of 3533; in 1885 it had grown to be a place of 9683; this was increased to 26,740 up to and including the year 1889; the population in 1890 is given at 42,837; in 1892 it had grown to 57,540, and in 1899 to over 86,000. It is confidently predicted that by the year 1910 the population will easily reach 300,000. The city at the present time has 60.45 miles of sewers and 101.59 miles of graded streets. The water system, which furnishes a very superior quality of pure water (and which is quite adequate for a city of the present size) is being augmented in a very substantial way, and a supply will soon be accessible for double the present population. It is brought in from a long distance, and secured from streams having their source in the Cascade Mountains, and is therefore absolutely pure and wholesome. The city is supplied with both gas and electricity in abundance, at rates which are considered very moderate compared with many cities of its size.

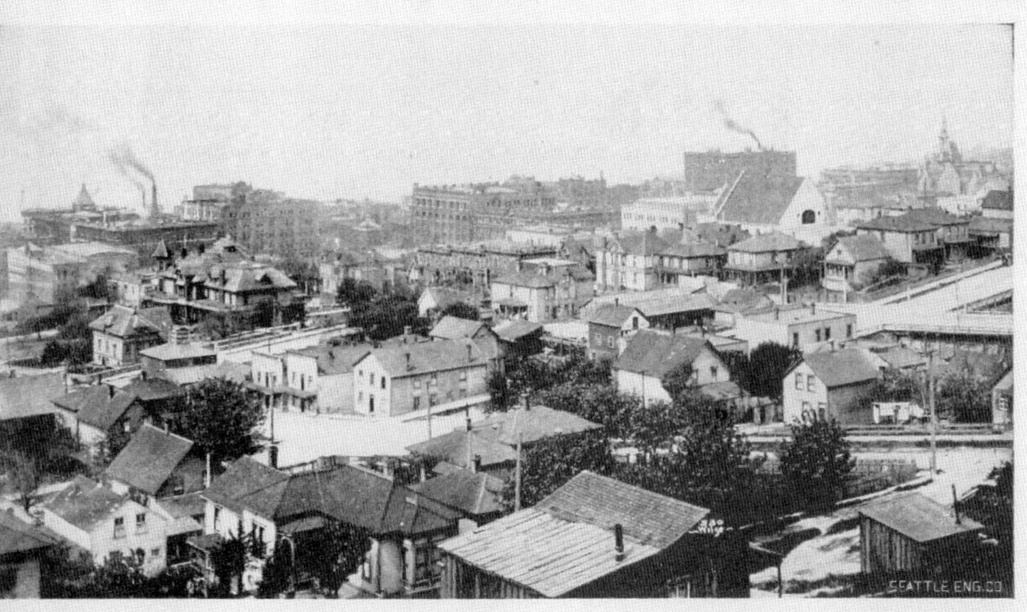

OVERLOOKING THE CITY FROM BEACON HILL.

Lake Washington, which forms the eastern boundary of the city, is two and one-half miles east of Elliott Bay. It is twenty miles in length and from two to five miles mide, with an area of forty square miles. It is from sixty to 222 feet deep, and is fed chiefly by the Samamish River, a stream flowing from the Cascale Mountains. Green Lake, a small body of water lying to the west of it, empties into Lake Washington. In the center of Lake Washington is Mercer's Island, five miles long by one mile in width, upon which East Seattle is located. Lake Washington is twenty feet above tide water, and is one of the many picturesque places which surround Seattle. Lake Union, wholly within the city limits of Seattle, lies one mile from Elliott Bay, and is twelve feet above tide water; it is from eighteen to forty-eight feet deep, having an area of two and one-half square miles. Green Lake, which is a little north of Lake Union, is four miles in circumference, and from thirty feet to forty feet deep. It is 160 feet above tide water. Ultimately there will be a tidal canal between Puget Sound and Lake Washington, into which deep water vessels will be permitted to enter. When completed it will afford a very advantageous arrangement for vessels of every character. It is probable that within the next few years this canal will be completed, and its worth to the general shipping interests will be almost incalculable.

REAL ESTATE.

One striking indication of the great prosperity of a city is the volume of its real estate transactions. During the year which closed on the 1st of January the volume of business has been steadily on the increase, until it is stated by conservative calculators that the transactions for 1899 reached the goodly proportions of $10,853,397. This showing will indicate more clearly than anything else which can be said that Seattle real estate is being greatly sought after by all classes of investors; and without doubt the close of the year 1900 will witness a very marked increase over that of 1899. The renewed confidence in land values in and about Seattle expressed by every one, and the faith in its continued growth until it becomes a city many times its present population, is having its influence upon many hundreds of investors, with the result that all kinds of real estate, no matter where located, is finding a ready sale at good prices. The depression which came in 1893 and lasted until 1897, had the effect of causing a general collapse of real estate values throughout the entire West, although Seattle probably suffered less than her sister cities on the Coast—consequently, on the return of good times investors realized that Seattle realty offered a most attractive field for investment, as well as for speculative purposes. Then by the infusion of several millions of Alaskan gold, real estate began to move very freely, and likewise created a demand for additional buildings, and improvements became active in the same proportion that sales of real estate were made. During the year 1899 fully 1200 new residences have been erected, to say nothing of the number of new business blocks of various kinds and descriptions which have been put up. It is probably sufficient to assert that real estate has advanced 25 per cent over the prices that were asked a year ago, and that the population of this city has increased by at least ten thousand people. Very considerable sums of outwas witnessed last; and some go so far as to predict that the present year will see a revival of the days of 1891, when real estate transactions were most extraordinarily lively. Two of the most notable sales during 1899 side capital are now coming to Seattle seeking investment, not only in real estate, but in everything else which promises a reasonable return. Some real estate dealers predict a more rapid purchase by a New York party of the Squire property, aggregating over $800,000. Even the most conservative realize that real estate anywhere near

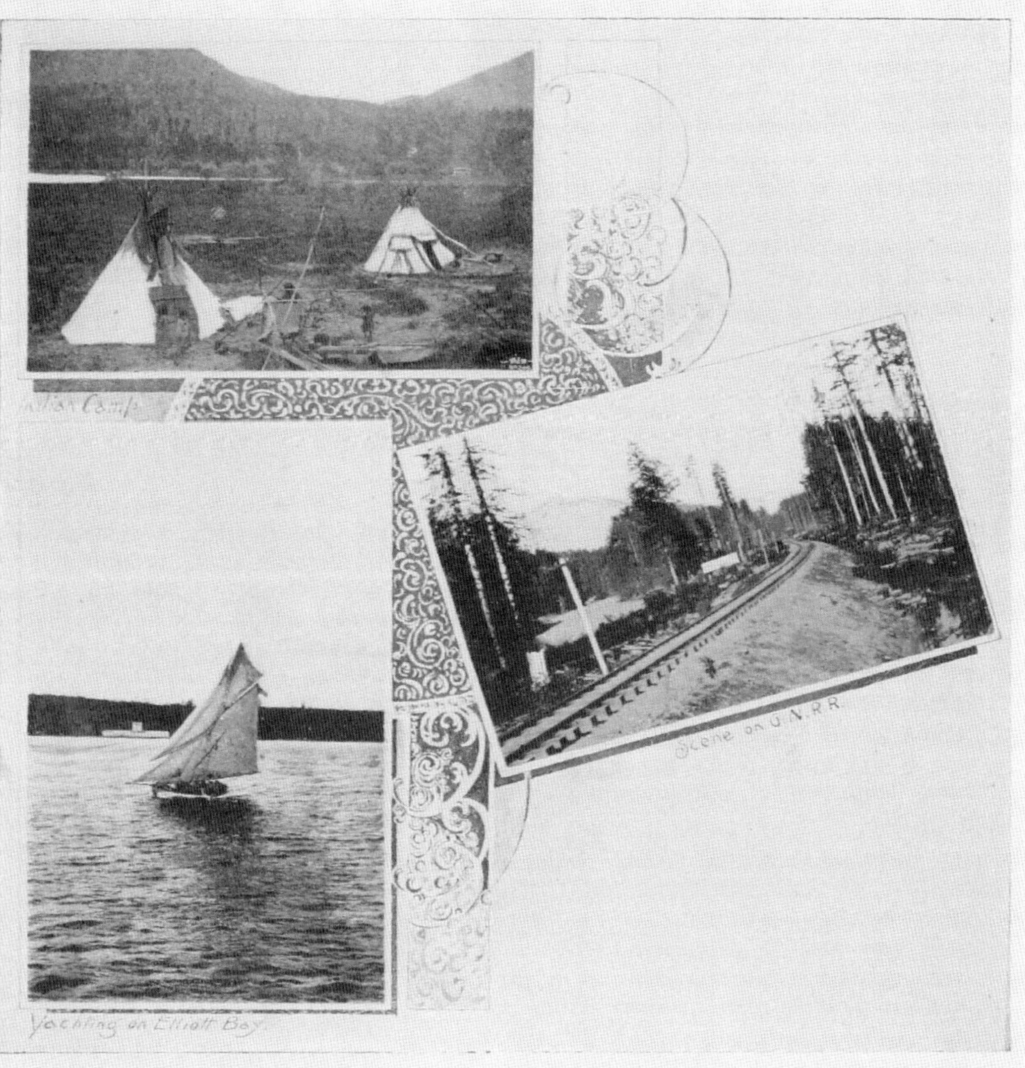

INTERESTING SCENES IN WESTERN WASHINGTON.

advance during the present year than were the purchase for $1,000,000 by the Northern Pacific Railroad Company of various water front properties, and the Seattle is a safe investment, as it is confidently predicted it will have three hundred thousand population by the end of the present decade.

THE CLIMATE VERY FINE.

It might not be out of place in speaking generally of Seattle to have a word to say in regard to its climate. The mild, equable climate that prevails on Puget Sound the year around is simply marvelous to those people who make their first visit here from the East. The mean temperature as deduced from nearly ten years' records of the United States Weather Bureau of this city is 51.5 degrees, and the highest temperature of which there is a record occurred on June 29, 1892, when the mercury registered 94 degrees; and the lowest, 3 degrees below zero, occurred on January 31, 1893. A comparison of the records shows that only during 1893 and 1894 did the temperature go below 20 degrees, and during both years there were periods of unusual cold weather for this locality. As a matter of fact, the temperature during the summer months averages about 59 degrees, while during the winter the average is about 44 degrees. The highest mean temperature for any three consecutive days was 75.3 degrees, which occured during July, 1899, and the lowest mean temperature for any three consecutive days was 29.3, in February, 1893 and 1899. The average precipitation at Seattle is 37.27 inches, divided as follows: The wet from November to April inclusive and the dry from May to October inclusive. During the wet season the average rainfall is 27.45 inches, while during the dry season but 9.82 inches falls. Comparatively speaking, very little snow falls on Puget Sound and it frequently occurs that no snow falls during the winter. The locality is remarkably free from severe local or general storms, and the highest velocity of which there is any record is forty-two miles. On the whole, the climate is bracing and salubrious, and the health of the people on the average exceedingly good.

SEATTLE AS A PLACE OF HOMES.

There are very few places on the Pacific Coast where living the year round is more ideal than on Puget Sound. The home life in Seattle is made as comfortable as in any of the older cities in the East. There are many hundreds of elegant residences in all parts of the city, and both in point of architectural beauty and general surroundings the homes are superior to many other places on the Pacific Coast.

To begin with, the City of Seattle is very charmingly situated, and during the past few years many hundreds of people have availed themselves of the opportunity of not only erecting substantial and costly homes, but have done their utmost to take advantage of what nature has already done for this city, with the result that the city is becoming well paved with good streets and considerable effort at adornment has been carried out.

There are over seventy churches in the city, all of which have fair congregations and a general attendance probably equal to any other city of ninety thousand inhabitants.

The educational system of Seattle is excellent. The public school buildings would be a credit to any city, both from a sanitary and an architectural standpoint, and likewise for modern educational apparatus. In addition to a very excellent high school, at which upwards of 1200 pupils attend, the State University is located within the borders of the city limits, and is of itself a very excellent educational institution, equal to similar seats of learning in the older states. In addition to these public schools there are several first-class business colleges.

Socially speaking, Seattle stands very high. The place is well provided

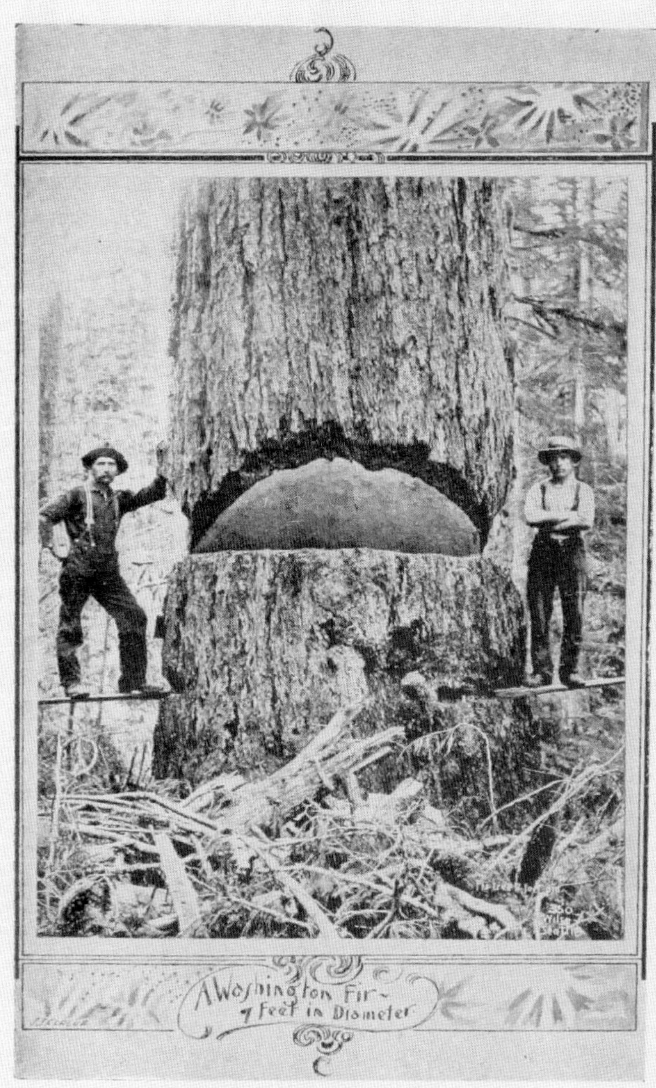

SOME OF OUR RESOURCES.

with numerous clubs of all kinds. In fact, it might be said that social life in Seattle cannot be excelled anywhere. One has only to pay a visit here to be thoroughly impressed with that fact.

TRIBUTARY COUNTRY.

The country which lies tributary to Seattle, and by that is meant the country over which Seattle carries on trade relations, consists of all of Western Washington, the greater part of Eastern Washington, portions of British Columbia, and all of Alaska Territory. Practically speaking, the tributary country to Seattle is greater in extent and wealth of resource than a like area tributary to any other city in the United States. The country lying upon Puget Sound is naturally very closely allied to Seattle, while the more remote portions, like that of Eastern Washington, seek this place through the channel of its wheat trade, and other commodities which it desires to place in this market. The trade with Alaska naturally consists in outfitting prospectors, miners and settlers to that region, and in furnishing supplies for those people who are already there, and in furnishing such machinery as is needed to carry on mining operations. Seattle to all intents and purposes is the head center of developments in Alaska and will continue to be such, probably, for all time to come. Its superior position on Puget Sound naturally makes it the center of a great tributary region. It is because of this fact that Seattle has attained its great importance in the Western world.

THE COMMERCE OR SHIPPING OF SEATTLE.

In speaking of the commerce of Puget Sound, it is perhaps necessary to again refer to the easy manner in which vessels of every size and character can enter or depart from this great inland body of water. As before stated in another article which appears elsewhere, Puget Sound has its inlet or outlet by way of the Strait of Juan de Fuca, to all practical purposes an arm of the sea itself, which extends eastward from the Pacific Ocean a distance of full eighty miles. It is so roomy and so free of obstruction that sailing vessels have no difficulty whatever in sailing in or out, although an admirable tug boat service is maintained to render expedition to vessels which do not carry their own steam. Without going into details, Puget Sound can be classed as the most magnificent harbor in the world, a fact which will probably not be gainsaid by any one at all familiar with nautical affairs. This one great fact stands out in very bold relief and gives Puget Sound a prominence in the matter of commerce not possessed elsewhere on the Pacific Coast. The principal cities bordering on the Sound are Seattle, Tacoma, Whatcom, Everett and Port Townsend, being in size and importance in the order in which they are named. Passing over the importance of the other places named, and speaking more directly of Seattle, it can be stated very briefly that at the present time it is the terminus of four transcontinental railways, several Oriental lines, and the entire fleet of vessels engaged in the Alaska traffic, besides an enormous "mosquito fleet," which ply between Seattle and various other Sound ports. Seattle is the chief manufacturing city on Puget Sound, to which some considerable space is devoted more particularly elsewhere, and as a shipping point on the Pacific Coast it is outclassed only by San Francisco, whose only rival it is, especially in the trade with the Asiatic ports. The Great Northern Railway, which has done so much for the Northwest, has its terminus in Seattle, and here its cars are unloaded into ships which carry the products of the country to the Orient. The construction of the Great Northern terminals has but just been completed, and the monster docks, warehouses and wheat elevators and miles of trackage are the first things that catch the eye of the traveler as he enters the city from the north. That company has just now in contemplation the building of a passenger depot, freight sheds and trackage facilities in the southern part of the city,

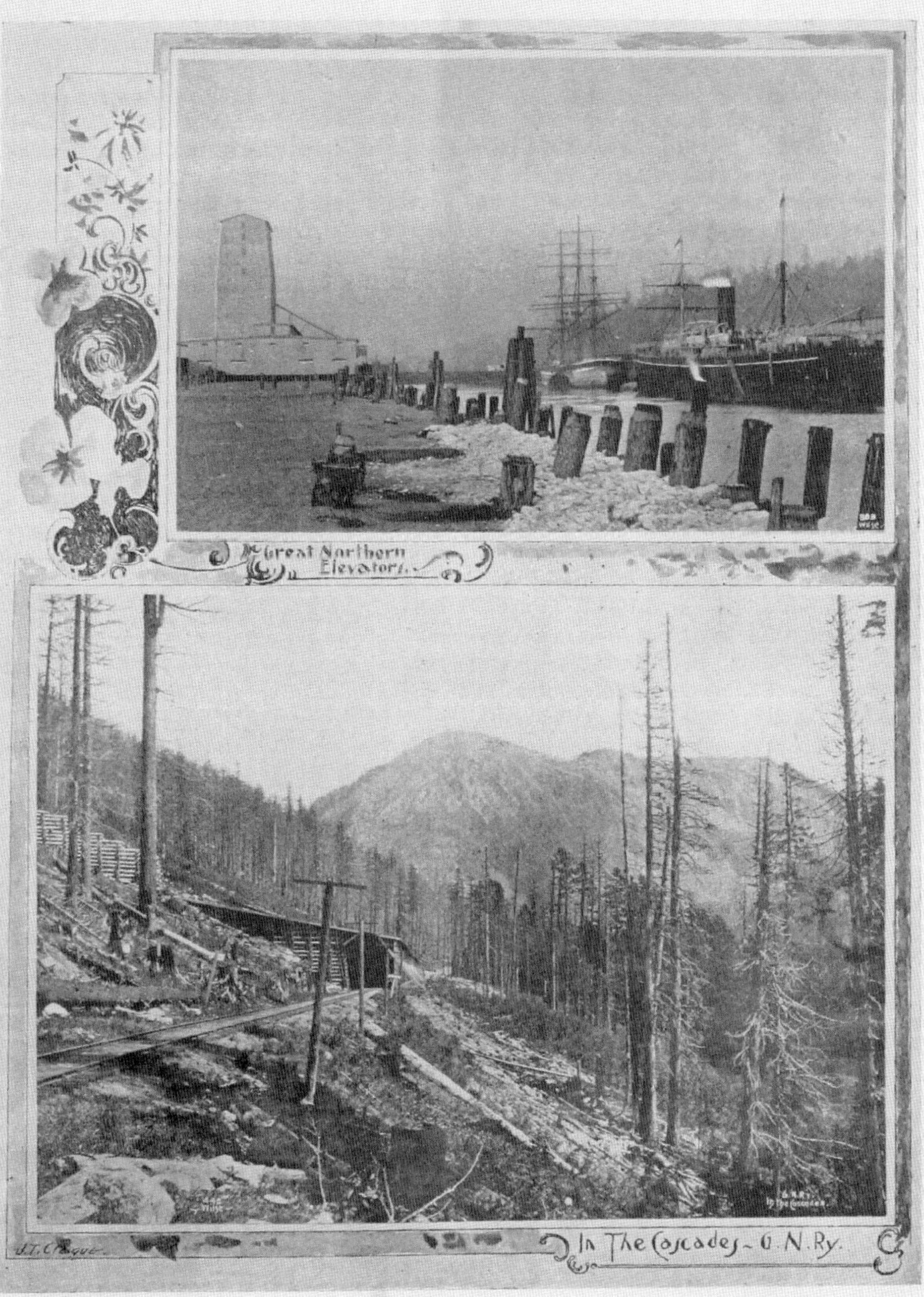

ACROSS THE MOUNTAINS TO TIDE WATER.

which will cost over $500,000. The extensive warehouses already completed and used for the storage of incoming and outgoing ocean freight, are so large that entire trains can be unloaded under their roofs and loaded into the lines of Oriental steamships, which leave these docks for Oriental ports. The erection of the great wheat elevators means that Seattle will be the greatest wheat exporting port on the Pacific Coast. In addition to the great elevators of the Great Northern Railway in North Seattle, there are extensive elevators here owned in West Seattle, on the western shore of Elliott Bay, by the Seattle & San Francisco Railroad; and from the present outlook the near future will see a number of others equally as extensive erected. The trade with Alaska has assumed very great proportions, and the fleet now engaged in that traffic is very large. The Harbor Master's report for the year 1898 shows that 1734 deep sea vessels passed in and out of Seattle harbor landing cargoes of gold, merchandise, Oriental goods, teas, silks, curios, etc., and taking away vast loads of coal, flour, wheat, lumber, Alaskan outfits and merchandise generally. Of this vast fleet 1297 were steamships and 437 sailing vessels, and their net tonnage combined reaches the large sum of 1,455,596 tons. This fleet was composed of almost every conceivable ocean going craft, and the entries and departures were to and from all parts of the world. This list does not include, however, the Sound steamer of any description or any of the numerous "mosquito fleet." During the year over two million tons of coal were shipped from Seattle and over 2,500,000 bushels of wheat, and over a billion feet of lumber was shipped out of Elliott Bay. The salmon pack, to which reference is made in another article, for 1898 reached 425,000 cases.

To give an idea of the travel between Seattle and Alaska it can be stated that from January 1, 1899, to July 25, 1899, there were 9,250 persons who took passage to the north from Seattle, and who took in excess of 34,000 tons of freight and supplies. The number of vessels engaged in this traffic was 163. Seattle is headquarters for all traffic to and from Alaska and the Northwest Territory, and generally speaking all supplies are purchased in this place.

Across the bay from Seattle is the Puget Sound Naval Station, where the largest dry dock in the United States is to be found. Many of the vessels of the American Navy have been docked there, and the fact that the United States Government realizes the importanc of Puget Sound lies in the fact that the largest dock on the Pacific Coast is located here.

SCENERY ON PUGET SOUND.

Very little has been said by the newspapers published in Western Washington on the scenery of this great state. It is only when a visitor from the East or elsewhere arrives here and goes into ecstacies over the remarkable scenery that is here found that those who live here really appreciate the wonderful scenic effect of this state. As a matter of fact Puget Sound possesses greater scenic attractions than any other state in the Union, and it is very much doubted if any other spot on earth can excel it. The City of Seattle is built upon a succession of gently sloping hills, which extend back from the waters of Elliott Bay until they rise probably five hundred feet, when the ground gently slopes to the eastward to reach the shores of a magnificent body of water called Lake Washington. One can stand upon the summit of this divide and while overlooking the entire city with Elliott Bay and Puget Sound upon the right hand, he can face the Cascade range of mountains, several of whose peaks are perpetually covered like four or five miles in width by ten or twelve miles in length, and surrounded, as it is, by evergreen forests and gently undulating hills gradually rising until they meet the foothills of the Cascade Mountains in the distance,

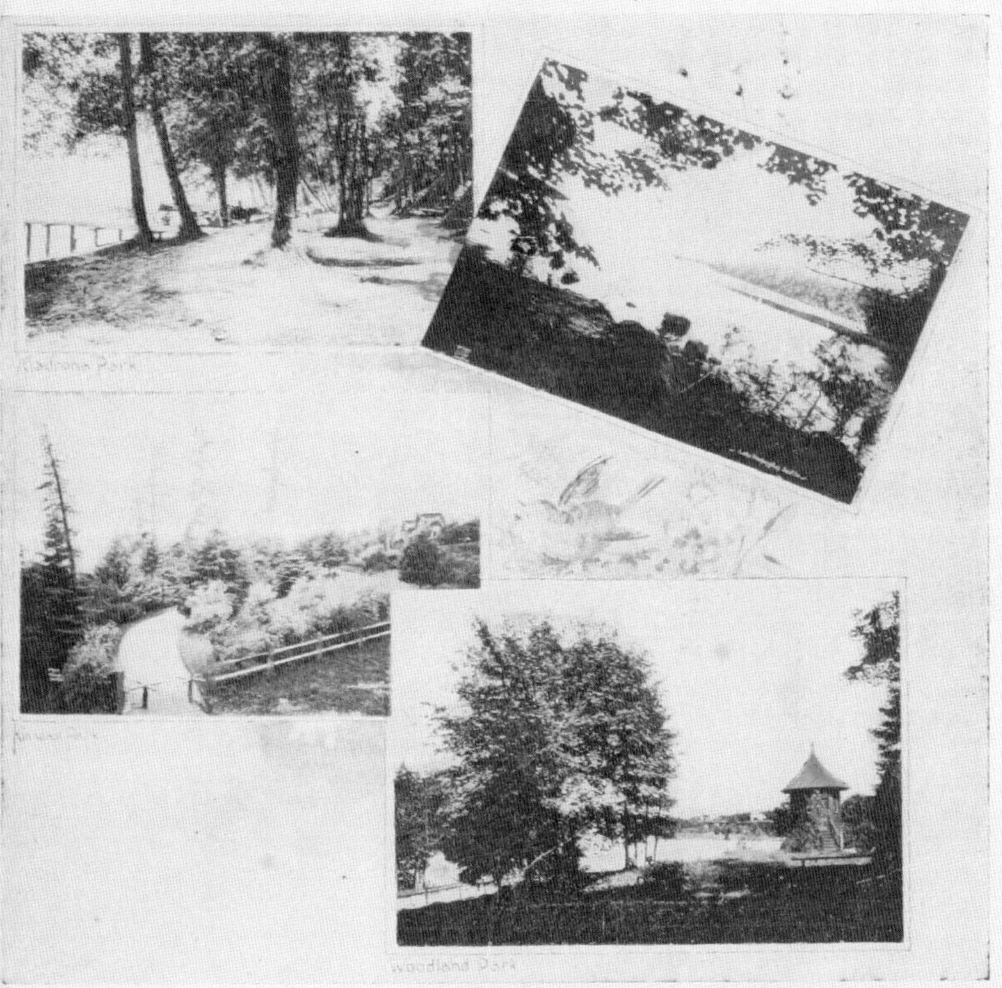

THE PARKS OF SEATTLE.

with snow, and see one of the finest, grandest panoramic view that ever stretched before man. On the left hand is Lake Washington, a body of clear, pure water, which is fed from mountain streams, which is something one can conceive of no finer or more entrancing place in which to make a home. Upon a clear day, while standing from the same crest, one can look across Puget Sound and see clearly and sharply defined the Olympic range of mountains on the west side of Puget Sound. This is a short range, which lies between the Sound and the Pacific Ocean. They are bold and rugged, and their extreme summit is covered with perpetual snow; and with the waters of the Sound in the foreground, and a fringe of emerald green at their base, they unquestionably form a bit of mountain scenery the equal of which is difficult to find. In the Cascade Mountains, lying a little east of south of Seattle, is the magnificent Mount Rainier, rising to a height of nearly fifteen thousand feet. A little farther south is Mount St. Helens, rising to a height of something like 13,000 feet, and still to the north, less than one hundred miles in an air line, is Mount Baker, twelve thousand feet in height.

Some of the pictures which are reproduced herewith, will give an idea of the scenes herein described, or as nearly so as an ordinary photograph can do so, but to be thoroughly appreciated one must visit these scenes and take in their beauty first hand. Not only is the mountain effect very sublime and very grand, but Puget Sound itself lends an added charm, and this can only be realized and appreciated by taking any one of a hundred different pleasure trips. It is filled with varying sizes of islands from one acre in extent up to the size which forms whole counties; in fact, it very much resembles the thousand islands of the St. Lawrence River, and the day will yet come when Puget Sound will be sought as much as a health and pleasure resort as for its untold business opportunities at the present time.

EXPORTS AND IMPORTS.

The exports from Seattle for 1899 were as follows: Coal by ship, 1200 tons per day; lumber by ship and car, 200,000 feet per day; shingles by car, 1,100,000 per day; flour by ship, 1000 barrels per day; wheat by ship, 5000 barrels per day; vessels built, $1000 per day; vessels repaired, $1000 per day; merchandise to Alaska, 420,000 per day; merchandise to British Columbia, $1000 per day; merchandise to Orient, $1000 per day; merchandise to Honolulu, $1000 per day; fish products, $1000 per day; oats, $100,000 per annum; hops, $100,000 per annum; beer, foreign, $100,000 per annum—or a practical total of $4,657,403, of which $349,139 was exported in January, and $508,715 was exported in December, showing a very substantial gain for the last month of the year over the first month.

The import trade is rather difficult to state accurately—the figures obtained only relate to foreign countries. The duties paid at the local customs house in 1899 amounted to $200,000, indicating the imports for local consumption of about $600,000. These were chiefly cement from Great Britain, Chinese and Japanese merchandise, tropical fruits and other productions. The domestic imports include vast quantities of fruit and vegetables, largely from California; California dairy products, meats, groceries, cloth, furniture, machinery and other articles which go to make up the lines of business usually carried on in an American city. The chief import was the gold from Alaska, which aggregated over thirteen million dollars. Roughly speaking, then (of course leaving out the gold product), the imports reached a total of $5,868,620.

SEATTLE PARKS.

If there is one thing more than another that Seattle can boast of it is its magnificent array of parks. They lie at all points of the compass from the center of the city, and are easily reached by any number of street railway lines. Kinnear Park, one of the most handsome, which lies at the terminus of the North Seattle Electric Line, is a park quite unique in the way it has been laid out. It consists of a narrow rim of a half mile or so in length along the cliff two hundred feet above the Sound, and the handsome landscape gardening, and here and there the assistance to nature has created a park of unusual beauty. From this spot, practically the entire city can be overlooked, including all of Elliott Bay, Mount Rainier, the Olympic range and a great portion of Puget Sound itself.

Woodland Park is another very beautiful spot; it consists of about 200 acres and borders the west side of Green Lake. It is reached by the Green Lake car line.

Ravenna Park lies out past the State University, and is a very ideal spot at which to spend a quiet summer day.

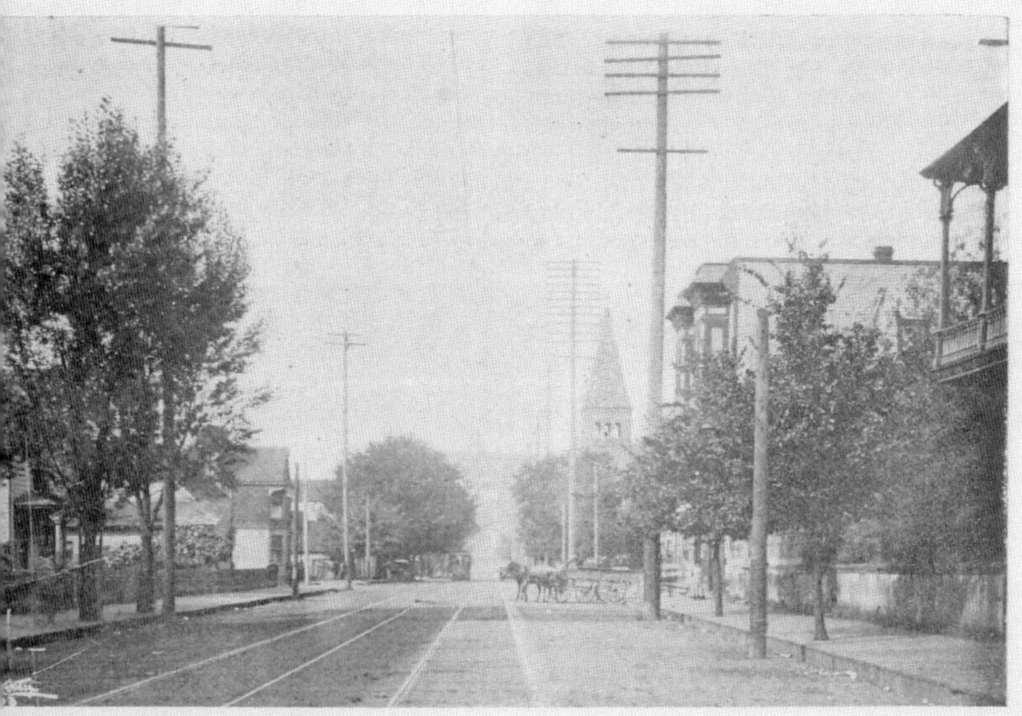

LOOKING NORTH ON THIRD AVENUE.

Then there is Leschi, Madison and Madrona Parks, all on Lake Washington. Denny Park and a number of others are scattered about here and there, on one or another of the lakes, all of which make attractive places for the visitor. The street railways reach all these fine resorts, and one can start from the center of the town and reach any of these places by a twenty minutes' ride.

COAL MINES

The coal mines of Washington, all of which are tributary to Seattle, form a very important industry of this state. The coal fields themselves cover an area of several thousand square miles and when fully developed will be practically inexhaustible. The several separate districts are as follows: Newcastle, Renton and Green River districts in King County; Wilkeson district in Pierce County, and the Roslyn district in Kittitas County. The Northern Pacific Company's mines at Roslyn are the largest in the state. The product is a high grade steam and domestic coal. Last year 635,318 tons were mined, of which 40,000 tons were exported to Honolulu. They employ one thousand men, and at present are mining 65,000 tons per month. The Pacific Coast Company's mines in King County produce 365,634 tons a year at present, and 650 men are employed; the product is a high grade steam coal. The Wilkeson Coal and Coke Company have fifty coke overs in constant operation, from which they manufactured 26,300 tons of coke in 1899. The Carbon Hill Coal Company mined last year 288,000 tons, and employed 500 men. In 1898 there were nineteen mines, which were shipping coal which had a daily product of 1,775,257 tons; the output for 1899 exceeded this by 2,000,000 tons. There is not a mine in the state that it not worked to its full capacity, and at present about 4500 men are engaged in coal mining, at an average of $2.50 per day per man. The present year will probably see an output of 2,500,000 tons.

GOLD FROM ALASKA.

Since the excitement in Alaska over the recently discovered gold mines, fully eighteen million dollars of gold has been received by the Seattle Assay Office. This amount has been brought out by just 8209 miners. The fact that Seattle is the practical starting point for all the region lying to the north of us, including both Alaska and the Northwest Territory, and is the first place to which the returning miner turns his face upon leaving that country with his gold dust, demonstrates that the development of the gold industry of that region will prove of very considerable importance to this city. This is easily demonstrated by calling attention to the amount of money which has already passed through the local Assay Office. While all this money does not remain in Seattle, enough of it goes into circulation to have a very considerable effect upon business. Alaska, like the Orient, is yet but in its infancy, and the future development of that country will simply be marvelous.

PUBLIC LIBRARY.

Seattle has a Public Library which contains 20,080 volumes. Of these 2000 volumes were added during the past year. The records show that 9100 persons last year secured the privilege of borrowing books for home reading, and that the home circulation now reaches 12,000 volumes per month. The library building is located in a very convenient part of town, in what was formerly the residence of H. L. Yesler, a pioneer of very considerable note who assisted in many ways to make Seattle what it is today. The income for the library for the past year amounted to $14,000. After paying the running expenses something like $6400 was left with which to purchase new books.

EXTENSIVE MERCHANDISE BROKERS.

The firm of Spencer-Clarke Company are the most extensive merchandise brokers in the Northwest, and the illustration that is published on adjoining pages will indicate the character of the premises they occupy, and they are located at 311 Occidental Avenue, and have a building 30x120 feet, three stories in height in addition to a basement. They have been established since 1894. Their trade is almost wholly confined to the wholesalers of the city and to the handling of canned salmon in the East. They are the direct agents for a number of very heavy Eastern manufacturers, and consequently a very heavy volume of trade passes through their hands. There is no firm in the Northwest which enjoys a higher rating or has a higher standing in the community than the firm of Spencer-Clarke Company.

BICYCLE PATHS.

It is estimated that Seattle has 5000 bicyclists. During the past year or two a great many miles of bicycle paths have been opened in and about the city and surrounding country, and it is now estimated there are fully thirty miles of cindered pathways winding in and out around the city. It is stated that no other section of the country affords so many pleasing bicycle paths as are found leading out of Seattle.

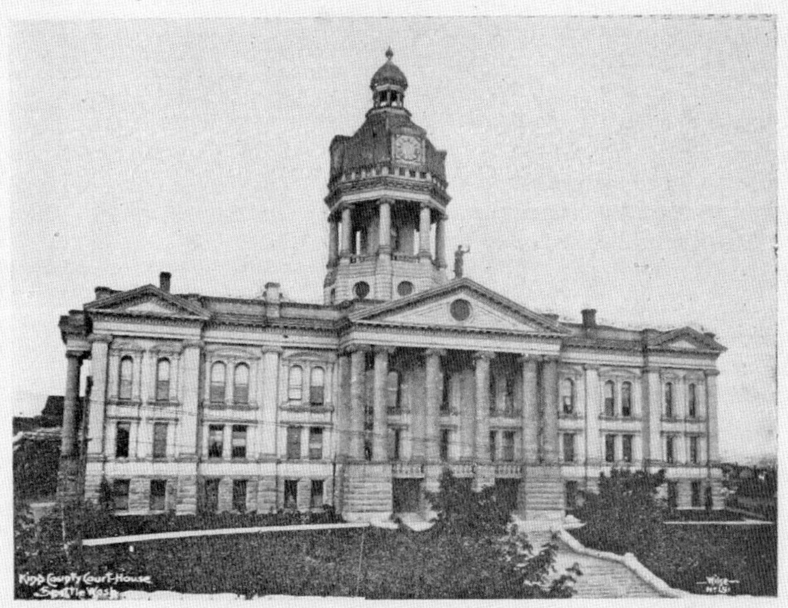

KING COUNTY COURT HOUSE.

SEATTLE'S FINANCIAL STRENGTH.

Nothing indicates the financial strength or character of a city quite so much as its bank clearances—in fact, bank clearances are a barometer which shows its prosperity. In this respect Seattle takes pardonable pride in showing a gain of fully 50 per cent in 1899 over the year 1898, or nearly 200 per cent over 1897. It was in 1897 that the pendulum of depression began slowly to move backward, and from that time can be marked a general upward tendency of prosperity for Seattle. The banks of Seattle today are among the strongest financial institutions of the West, and each shows a most flattering state of affairs. As an illustration of this can be cited, that in the latter part of last year, during the temporary shortage of funds in New York City, Seattle was enabled to loan a half million dollars of its surplus to New York City banks in order to tide over the momentary flurry there. This statement when published, was received with some scepticism, but when it was confirmed it created a profound impression and probably did more to strengthen Seattle's financial firmness than almost anything else that could have happened. Nothing shows more clearly the great volume of business done in banking and commercial circles than the clearing house. Some one has compared the clearing house to the pulse whose beat indicates unerringly the circulation of the blood through the veins and arteries of the body financial. Other writers have called it a barometer, whose rise and fall is an index to the financial weather. Both illustrations are apt and forcible. The truth is, that when the returns of the Seattle clearing house first began to show the rapid yet steady growth of the business in this city Eastern financiers themselves were sceptical, and some insinuations and even direct charges were made to the effect that the returns here were being "doctored" in order to make a favorable financial showing. Actual investigation, however, and the character of the men who stand back of this institution soon convinced the world of the falsity of such insinuations. The records of the clearing house will speak for themselves, and need little in the way of comment or explanation. The following tables for the years 1898 and 1899 show the wonderful gains that have been made:

For 1898 the record was as follows:

January	$ 5,673,0[illegible]9.58
February	5,549,520.98
March	7,361,365.35
April	6,456,461.17
May	4,960,182.90
June	5,516,238.19
July	4,545,357.12
August	5,308,357.63
September	5,039,647.63
October	5,872,473.11
November	6,108,860.22
December	6,020,151.30
Total	$68,414,635.78

For 1899 the record was as follows:

January	$ 5,026,965.43
February	4,689,849.55
March	6,065,546.84
April	6,370,180.36
May	7,440,292.73
June	7,565,028.72
July	8,791,153.81
August	12,955,927.85
September	13,584,924.31
October	11,589,619.01
November	10,705,114.12
December	8,642,984.74
Total	$103,327,617.47

In other words, the clearances for the current year exceed those of 1898 by more than $34,000,000, or about 50 per cent, while they exceed those of 1897 by about $66,000,000, or nearly 200 per cent.

As showing what a very considerable financial center Seattle has grown to be it can be stated that it has ten banking institutions—six national and four state banks. These banks on Jan. 1st, 1900, had a total of $14,000,000 on deposit. This is an increase of nearly $10,000,000 over the period of extreme depression following the panic of 1893. A more detailed showing of the more important institutions is made in succeeding pages.

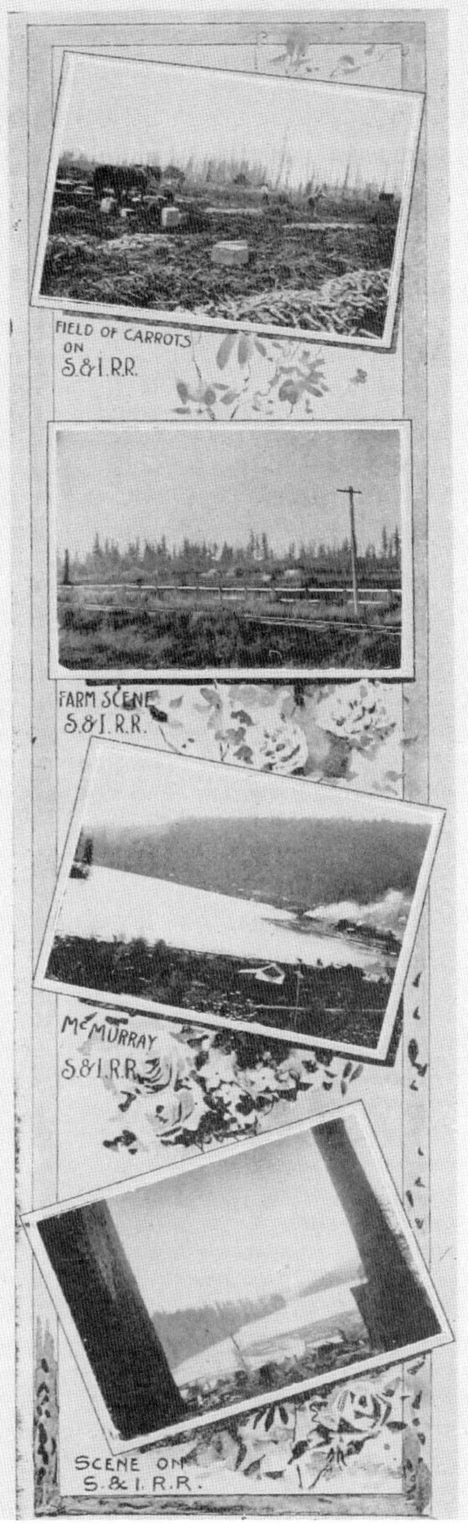

SEATTLE INDUSTRIALLY.

By "Seattle Industrially" is meant that which goes to make up its industries with particular attention to its manufactures. When one attempts to enumerate the various manufacturing establishments which are found within the borders of Seattle, it at once becomes apparent that the establishments of that character not only occupy a wide range, but are more numerous than one would suppose at first glance. Some idea can be formed of their great importance when it is stated that Seattle gives employment to more than 3000 people in lines which are classed as those of manufacturers, and the value of the product which is turned out reaches a very high figure. Aside from the manufacture of lumber and shingles the largest single industry is that of ship-building, at the head of which stands the firm of the Moran Brothers Company, who give employment to more than 500 men about their great establishment, most of whom are engaged in ship-buliding and kindred lines. Leaving the ship-building and passing on to the other industries, without going into enumeration of them all, it is found that almost every article, with the exception of raw material, is made here. A half dozen manufacturing machine shops are in operation, which employ fifty to 150 people; besides several breweries, bottling works, ice factories, candy factories, cracker factories, box factories, meat packing establishments, fish canneries, furniture factories, tents and awnings, flour mills, coffee, spice, flavoring extracts and baking powder establishments, evaporating fruit and vegetable factories, woven wire works, tinware, saw works, soap works, paints and varnishes, and in fact almost every conceivable article used in the ordinary course of consumption by people in the West. Some of the factories, to be sure, are small and give employment to but few people, while others give employment to a great number of hands. The sum total will reach the figure named, and it will at once be seen that Seattle's industrial army is a very striking one.

Among the number which are not already enumerated and spoken of in conjunction with photographs bearing directly upon their line is that of the candy manufacturing concern of E. M. Thurlow at 906 Western Avenue, who gives employment to thirty hands, and makes a product which he sells all over Western Washington and into Alaska; the Pacific Door Company, on Railroad Avenue and Pine, which gives employment to twenty-five men in the manufacture of doors, which are sold generally throughout the West; the Washington Wood Pipe and Stave Company, at the same location, which is engaged in the manufacture of wood pipe and tank stock employing fifteen hands, and which ships its product both to the East and points on the Pacific; the Seattle Cereal Company, at 304 Railroad Avenue, which is engaged in the manufacture of rolled oats and other cereals, employing twenty-two hands, and whose product is sold throughout Washington and as far South as California; the Seattle Ice Company, having a capacity of fifty tons, employing fourteen hands; the Queen City Trunk Factory, at 702 Second Avenue, which employs six hands; the Seattle Brick and Tile Company, located in South Seattle, which employs twenty-four men and eight teamsters, in the manufacture of brick and tile, whose product is sold throughout the Puget Sound country and into Alaska; the Gilbert Soap Company, that employs six hands; the Pacific Wagon Company, at Third Avenue South and Main Street, which employs twenty-five hands; the Hill Syrup Company, at 214-216 Jackson Street, which employs eight hands; George T. McGinnis & Co., 826 First Avenue South, doing a general bottling and manufacture of soda water, which employs nine hands; the Seattle Mattress and Upholstering Company at 924 First Avenue South, which employs thirty hands, and which expects to soon increase its capacity so that it will employ sixty in the manufacture of mattresses and all kinds of upholstered goods; the Washington Shoe Manufacturing Company, at 902 Jackson Street, which employs eighty hands, and which sells its product throughout the entire Northwest country; the Denny-Clay Company, which employs from eighty to ninety hands and manufactures sewer pipe, and which already does a very large trade with South Africa, the Philippine Islands, the Hawaiian Islands and points on the Coast and in the East; the Westerman Iron Works, at 1112 First Avenue South, which employs thirty hands. These are a partial list of the great number of industrial concerns which are making Seattle a very considerable center for manufactured products.

THE POLSON-WILTON HARDWARE COMPANY.

The Polson-Implement Hardware Company, which do a wholesale agricultural implement business, and who are located at 806 and 808 Western Avenue in a 50x100 four-story building, are one of the very considerable firms doing business in Seattle. They have been established since 1892, and are now doing business through all parts of Western Washington, and also over a portion of Eastern Washington along the line of the Great Northern Railroad. They give employment to ten men in their establishment, and keep representatives on the road in their interest. In addition to the house in this city they have a branch at La Conner and also have an interest in the Wenatchee Hardware Company at Wenatchee. As indicating a very substantial increase in their business it can be stated that it was fully 40 per cent in excess of the business

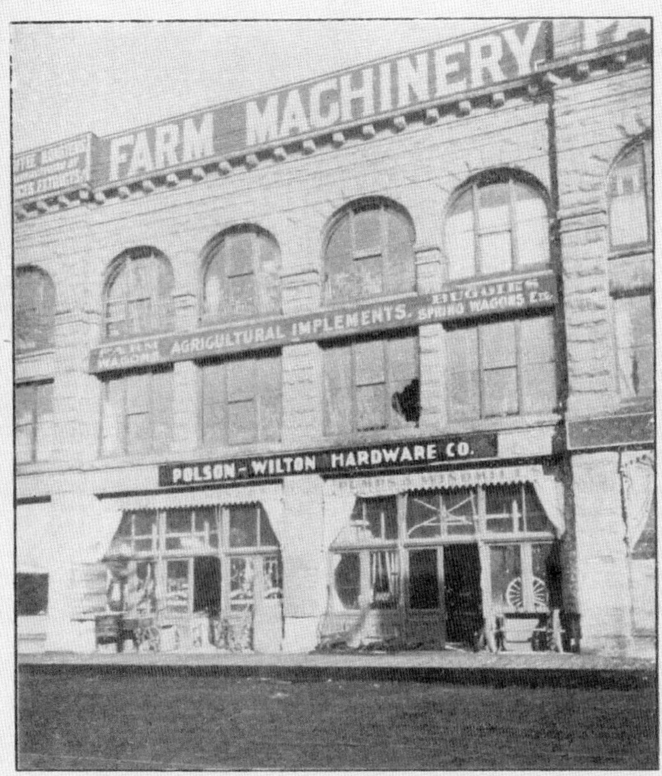

STORE OF POLSON IMPLEMENT HARDWARE CO.

of 1898, a statement which speaks volumes for the manner in which they are pushing their trade. They handle practically everything in the agricultural implement line, including a very heavy line of vehicles and farm wagons of all kinds. A very fine illustration of their place is shown herewith.

PUGET SOUND FOOD FISHES.

The fish product of Puget Sound waters and the magnitude of the fish industry, including the cultivation of oysters, is just beginning to be realized. Where but a dozen years ago practically no revenue was derived, the industry in fresh fish alone has reached a point where a revenue of fully $1,000,000 a year is now realized. Take the oyster industry and the fish industry and the value of the combined product will approximate fully 5,500,000 per year, at a very conservative estimate. Fresh fish from Puget Sound waters are now being shipped in cold storage to practically every state in the Union, and the product in smoked, salted and canned fish is finding a market in all of the civilized countries of the world. The total pack of all classes of fish reached a total of 930,000 cases, and exceeded by 500,000 cases that of the previous year.

The eighteen canneries on Puget

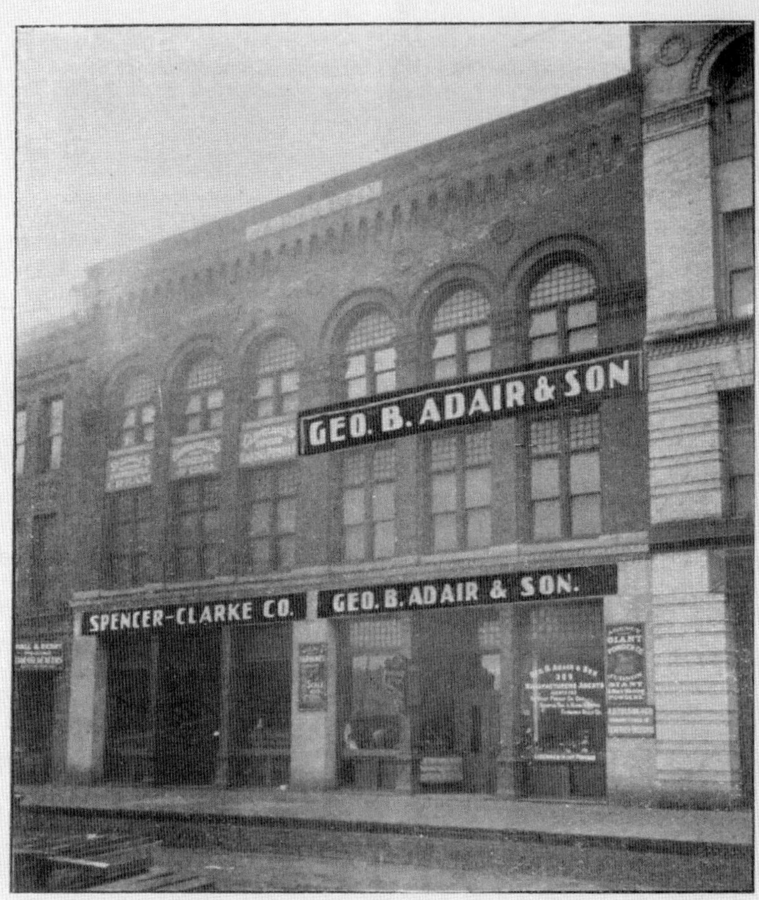

BUSINESS HOUSES OF SPENCER-CLARKE CO. AND GEO. B. ADAIR & SON.

Sound packed the following kinds of fish:

	Cases.
Sockeyes	528,000
Spring salmon	22,600
Cahoes....	103,500
Humpbacks	256,300
Chums	19,400

On the Columbia River the eighteen canneries packed 374,500 cases, of which amount the five canneries on the Washington side of the river put up 68,500 cases, as follows:

	Cases.
Chinooks	53,500
Steelheads and bluebacks	5,500
Fall salmon	9,500

On the British Columbia side the seventy-one canneries put up a total of 766,000 cases, of which the forty-nine canneries on the Fraser river put up 528,000 cases, and the northern pack was 238,000 cases.

This shows the Puget sound canneries packed nearly double the amount of any other locality.

In comparing the capacty of the canneries in the various districts, the following table shows the capacity of the largest cannery in each district:

In comparing the capacity of the largest canery in each district:

	Cases.
British Columbia	27,000
Alaska	69,000
Columba river	37,000
Puget sound	118,000

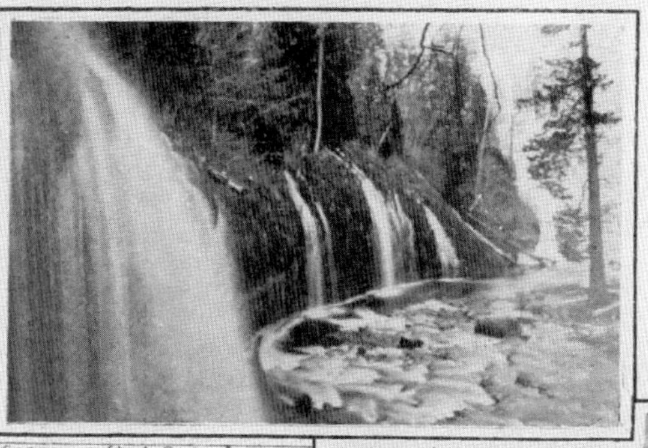

Scene on Shasta Route - S.P.R.R.

The Sound also has several canneries of 40,000 to 50,000 annual capacity.

For the state the salmon pack is shown to be valued at $4,500,000, divided up as follows:

	Cases.
Puget Sound	930,000
Columbia River (Washington side)	68,500
Grays Harbor	16,200
Willapa Bay	17,400
Total	1,032,100

Making in all one-third of the entire Pacific coast pack, which for the year 1899 was valued at $14,000 000.

In addition to the canned salmon, there were shipped from Puget sound as frozen, fresh, salt and smoked salmon 16,000,000 pounds, valued at over $450,000; 2,500,000 pounds from the Columbia river, valued at $125,000; 630,000 pounds from Willapa bay, valued at $16,000, and 1,600,000 pounds from Grays harbor, valued at $40,000, making a total of $631,000 to be added to the output of the canneries, or $5,130,000 for salmon alone.

When to this is added the value of the halibut, cod, sturgeon and other fish, with the oyster, crabs, clams and other fishes, the importance of the fishng interests of the state take a front rank.

Over 50,000,000 cans are used for putting up the salmon pack.

TRANSPORTATION LINES.

The transportation facilities, which consist of both rail and water lines, which center in Seattle, form a very conspicuous part in the material progress of this region. In railway lines, Seattle now possesses practically four transcontinental lines of railways as follows; The Great Northern, the Canadian Pacific, the Northern Pacific and the Southern Pacific. While in the strict sense of the word the Southern Pacific line does not enter Seattle, it is still a part of the railway system of the city, and is doing a very

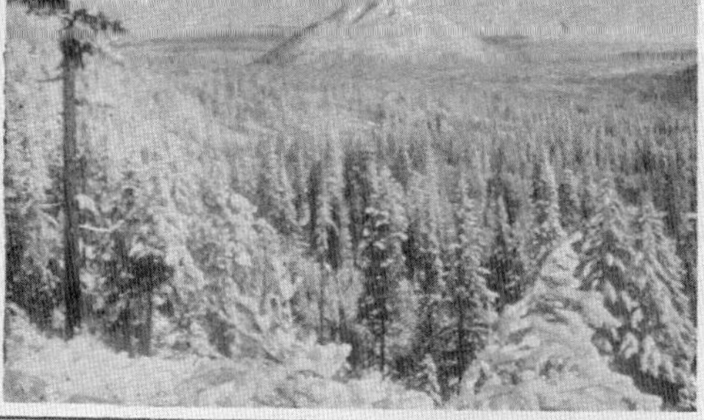

Scene on Shasta Route - S.P.R.R.

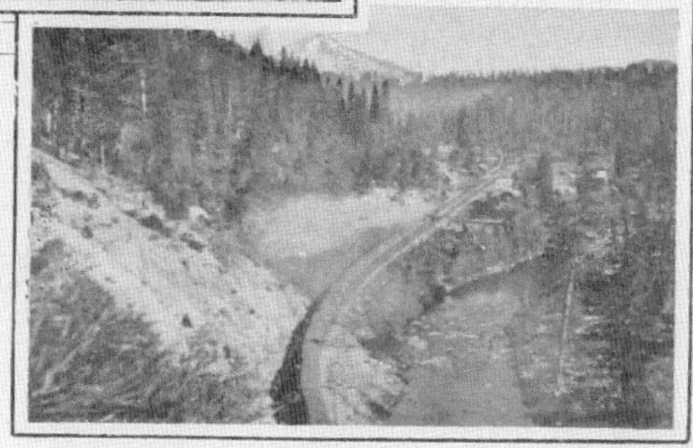

Headwaters of the Sacramento River

OVER THE SOUTHERN PACIFIC RY. TO CALIFORNIA

considerable business in direct shipments to and from over the line between here and Portland of the Northern Pacific Railroad. By its route Seattle has intercourse with California, and thence eastward by either the Central Pacific or Southern Pacific through Arizona and the Southern states. The Northern Pacific has its direct terminals here, and during the past year has expended over one million dollars in buying lands sufficient to carry on its increasing traffic. The Great Northern also has its Western terminus in Seattle, and has already expended hundreds of thousands of dollars in equipping itself in order that it may handle the thousands of tons of merchandise which it hauls to and from. The Canadian Pacific, while officially terminating at Vancouver, British Columbia, has track facilities over the Seattle & International, and to all intents and purposes has its terminus at Seattle. It will thus be seen that in the matter of rail accommodations Seattle is superior to any other city on the Pacific Coast, and in thus briefly passing over such an important element as railroad facilities, it is taken that the facts are sufficiently clear to occasion no lengthy comments.

Its water lines are even more numerously represented. First in importance is the Pacific Coast Company, which operates a line of magnificent steamers between Seattle and San Francisco and other points along the Coast farther south, and it also operates a line of steamers to Alaska. This company has its headquarters here, and maintains its general offices in this city. There are three separate lines of trans-Pacific steamships which are carrying on business with the Orient, and there are more than a dozen companies engaged in operating from one to three ships each between Seattle and points in Alaska. These do not include in any respect the vessels which ply irregularly between this port and the Orient and the various other places in the world, both of steam and sail. It will convey some general idea of the magnitude of the transport business without going into further detail.

ARE DIRECT FACTORY REPRESENTATIVES.

The firm of George B. Adair & Son at 309 Occidental Avenue are the direct representatives of ten factories located in various parts of the United States, in part as follows: The Giant Powder Company; Fairbanks Scale Company; Fairbanks, Morse & Company, railway supplies, gasoline engines, etc.; the Curly Handle Company, ax, pick and sledge handles; the Champion Tool and Handle Works; the Hartz All-Steel Tackle Blocks; Chisholm-Moore Manufacturing Company, differential chain blocks and anti-friction hoists; McCaffery File Company; the Anti-Chlorine Pipe and Boiler Company; James McBeth & Company, electric blasting apparatus, and the McNeale & Urban Safe and Lock Company. Through these firms or manufactories George B. Adair & Son do an extensive business. Their increase last year was fully 40 per cent over the year previous, and compelled them (about the first of the present year) to move into new quarters, where they are now located. They occupy two floors, each 30x115 feet in size, and give employment to five men in their store, and keep one man who represents them on the road. Their trade extends from Alaska to the Columbia River. Mr. George B. Adair has been in Seattle since 1883, and the head of the present company since 1894. He is probably one of the best known merchants in the city.

THE SNOQUALMIE FALLS POWER COMPANY.

As a preface to a resume of the manufacturing interests of Seattle, nothing could be more appropriate than a brief description of one of the greatest water powers and its use as an electrical power generator to be

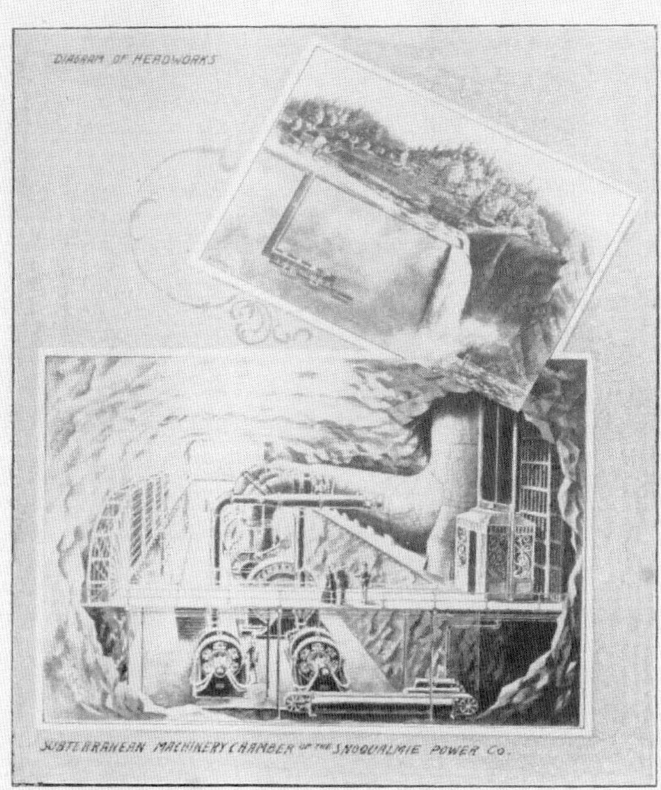

THE SNOQUALMIE POWER CO.

found in the Western Continent. This is the famous Snoqualmie Cataract, located thirty-one miles from Seattle, and which has been successfully harnessed by the Snoqualmie Falls Power Company. This company, which began operations some two years ago, now furnishes power to Seattle and Tacoma, and likewise soon to Everett, and have solved the problem of cheap and abundant power in a most highly satisfactory way.

In October, 1897, Snoqualmie Falls was purchased by Charles H. Baker of Seattle, and with this purchase the conception of the power transmission enterprise began to have practical significance. Thomas T. Johnston, a hydraulic engineer of Chicago, and the consulting engineer of the Chicago drainage canal, sent out here by Mr. Baker to examine the water power and make a preliminary estimate as to the costs and the practicability of utilizing this vast amount of energy, which was represented in the falls of the river, made a favorable report, and in the early spring following, or in 1898 to be precise, the company was organized, a heavy construction plant consisting of large boilers, steam hoisting machinery and a ten-drill air compressor was quickly installed, and the first big drill began operation April 17, 1898, and from that time forward work was prosecuted

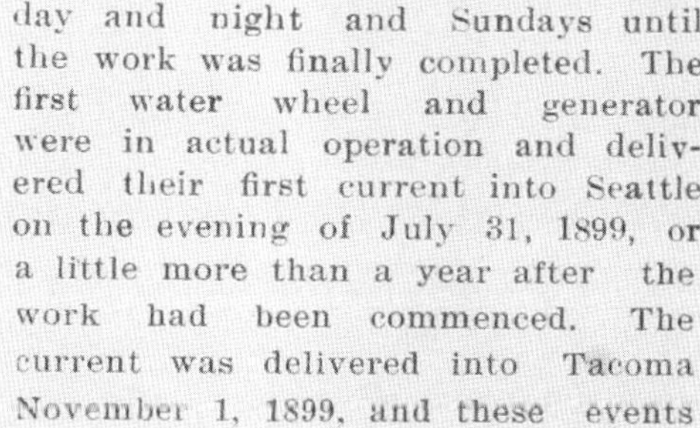

day and night and Sundays until the work was finally completed. The first water wheel and generator were in actual operation and delivered their first current into Seattle on the evening of July 31, 1899, or a little more than a year after the work had been commenced. The current was delivered into Tacoma November 1, 1899, and these events naturally mark the successful completion of the project, which throughout had been unattended by any fatality or serious accident. The design and execution of this plant is replete with original features, never before exploited in power transmission, conspicuous among them being: First, a subterranean power house; second, a cycloidal water wheel, a very efficient water motor; third, use of aluminum wire in long distance transmission. To give one some idea of the undertaking a very brief description will be given. The falls, which, by the way, are 270 feet high, over which the entire volume of the Snoqualmie River falls in one mighty cataract, is utilized in the following manner: About 500 feet back from the brink of the falls a shaft has been sunk in the bed of the river, which descends 270 feet to the level of the river below the falls. Concurrent with the beginning of the shaft above the falls a tunnel 12x24 feet, with an upward slope of twenty feet in its length, was drifted in from the face of the ledge below the falls to an intersection with the shaft, a distance of 650 feet. Beginning at the shaft and extending over and along the tunnel a huge chamber 200 feet in length, forty feet wide and thirty feet high, with the floor at the elevation of high water below the falls, was excavated out of the solid rock, and this cavity, nearly 300 feet below the surface of the earth, is the machinery room in which the water wheel and electric generators have since been installed. At average stages of the river, the tunnel is submerged about two-thirds its depth, while during the flood seasons it is entirely submerged. The water is diverted from the river by an intake constructed of concrete masonry, the walls of which are six feet in thickness and twenty-five feet high, and resting on the native rock, which diverts the water into the shaft above mentioned. In order to keep this bay free of obstructions, heavy timbers have been so arranged that all debris is kept from floating into it—in other words, it is a grating made of timber, and as an extra precaution a heavy steel wire screen adds further precaution to the waters coming into the intake. A rudder boom 300 feet in length is moored up stream on the intake side of the river and reaches past the intake. By turning the capstan at the head of the boom, the rudders are thrown out, which causes the boom to swing out into mid-stream and serves as a fender for floating logs, etc. The river is 150 feet wide at this point, and about fifteen feet deep at ordinary stages. It is contemplated to build a concrete dam diagonally across the river from the down stream pier of the headbay to the opposite shore at the next low water season, which will have a length of about 400 feet, and which on account of its long crest will not cause backing up of flood waters, and at the same time will raise the level of the river at the intake six feet and permit of a better inflow, and equalize the daily flow of water during the period of extreme low water.

Returning again to the shaft, into which the waters have been diverted: A steel penstock seven and one-half feet in diameter rises through the excavation into the bottom of the intake, the top or expansion joint of which is made tight with the rock walls of the shaft, so that a water tight roof is afforded to the shaft, leaving the only escape for the water down through the penstock. A steel bulkhead 8x10 feet, rises beside the penstock and behind the center pier, and this bulkhead, surmounted by a neat little house, is the front door of the subterranean power house. Through it the elevator travels for the convenience of the operation of the works, and through it the electrical conductors descend. The penstock

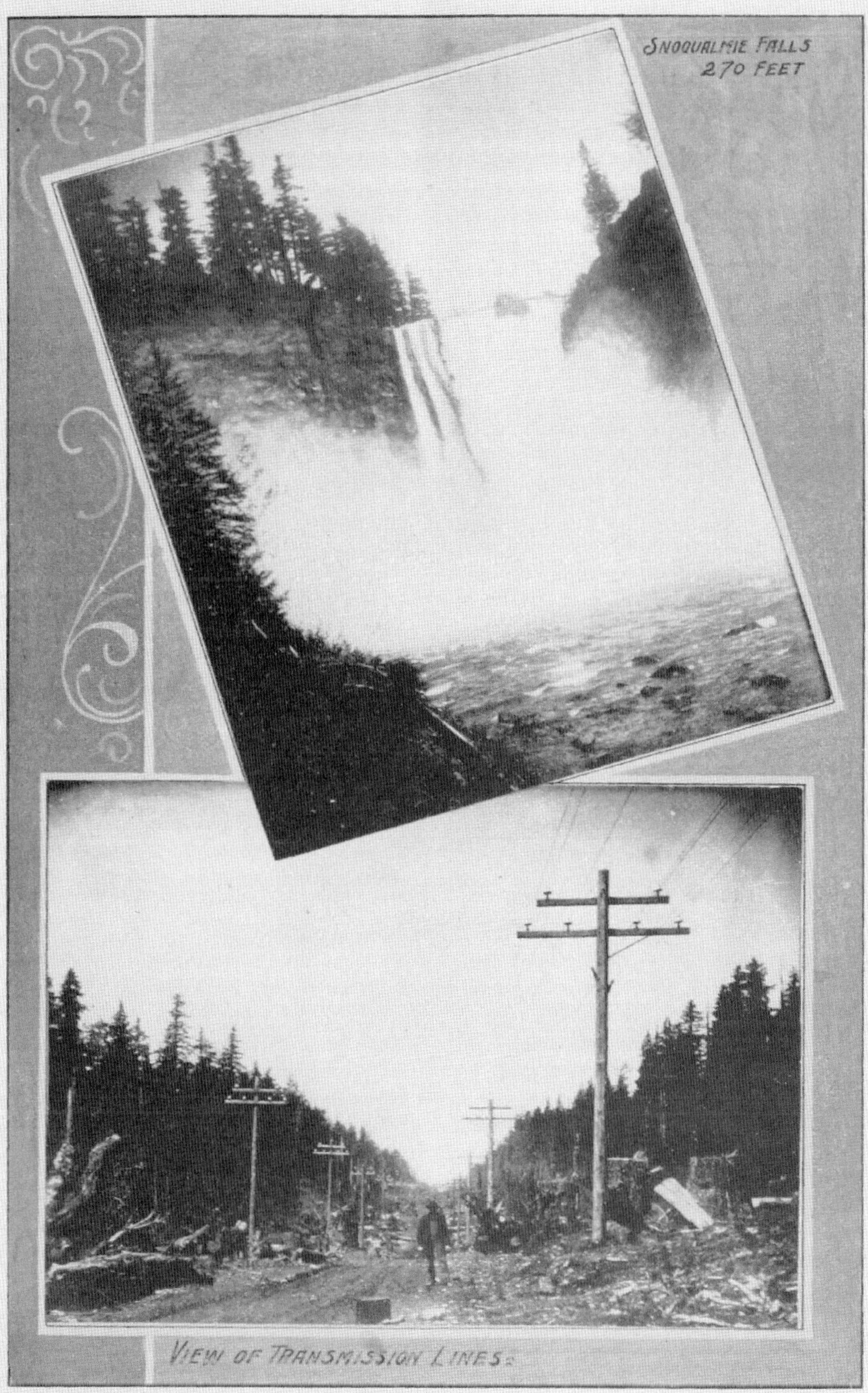

THE SNOQUALMIE POWER CO.

descends 250 feet until the cavity is reached, where it makes a right angle turn to the horizontal position and enlarges to a diameter of ten feet, reducing again to eight feet at the middle section, which horizontal construction is known as the receiver. The receiver and lower half of the penstock are made of rolled steel eight-foot plates, one inch thick. The upper half of the penstock is made of half-inch plates. The whole construction is calked bottle tight. The receiver lies upon a rock bench left in the cavity along its north margin, twelve feet above the floor. The penstock and receiver weigh 450,000 pounds, and the water column in the penstock weighs 340,000 tons—in other words, the 340,000 tons of water which the penstock holds is what furnishes 12,000 horse power of electric energy that the company are now furnishing to consumers. The shaft was made large enough for two penstocks in view of doubling the capacity besides leaving room for the elevator to travel between, as well as for space for outgoing electric conductors. The receiver branches at four points along its length, with four-foot openings, each branch being opened or closed by an immense Rensallaer valve weighing 23,000 pounds, being the largest in use under so great a pressure. Each of these branches is connected with a 3000 horse power Snoqualmie water motor, resting upon the rock floor of the cavity below, under which the tail race extends the entire length and receives the discharge from the motors. Each water motor is directly connected with a 1500 K. W. Westinghouse triphase generator. The current passes from the generators to a marble switch-board, and ascends the shaft on cables of twisted aluminum wire to the transformer house above at a voltage of 1000. The motors in use by the Snoqualmie Company are the invention of the chief engineer of the company. Without going into a technical description of the motors, it can be said that they revolve at a speed of 300 revolutions per minute, and have a capacity of 3000 horse power in the water column; they are simple in construction, cheaply built, and can be designed for any head. The transformer house, of which mention has been made, is fire-proof, built of brick and iron, with a concrete floor having an area of 40x60 and 30 feet high; it stands just east and contiguous to the intake. In this building the current is received at an initial voltage of 1000 and is then passed into a series of step-up transformers, where the voltage is raised to 30,000, which is the voltage of transmission. While at the present time the power which can be generated is estimated at 30,000 horse power, the company estimates that in the event that it was required they would be able to develop 200,000 horse power—enough to furnish Seattle, Tacoma and Everett with all the power necessary for the next fifty years. They own the rights-of-way for the total line leading to both Seattle, Tacoma and Everett, with the exception of several stretches along county roads, over which they have franchises. The right-of-way is patrolled daily by men on horseback, each having a distance of ten miles to go, to see that nothing befalls the line, and in this way they keep a perfect care over their entire lines, and are able to prevent any serious trouble to occur. The circuits used are of aluminum, the first in use for long distance transmission, and they have given very great satisfaction, as aluminum is lighter and is non-corrosive. Excellent cedar poles have been used, and every care has ben exercised in building the works at the falls and in erecting the lines, to put in nothing but the very best of material, regardless of any expense. The result is a very satisfactory power transmission plant, and one which will aid very materially in developing manufacturing interests in the cities to which it is supplied.

In Seattle the company has built at the corner of Main and Second Avenue a very substantial stone and iron building, which is used as a terminal substation and for general offices of the company. The machinery occupies the underground basement, while the company's offices and tenants occupy the street floor space above.

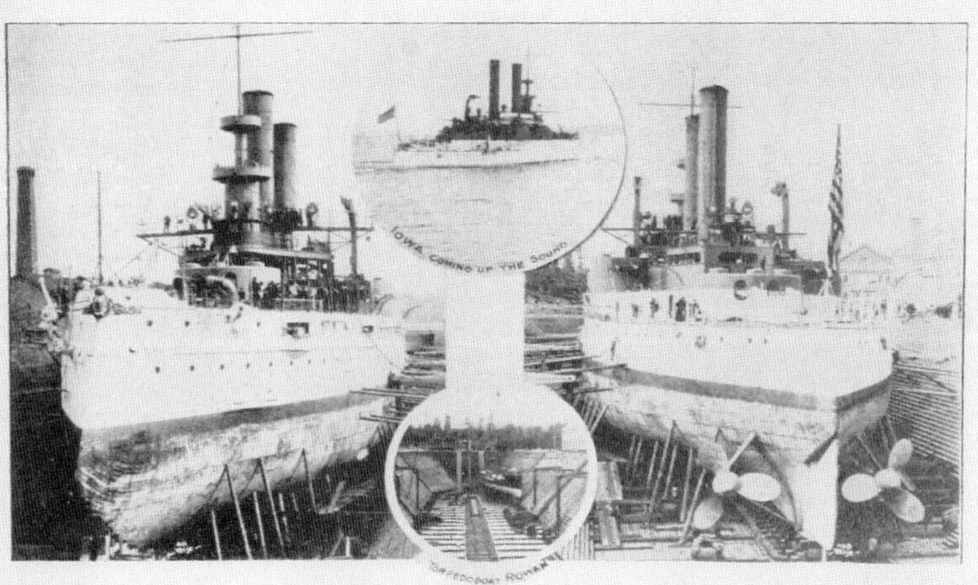

IN THE NAVY YARD OF PUGET SOUND.

Among the large consumers already taking power in Seattle is the Centennial Mill Company, which is now operating two 200-horse power motors, the current from which is supplied by this company. The functions of the company will be to furnish power for all purposes, and it is not unreasonable to believe that almost every wheel turning in Seattle and Tacoma will soon be propelled by the power from Snoqualmie Falls, as well as the power for electric lighting and railways for both towns, and naturally a very great future is in store for it. The constructional operations of this great power project have been conducted throughout by Charles H. Baker, its president and manager, and Thomas T. Johnston, its chief engineer.

PUGET SOUND FISH.

Of the various industries or interests which center at Seattle none has made a more remarkable growth within the past few years than its fishing trade. It has grown from a very insignificant start to a business which gives employment to several hundred people at the present time. The illustrations shown herewith give a view of the wholesale fish house of Frank V. List, formerly George S. List & Brother. It is located at the foot of Lane Street, south of the Stetson-Post Mill Company's property, and has very advantageous arrangements for receiving fish from steamers and shipping by rail. The house has been established three years, and is doing a very extensive business, principally shipping from their fish in cold storage to the Eastern market. Last year the increase was fully 50 per cent. This year Mr. List contemplates operating his own steamboat, and will then be able to greatly increase the amount of product he handles. He now buys fish all the way from Olympia to Alaska, and employs anywhere from ten to twenty-five men. The market in the East for Puget Sound fish is very large and no difficulty is experienced in finding a ready sale for all the fish that can be procured.

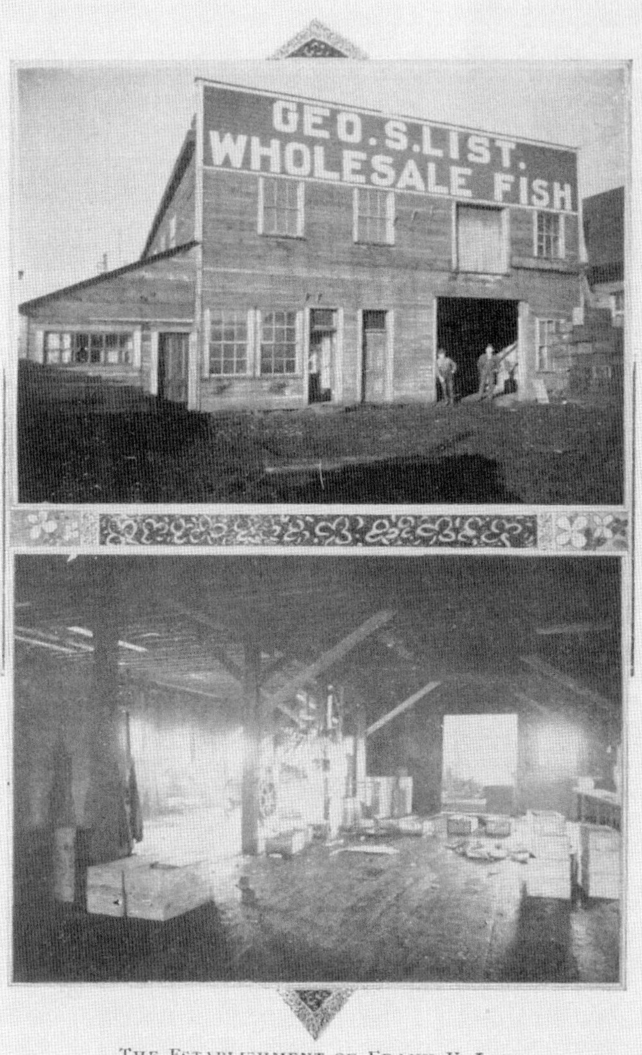

THE ESTABLISHMENT OF FRANK V. LIST.
(Formerly owned by Geo. S. List.)

THE TIMBER OF PUGET SOUND.

Very few people outside of the State of Washington realize the vast importance of the timber wealth of this state. It might also be stated that few people outside of those very familiar with the subject, even in the State, realize the importance of the great lumbering industry now carried on. Directly employed, there are, approximately, 22,000 people engaged in the lumbering business in the western part of Washington, fully two-thirds of whom are upon Puget Sound, and the value of the product which is turned out will reach into the millions. There is not a country in the civilized world which is not now using lumber shipped from Puget Sound; there is hardly a state in the Union but what is receiving lumber or shingles from Puget Sound, and the demand has grown so large (due most largely to its superiority) that it is with much difficulty that the supply is maintained.

The foreign trade which is now developing into very great proportions, and which, by the way, is handled by those mills which are accessible to vessels plying the Pacific, promises to steadily increase as time progresses.

In the State of Washington there are 23,588,512 acres in timber, almost nine-tenths of which lies in Western Washington. The value of this timber, roughly speaking, is probably not far from one billion dollars; and the further the inroads the lumberman makes upon the supply, the more valuable will the remainder become. To give an idea of the shipments from Puget Sound by water it can be stated that 2,250,000 feet per month were shipped for 1899. Over 20,000,000 feet have been shipped from Seattle to coastwise points during the year, and fully 6,000,000 feet went to foreign ports; more than 35,000 cars were loaded and forwarded to Eastern markets, and had it been possible to secure a sufficient number of cars, it is estimated that at least 20 per cent more business would have been done. There are now upward of nearly five hundred small lumber and shingle mills distributed along the lines of railroads centering in Seattle as follows: On the line of the Great Northern, 305; Seattle & International, 75; Seattle & Northern, 10; Northern Pacific, 165; Everett & Monte Cristo, 6; Bellingham Bay & British Columbia, 10; Columbia & Puget Sound, 4; in Seattle, 4; other points, 120. The aggregate daily capacity of these mills is 7,000,000 feet of lumber and 30,000,000 shingles. The number of men employed in logging camps and about the mills during the past year is about 22,000, and the amount of money which the lumbering industry pays for labor is more than one million dollars per month. Nature has supplied the Sound country with suuch a vast quantity of timber that its forests cannot be removed during the next fifty years, and the manufacture of the many kinds of wood will remain, as it now is, the leading industry of Puget Sound. Only the manufacture of fir and cedar has as yet been caried on extensively, but in addition to these valuable woods the forests of Western Washington contain spruce, hemlock, pine, tamarack, yew, maple, alder, cottonwood, vine maple, oak, ash and dogwood, any of which are adapted to the manufacture of all kinds of furniture, barrels, tubs, pails, etc. During the year 1899 there have been about 15 new shingle mills established in the western part of this state, 20 new lumber mills, and 25 logging camps. As stated above, the cut of lumber has averaged about 7,000,000 feet per day. This product represents the labor of one man in the woods, also one man in the mills for every thousand feet of sawed lumber.

IN A WASHINGTON LOGGING CAMP.

A lumberman from the East, suddenly transplanted to the depths of a Washington forest, would throw up his hands, sorrowfully shake his head and loudly bewail his inability to successfully bring the giant conifers to a bed in the saline waters of Puget Sound.

And it is no small task that the lumberman of the Coast undertakes, when one considers the height and girth of the trees with which he must cope. Eastern methods of logging, while unexcelled in their own territory, would be worse than useless on the Coast, and many a logger from the white pine districts has found to his cost that the seemingly crude appliances in vogue in Washington are the only successful methods of operating in such mighty timber.

It may be well to take a bird's-eye view of the work as carried on by the

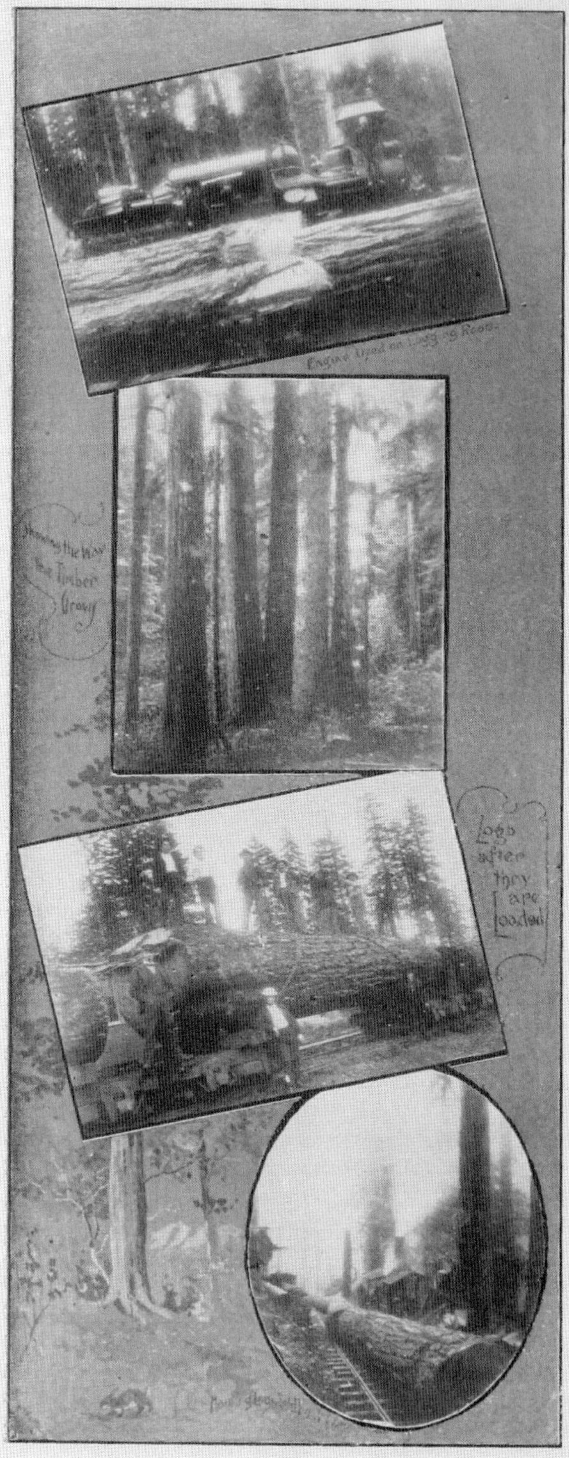

IN CAMPS OF SIMPSON LOGGING CO.

largest concern in the Pacific Northwest, and it is not impossible, the largest individual institution of the kind in the world—that of the Simpson Logging Company.

The company maintains a corps of surveyors, who in addition to their work of "running the lines" of the tracts of timber selected as the next victim of the woodman's axe, select and determine the routes for the extensions of the logging railroads, estimate the cost of bridges, fills and cuts and perform the same duties as of other railroad companies. On their report depends the location of the railroad and the scope of country which can be embraced by the proposed branches.

When the line of road has been fully determined upon and the graders at work, the camp foreman carefully traverses the ground and locates the site for the permanent camp; having reference to its accessibility to the timber, water supply, etc. Formerly camps were built of logs, but with improved methods of transportation which the logging railroads afford, lumber is now chiefly used as a building material. While the picturesque feature of the old-time camp is lost, the ease of construction is greatly increased, and having only mild winters to contend with, the warmth of a log house is unnecessary. In the operations of the company in question portable camps have been utilized with great success. When the timber in reach of the camp has been removed, it is but the work of a few hours to take down these structures, load them on the cars and erect them in some new spot.

With the building of the camps, the grading of the railroad and the selection of his men, the camp foreman has his hands full, but when these necessary adjuncts are once complete, the serious work of logging commences. After a survey of available grades for the skid roads, one crew is put at work cutting out the right of way, grading the road and laying the skids. These skids are small logs from 12 inches to 18 inches in diameter and are sunk one-half their thickness in the ground, being spaced nine feet apart. These skids form the bearings on which the logs are dragged, and as nothing shorter than a 20-foot log is hauled, nine feet centers give each log two bearings and prevents tipping up and tearing out the road.

Another crew is busy preparing the landing or rollway from which the logs are loaded on the cars. When these components of operations are in readiness, the sawyers are set to work and on them depends largely the success of the work. A good head faller can in falling his timber throw a tree in any direction, taking into consideration, of course, its lean and sweep. An incompetent workman can waste his wages many times over by dropping a tree on to a stump, breaking and shattering the timber; or he can place it in such a position that the bucker or man who cuts the fallen monster into log lengths will have to upcut it, thereby losing valuable time, or he can fall it so that great trouble is experienced in yarding it out to the skid road. He is a picturesque figure in red shirt, bare headed, bare armed and brawny chested. Perched on his spring board sometimes twelve and fifteen feet from the ground, he pierces the vitals of the fir with the steel, which gives forth a dirge for the leviathan which it is about to bring to earth.

Slowly, but surely, the saw makes its inexorable way, and finally with a few sharp blows on the wedge, the masive top shivers, sways and bows its head to the mighty will of man.

Following, comes the bucker or sawyer, and on him also depends much. He measures the tree, decides what length of logs it will make, having always in mind his foreman's instructions relative to the lengths wanted for the boom then in preparation. He knows instinctively how to so place his cuts that no defects show on the ends of the log for the scaler's watchful eye to fall upon and he labors from morning to night, a machine of human intelligence. With the last coarse note of his saw through the under bark, comes the hook tender, or man who shall decide in what direction and in what way the log shall be "yarded" or hauled to the skid road. After a careful survey of the conditions of the ground obtaining, this skillful general issues his orders to his subordinates, and soon a fairly clear pathway is hewn from the log to the road.

Carefully, deliberately, with no undue haste, comes plodding a faithful horse; stepping over obstacles, avoiding pitfalls, browsing on a tempting bit of scrub he comes, dragging one end of a seven-eighth-inch wire cable, the other end being no man knows where. By this time steel dogs are driven into the log and everything prepared for its initial journey to tide water. The barkers have hewed the ride (the portion which rides the ground), the snipers have bevelled the end so that the sharp corners may not catch on roots or other impediments, and the pounders have seen that the dogs are so driven that they shall not pull out. One end of the line is hooked to the dog, blocks rove to carry the line around obstacles, and with a stentorian roar the hook tender gives the signal to the waiting "donkey" or winding engine to whose drum the invisible end of the line is fastened, to "go ahead," and with a groan, a shiver and a heave the line taughtens, the blocks raise from the ground, and the log starts forward on its first stage to the water. Many are the obstacles in its course, and skillful the manner in which the hook tender removes the same. Now, by a "lead" with a block, a stump is avoided, again by a change in "hold" a roll is given that takes it over a windfall, until the clear road is reached and the yarding donkey's labors are over.

Coupling dogs are driven, and linked to three, four or even seven of its fellows, the great bole glides slowly off impelled by the insistance of the road donkey at the other end of an inch in diameter steel cable. This road donkey engine may be a mile and one-quarter from the log when first it starts on its journey, but the inevitable steel rope curls its devious way guided by rollers around the tree trunks, rocks and hills, the log following the gentle sheer given by the skids, until with a final pant the engineer shuts off steam and the log rests on the rollway or platform, preparatory to being loaded on the cars for the final stage of its journey to salt water. This rollway holds from one hundred to one hundred and fifty thousand feet of timber, and is elevated the height of the bunks on the logging cars from the track.

The logging trucks are placed in position, the loading donkey's cable is wrapped around the log, and the giant rolls gently onto the trucks and brings up hard against the chocks which prevent its gaining the ground on the other side of the car. Car after car is loaded, and when the locomotive with its train of "empties" comes puffing in sight its return load of from sixty to seventy thousand feet of logs stands ready to "hit the trail" for its final resting place.

The balance of the journey is fraught with not a little danger, and the men manning the log trains have many

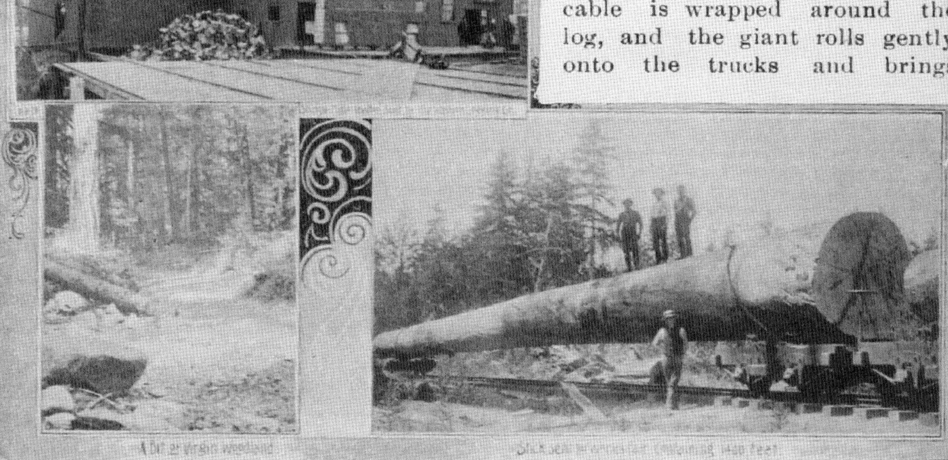

THE SIMPSON LOGGING CO.

more perils to contend with than their brothers of the strictly mercantile rail. Chocks and "dutchmen" get loose, dogs pull, rails spread and trees fall across the track, and with the sharp curves, heavy grades and the necessity for hand breaking, a job on a logging train is no sinecure.

The method of unloading the logs from the truck and their final deposit in the waters of the Pacific is one peculiar to the coast. On a parallel track to the one on which the loaded train stands is a box car in which is mounted a hoisting engine and crane. A rope rove through its extremity carries a swamp hook which engages with the log and a few turns of the drum of the engine is sufficient to roll the log from the car and dump it into the water. The "unloader" by a system of transmission chains propells itself to the next car when the operation is repeated, and in a surprisingly short time the trucks are clear and ready for their return to the woods.

Modifications of the above method of logging of course are employed in some camps of the company, whose operations are outlined above, horses being used instead of steam, but they are gradually being supplanted by the latter contrivances.

To give some idea of the magnitude of the operations of the largest logging concern on the Coast, the following may be of interest. The Simpson Logging Company of Seattle, Washington, whose works are chiefly in Mason County, operate seven camps, two lines of standard-gauge railroad, one with its branches and ramifications comprising about forty miles, while the other with sidetracks and switches covers at least sixty miles of grade. For the operation of these roads ten locomotives are used, varying in weight from twenty-five to sixty tons. Of these three are used for yarding purposes or taking the loaded cars from the branches to the main lines, where they are made up into trains for the salt water trip. These yarding locomotives are of the geared type, and can haul a train load of empty trucks up a 12 per cent grade and a train of loaded cars on 5 per cent grade without "turning a hair." In the preparation of the logs for the train twenty-two donkey engines and eighty horses are used. The donkeys winding from 1000 to 6500 feet of seven-eighth-inch to one-inch steel cable. This company also utilizes a device for taking logs up and down steep places in order to do away with the use of "chutes." This use of chutes permits of the descent of the log from a high level at terrific speed, fills the timber with gravel and stones, damaging the mill saws and lessening the marketable quality of the logs. To obviate this, a heavy boiler and hoisting engine of peculiar construction are mounted on a flat car. Around a wheel rigged with grips passes a wire cable, whose ends are made fast, one at the foot and one at the summit of the grade to be overcome. The logs are rolled on the track ahead of the machine, and coupled to the same. When started the machine acts as a brake and brings them to the bottom of the decline without hurt. It then winds itself up the rope to its proper place at the top of the declivity. If necessary the operation can be reversed and the logs hauled up as high as a 7 per cent grade.

The seven camps of the company are all connected with the central office by telephone, so that instructions can be given to the several foremen without loss of time. The pay roll comprises some 500 names beside the heads of the different departments. In connection with the actual business of logging, the company furnishes supplies for its camps and employes from two large general stores, and three large steamers are employed in its transportation service. Its annual output aggregates 100,000,000 feet of logs per year, and its large shingle mill has an annual capacity of 50,000,000 shingles in the same time.

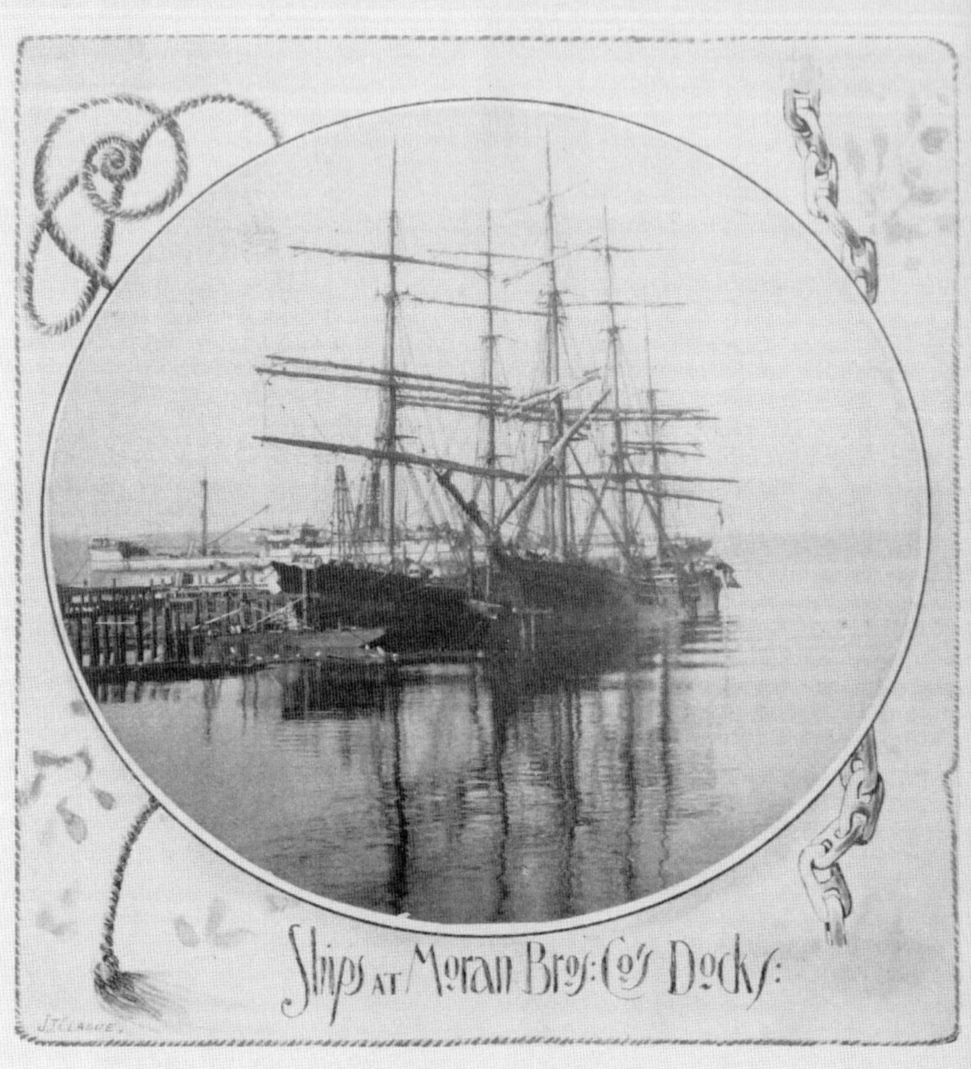

Ships at Moran Bros. Co's Docks.

The head, originator and active principal in this enormous business is S. G. Simpson, who ten years ago started the ball rolling with six horses and twenty men. The foregoing article shows what has resulted from this small beginning. Showing the progressive tendencies of the man it is only necessary to state that Mr. Simpson inaugurated engines in logging, and the first donkey engine ever installed in the woods was operated by him.

From this small beginning sprang the immense business of the present day, and as an example of push, energy and sound business sense, Mr. Simpson is "facile princeps."

FRANCIS ROTCH.

SHIP BUILDING ON PUGET SOUND.

Moran Bros. Company Building Up a Great Industry.

Ship building on the Pacific Coast, although in its infancy as yet, promises to become ere long equal in magnitude to the long established industry of like nature along the Atlantic Coast.

Several yards in California have been established many years, and have built many of the fine vessels now in service on this Coast.

Yards on Puget Sound have also been active in building vessels for all kinds of service.

To Seattle belongs the distinction of possessing among its many growing and prosperous industries, a ship yard and engine building works which for rapid growth has outclassed many sister enterprises. Moran Bros. Company's business was established in Seattle in the year 1882, with a small capital, and its present large proportions represent the natural outgrowth of such an enterprise where it is backed by industry and energy.

This company built its first vessel, the fireboat Snoqualmie, only ten years ago.

Several years elapsed after building this vessel without opportunity for this company to secure ship building contracts, and during which time it acquired a reputation for designing and building high-class machinery and general structural work, but since 1895 the company has come foremost as a ship building concern of the first class.

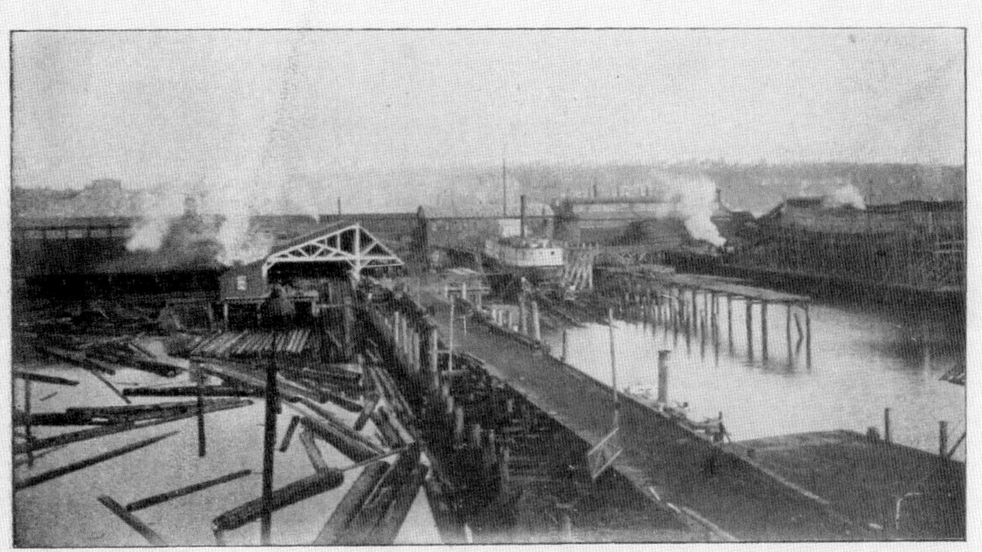

MORAN BROS. CO —OVERLOOKING WORKS FROM OUTER WHARF.

The first steel vessel constructed in the Pacific Northwest was built and equipped at the works of the company in Seattle, and several steel vessels have been built there since, fully establishing this plant as a successful steel ship building yard.

Only a year ago the company, realizing the growing importance of wood ship building, decided to build large saw and planing mills in connection with a modern wood ship yard, all of which has been accomplished, the mills and ship yard having been in operation for several months.

This company's business has covered a wide range of work, including vessels for the United States Navy Department, also revenue cutters, river boats, Sound steamers, ocean going steel and sail vessels of both wood and steel construction.

Moran Bros. Company's specialty is rapid work, and its ability to handle work of magnitude on short time contracts was well demonstrated in the early part of 1898, when it built and equipped ready for service twelve large passenger river steamers for the Yukon River trade in the short time of four months. Each of these vessels was of the following dimensions: 175 feet long, 35 feet beam, 6½ feet depth of hold, and each fitted with two engines with 20-inch diameter cylinders, 7-foot stroke. These vessels were taken under their own steam from Seattle to St. Michael, Alaska, which contemplated an ocean voyage of approximately 4000 miles. Eleven of the twelve steamers were delivered at St. Michael in first-class condition, and entered upon service on the Yukon River. Moran Bros. Company have built practically all of the vessels now navigating those waters. The above feat of river boat building, taken into consideration with the voyage from Seattle to St. Michael, Alaska, and the shortness of the time within which it was accomplished, is probably unparalleled in the history of the world in that line of work.

There is now building at the company's new yard a wooden steamship for the Pacific Clipper Line, to be used in its Cape Nome trade. This vessel will be thoroughly finished and equipped for first-class passenger service, for which the time allowed from the sawing of the first timber to the completion of the vessel is 120 days.

This vessel is nearly 250 feet in length, is heavily built and the finishing throughout is to be artistic as well as substantial. To those acquainted with the work of building such a vessel the short time mentioned will be thought remarkable. They also have under construction a large four-masted schooner for the same company.

During the past year large extensions have been made to this company's plant, which now includes steel and wood ship building in all its branches, saw mill in which the largest and longest timber can be cut, including sticks as large as 48 inches square and 125 feet long.

The company also operates the largest and best equipped foundry, machine shop and boiler shop and forge on the North Pacific Coast. The boiler shop and forge are equipped with the largest and most modern tools on the Pacific Coast, equal to any requirements. The plant covers an area of sixteen acres, with nearly a mile of dock frontage, and with all transcontinental railway tracks connected direct to the shops and yards.

On the deep water dock there is constructed a seventy-five-ton electric shear for transferring heavy machinery from the cars to vessels, or vice versa. This plant, taken as a whole, is probably the most complete of any on the Pacific Coast today, as within itself it has the facility for the construction of any work, the hull and machinery of either wood or steel vessels, also including cabin work and the larger part of the equipment, making the plant independent of any outside source of supply.

To those who are unfamiliar with the process of building a steamship, a short description of the work may prove interesting. The owner having determined on a certain capacity for any desired service, the designer lays out the lines of a hull of the required displacement; the general form or degree of fineness of water lines being suited to the speed desired. Calculations are then made to ascertain the power and type of machinery. The general outline having thus been determined, the arrangements of the vessel's framing and plating or planking are then laid out on a scale model, and the detail drawings of the hull construction may then be made.

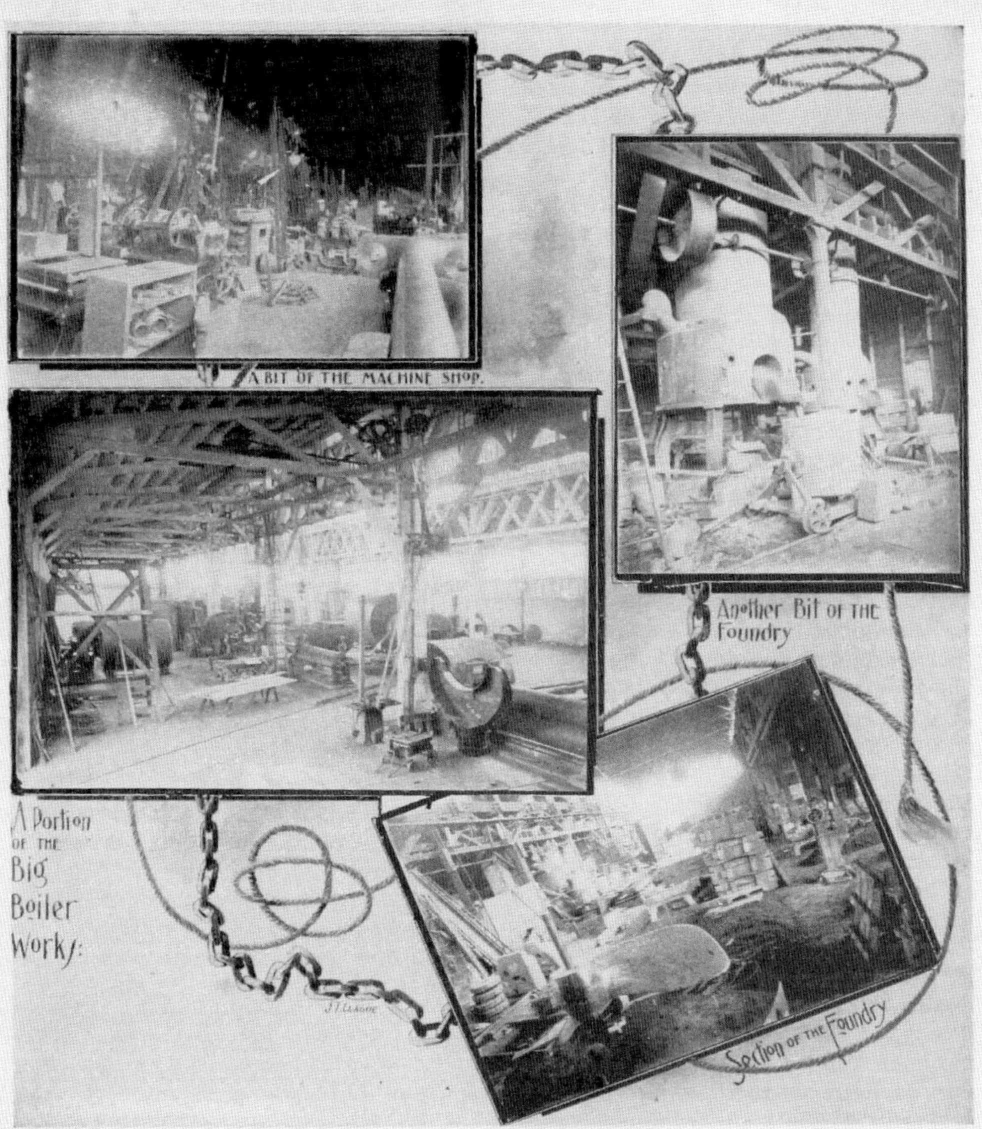

In Moran Bros. Co.'s Ship Yards.

The work of laying down the lines full size on the mold lift floor is next in order, after which the molds are "lifted," which means that a portable mold or pattern of each of the vessel's parts is made from the lines on the floor for the purpose of transferring the shape to the respective pieces of the bulk material.

Meantime the detail plans of shop drawings of the machinery and hull trimmings are being made so that by the time the keel of the vessel is laid the entire work is well in progress.

The assembling of the vessel's parts, plating or planking, installing of machinery and general finishing and equipment are all operations with which the reader is more or less familiar. Each respective detail requires most careful study and attention, so as to insure substantial work and compliance with the requirements of all laws and regulations. The launching of a vessel is generally a source of excitement in the ship yard, and to see a ship enter the water always gives the builder a sense of pride and satisfaction. The preparations incident to launching the vessel are attended with much care and vigilance on the part of the constructor, as the least neglect or error in the arrangement of the details might render the launch a failure, or cause irreparable injury to the work so carefully done on the cradle.

Not least among the builder's trials is the trial trip of the vessel, when her machinery and framing are tested to their full capacity to satisfy the owner that no part of the work has been slighted or errors made in the original design, and a successful trial fully repays the builder for his care and anxiety during construction.

Moran Bros. Company have a clean record of trials of vessels built at its works, all requirements having invariably been exceeded, and it is a gratifying pleasure to the citizens of Seattle and the Pacific Northwest to note that this company's plant is rapidly expanding and to offer their wishes of success and prosperity to the men whose enterprising spirit has been the foundation of an industry destined to become a source of pride to all.

There is also under construction at the present time a large two-section floating dry dock, which is of the following general dimensions: 400 feet long, 100 feet wide, and with a lifting capacity to dock any vessel of this length. The company also operates a marine railway with a capacity for docking vessels of 1500 tons and less.

All of the shops are equipped with electric traveling cranes and other labor saving appliances, including compressed air and hydraulic tools of every description.

A few details of the Moran Brothers Company's shipbuilding yards will prove of interest to the ordinary reader, or at least those who take an interest in the building up of a great big industry such as this is proven to be. Beginning at the office of the company, if the visitor should desire to make a trip through their establishment, going first through the machinery shop, and then around by way of the ship yard and saw mill, he would be most thoroughly impressed with what he saw. The first buildings to the left are the machine shops, in which are located the most substantial character of iron working tools. As at present arranged, a little to the south and under the same roof, is the foundry. In order to expedite work, an over-head traveling crane is operated, capable of lifting fifteen tons of metal. For instance, if an iron bar or a heavy casting is desired to be placed upon a lathe or planer, the man who has charge of the crane is given the order and with his independent engine which shifts the crane from one position to another or lowers the great block and tackle, the piece of casting or iron bar is picked up and transported to the position desired, all in the space of a very few moments. Everything is conducted in order to expedite time and for the relief of great bodily exertion.

Passing through the machine shop one comes first to the copper smith shop, where the various articles in use about a ship are constructed. In the rear of this shop are the store rooms, where all conceivable articles of marine hardware are stored. Still further south of this is the pipe-fitting works, and across an open driveway principal reason being that the articles purchased are not of the high standard or equal to those they can manufacture. When one has reached the pattern shop they have practically finished with that portion of the shops erected at the organization of the company. Between this space and the new boiler shops there is a warehouse and a shed; to the left of this is the blacksmith shop, in which the heavy forging and various other work is done. Probably the most interesting place to visit

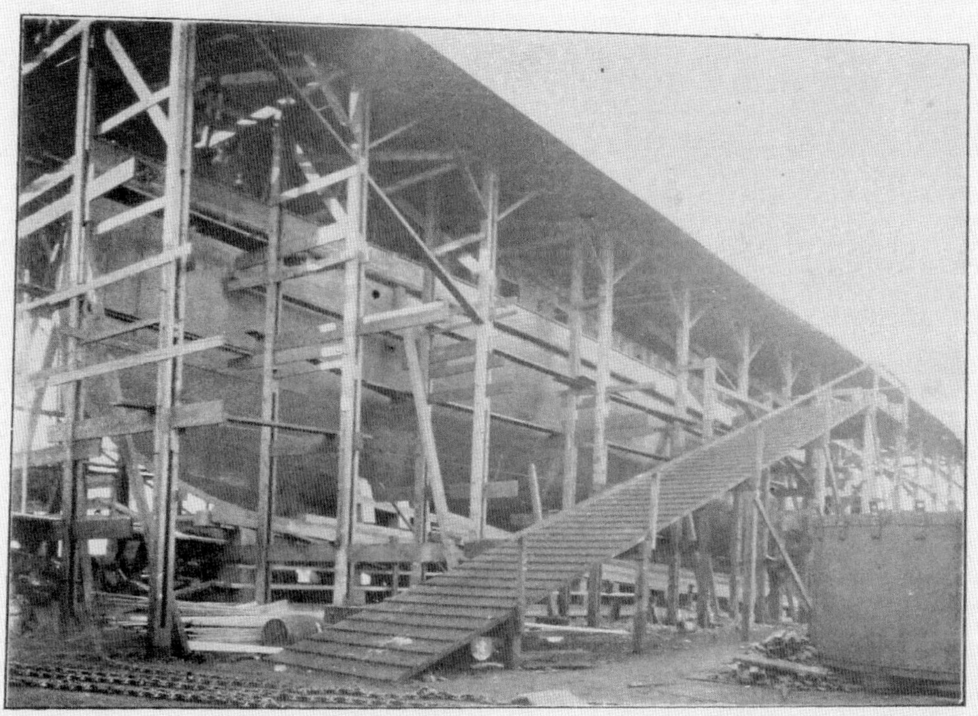

WHERE THEY BUILD STEEL SHIPS.

is the brass or copper foundry. Still farther along is the pattern shop and furniture factory. The visitor would probably be surprised when he is told that in the furniture factory practically everything in the shape of wood work or furniture to be used in fitting out the interior of a ship is constructed. Even such articles as the wheels in use, the settees and other innumerable articles. The company, no doubt, could purchase these things as cheaply as they could make them, but it does not follow out their line of policy, the is the shop one will enter from this point—the new boiler works. This is a portion of the new works which is contemplated and for which plans have been drawn some little time. The building is built after the most improved plan and is most substantially constructed, having plenty of light and room enough for carrying on all works without obstruction, and so arranged that machinery will work to the utmost advantage. Running the full length of this shop is a traveling crane, operated by electricity, which has a lifting capacity of thirty tons; it is quick acting and will do the work much more speedily than the old style or those which are operated by steam power. The shop is supplied with practically every modern machine, including a compressed air and hydraulic plants, which furnish power for rivetting, drilling, etc., and is easily transported by means of a hose and pipes from various parts of the building, or can be carried on to adjacent places on the premises. There are also gigantic punches, one of the largest set of rolls for rolling sheet iron in the United States, enormous shears for cutting up plate used in the construction of boilers—and, in fact, almost every conceivable device for expediting the handling of the parts which go to make up boilers. From this building one turns to the west and follows the wharf out to the ship yards. A portion of the sheds, which will be extended clear to the outer limits of the wharf, have already been constructed, and some idea can be formed of the way it will operate when completed. To be brief, it contemplates an electric traveling bridge, which will be sufficiently high to move above vessels which are being built in the yard, and modeled much after the steam or power cranes; it will enable the operator to pick up a stick of timber or other heavy material which now requires a great deal of bodily exertion, and place it in position upon the vessel required, in a fraction of the time it now takes to perform this task. This traveling crane will move over the section allotted to shipbuilding purposes; in other words (using the picture of the George W. Dickenson which is shown in a picture herewith as an illustration) this bridge will be able to move above such vessels, and one can readily appreciate the enormous advantage of having such an auxiliary to the work in hand. This portion of the yard will probably be devoted to wooden shipbuilding and has ample capacity for several vessels on the stocks at one time. A waterway sufficiently wide to permit of egress and ingress will be left, and on the opposite side, near where the present marine railway is situated, will be located a floating drydock of size and capacity sufficient to life up any vessel which may desire to take advantage of it. The machinery for this dock is now being built by the company, and it will be constructed as speedily as possible. At the present time the whole works, from one end to the otner, are going through a transitory state. The plans contemplated call for the most modern and complete shipbuilding plant in the country, in which both steel and wooden ships can be advantageously

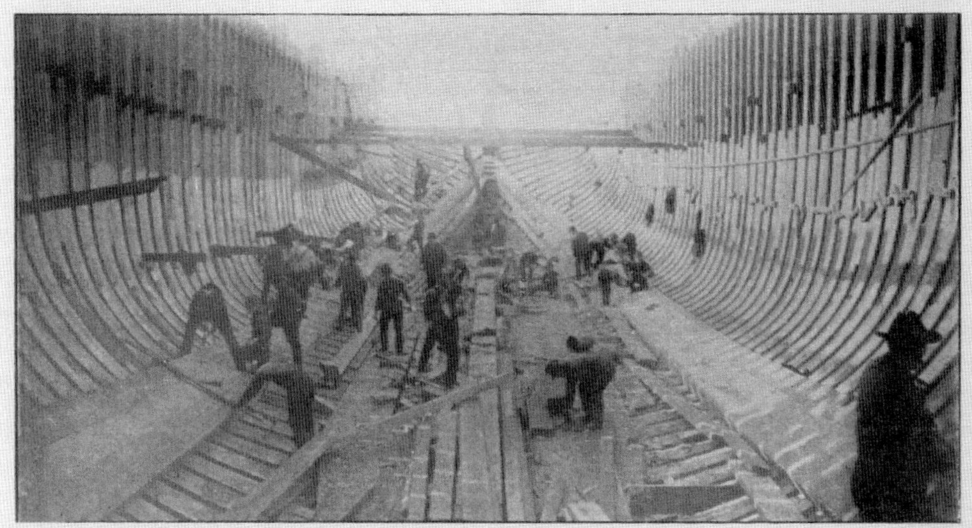

MORAN BROS. CO.—HOW A SHIP LOOKS ON THE INSIDE WHILE IN FIRST STAGES OF CONSTRUCTION.

built. It will be possible when finished—in fact, very shortly—to do the labor that now requires a dozen men to perform, with the assistance of but one or two; for instance, a large steam crane will be constructed on the outer end of the northern wharf, which will be capable of lifting seventy-five tons. Upon the completion of a boiler weighing fifty or sixty tons, it will be lifted from the floor of the boiler shop upon a car, and this car will run out through the works upon the wharf alongside of the waiting vessel, and this great, immense crane will pick it up and lower it in position, doing the work in half a day that under ordinary circumstances requires several weeks. It is intended to build the shops, or an extension of the boiler shops, through to the northern entrance, or, practically speaking, where the offices now stand, in which will be located the machine shops, the foundry, blacksmith shop and various establishments now located in the various buildings, all in this one great establishment, with the exception of the pattern shop and furniture factory. The building then will have an approximate length of 580 feet. The present offices will be torn away, and a brick building erected in their place, with ample quarters, and specially guarded against any possible fire. There will be railroad side tracks for the receiving of freight, built into yards, and trackage facilities throughout the yards for the transporting of their own material from one point to another, operated by their own locomotives; and by being able to manufacture not only in wood, but in all kinds of metal, everything practically used in the construction of a ship, down to the minutest detail, the Moran Brothers Company will have an establishment which will exceed anything at present on the Pacific Coast. The saw mill which was recently constructed by them and is now in operation, having a capacity of 80,000 feet of lumber per day, gives them the advantage of getting out just such lumber and such wooden materials as are best needed for all purposes.

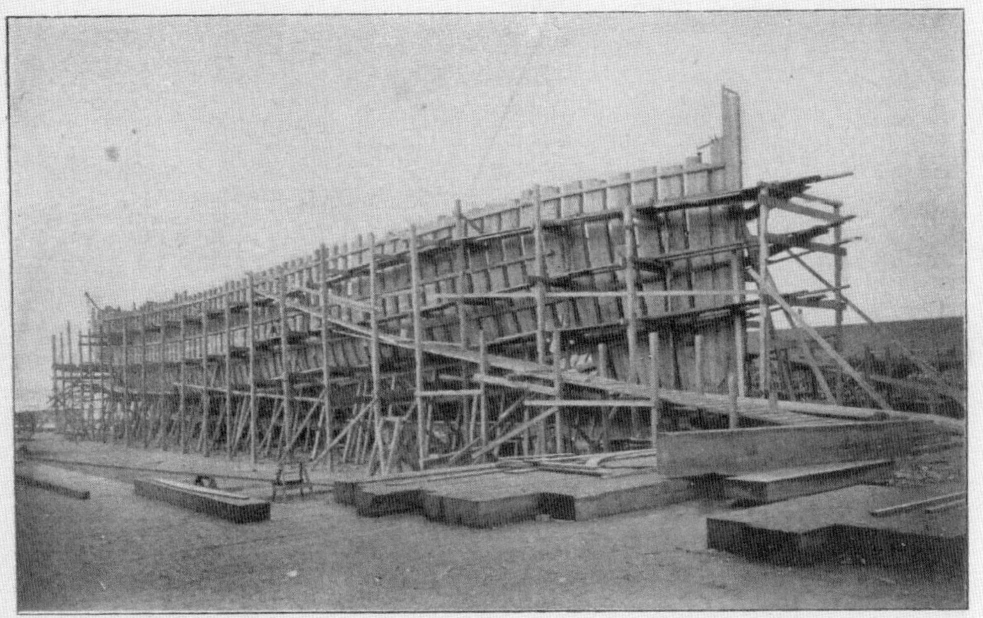

MORAN BROS. CO.'S SHIP YARD.—THE FRAME OF STEAMER GEO. W. DICKINSON 30 DAYS AFTER LAYING KEEL.

To give an idea of the magnitude of the foundry which they have in operation, it can be stated that a few days since a single casting was made which contained 32,000 pounds of metal. It is doubted if any larger castings were ever made on the Pacific Coast than this. But to describe the whole establishment in the minutest detail would occupy a very considerable space and probably be so technical that the average reader would not understand it. It has been more the purpose of this article to give some general idea of what shipbuilding in Seattle is destined to become, rather than to go into the finer details.

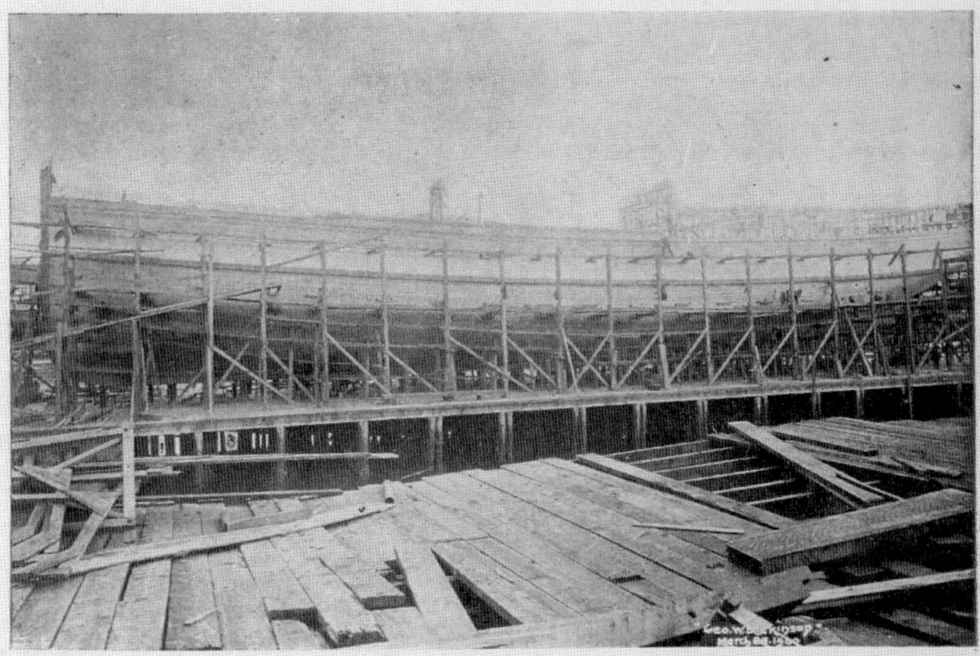

MORAN BROS. COMPANY.
View of Steamer Geo. W. Dickinson 50 days after her keel was laid. She is being built for Pacific Clipper Line.

GALBRAITH, BACON & COMPANY.

One of the extensive commodities that is shipped from Seattle to Alaska and to the Orient, and which has grown considerably during the past year, is hay and mill feed. Through a process of compression Galbraith, Bacon & Co., who occupy the Galbraith Dock at the foot of Washington Street, upon the water front, are enabled to compress hay into one-half the volume or space formerly required to put up this commodity, and during the past year they have developed an enormous trade. They are wholesale dealers in feed, grain, hay, building materials of all kinds, such as lime, plaster and cement, and their increase last year over the previous year was equal to 35 per cent. The company has been in business here for nine years, and now has a trade which extends all over Western Washington, down to the Hawaiian Islands, into California and into Alaska. J. E. Galbraith is the senior partner and manager and is represented as one of the very substantial merchants doing business in Seattle. He occupies a very beautiful residence at No. 109 Fifteenth Avenue North, a picture of which is shown in future pages of this volume. Their warehouse is one of the busy places in the city. Eleven steamboats make a landing at this place, and have intercourse with all points on Puget Sound. About their wharf and in their warehouse they give steady employment to thirty people, and during the year they will probably increase this number, at least to the extent of putting representatives on the road to travel in their interest.

ROHLFS & SCHODER.

Seattle has one of the largest bank and office fixture manufacturing concerns in the Northwest in the firm of Rohlfs & Schoder. They are located at 610 to 620 First Avenue South in a building 150x150 feet in size. They have been established here since 1889 and are really the successors of the Hall & Polson Furniture Company. At the present time they give employment to forty people and the extent of their trade is very considerable. Their product, as above stated, consists of bank and office fixtures, which means practically the manufacture of counters, steamboat fixtures, and all kinds of stationary furniture, such as is used in banks, offices, steamboats and stores and covers a pretty wide range. The firm is one of the best known on Puget Sound, and the fact that their establishment is crowded with orders and their mill is about one of the busiest places in Seattle is evidence of the standing they possess. An illustration is shown herewith which will give some idea of the size of the building they occupy, but to thoroughly appreciate the great amount of industry manifested one is compelled to make a visit through their place.

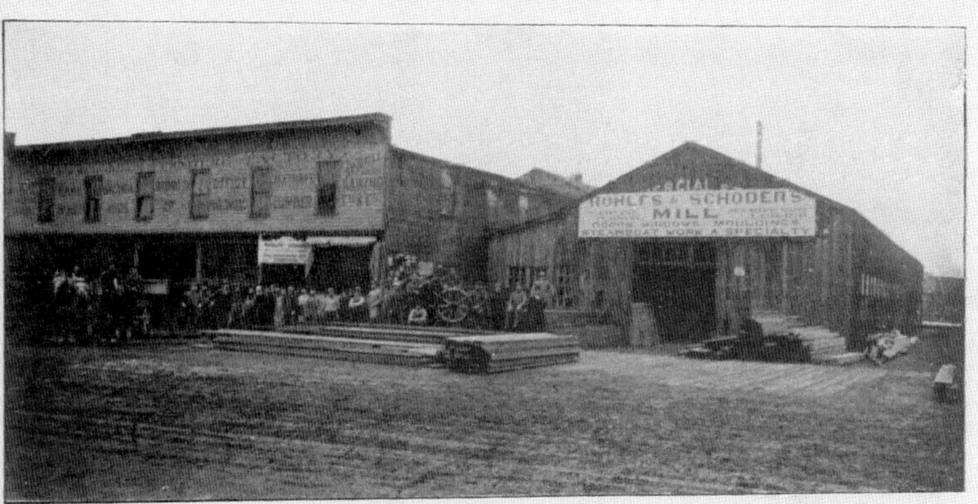

FACTORY OF RHOLFS & SCHODER.

ONE OF THE BIG MACHINE WORKS.

One of the largest and best known machine works on the North Pacific Coast is that of the Washington Iron Works Company, which occupies two and one-half blocks of land on Grant Street, in the southern part of the city. Some illustrations accompany this article, which will afford an idea of the magnitude of the plant. The one of the exterior view does not take in the entire establishment, because of the fact that the buildings in which are located the foundry are some little dis-

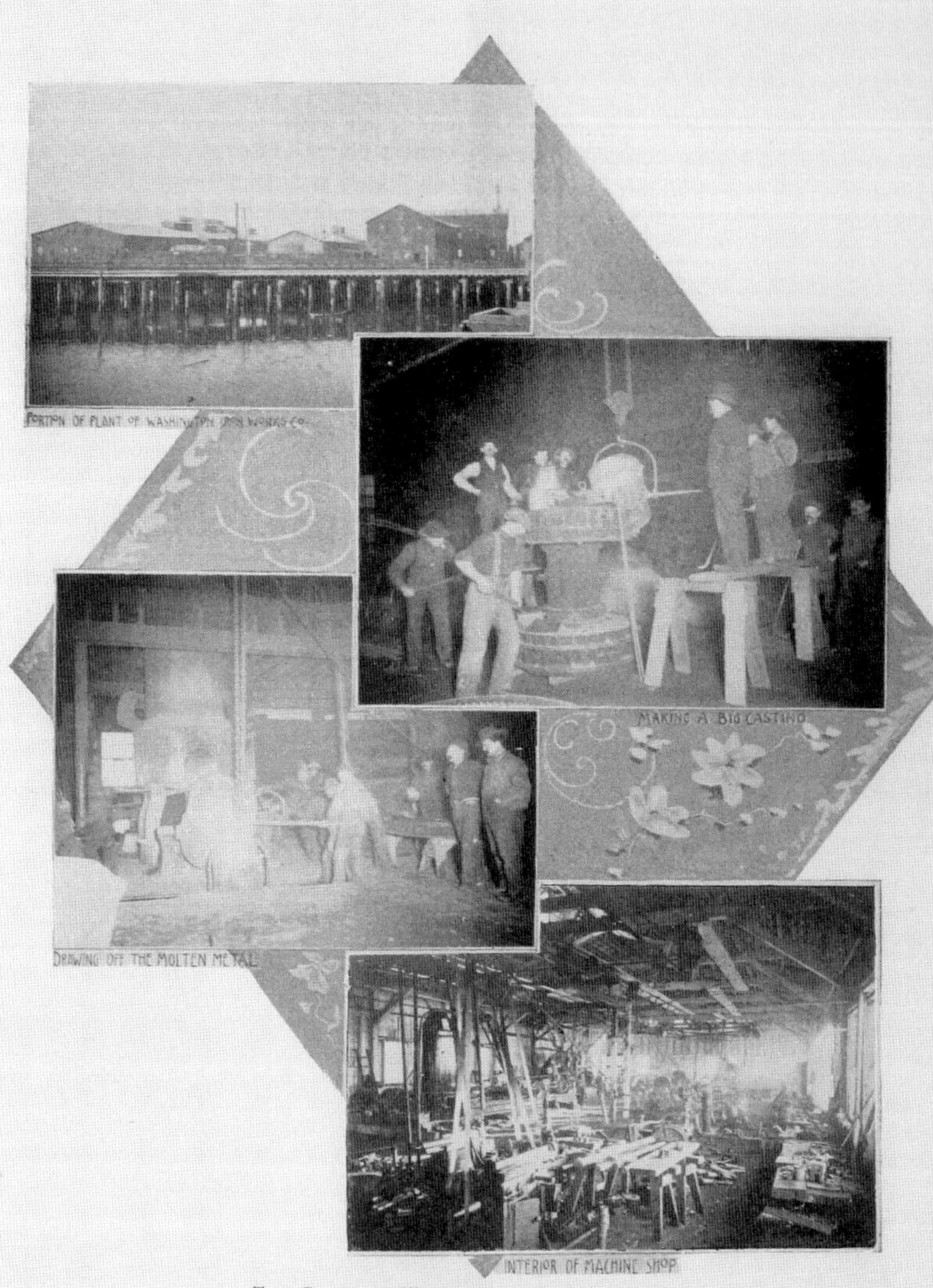

THE PLANT OF WASHINGTON IRON WORKS CO.

tance away on the opposite side of the street. Illustrations, however, do not always tell a complete story in themselves, but help to emphasize their character and magnitude. The Washington Iron Works was established in 1882, and has steadily grown from that day to this, until it now occupies a foremost position in the manufacture and repair of all kinds of machinery. The principal product of this concern is the manufacture of engines and exceed that this year. The company give employment to over 140 men in their various departments. One of their specialties, if it may be called that, is the building of a logging engine along the lines of great superiority. The demand by loggers throughout the Coast for this particular engine has been so great that it has been almost impossible to supply the demand. J. M. Frink, president and general manager of the company.

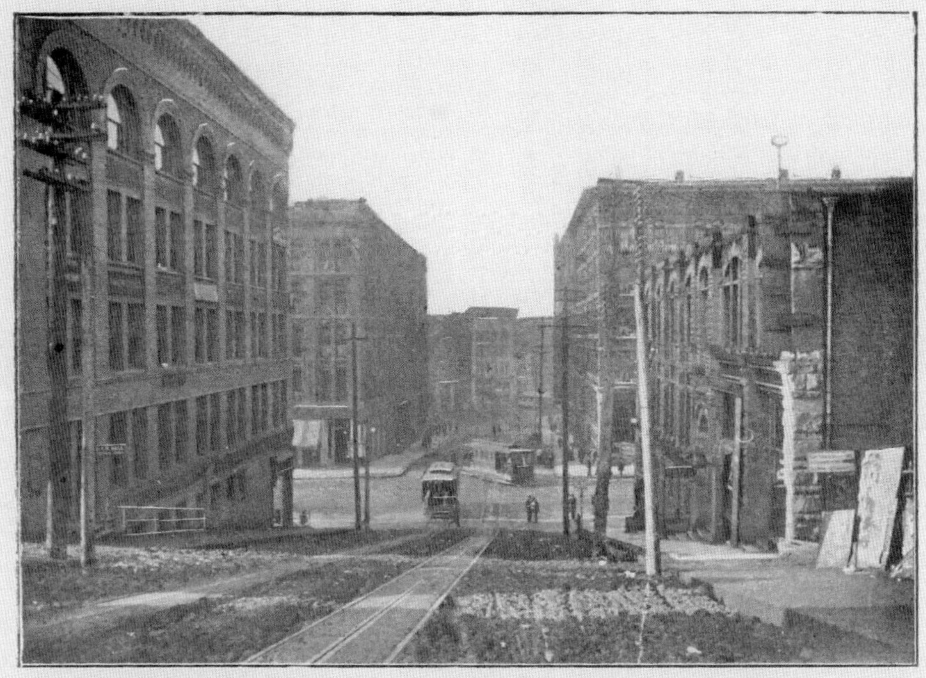

JAMES STREET, LOOKING TOWARD PIONEER SQUARE, SHOWING SEATTLE HOTEL ON LEFT.

boilers, as well as all kinds of mining, milling and logging machinery. Their product has been sold in the Northern territory on the one hand, and as far south as Nicaragua on the other. Because of their general increase in business they contemplate a general enlargement and are now engaged in installing considerable new machinery, two car loads of which recently arrived from the East. Their increase last year over the previous year amounted to fully 20 per cent and it will probably states that these engines are sold faster than they can be made, and that he looks forward to a very big year's business for 1900.

It is establishments like this wnich give very great prestige to the manufacturing industries of Seattle and give the city a high reputation among all classes of people. The foundry belonging to the company is one of the finest on the Coast and is fitted out with every modern convenience for the handling of all kinds of castings, including those of very great size.

THE J. E. FOX SAW WORKS.

The only plant for the manufacture of saws upon the Coast is located here in Seattle. It is the establishment of the J. E. Fox saw works. The manufacturing establishment or works are located at 901 First Avenue South, while their office and warehouse is located at 112 Washington Street. The works occupy a building 60x180 feet, two stories in height, a picture of which is shown among other industries. The concern manufacture all kinds of circular saws and saw teeth for use of lumber and shingle manufacturers, and as this place is the centre of a very large lumbering industry, the saw works have developed a very extensive business. They have been established here six years. Last year the increase in their business was fully 200 per cent in excess of the year previous, and this year it is contemplated to greatly enlarge the plant and afford a much greater capacity. At the present time twenty-two men are employed, in addition to one man who travels upon the road in the interest of the concern. The saws made by the Fox saw works are used all over Washington, and in many places outside of the State. Practically speaking, the firm have had all the business they could do, and in order to keep up with the demand are compelled to increase their capacity.

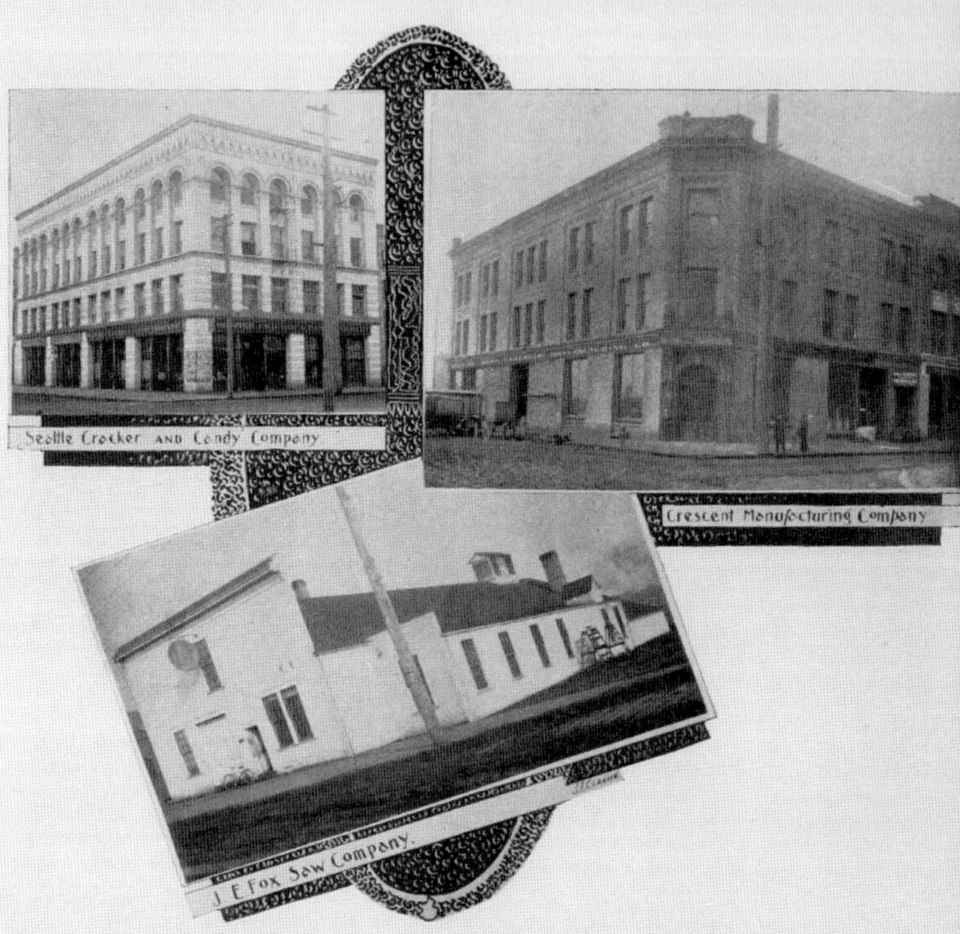

A Group of Seattle Manufactories.

THE CRESCENT MANUFACTURING COMPANY.

An illustration is shown, among other manufacturing concerns of this city, of the building occupied by the Crescent Manufacturing Company at 315 Occidental Avenue. The company occupy the entire three floors and basement, the building being 60x120 feet in size. The character of the business consists in roasting and packing coffee, manufacturing the Crescent baking powder and extracts, and in the grinding of spices. They have been established here twelve years. Their business last year shows an increase of 25 per cent over the year previous. At the present time over thirty people are employed in the establishment and five men are kept upon the road introducing the company's product to the trade throughout the State of Washington and in Alaska. They make a specialty, aside from the coffee and spice business, of putting up a superior quality of baking powder and extracts. Their representatives while on the road are constantly making demonstrations of their brand of baking powder in conjunction with brands of other well known makes, and in every instance the Crescent people are able to make a better showing. It is the same way with the extracts they put up; and the time will certainly come when the goods which are manufactured by this firm in Seattle will take precedence of those articles which are shipped in here from abroad, which indicates very clearly that Seattle manufacturers are able to thoroughly cope with the problem of manufacturing, and will in time be able to occupy this field entirely themselves. Not only is the stock equally as good, but the manner of putting up is equally as attractive and does the local concern very much credit. They also put up considerable tea under their own brand, and also for local firms who purchase from them.

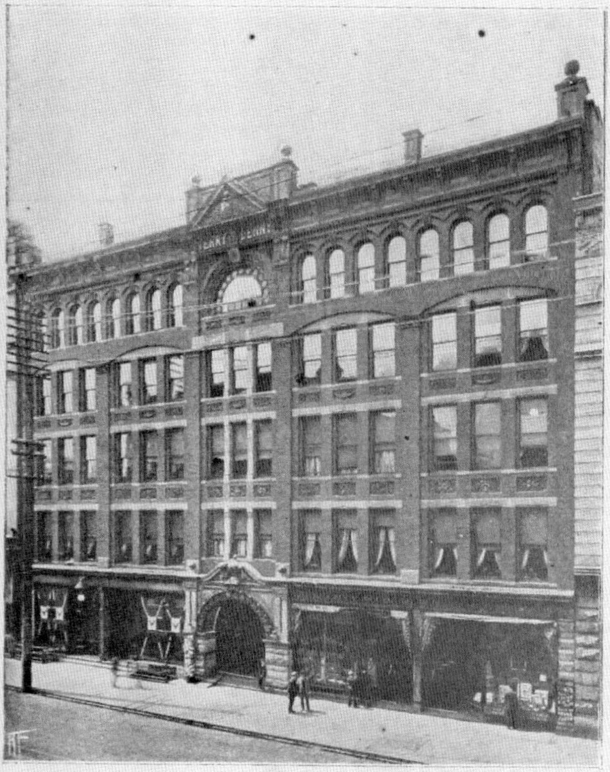

THE NORTHERN HOTEL ON FIRST AVENUE SOUTH.

HALL BROTHERS' SHIP YARD.

Hall Brothers' ship yard which is locatep across the Sound from Seattle, at Port Blakeley, is one of the pioneer shipbuilding coucerns on Puget Sound. Hall Brothers have been engaged in business here for twenty-seven years, more than twenty of which have been spent at Port Blakeley, and many of the first-class wooden ships which are plying the waters of the Pacific Ocean today are the product of their yards. During the past few years, particularly, they have been exceedingly busy; and the illustration shown herewith shows three vessels upon the stocks which have since been launched and are now in the service. At the present time three vessels are under course of construction, and will be ready for launching during the next few months. Hall Brothers probably have the best reputation for the building of wooden ships of any concern engaged in shipbuilding upon the Pacific Coast, and have more fine vessels to their credit than any other concern. During the year 1899 three four-masted schooners were built and launched from their yards, as follows: Winslow, William H. Smith and Lottie Burnett, practically of the same size and tonnage. The registered dimensions of these vessels were: Length, 107 feet 4 inches; breadth, 37 feet 6 inches; depth, 12 feet 8 inches; gross tonnage, 566, net 496; lumber-carrying capacity, 750,000; dead weight, 1000 tons. They have recently launched a four-masted schooner, which was built for Allen & Robinson of Honolulu, with registered dimensions as follows: Length, 202 feet 2 inches; breadth, 40 feet 2 inches; depth, 15 feet 9 inches; gross tonnage, 950, net 839; lumber-carrying capacity, 1,100,000; dead weight, 1850 tons. Altogether the vessels which this firm has turned out, including those which are now on the stocks, run up to ninety-six, a record which is rather difficult to beat by any concern, no matter where located. The very great demand for ships of all kind and character is giving them all the work they can possibly do at the present time. They are now employing something over 100 hands.

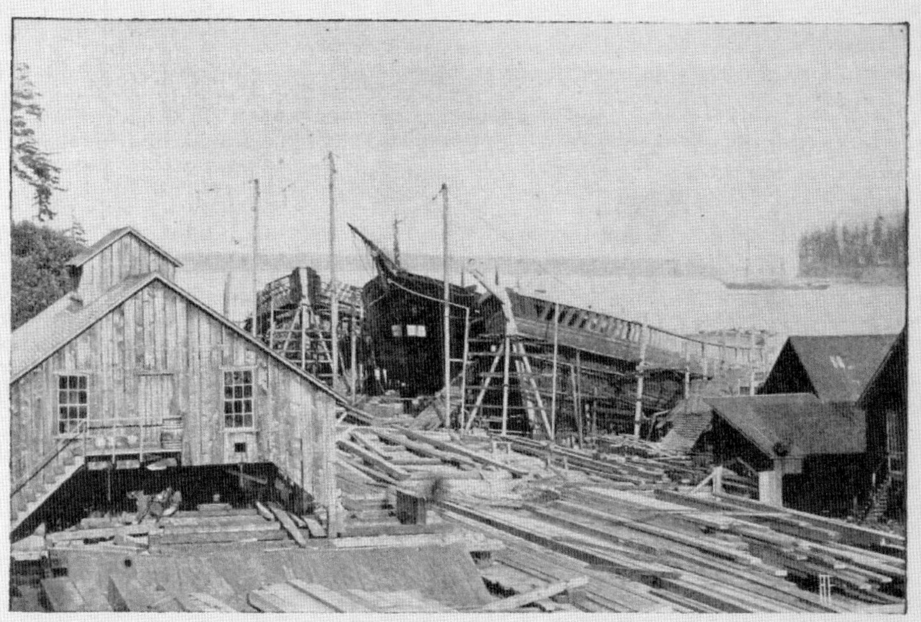

HALL BROTHERS' SHIPYARD, PORT BLAKELEY.

THE PUGET SOUND NEWS CO.

The Puget Sound News Company, a branch of the American News Company, of New York, was established in 1894. The company does a general business in newspapers and periodicals covering Oregon, Washington, Idaho, all the Northwest Territory and Alaska. They also supply the railroad train service north of the Columbia river. The Puget Sound News Company also receives and handles subscriptions for papers and periodicals of every description and in every written language. Their business association with the American News Company, which has branches and correspondents in all parts of the world, affords them unrivaled facilities for promptly filling orders for publications from any country. The company assumes responsibility for all monies received on subscriptions.

This company also conducts a comprehensive wholesale stationery and book business, their paper-covered book trade being the largest on the Coast north of San Francisco. The three floors of their establishment in the elegant stone block opposite the railway passenger center of the city, at the northwest corner of Columbia street and Western avenue, are crowded with their constantly changing and immense stock of stationery, books, periodicals and newspapers.

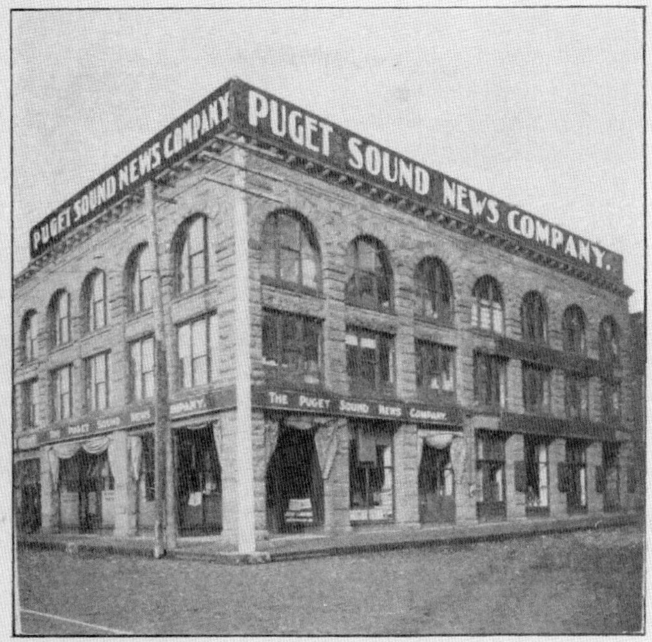

SEATTLE BREWING AND MALTING COMPANY.

It is a gratifying fact that the product of the Seattle Brewing & Malting Company has reached that point of excellence and celebrity where it is placed in competition with all beers of the world. Their "Rainier Beer" is now to be found in the markets of nearly every country bordering on the Pacific. The company have numerous testimonial letters, received from disinterested parties in Hongkong, Shanghai, Tokio, Manila, Bankok, Honolulu, Guatemala, San Salvador, San Francisco and many other places, which speak in the highest terms of "Rainier Beer," lauding both its palatableness and its purity. The company feels a pardonable pride in the fact that their product is free from any of the deleterious substances oft-times, for the sake of economy, made to take the place of malt and hops in beer manufacture.

A small army of employes is required to perform the multiple duties of brewing, ice-making, bottling, labeling, packing, selling, shipping, delivering, etc., together with the large office force. The plant is equipped with every facilily and modern appliance to expedite the work. The company malts its own barley and makes its own ice. Their bottling department has of late been greatly enlarged to meet the growing demand. This department is a great enterprise by itself. The phenomenal success of the company is due in a great measure, to the indefatigable efforts of General Manager E. F. Sweeney, who is a brewer to the manor born, having been in the business since childhood. The officers of the company are: Andrew Hemrich, president; E. E. Sweeney, vice-president and general manager; J. F. Campion, treasurer, and J. G. Fox, secretary.

The export business of the institution is constantly on the increase. Nearly every steamer to Alaska, to Honolulu or the Orient carries a good sized consignment of Rainier beer. The title "Rainier Beer," which is now familiar to every shore washed by the Pacific, was chosen by the company, as the name naturally suggests superiority and purity. Rainier, the grand old mountain, robed in purest white, rises sublimely above all surrounding peaks; this excellent beverage enjoys an eminence in popularity and purity combined which no rival on the Coast has yet attained.

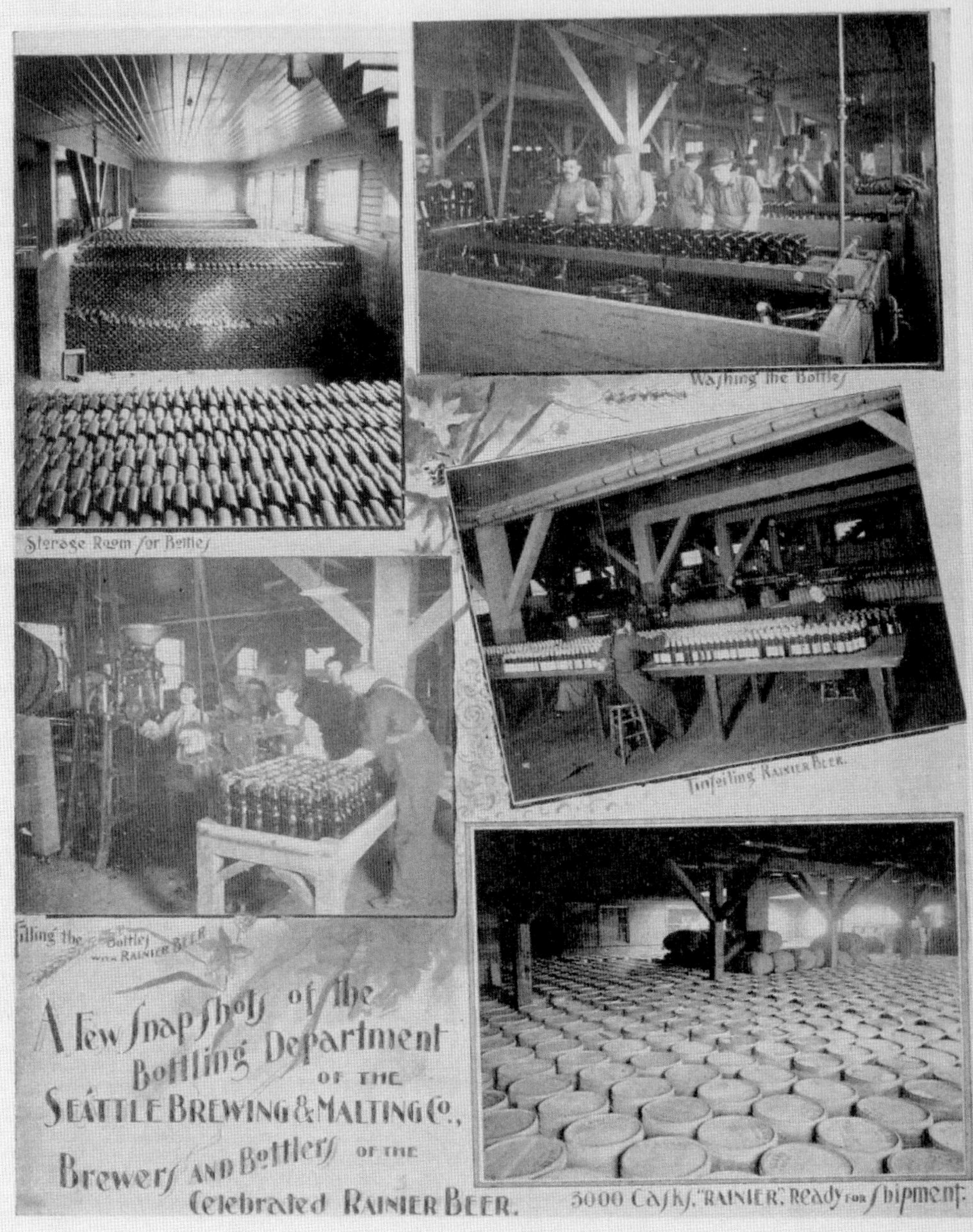

WHERE RAINIER BEER IS MADE.

THE STETSON-POST MILL COMPANY.

The Stetson-Post Mill Company is one of the pioneer lumbering concerns of Seattle; in fact, when the mill was built away back in 1875 on its present site just below the coal bunkers in this city, they were practically alone in the lumber trade, save for some very inconsiderable concerns located on this side of the bay. Their site in those days was considered quite a ways out of town, comparatively speaking, but the city has now grown around them so completely that they are already crowded for room, and are, practically speaking, doing a saw mill business right in the heart of the water front. They own the site of nine acres on which their mill is located; in addition to their big mill they have a sash and door factory—recent improvements have been made to this at a cost of $12,000 and they are already taxed to their utmost to supply the demand made upon them. Mr. Stetson, in the course of an interview upon the lumber trade, stated that the increase last year was a very substantial one, and both the mill and the sash and door factories were running at their full capacity. They give employment now to over one hundred men, two-thirds of whom are employed in the saw mill proper. About one-third of the product of the mill goes East by rail, the balance being used for local consumption; the product of the sash and door factory is all used locally. Among other improvements which have been made during the past year was a large shed used for planing machines. The illustration which accompanies this article gives a rather comprehensive view of the property of the Stetson-Post Mill Company and shows the magnitude of the concern as it stands today. The property owned by the company is one of the most valuable in the city.

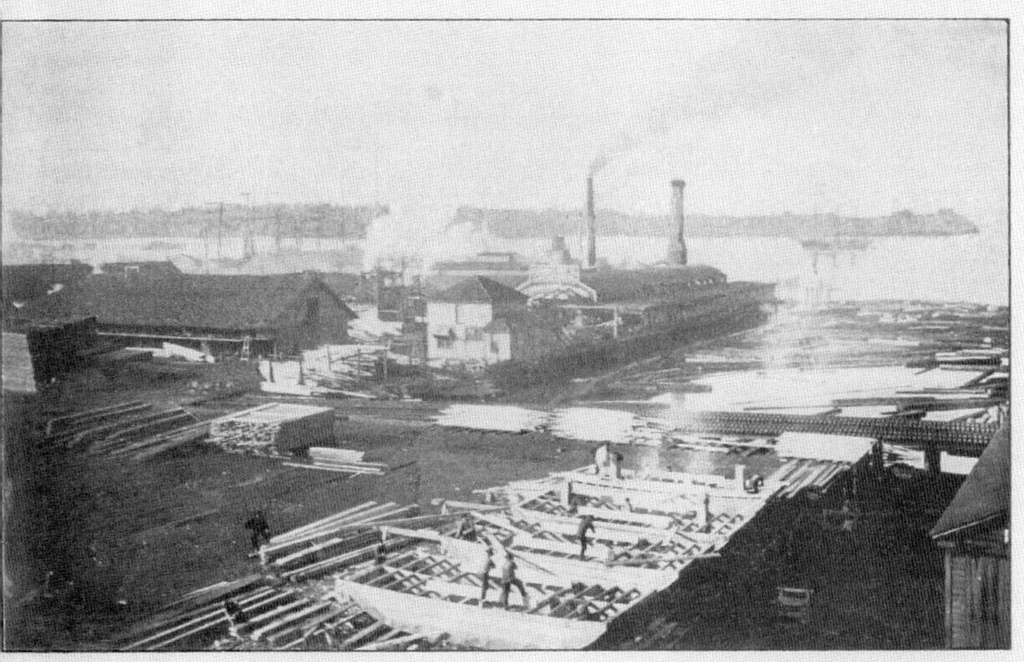

MILL AND YARD OF THE STETSON-POST MILL COMPANY IN SEATTLE.

THE DIAMOND ICE COMPANY.

One of the very considerable cold storage plants and ice factories located upon the Pacific Coast is that of the Diamond Ice Company, which is located on Western Avenue and Union Street. An exterior picture of the building, together with an interior picture of the methods used in manufacturing ice, is shown in this article, and will give an idea of how extensive this establishment has become. They have been established here since 1893 and have built up a very large business—the increase last year shows a gain of 25 per cent, and with additional machinery they will increase the capacity this year by 50 per cent. Twenty people are employed about the place in various capacities. In addition to the manufacture of ice, which at present is thirty tons per day, they have a very extensive cold storage warehouse, in which butter, eggs, beer, cheese and fish are kept for local dealers, which has a capacity of 150,000 cubic feet. The largest portion of their cold storage plant is devoted to the freezing of fresh fish; this has a capacity of two carloads or 40,000 pounds per day. The system in use for making ice is what is known as the Pusey system. The ice is made upon plates and is sliced off first in cakes 22 inches by 11 inches thick and 66 inches long, making a cake that weighs 500 pounds; it goes from here to the recutter and there is cut into three cakes of 150 to 175 pounds, and in these sizes is stored in the ice house.

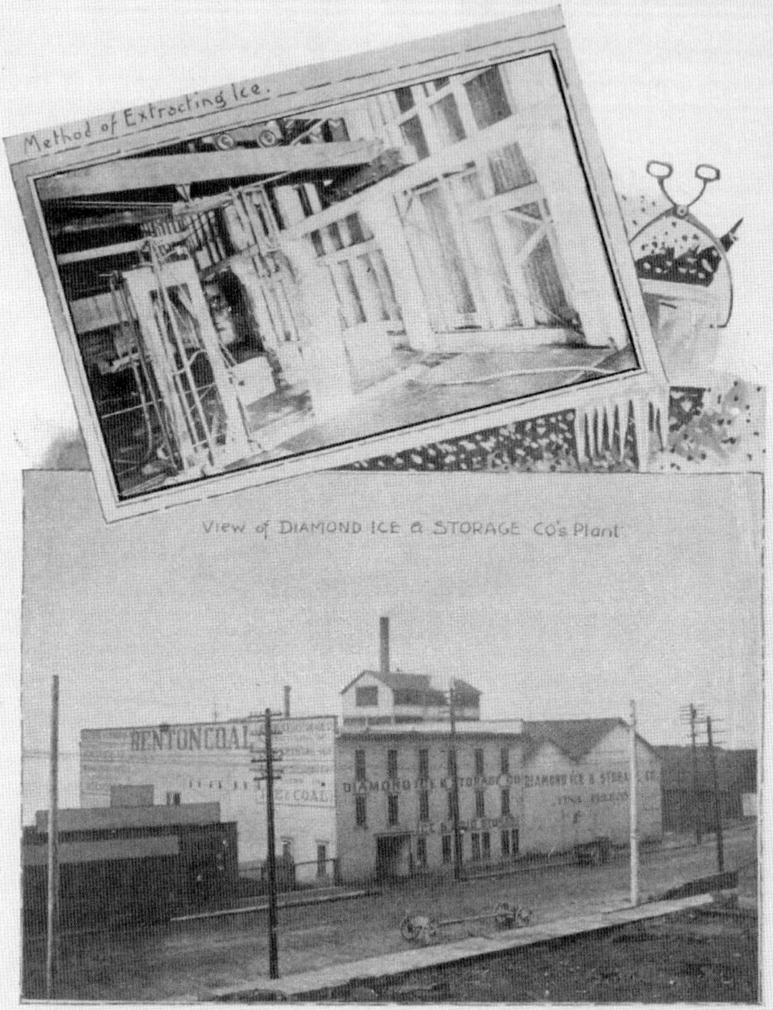

THE ESTABLISHMENT OF THE DIAMOND ICE CO.

The ice is all made from distilled water and is as pure as any natural ice that can be found. The capacity for storage purposes is fifteen hundred tons. It is probable that their capacity for filling orders is not exceeded by any other concern in the country. Last season they received in one day an order for 125 tons of product, makin a whole train load. It was filled within eight hours and started off on its journey, a record that would be very difficult to beat.

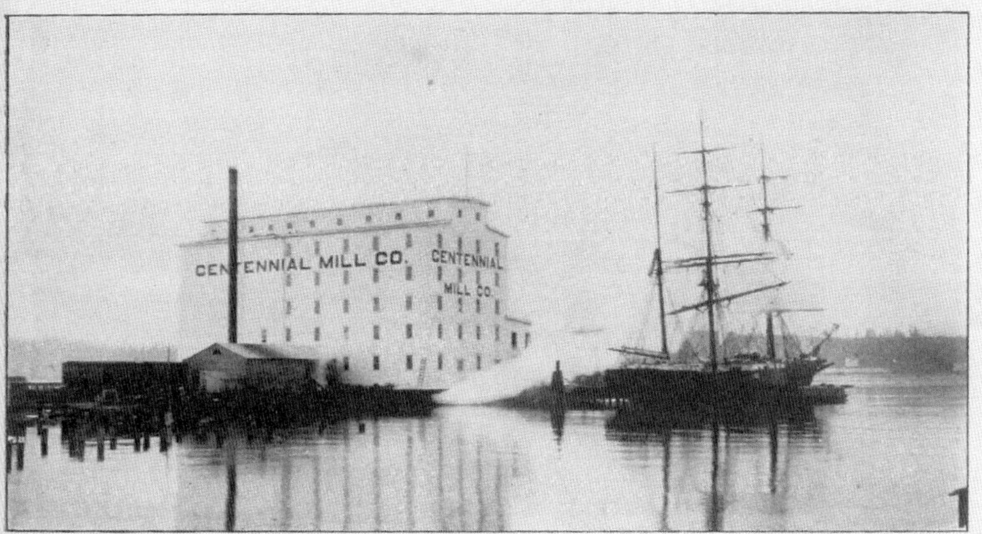

THE PLANT OF CENTENNIAL MILL CO., SEATTLE.

THE CENTENNIAL MILL COMPANY.

The Centennial Mill Company, which has now been established in this city for two and a half years, is already reaching out for a very considerable Oriental trade. They have already shipped a good many cargoes direct to the far East, the last two of which, amounting to nearly 6000 tons, having gone to Siberia. In this city they own six and one-half acres of land very advantageously located upon the bay and have a flouring mill with a capacity of 1800 barrels per day; they also own a mill at Spokane with a capacity of 700 barrels per day, and aside from the product which is furnished for domestic consumption in both places, the balance is all shipped foreign, and already a trade has been developed with China, Japan, Siberia and Hawaii. The increase last year was fully 50 per cent over the year previous, and the near future will probably see further increases in the quantity manufactured. Mr. Thomson, the president of the company, has already made several trips to the Orient and has succeeded in establishing himself there very firmly.

A VERY EXTENSIVE FIRM.

The firm of M. & K. Gottstein, located at 806 Yesler Way, in a five-story brick building 30 by 120 feet in size (a fine illustration of which is herewith shown),is one of the very considerable wholesale houses in the Northwest.

They probably carry the largest line of liquors, wines and cigars of any firm in Washington; they are also one of the oldest firms in Seattle, having been established since 1883. Their increase last year over the previous year is fully 25 per cent, and from present indications they will show a more marked gain this year. They have eleven

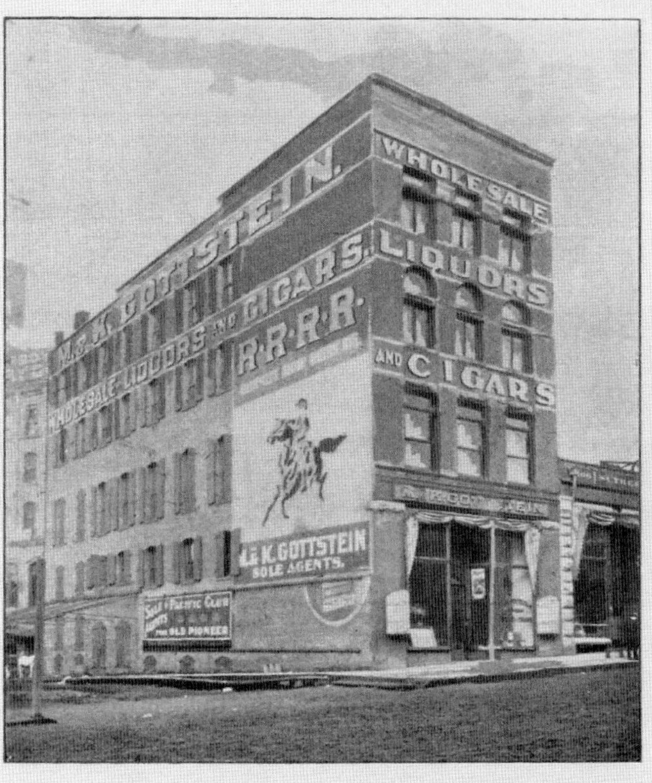

WHOLESALE HOUSE OF M. & K. GOTTSTEIN.

men employed in their establishment and keep three men traveling upon the road and are now selling goods in Alaska, all over the State of Washington, and over a portion of Oregon; with the beginning of the present year they are developing a trade with Japan, shipments to that country having already been made. They believe thoroughly in expansion and think that within a few years Seattle will be doing a very large trade in all of the principal points in the Orient.

OUR BIG IMPORTERS.

One of the largest importing firms in this city dealing directly with Oriental countries is that of the Wa Chong Company, who occupy their four-story brick building, located on Third Avenue South. The principal articles which they handle are tea and rice and Chinese merchandise. They operate their own rice mill in their establishment in this city, which has a capacity of seven tons per day. In addition to the house in Seattle, they have houses in Montana, and supply very much in the way of tea and rice and general Chinese merchandise to points in that section. In addition to being very extensive importers, they buy very large quantities of American flour and export it to their Oriental connections. The head of the firm, Wa Chong, is one of the oldest and best known citizens in Seattle and has a high standing in the Western commercial world.

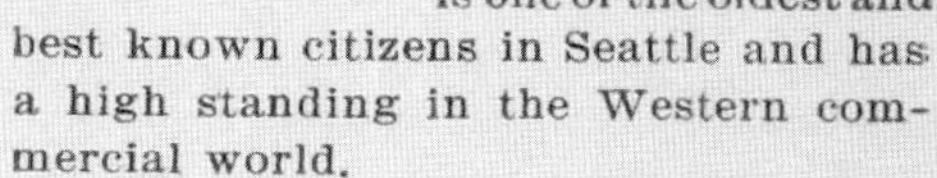

THE NEWELL MILL COMPANY.

The Newell Mill Company occupies the most southern portion of Elliott Bay, having a capacity of 50,000 feet of lumber, 70,000 shingles and 10,000 lath a day. Its location is in South Seattle upon a site of land which comprises ten acres. Mr. George Newell, the president, established the mill sixteen years ago and is one of the shining examples on Puget Sound of success in the milling business. Like most energetic men he has had his ups and downs, fire having visited his place once, but still he has succeeded beyond his most sanguine expectations builders, but furnish free steam and, incidentally, the use of more or less machinery. Were it not for the Newell Mill Company, South Seattle would not be as important as it is today. The fact that they give employment to over fifty men, the majority of whom own their own homes, makes it a thriving little place. Most of the product of the mill is sold locally.

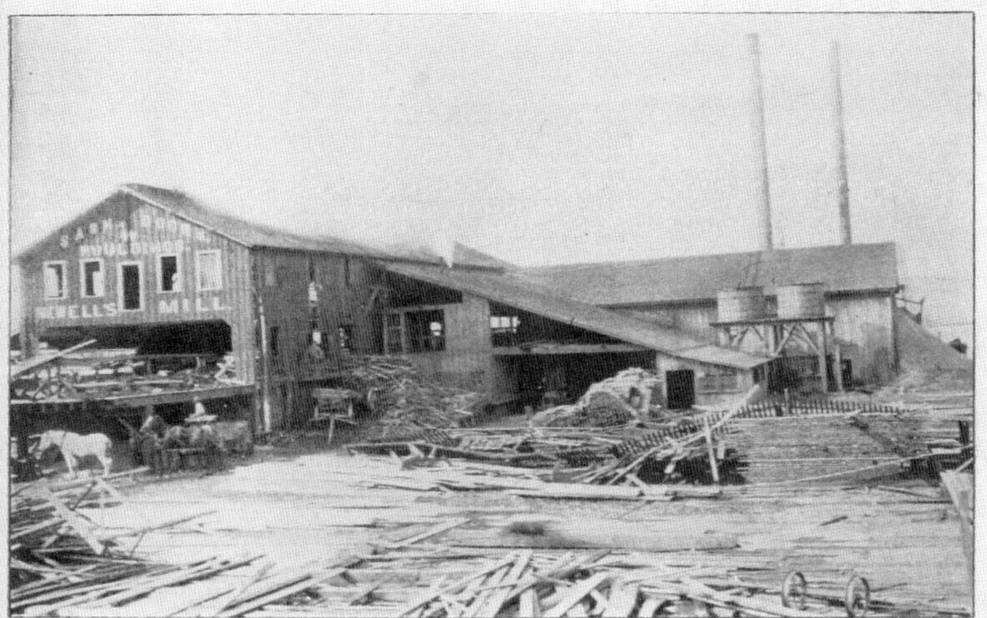

THE PLANT OF THE NEWELL MILL CO., SOUTH SEATTLE.

and today, together with his son Fred W., who is the secretary and manager of the concern, occupies a position of absolute independence.

Alongside of the mill, of which a very excellent picture is herewith shown, the mill company has a shipyard, and although not running it themselves, usually have one or more vessels in course of construction most of the time. In fact, they rather encourage any kind of industry and not only give the ground rent free to ship

TAX RATE.

The tax rate in Seattle, including State, County, City and School is 21½ mills upon a valuation of about three-fifths of the market value of the property. This is a reduction of about 11 mills since 1893, and shows a very gratifying state of affairs. The city's credit stands high, both locally and with financial centers of the East, and no difficulty has been experienced in disposing of its bonds at a very substantial premium. The city is on a cash basis and has no floating debt outside of that for which bonds have been issued. The greater part of these bonds bear 5 per cent interest.

COMMERCIAL STREET BOILER WORKS.

The Commercial Street Boiler Works, of which H. W. Markey is the proprietor, and which is located on First Avenue South and Lane Street, occupying a building 45x138 feet in size, is an establishment of very considerable magnitude. As an instance of this fact it can be stated that Mr. Markey has just completed one of the biggest contracts of modern boiler repairing ever done in the North. It consisted in overhauling and putting in thorough repair the boilers of the steamship Oregon, which involved an expenditure of upwards of $50,000. Mr. Markey received this contract, and at once put fifty men at work upon it, and rushed the work through with great expedition. This one point illustrates the fact very clearly that Seattle is able to do any kind of contract work in matters of this kind, and her establishments are as thoroughly advanced as those in San Francisco. The Commercial Street Boiler Works has been established here thirteen years. The business the past year has shown a very great increase, being fully 75 per cent in excess of the previous year, and it has necessitated putting on a new addition thirty feet in extent, and the purchase of new rollers and a new steam punch and the replacing of older machinery with that which is more modern and up to date. The works send men to the Eastern part of the state and generally to all parts of the country in doing repair work, or in building new boilers. Something over sixty men are employed by Mr. Markey, and the boilers which he makes are used for all purposes.

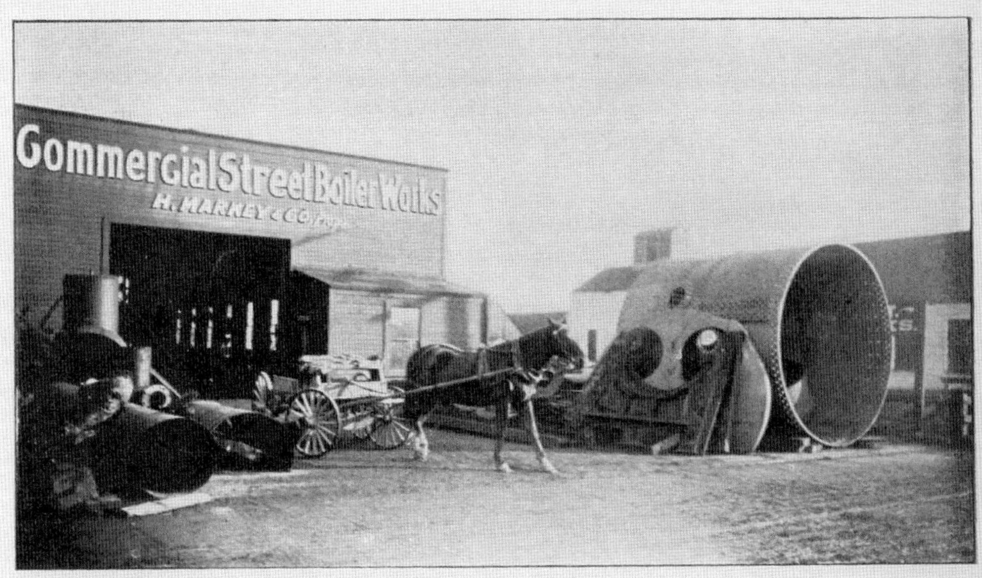

THE COMMERCIAL STREET BOILER WORKS.

THE HEMRICH BREWING COMPANY.

The Hemrich Brewing Company, incorporated in 1899, by Alvin and Louis Hemrich of Seattle, has already acquired a solid footing in commercial circles on the Coast, owing to the excellence of its wares and to the wide experience of the incorporators and their extensive acquaintance on the Sound. The name of "Hemrich" has been connected with all the various brewing concerns of Seattle from its early history. The brothers were connected with the old Bay View Brewing Company, and later with the Seattle Brewing & Malting Company. After the consolidation of the various Seattle breweries the Hemrichs bought the old Slorah steam brewing plant near Lake Union, converting it into a lager beer plant, since which time they have put on the market a quality of beer unexcelled on the Coast, in the manufacture of which only the best materials obtainable, are employed. The increased demand for their product has recently necessitated the doubling of their capacity. The enlarged plant, equipped with the best modern machinery and appliances, is now complete and in operation.

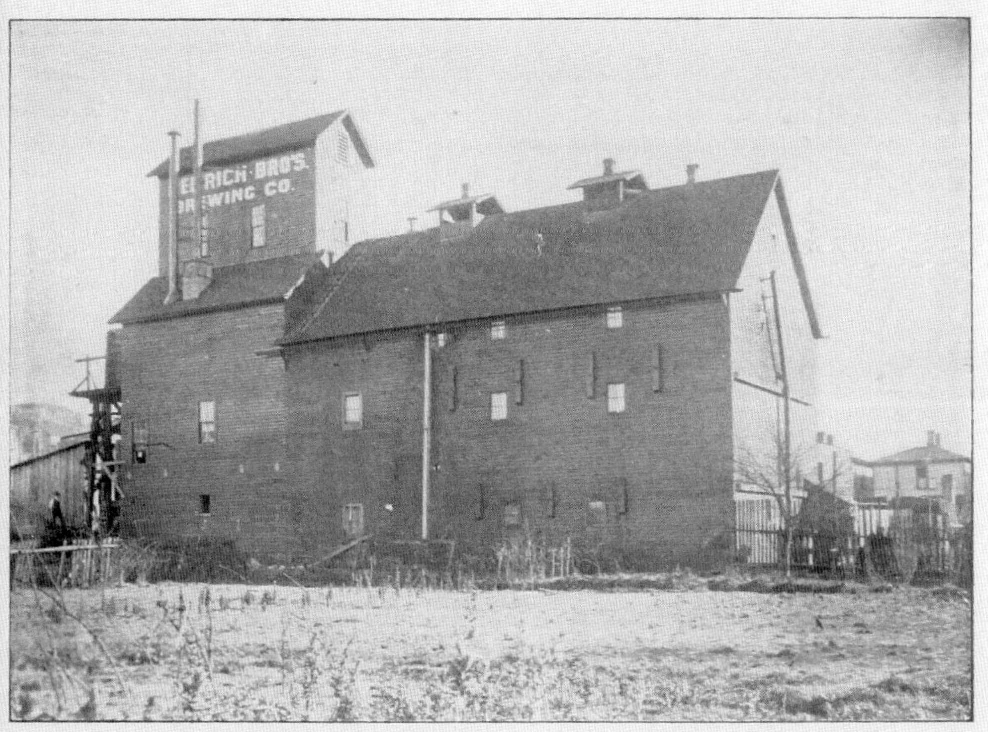

THE BREWERY OF HEMRICH BROS., NEAR LAKE UNION.

The following excerpts from the American Journal of Health, of New York, are self-explanatory: * * * "A few days ago we made an analysis of the beers manufactured by the Hemrich Brothers Brewing Company of Seattle, Wn., and we found no trace whatever of any ingredient that should not enter into the composition of a perfect beer. But such a beer must be classed among the rare exceptions, as very few articles of manufacture are adulterated to a greater extent than this beverage, for the temptation to use the cheaply prepared drugs in the place of the more costly malt and hops * * * is very great * * * and the effect of such beverages * * * is injurious. * * * We give an unqualified editorial endorsement to the beer brewed by the Hemrich Brothers Brewing Company, and it is the intrinsic worth of the product that enables us to do so."

A similar endorsement, under date of September 9, 1899, has been received from E. A. McDonald, state dairy and food commissioner of the State of Washington.

This company also makes a superior article of porter which finds growing favor on the Sound.

THE STREET CAR SYSTEM OF SEATTLE.

Seattle is probably better supplied with an efficient street car service than any other city of its size in the country. A recent consolidation of a majority of the lines in the city under one general management will vastly improve the general service and put the various lines in far better condition than they have ever been before. At the present times there are sixty-four miles of road, divided up, before the time of consolidation, between nine different companies, six of which have passed into the hands of the new company. It is the purpose of the new company to continue improvements and extensions until the lines of Seattle are put in thoroughly first-class shape. These improvements, together with the purchase price, represent an outlay of about five millions of dollars. Employed by the nine companies there are something like 418 men, who are paid $25,000 a month in the shape of salaries. At the present time ninety-four cars are employed in transporting passengers to the various points of the city.

An efficient street car service probably attracts more favorable attention from possible investors than anything else in a city, with the possible exception of its bank clearances, and the fact that Boston and Eastern capitalists have taken hold of the various lines in the city with the purpose of expending so much money is pretty good evidence that Seattle has a most excellent rating, and that the business of operating street car lines is looked upon with favor. It is sufficient to say that within the next year the new consolidated company will have a service upon its various lines which will not be equaled by any other city on the Pacific Coast.

THE N. W. RICHMOND PAPER CO.

The H. N. Richmond Paper Company, which is located at 213-215 Occidental Avenue, is the only exclusive wholesale paper house in Seattle. The company is a very considerable concern and practically occupies five full floors, including basement, at the premises where it is located. They have been established here for eleven years and their trade now reaches all over Washington, portions of Oregon, Idaho, Montana and into Alaska. Some thirteen people are employėd in their store in this city, and three men are kept traveling upon the road in the interest of the company. Last year the business showed an increase of fully 25 per cent over the previous year, and it is safely predicted that the present year will show equally as marked an improvement. The company unquestionably does as extensive a business as any other wholesale paper house on the Coast.

THE RAINIER CIGAR COMPANY.

In a city like Seattle where so much money is expended by smokers for cigars and tobacco there ought to be more home manufactured goods sold than these are. As an evidence of the fact that Seattle is able to manufacture and sell quite as good an article as can be produced elsewhere, the Rainier Cigar Company, of which A. A. Wright is the manager, located at 1004 First Avenue, is given as an illustration. The factory, while making several brands of cigars, pay particular attention to the "Rainier" brand, made in two grades, selling for 10 cents straight and two for 25 cents, and which, by the way, are equal to any cigar made in the country and superior to nine-tenths of those which are imported here and sold under the guise of strictly imported goods. The Rainier Cigar Company ought to have more encouragement than they have—in fact, they, as well as every other manufacturing concern in this city, ought to be patronized more extensively, particularly when equally as good goods are made as those which can be purchased from other quarters. This company has been established here now five or six years. Last year the increase of the business was very large; this year it will be still greater. They are now employing twelve people in the factory, and in addition to supplying this city are also selling goods to Alaska.

In regard to the manufacture of cigars a few statistics compiled by The Tobacco Leaf, a New York journal devoted to tobacco interests, show that during the last five months of 1899 revenue tax in the United States was paid on an average of about 500,000,000 cigars per month. Averaging these same ratio, viz., 40 per cent, would pay the laborers in cigar factories $24,000 per month. Probably not more than 20 per cent of the amount used here are manufactured here; but $4800 per month to cigar makers alone is quite a little amount even for a city the size of Seattle. The above figures are on cigars alone, not including cigarettes or other tobaccos.

The internal revenue reports for 1899 on tobaccos of all kinds averaged very nearly $5,000,000 per month. The

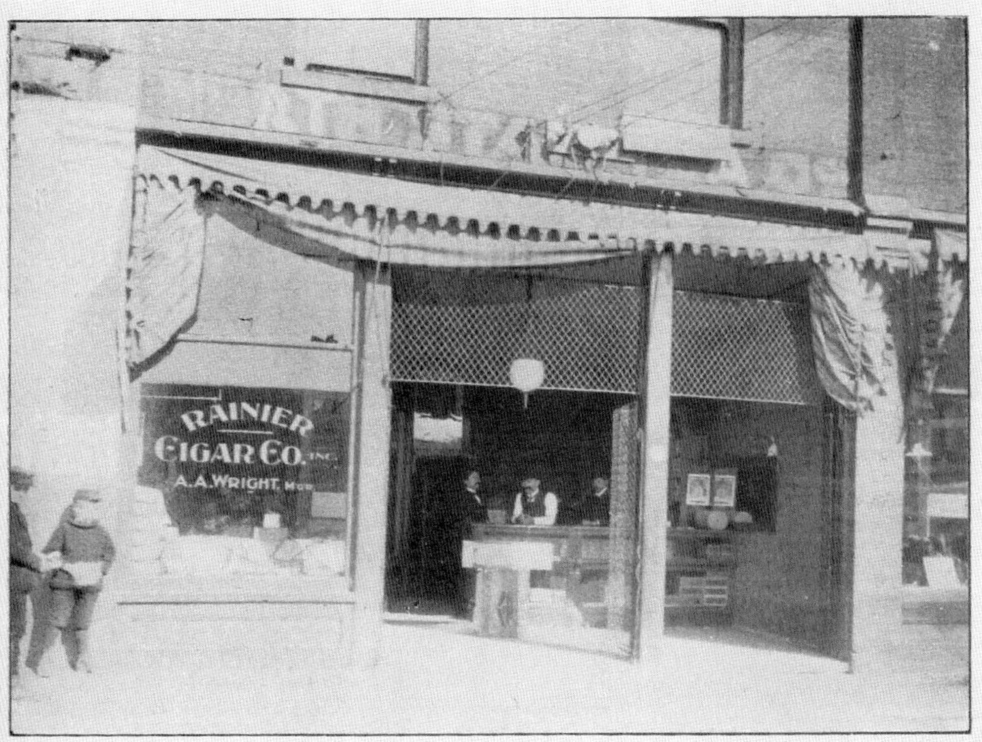

THE STORE AND FACTORY OF THE RAINIER CIGAR CO.

cigars at $50 per thousand, a conservative estimate, the selling price of these cigars amounts to the enormous sum of $25,000,000 per month. As the cost of manufacture alone amounts to about 40 per cent of the selling price, it will be seen that the various cigar factories of the United States pay their employes $10,000 per month for labor.

In Seattle a conservative estimate gives the number of cigars sold each month at 1,200,000, which at $50 per thousand amounts to $60,000. If they were all manufactured here, this at the actual number of cigars manufactured in the United States for the six months ending December 31, 1899, was 3,059,468,663.

COOPER & LEVY.

One of the oldest grocery firms in the Queen City is that of Cooper & Levy, located at the southeast corner of Yesler Way and First Avenue South. They occupy three floors, each 40x110, with an immense stock of goods, besides having large warerooms elsewhere in the city. They do a retail grocery business as well as handling certain lines of hardware and house furnishing goods. The house was established in 1890 by the present partners, Isaac Cooper and Louis Levy, both of whom continue to take an active part in the business. The firm employs upwards of thirty persons and six wagons. Their trade, while largely confined to the city, is immense and is expanding rapidly. They do a strictly cash business, which insures patrons the very lowest prices and best goods. A number of their leading articles are put out under their own brand.

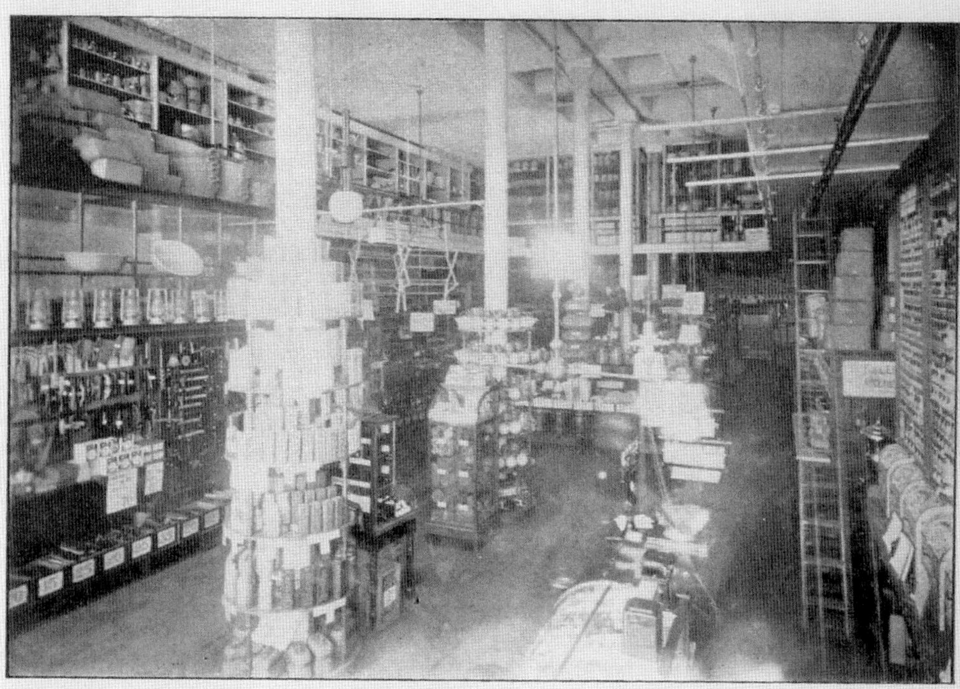

INTERIOR VIEW OF THE STORE OF COOPER & LEVY.

A feature of their business is shipping goods to families in considerable quantities on orders by mail from the surrounding country, from British Columbia and Alaska. They issue and mail to their patrons an illustrated 80-page price list monthly, containing a list of upwards of 400 articles, with prices of same, enabling outside people to get their goods as close as residents of the city.

The firm attributes its uninterrupted success to close attention to business, selling at right prices, keeping the best grade of goods, the largest assortment in the city and employing efficient help.

THE SEATTLE TRANSFER COMPANY.

Some idea can be formed of the traffic carried on in Seattle when it is stated that a single transfer company gives employment to 85 horses and 79 men. The whole story is told when these figures are given. The company referred to is the Seattle Transfer Company. They occupy their own building, which is 120 feet square, and consists of two floors, located near the Northern Pacific freight depot, in the southern part of the city. They have been established here since 1888, and in addition to a general transfer business, such as handling baggage and express from all the trains, to and from incoming ships, railroads and the like, they do a very large dray business and also a very large business in furnishing carriages and hacks. In the freight business they employ fourteen trucks and two drays, and in handling baggage they have twelve wagons. They also have ten carriages or hacks. The stable which they occupy is pronounced one of the most complete, elaborately arranged transfer barns in the West. The lower floor is occupied by the various vehicles of the company, harness room, drying room, place for washing wagons and by offices. The upper portion is used for the horse stalls, in which they now give accommodation to 107 head. It is divided off in a stall for each animal, with several box stalls for infirmary purposes. There is also a convenient place for the veterinary. All the refuse is carried to the rear of the building and from there dumped into the Sound, the waters of which rise with each succeeding tide. On the whole, it is most elaborately arranged. The Seattle Transfer Company also have two large omnibuses of their own, which they run to and from various trains and steamers. They were the first people in town to adopt rubber tires on their carriages. One of the features which they have recently added to their business is that of furnishing delivery wagons complete, including driver, to any merchant who desires the same, the payment for the service being made once a month. In this way the transfer company furnishes the entire equipment, keeps the wagons in order and stands all risk, the merchant simply paying for the service in a lump sum. It is becoming quite popular, and they already have four customers, one of whom uses four wagons. The company has the right (in fact, are the only people in Seattle who have it) of boarding all incoming vessels and trains and soliciting baggage, and this feature of their business has grown to very large proportions. The president of this large concern is E. C. Neufelder, president of the People's Bank, while R. J. Reekie is secretary and treasurer and looks after the active management.

THE SEATTLE HARDWARE COMPANY.

Among the big houses which have given Seattle a reputation throughout the West as a jobbing center, the Seattle Hardware Company takes a leading place. In order to emphasize the size and importance of their establishment several illustrations are herewith reproduced, showing both their wholesale department and their retail store. The company has a capital of $200,000 and are shipping goods all over the State of Washington, Alaska, British Columbia and into Idaho. In order to cover this territory five men are constantly upon the road, and the goods and stock handled by this well known firm finds a very wide distribution. Some idea can be formed of the enormous trade carried on when it is stated that ninety people are employed, and although established but fifteen years they now take rank with any of the big concerns doing a like busi-

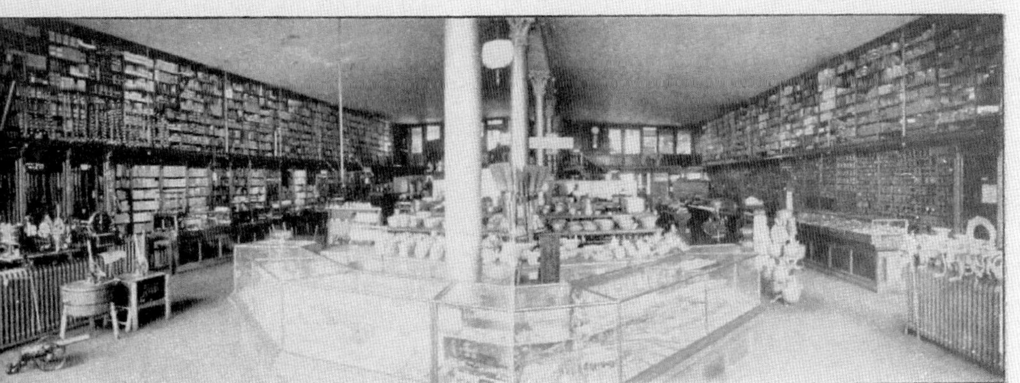

INTERIOR MAIN STORE OF SEATTLE HARDWARE CO.

ness in San Francisco, and practically are able to drive out all competition from the southern metroplis, and it will only be a question of a very short time when this firm will be able to enlarge its field of action and be selling goods direct to the various points in the Orient. The floor space occupied by them amounts to something like 50,000 square feet. Last year the increase in business was 10 per cent in excess of the year 1898, a very large showing when it is taken into consideration with the fact that the year 1898 was considered a banner year. One of the notable undertakings which this company have just accomplished is the issuance of a 1100-page illustrated catalogue, which has been printed at a cost of $12,000. Such an undertaking has never before been attempted on the Pacific Coast, and this fact lends all tne more weight to the enterprise and energy displayed by the Seattle concern and shows that houses here are fully alive to the demands that are being made upon them and that they will easily and successfully be able to do the enlarged trade which it is confidently predicted will ensue by closer trade relations with our Oriental neighbors.

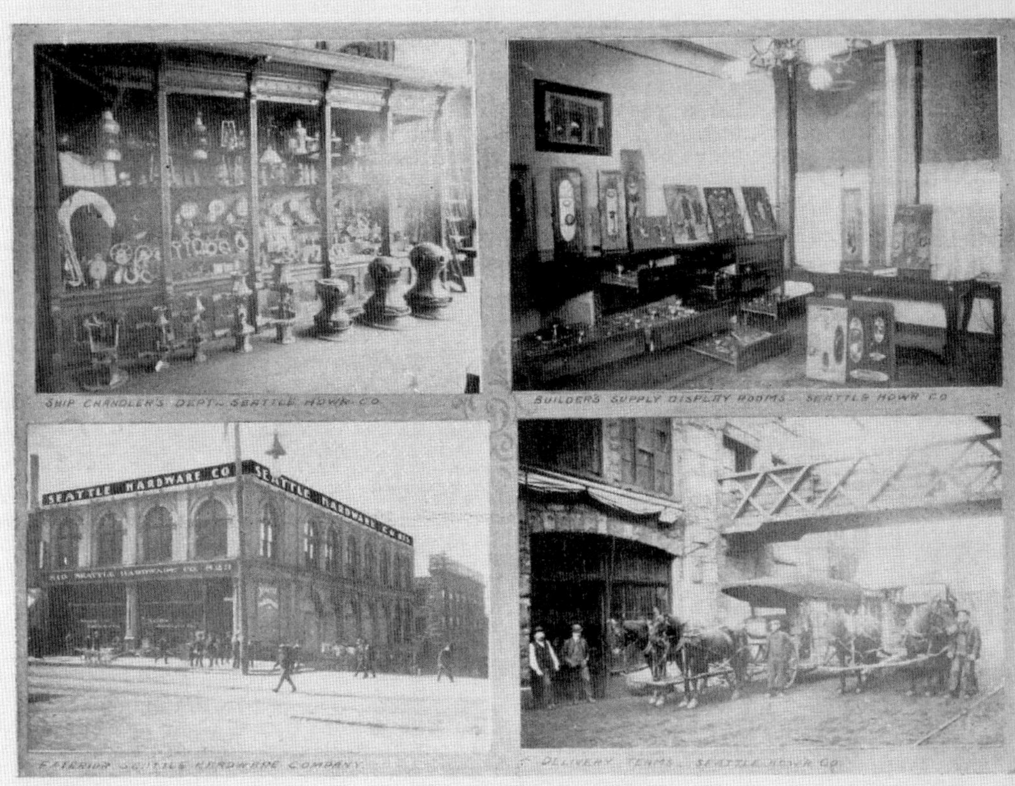

SOME GENERAL VIEWS OF SEATTLE HARDWARE CO.

THE PACIFIC COAST COMPANY.

The Pacific Coast Company, which now has its general offices and headquarters in this city, is one of the largest steamship companies on the Pacific Coast, and in order to get a comprehensive idea of how extensive they are, the following list of vessels which they operate is enumerated: Steamships Queen, Santa Rosa, Cottage City, State of California, City of Topeka, Coos Bay, Santa Cruz, Walla Walla, City of Pueblo, Corona, Coracao, Alki, Bonita, Gipsy, Umatilla, Senator, Orizaba, Alex. Duncan and Willamette, having a total carrying capacity of 32,-

495. The routes operated are practically five in number, as follows: California, southern coast, between San Francisco and San Diego, California, at which all the ports, large and small, lying between those places are visited; the next is the San Francisco, British Columbia and Puget Sound, between San Francisco and Seattle, which also includes Victoria and Vancouver, British Columbia; the next route or division is the line plying between Puget Sound and Alaska, which includes all points on Lynn Canal, as far north as Sitka; the next is San Francisco to Humboldt Bay, a distinct service being performed between the southern metropolis and Eureka, California; then there is the San Francisco and Mexican route, which consists of a line of steamers plying between San Francisco and Guaymas, Mexico, and various intermediate ports. In addition to these steamship routes, the Pacific Company has several lines of railway, which they also operate—one of these the Columbia and Puget Sound Railroad is used largely for coal purposes out of Seattle, and was, by the way, the first railroad that Seattle ever had. In addition to this line, they operate the Port Townsend and Southern under the head of the Port Townsend division and the Port Townsend Southern under the title of Olympia division. Besides these roads they also own and operate the Seattle and Northern, which forms important connections between points in Skagit County and Anacortes. They also own a very extensive line in California, which they operate in connection with the Southern California steamship service. The enumeration of these facts will convey to the reader that the company is one of very considerable extent, and entering so largely into transportation facilities, wields a very considerable influence upon a city like Seattle. Some illustrations which are shown will give an idea of the character of the ships; one in particular shows two of their big ships, which ply between here and San Francisco, lying at their own dock at the same time, both engaged in taking on or discharging cargoes. The company this season will enlarge its Alaska business by the establishment of a line running to Nome and Cape York, putting into this service some of their largest and best vessels. Up to a few years ago the company kept their headquarters in San Francisco, but within the past few years the general offices

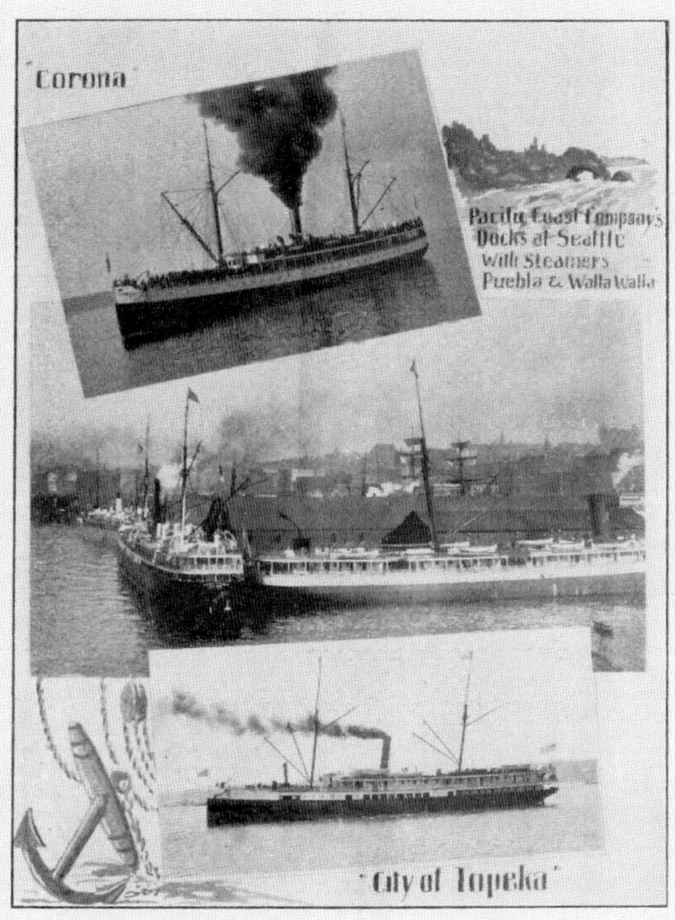

SOME SHIPS OF THE PACIFIC COAST CO

have been removed to this city, and that fact is naturally of considerable importance as increasing the prestige of Seattle as the home of one of the big Pacific steamship lines. One of the features of this company has been the inauguration for some years now of an excursion steamer at regular periods to interesting points in Alaska. The steamer Queen has been the one which is doing this service, and in this way thousands of people all over the United States have occasion to get brief glimpses of the "land of the midnight sun" and the land which has been made famous during the past few years by its phenomenal harvest of gold. The Queen is a very fine ship, having a capacity for 250 first-class passengers, and is supplied with all modern improvements and appliances, and has become very famous by reason of the great number of people all over the United States which she has carried. It is probably safe to say that the Queen has carried more distinguished people than any other steamship in the service at the present time.

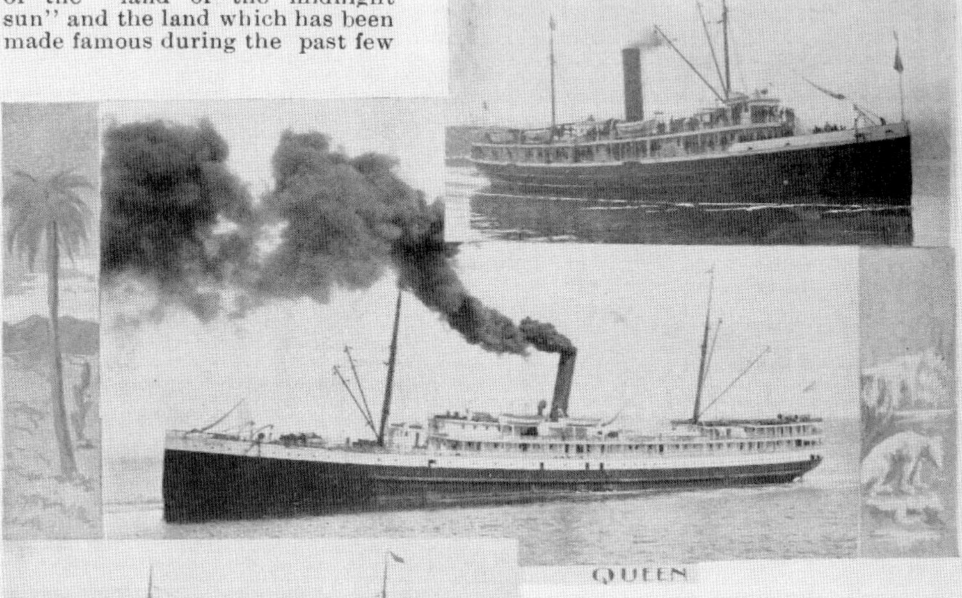

SHIPS OF THE PACIFIC COAST CO.

DO A BIG EXPORT TRADE.

O. D. Colvin, sales agent at Seattle of the American Steel and Wire Company of New York, Chicago and San Francisco, came to the State of Washington in 1888 and settled in Seattle in 1890. For a number of years Mr. Colvin was connected with the county offices of King County. In 1895 he was appointed auditor of the Seattle Consolidated Street Railway Company, as well as auditor of the Rainier Power & Railway Company. In 1896 he was appointed receiver of the Front Street Cable Railway by the Federal Court, which position he filled with such credit for four years that, on the reorganization of the company, at the expiration of that period, he was appointed as general manager of the road by the new organization. Mr. Colvin remained in this capacity until August,

1899, when he severed his connection with the road to devote his entire time to the business of the American Steel and Wire Company.

The American Steel and Wire Company controls about 95 per cent of the manufacture and sale of nails, barbed and plain wire, etc., manufactured in the United States. The company is practically a consolidation of nearly all the mills manufacturing wire products in this country. It owns and operates forty-two distinct manufacturing establishments in different States in the Union. In addition to the above lines, the company manufactures extensively steel sheets and plates, chains, horseshoes, boat and track spikes, polished shafting, field fencing, woven wire fencing and, in the Washburn & Moen department—which was purchased outright in 1899 by the company—manufacture and market electrical wires, bare and insulated copper wire, trolley wire, submarine cables, telegraph and telephone wire, steel spring wire, special wires, coil springs of all kinds and wire rope and steel hawsers, etc.

Frank L. Brown, of San Francisco, is the Pacific Coast sales agent, covering the Pacific States, as well as Idaho, Utah, Montana and Nevada, and Alaska, British Columbia and Northwest Territory. The Seattle agency reports to San Francisco and its territory embraces Washington, British Columbia, Northwest Territory and Alaska.

The business at the Seattle agency has increased wonderfully during the past year. Mr. Colvin has recently fitted up an elegant suite of offices at 108 West Washington Street, the offices being connected with a store room, where electrical and special wires are carried in stock. The heavier stock, such as wire rope, nails, barbed wire, etc., are kept at their large warehouse elsewhere in the city.

By reason of Seattle's geographical position, the agency here is able to do business throughout British Columbia and the Northwest Territory, and hence commands all this trade. From San Francisco a very heavy export business is carried on in which all Pacific countries are supplied. In time, naturally, much of this export trade will be supplied through Seattle.

THE SEATTLE GAS AND ELECTRIC COMPANY.

This city unquestionably possesses the most complete and elaborate gas lighting and heating plant on the Coast. It is conceded to be conducted upon more systematic and business-like principles than that of any other company in this region of the West, and as a result the Seattle Gas and Electric Company is giving a service which cannot be excelled. People may make complaints of other corporations supplying general utilities, but it is rare, indeed, when anything is directed against the gas company. General Manager C. R. Collins came out here from the East a few years ago, and at once proceeded to lay a foundation for doing business. He possessed what few other men in the West possessed—a thorough knowledge of the gas business. He was practical. As a result, he began, as soon as possible, to make gas which had the proper illuminating powers. When he got the product he put it upon the market, so to speak. He made it a business matter, and, unlike gas corporations, he exacted only what was just and reasonable. He moreover met the people half way. If they had complaints he listened to them; if possible, they were speedily set to rights. No one was asked to pay for gas he did not burn. Meters were regularly inspected and patrons given to understand that the company only wanted what was just. People were also assisted in many ways. New devices were added for convenience. Prepayment meters, the first on the Coast, were put in so that a customer can pay for his gas just as he uses it. The latest in the way of ranges were secured and sold to patrons at cost. That these up-to-date methods have been appreciated is evidenced by the fact that today in the city of Seatttle there are over 2500 gas ranges in use. There are also 25,000 Welsbach burners in use.

Some illustrations are shown in this article which will give a good idea of the company's plant at Fifth Avenue and Grant Street and of the size of the big 860,000-foot holder, one of the largest in the country. The other pictures are of the offices and sales room. The company has a total of sixty miles of gas mains. The rapid growth of the city will compel an increase of 25 per cent to this number of miles. During the past four years the whole plant has practically been rebuilt, mains either have been increased in number or relaid entirely; the big gas holder built and a general increased standard of excellency maintained. Besides the gas business, they supply a very considerable number of arc and incandescent electric lights from their own plant. Their general offices and sales room is at 216 Cherry Street. Besides the offices, they have a stock of stoves, heaters, gas and electric fixtures, and, in yards and unloaded in their own coal bunkers.

The intricate details of the business are more interesting, but space in this article is too limited save for a general cursory view of the whole system, and is intended only to show in a general way how thorough the system is conducted and maintained under its present management. Speaking in general terms, Seattle has the most up-to-date gas company in the whole West, and forms an interesting chapter to Seattle's progress.

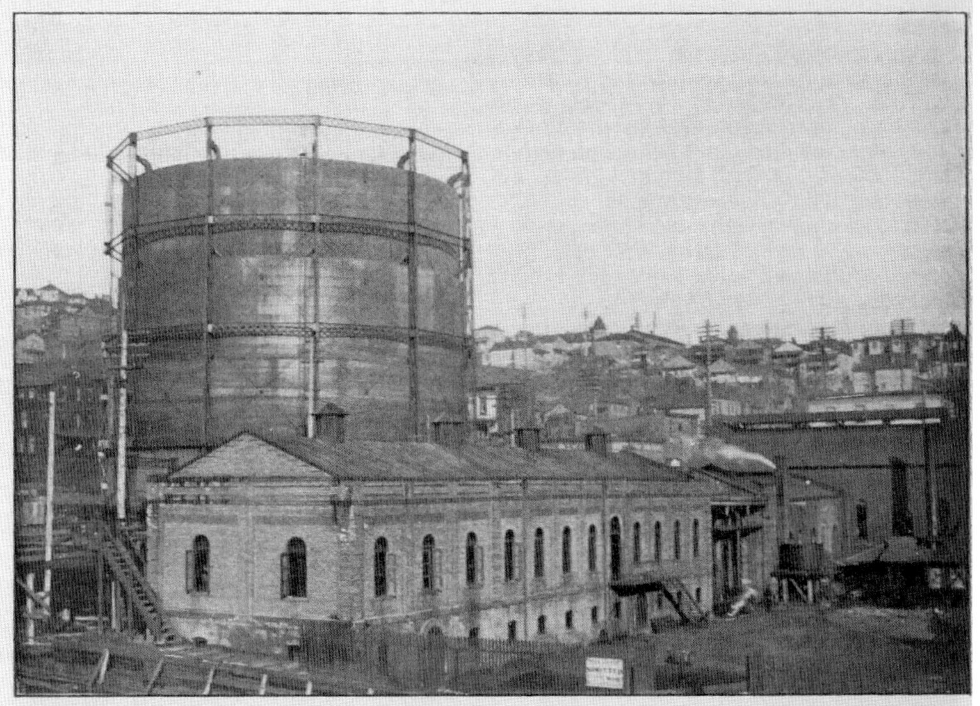

GENERAL VIEW OF WORKS OF SEATTLE GAS & ELECTRIC CO., SHOWING A GAS HOLDER WITH A CAPACITY OF 860,000 FEET.

fact, every conceivable kind of appliance known in gas heating. The lower floors are used for store rooms and for work shops.

The company employs from eighty to 100 men in various capacities, including those about the works. The coal used for manufacturing gas all comes from Washington mines, the cars bearing the coal being run right into the

Speaking about the prepayment meters, which are becoming so popular with householders, Seattle is the only city which takes kindly to them, so far, it is said. This is because the people of Seattle like to pay for what they consume as they go along. Other cities find it slow to have them used, but here they are preferred.

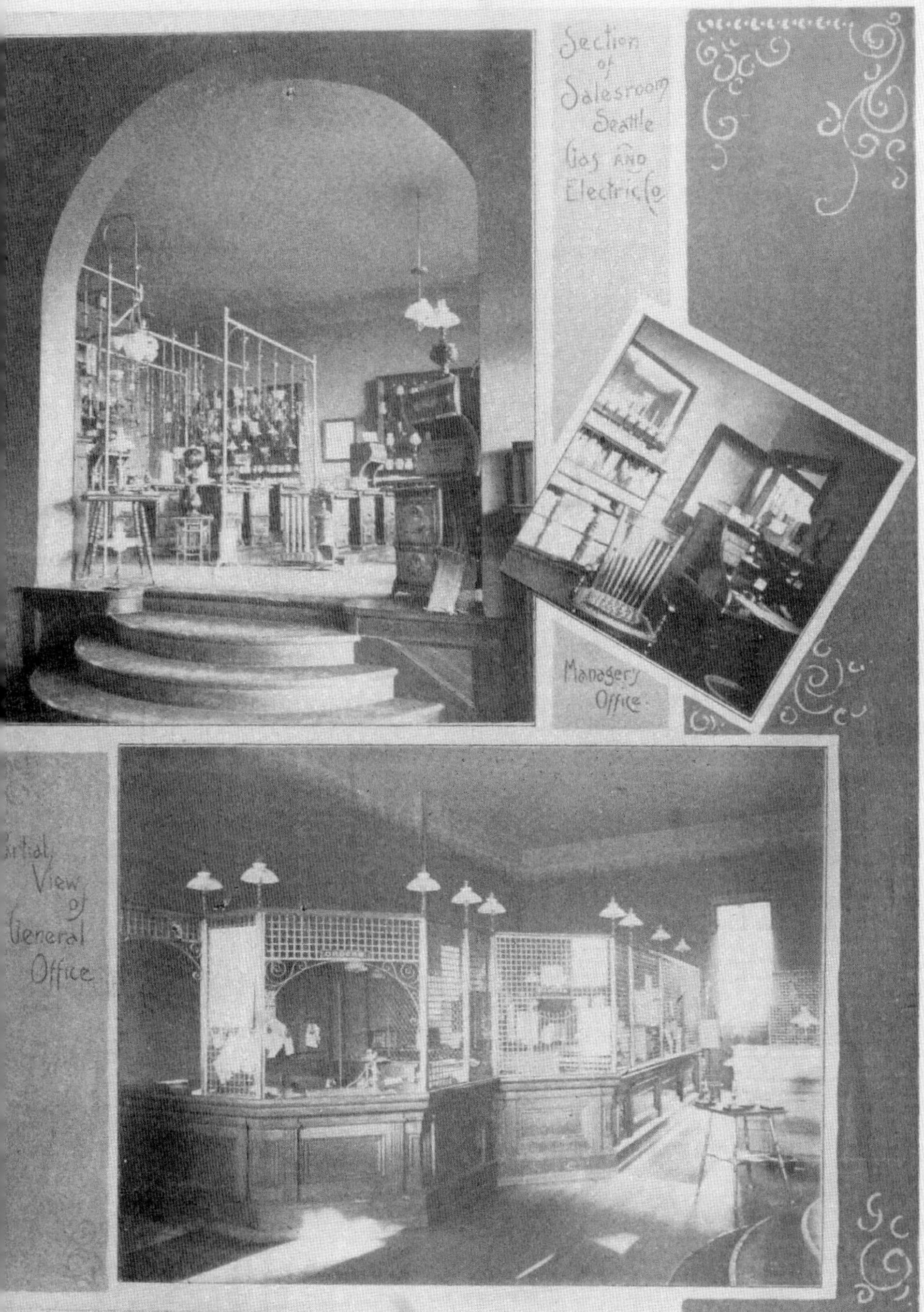

OFFICES AND STORE OF SEATTLE GAS & ELECTRIC CO.

WE TAKE TEA AND SILK.

The leading articles imported by this country from Japan are raw silk and tea. The value of the silk imports for the fiscal year ending June 30 were $10,010,885 in 1897, $16,510,502 in 1898, and $14,920,787 for 1899. The tea imports in pounds were 45,465,161 in 1897, 26,233,407 in 1898 and 29,277,798 for 1899. The tariff on tea has cut down our tea imports from Japan about 40 per cent. Bradstreet's states that the Japanese delegates now in this country for the purpose of getting our tea duties removed or modified claim that said duties greatly hamper and likewise threaten the trade relations of the two countries. "Last year," says this authority, "the average price of tea in the Japanese markets was $12.50 per 133 pounds, while the tax on tea is $13.30 for the same amount, so that the tax amounts to more than the original price of tea."

The principal exports of this country to Japan for the fiscal year ending June 30 last were, in order: Cotton, $5,775,784; petroleum, $2,461,475; tobacco, unmanufactured, $2,414,482; wheat flour, $722,910; manufactured tobacco, $512,218; scientific and electric instruments, $232,892; clocks and watches, $188,602; vehicles, $142,301. The aggregate of iron and steel exports to Japan is also large, the exports of railway iron last year from this country to Japan being $1,150,766. The new tariff of Japan cut down Japan's total imports of manufactured goods for the first seven months of the year 37 per cent and the imports from the United States 18 per cent.

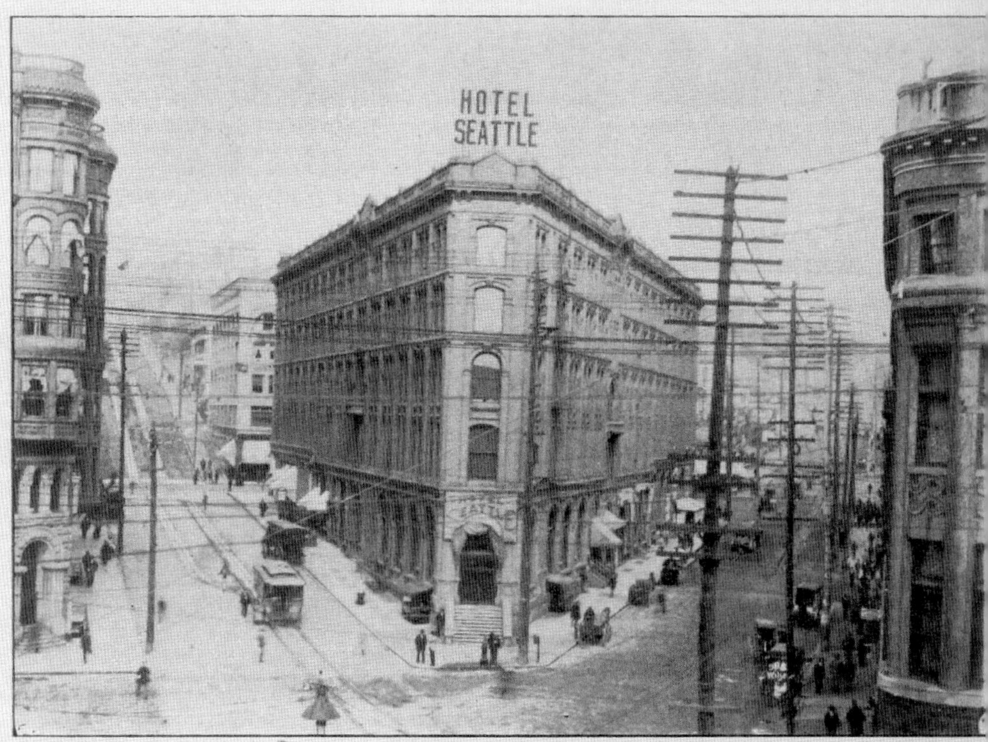

HOTEL SEATTLE, JUNCTION OF YESLER WAY AND JAMES ST., KNOWN AS OCCIDENTAL BLOCK, ERECTED AND OWNED BY JOHN COLLINS.

THE HOTEL SEATTLE.

Hotel Seattle is located at the intersection of James Street, Yesler Way and First Avenue, within from one to two blocks of all the railway passenger depots and principal passenger docks in the city. This hotel has 200 guest rooms, all outside. One hundred and sixty of these are strictly front rooms, all facing business streets. The rooms are all elegantly furnished and arranged with a view to comfort and convenience. The building is of brick and stone, and is five stories in height. The hotel office and lobby is large, well lighted, elegantly furnished, overlooking three streets and Pioneer Square. The hotel is located at the initial point of nearly all the street car lines in the city.

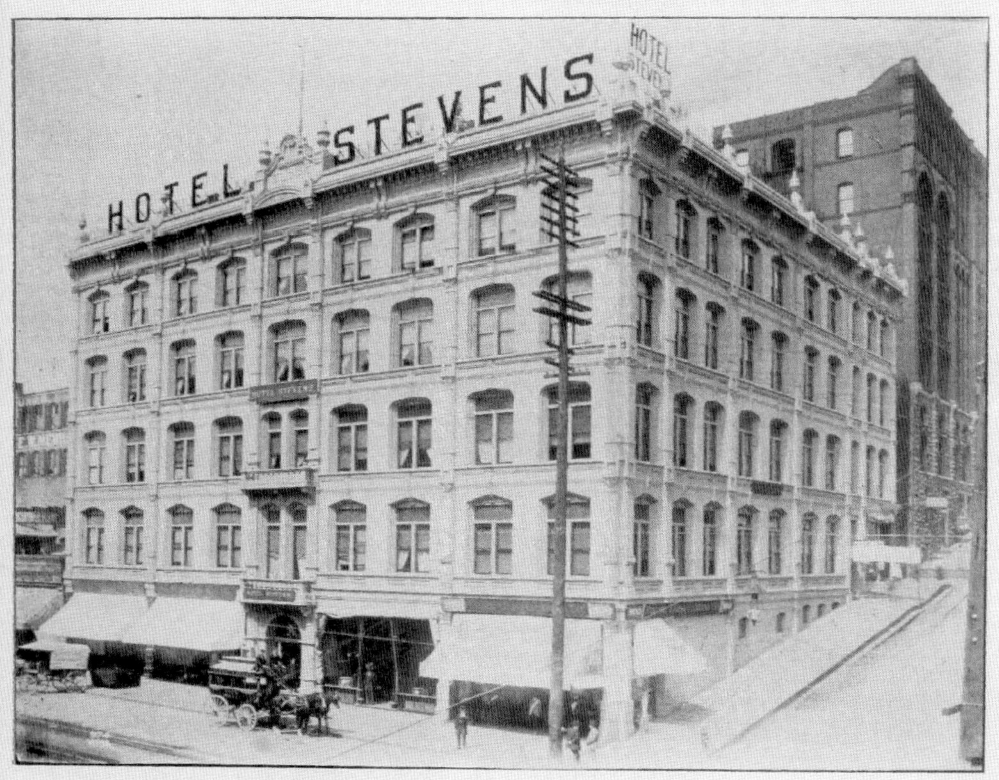

HOTEL STEVENS, ON FIRST AVENUE.

HOTEL STEVENS.

Hotel Stevens is run on both the American and European plans. It has 100 guest rooms, all first-class. A majority of the rooms at the Stevens are among the best in the city. This caravansary is also very conveniently located as regards railway and steamboat lines, being but two blocks removed from the depots and principal docks. The excellent dining room in connection with the Stevens is run by Mrs. Wescott, whose wide experience in this line especially fits her for the business.

THE KERRY LUMBER COMPANY.

An illustration is presented herewith of the Kerry Lumber Company's new sawmill, recently constructed and now in operation on the water front of this city, between Broad and Clay Streets. The alacrity with which this institution was rushed to completion and got down to the business of turning out the manufactured product, while surprising in itself, is characteristic of Manager A. S. Kerry's manner of doing business. The first piling for the mill was driven in October last, and on December 20 the mill was finished to its present stage and cutting timber. Before the mill is fully completed an additional engine must be put in place, which work is under way. There will also be dry kilns, a planing mill and factory built in connection with the sawmill as soon as men and money can rush them to a finish.

At present the capacity is but 50,000 feet daily; with the additional side in operation 90,000 will be a day's run.

The mill is a double affair, i. e., the same as two single sawmills, side by side, under one roof.

The mill proper is 256 feet in length by 56 feet in breadth, with two stories, the upper story for the manufacture of lumber and the lower story occupied by planing engines and a lath mill.

The boiler room is a separate building, to the west of the mill, with concrete foundation, corrugated iron sides, and gravel roof. There is a battery of four boilers, capable of developing 300-horse power.

A prominent feature of the Kerry Lumber Company's new sawmill is the large Berlin timber planer that will, at one and the same time, dress all four sides of a timber 20x30 inches in size. This planer is made by the Berlin Machine Works, Beloit, Wis. Its weight is 25,000 pounds. It will occupy a place on the upper floor of the main mill.

The piling under the mill is protected by the "Perfection" process, a home enterprise.

Besides the mill property the company also owns the tugboat Lady Lake and a number of large scows. When in full operation the company will employ about 100 men.

The new mill is so located as regards railroad trackage that it has access, free of switching charges, to all the railroads entering the city. This is a great advantage and one of the features of Seattle's railway facilities, for a manufactory located anywhere along the water front is accessible alike to all the great railway systems.

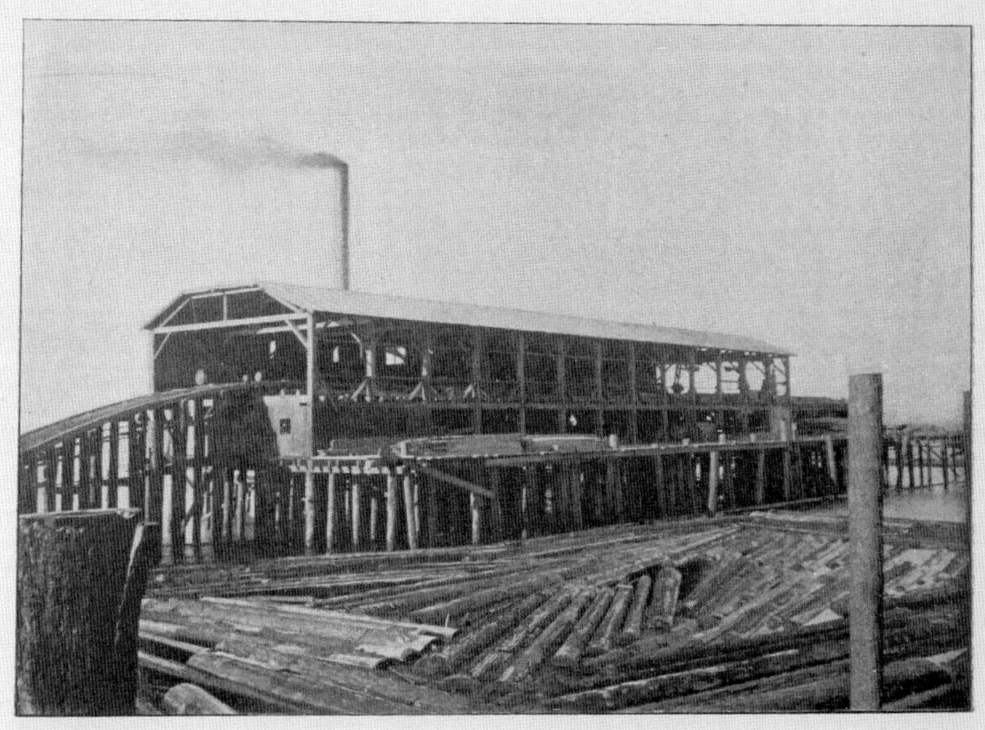

THE MILL OF THE KERRY LUMBER CO.

Separate from the mill land across the railway tracks, on the east side of Railroad Avenue, is the company's office, a neat building, 18x28 feet. The down-town office is in the Bailey Building.

When the plant is fully completed

there will be an overhead transfer, from the mill across and over the railroad tracks, to carry the output to the dry kilns and planers, which are to be located about 250 feet east of the sawmill, on the opposite side of Railroad Avenue. The lumber will be carried across on conveyors. There will also be a broad and substantial wharf built, extending to the west of the mill, so that the largest vessels can load or discharge alongside.

A. S. Kerry, president of the mill company, has been in the lumber business in Seattle for thirteen years. Previous to the destruction of the Kerry Lumber Company's mill on the tide flats, in 1897, they had branch yards in Juneau, Skagway, Douglas Island and Rossland, B. C.

THE TRADE WITH THE ORIENT.

But little has been said in this volume up to this time of our trade with the Orient, save in the course of a general discussion of its possibilities. The following information bearing directly upon the trade, showing, as it does, how important it is becoming, will be of interest:

The Pacific trade of the United States has advanced two thirds in volume during the past five calendar years. American imports of the products of Asia and Oceanica have increased 40 per cent since 1894, while American exports to the markets of Asia and Oceanica have grown 135 per cent, or multiplied nearly two and one-half times.

We are taking $48,000,000 of goods a year to the East Indies, as compared with $25,000,000 in 1894. We are taking $16,000,000 of sugar a year from the Hawaiian Islands, as compared with $8,000,000 in 1895. Our annual tea bill with China and Japan now runs to near 100,000,000 pounds, and our silk bill with these countries reaches $25,000,000 a year, comprising nearly all of our imports of unmanufactured silk.

We are shipping $18,000,000 of American products to Japan, where we sold only $3,300,000 in 1892, and over $12,000,000 to China, where we shipped $4,800,000 in 1893. Our exports to Hawaii have risen from less than $3,000,000 in 1893 to near $7,000,000 now, and our shipments of American wares to Australasia have grown in that time from $7,500,000 to $17,500,000 a year. Our Pacific exports of flour have risen in a few years from practically nothing to 2,500,000 barrels, and our sales of cotton goods to the Orient have grown from $4,000,000 in 1894 to $15,000,000.

American Trade with Japan.

The heaviest trade of the United States in the Orient is with Japan, whose people are known in the trading world as the "Yankees of the East." Our imports from Japan are larger than from any other Oriental country, unless it be British India, and our exports to Japan are heavier than to any other market on the Pacific, except possibly Australasia. As compared with our trade with China, both exports and imports with Japan are about one-third larger.

The rapid growth of American trade with Japan, the export feature in particular, is strikingly shown by the statistics of the past five calendar years:

Our Japan Trade of Past Five Years.

Year.	Imports.	Exports.	Total.
1894	$23,100,725	$ 4,001,962	$27,102,687
1895	27,430,678	5,356,454	32,787,132
1896	18,214,322	10,145,909	28,360,231
1897	28,085,123	16,009,471	44,094,594
1898	23,255,253	19,716,086	42,971,339

It is thus seen that American exports to Japan have grown from $4,000,000 in 1894 to $19,000,000 in 1898, multiplying nearly five-fold. The imports have fluctuated and have a little more than held their own. The aggregate trade has increased $15,000,000 in the five-year period, or a trifle under 60 per cent.

Recent Changes in Our Japan Exports.

The development of the manufacturing industries of Japan during the past five years has had the effect to increase American exports of raw material, like cotton and tobacco leaf, and keep down the exports of finished wares somewhat. The new tariff of Japan, which went into force about a year ago, is calculated to intensify this tendency.

What the Future Holds.

As regards the future of American commerce in the Orient, the trade with China is of the foremost interest. In population, extent of empire and natural resources and future possibilities, China is the colossal figure of the Orient, and its commerce during the next ten years will be the fighting goal of all commercial powers. The trade of the United States with China at present is second to that with Japan. We export more merchandise, moreover, to Australasia, and import more goods from the British and Dutch Indies. But the situation tomorrow may be—indeed, is bound to be—reversed, for China's commercial future will from this point develop rapidly.

For thirty years our imports of Chinese goods have averaged about $20,000,000 per annum, with a little variation. The $22,000,000 of imports from China in 1896 and the $18,000,000 in 1899, for the fiscal years ending June 30, give a fair idea of the fluctuation. Our new tariff tax on tea is responsible for part of this variation, the shrinkage in pounds being from 56,000,000 in 1897 to 39,000,00 in 1899. The hole made by our tariff on tea, however, was partially repaired by the increase in the imports of raw silk, the values being $4,364,000 in 1897 and $6,497,000 in 1899. The predominant interest of the United States in China is in the exports rather than the imports, it is true, but the shipowners bitterly complain that they cannot do a profitable business at low rates in carrying American goods to China unless they can get return cargoes of Chinese goods to the United States, and hostile taffiffs, treaties and other legislation greatly hamper their business and force them to collect higher rates than would be possible under unrestricted trade relations.

Remarkable Growth in United States Exports to China.

The most conspicuous feature of the trade of the United States in the Orient is the advance in the exports of American goods to China. From 1880 down to 1895 our exports to China were at almost as great a standstill as the commercial development of China had been during the centuries preceding. For the fiscal year ending June 30, 1880, we exported only about a million dollars' worth of American wares, and fifteen years later the exports were still the bagatelle of three millions. The vast growth during the five-year period, 1895-9, is represented by the following exposition in arithmetic:

United States exports to China, fiscal year 1895	$ 3,603,840
United States exports to China, fiscal year 1899	14,493,440
Increase of 1889 over 1895	$10,889,600
Percentage of increase in five years	302 pr ct.

China's Vast Natural Resources.

Before the London Chamber of Commerce, October 26 last, the British consul, C. T. Gardner, in discussing "The Trade of China," thus spoke of China's native resources:

"The vast territory marked on our maps as China proper and Manchuria, more than 1,500 miles from north to south, and then 2,000 miles east to west, is remarkably fertile and capable of producing all the vegetable products of which the world stands in need. This vast territory is remarkably free from desert tracts, such as the sandy deserts of Australia and India and the alkali deserts of America.

"It is now known that China is richer in mineral wealth than was supposed in 1859. The partial surveys made by experts up to the present time show that China is full of most valuable minerals. I need only refer to the extensive coal deposits all along the Yangtse, and to those a few miles west of Moukden in Manchuria. In fact, coal is now known to exist in almost every one of the eighteen provinces. Yet up to the present time, if we except a few mines worked in a primitive way in primitive native fashion, the Kaiping mines are the only ones that are beng worked.

"Iron exists all over the country; the hill of iron—Tieh-Kangshan—between Kiukeang and Hankow, is said to be the richest and most extensive iron field in the world. Gold is washed for in the river below Ichang, proving the existence of gold fields above that port; mercury, copper, tin, silver, lead and other valuable minerals have been found in many of the provinces; at present they are unworked.

"The population of China is now known to be as dense as was estimated in 1859. It is ascertained to number about 360,000,000, and is free from the blight of caste, the curse of such vast regions of India; it is free from the laziness of the African race, which has been such a curse in Africa, America and the West Indies. It is to Chinese labor, to a great extent, that Canada owes its present prosperity—the Chinamen gave most efficient aid to the construction of railways, for instance; the wealth of the Straits Settlements is due to the millions of Chinese laborers, working there in agriculture and mines—yet Chinese industry, which has done so much to increase the wealth and prosperity of our colonies, has done little or nothing for China itself.

"The Chinese are now known to have the instinct of trade and trade capacity to an extraordinary degree; every coolie who has a few 'cash' invests it in an article of trade to sell at a profit; the Chinese shopkeeper is reasonably honest, and the Chinese merchants proverbially so. At the small treaty ports the natives have captured the import trade, and at Hongkong, Singapore and Shanghai they are capturing it and doing away with the expense of the foreign middlemen, yet the demand for British staples has been stationary or even retrograde."

SOME PROMINENT CITIZENS.

POSTMASTER STEWART.

George M. Stewart, the present postmaster for Seattle, Wash., was born at Elmira, N. Y., May 16, 1850. Mr. Stewart came to the Pacific coast when but 16 years of age, staying in San Francisco for one year, when he left to try his fortune in the Comstock mines. He clerked in a grocery store in Virginia City, Nevada, for two years, when he engaged in the mercantile business on

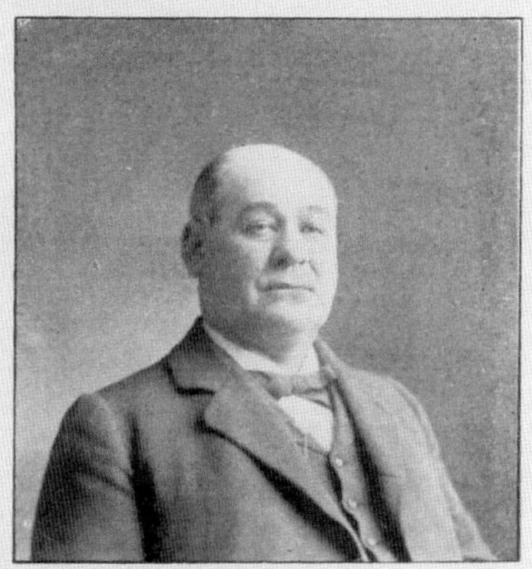

POSTMASTER GEO. M. STEWART.

his own account. Mr. Stewart next accepted a position in a large wholesale house in Sacramento, which he retained for six years. In 1889 he came to Seattle a move he had been long contemplating—and bought an interest in the undertaking firm of Shorey & Co., the style of the new firm being Bonney & Stewart, under which name it has since carried on a very successful business.

While in Nevada Mr. Stewart took an active part in politics. He was a hard worker in the Republican ranks and served on various state and county committees. Since coming to Seattle Mr. Stewart has taken an active part in the councils of his party. He has been for four years a member of the King county Republican executive committee. He represented the county on the state committee during the campaign of 1898 and has been treasurer of the state Republican organization since 1896. Mr. Stewart has always been a staunch supporter of Jno. L. Wilson. He was appointed to his present official position by President McKinley in 1899. He never sought and never held office before.

EDWARD P. EDSEN.

Edward P. Edsen, lawyer and author, is a native of Husum, Germany. After graduating at the Universities of Berlin and Heidelberg he spent four years in travel, bringing up in Portland, Oregon, in 1875. Being in need of money, he sought and obtained employment on a farm near Sandy postoffice, remaining until March, 1876, when he engaged for one season in salmon fishing at Brookfield, Wash. Afterward Mr. Edsen took a business college course in Portland, perfecting himself in English at the same time. For six months he worked as a deck hand on the Columbia River, followed by six months' lumbering at Walla Walla. In the spring of 1878 he found employment at Stohl's City brewery, Walla Walla, where, by reason of his faithful attention to business, he was rapidly advanced to the position of general manager. About this period he made an unfortunate investment of a large part of his savings in a mining venture.

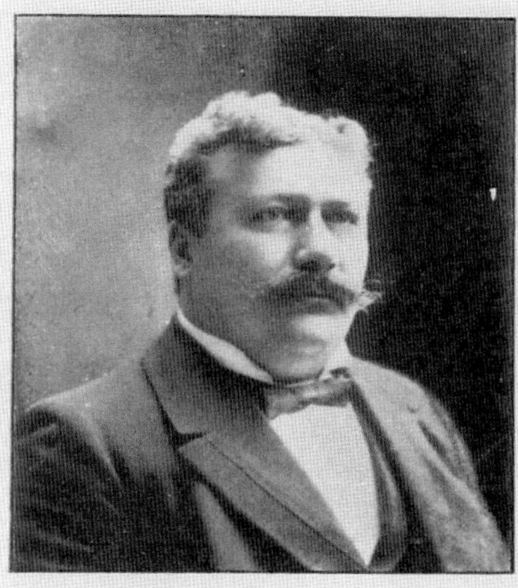

EDWARD P. EDSEN.

We next find the subject of this sketch, in 1881, conducting a real estate and insurance agency at Walla Walla in partnership with Judge V. D. Lambert. In the summer of '83 Mr. Edsen visited the Sound, finally locating at Seattle in December. In January following he was admitted to the bar. His mastery of no less than seven languages soon secured him the major portion of the foreign law business of the city. He readily gained recognition as one of the leaders of the bar, his business affairs prospered, while his popularity grew with his circle of acquaintances. In November, 1889, Mr. Edsen found a law partnership with Will H. Thompson and John E. Humphries, under the style of Thompson, Edsen and Humphries, which partnership continued for eight years developing into one of the leading law firms on the Coast.

Mr. Edsen has been an active factor in the militia organizations of the state. In 1884 he founded Company D, N. G. W., being its first captain. He is an expert drill master, his company as well as the Rainier Division 18, U. R. K. of P., organized by him in 1892, ranking among the best in many competitive drills. He is now serving his second term as judge-advocate-general of the Washington Brigade, which position he has creditably filled since 1892. In politics Mr. Edsen has ever been Republican, but, though a recognized party leader and though frequently urged to accept nomination for official honors, has steadfastly refused. He has been for several years, and is yet, state president of the German-American Republican Club.

His membership in social and fraternal organizations is extensive, and includes the three branches of the K. of P., Knights of Malta, Knights of the Golden Eagle, U. A. O. D., the A. O. U. W., the Royal Arcanum, the Order of Chosen Friends, four branches of the I. O. O. F. and the Fraternal Order of Eagles, for which order he wrote both of the Grand Aerie and subordinate Aerie Rituals, etc., as well as a complete code of laws. He was one of the founders of the Seattle Turn Verein, and since 1889 has been president of the George Washington Branch of the Irish National League. In 1894 Mr. Edsen was representative of the State of Washington at the World's Fair, Antwerp, being present at its formal opening by King Leopold II. on May 5. Mr. Edsen has made numerous creditable contributions to periodical literature in both prose and verse, having shown particular ability in the latter by his clever mastery of frontier and mine dialects. Of powerful physique and commanding presence, he is what he appears, a man of untiring energy and unlimited resources.

M. H. YOUNG.

One of the leading financiers in the chief city in Washington is M. H. Young, whose picture is given herewith and who occupies a suite of offices in the Pioneer Building, rooms 211 and 212. Mr. Young is general manager of the New England & Northwestern Investment Company, a director in the National Bank of Commerce, vice-president and director in the Seattle Gas and Electric Company and director in the Seattle Electric Company (Consolidated Street railways). He deals in real estate, and has the reputation of a careful, shrewd and safe investor.

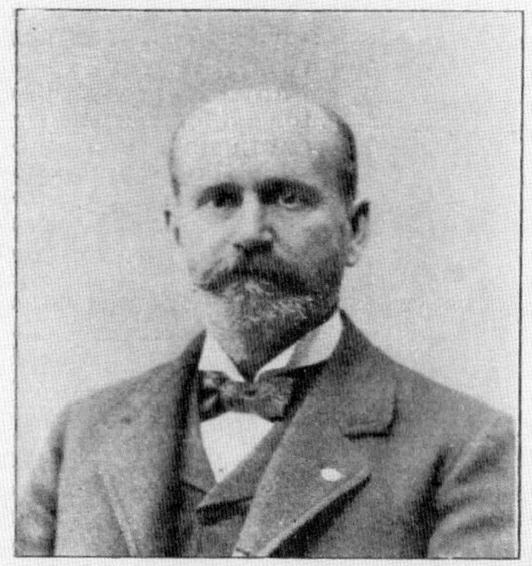

M. H. YOUNG.

Mr. Young has also been an active factor in building up the city, having built over 100 houses since coming here in 1890. He has built several fine business blocks and effected the Beacon Hill improvement. In company with R. R. Spencer, cashier of the National Bank of Commerce, Mr. Young has recently entered the import trade, bringing to this country the products of Japan and China.

Mr. Young was born at Graton, Mass., in 1846. He enlisted with the Union forces in 1863 and served throughout the rest of the war. From 1870 to 1872 he was connected with the C., B. & Q. Railroad, and from then till 1890 he was cashier of the Boston Manufacturing Company, residing at Waltham during the time. He was one of the organizers of the Waltham Electric Company, and when that company consolidated with the Waltham Gas Company he was a director in the new organization and was the first secretary and treasurer of the Waltham Co-operative Bank. He held the position until its affiairs grew so large that he could not attend to them with his limited time, when he resigned, remaining a director, however, till coming to Seattle. He was also a member of the Board of Aldermen of Waltham for two years, declining re-nomination. He served three years as chairman of the Sinking Fund Commission. Mr. Young moved to Seattle in 1890. He was president of the Union Trunk Line until its consolidation with the Seattle Electric Railway.

FRED RICE ROWELL.

Fred Rice Rowell was born in South Thomaston, Maine, December 29, 1856. He is a graduate of Colby College, Waterville, Maine, of the class of '81. He read law in the office of Hon. A. P. Gould, at Thomaston, Maine, and was admitted to the bar of Knox County, Maine, in September, 1883. He formed a law partnership with Hon. J. O. Robinson and practised his profession in Rockland, Maine, till 1888, when he removed to Seattle, where he has since continuously practised law. In 1890 Mr. Robinson joined Mr. Rowell in Seattle and the firm of Robinson & Rowell was reorganized and still continues. In politics Mr. Rowell is a Democrat and immediately identified himself with his party upon coming to Washington. He has received political honors from his party in Seattle and King County, having been at different times a candidate on his party

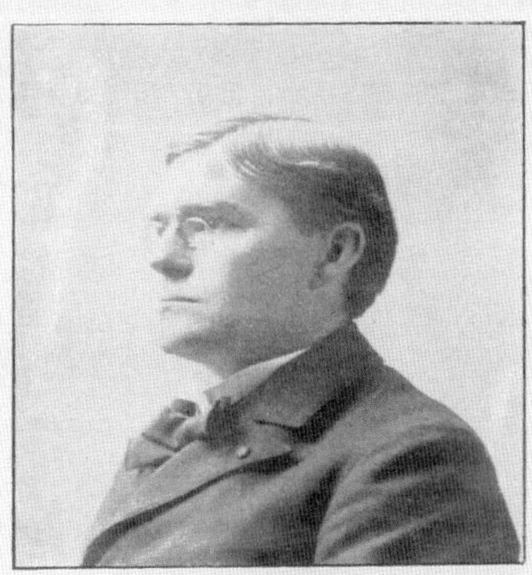

FRED RICE ROWELL.

ticket for Presecuting Attorney of King County, for Alderman of the Fifth Ward, and in the spring of 1898 for Corporation Counsel for the City of Seattle. His vote on the latter occasion was a very flattering testimonial to his popularity, as he lacked but a few votes of election on a ticket overwhelmingly defeated. Mr. Rowell married in January, 1884, Miss May Florence Stetson of South Thomaston. Both Mr. and Mrs. Rowell are members and communicants of St. Mark's Church, Seattle, having been confirmed during the rectorate of Rev. D. C. Garrett.

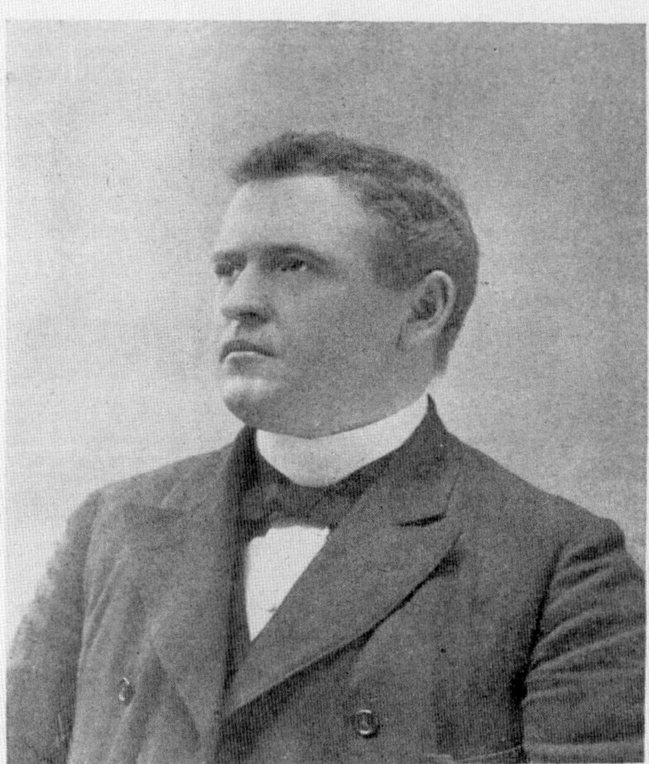

JAMES GRIFFITHS.

JAMES GRIFFITHS.

James Griffiths, whose portrait appears on this page, is president of the Griffiths & Sprague Stevedoring Company, Inc., of Seattle, and sole partner in the firm of Jones, Griffiths & Co., ship brokers and commission merchants, with head offices at 610 Bailey Building, and with branches at Tacoma and Port Townsend. This firm handles the exclusive stevedoring business of the Nippon Yusen Kaisha at this port, and also handle all Oriental freight from the cars of the Great Northern Railroad at Smith's Cove dock. They are also stevedores for the Centennial Mill Company of Seattle and Spokane. They recently loaded for that company the Japanese twin-screw steamer Nanyo Maru with 3800 tons offlour for the Orient in sixty-one hours, which is far and away the quickest dispatch ever given to the loading of a full cargo of flour at any Puget Sound port, and the feat speaks volumes for the facilities afforded at Seattle for the loading of large steamers, and the ability of this firm to put work through expeditiously. Their stevedore business extends to all ports on Puget Sound and includes stevedoring sailing as well as steam craft, with wheat, lumber or coal.

Mr. Griffiths resigned the local management at Seattle of the Nippon Yusen Kaisha to organize and operate the Centennial Alaska Transportation Company. This company purchased the Japanese steamship Takasago Maru, a screw propeller of 2075 tons register, and brought her to Seattle as the most suitable and convenient port in which to fit her out for the Alaska trade. Her name was changed to the Centennial, and she soon became a general favorite by reason of her speed and comfort. On the outbreak of the late Spanish-American war the free use of the Centennial was tendered to the Secretary of War for use as a government transport. In recognition of this offer Congress granted the vessel an American register and her transfer to the American flag was made in Seattle harbor on the 21st day of May,

1898, Old Glory being hoisted to the masthead by Mrs. W. W. Robinson, wife of Capt. W. W. Robinson, U. S. A., quartermaster for the district of Puget Sound. The Centennial is the only steamer registering from Seattle employed by the government as a transport.

In a personal visit to Washington, Mr. Griffiths rendered signal aid to Capt. Robinson in getting the War Department to recognize the advantages of Seattle's facilities for transport work and supplies.

FRED H. PETERSON.

Attorney Fred H. Peterson, whose portrait appears above, has been in active law practice at Seattle for six-has carried on a general practice and has had a wide experience in all classes of litigation.

During his long residence here he has held office but once, that was in 1886, when he was elected City Attorney, preferring to practice law rather than to aspire to wear official honors, although he has always taken an active part in politics, and particularly during the hot municipal campaign which re-elected Thomas J. Humes Mayor of Seattle, when he was chairman of the

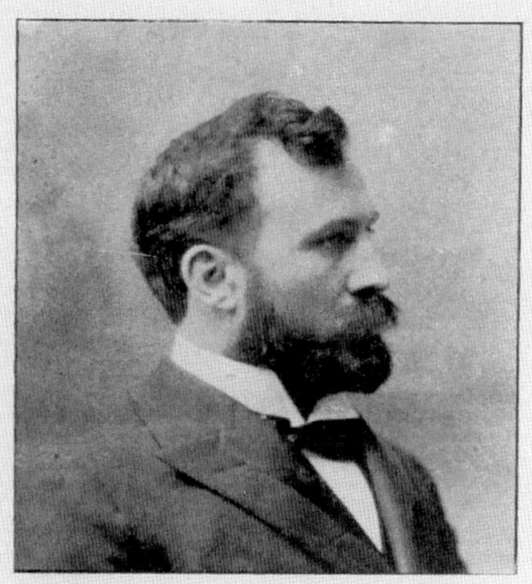

FRED H. PETERSON.

teen years. During that time he has been engaged in many important cases, and by industry and perseverance has established a reputation as one of the most successful lawyers in the city. He Republican Central Committee. The result of that election showed that he was as aggressive and successful in the management of a political campaign as in the conduct of a lawsuit.

Mr. Peterson has an elegant suite of offices at 410 to 413 Mutual Life Building.

P. SARTORI.

P. Sartori, the wholesale and retail liquor dealer, in the Occidental Block, is probably as widely known as any merchant at the present time in this

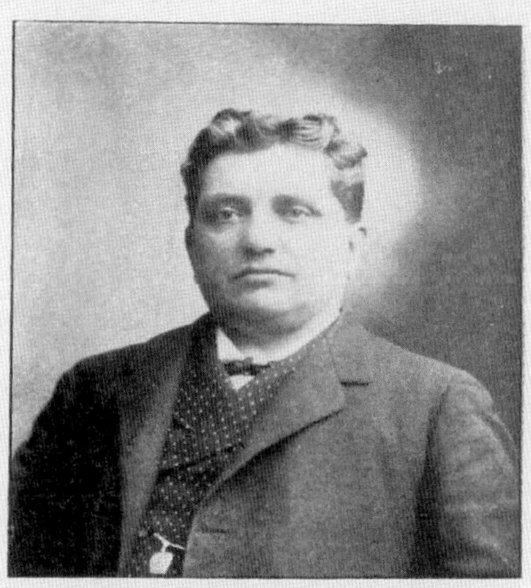

P. SARTORI.

city. Mr. Sartori came to Seattle in 1889 and went into business in the Bell Block, where he continued for three years, being unable at the time to get adequate quarters nearer the central business portion of the city. Seven years ago he moved his business to the Occidental Block, on James Street, where he has since remained. Mr. Sartori has a patronage that extends not only to all parts of Washington but all throughout Alaska as well. Once every two years Mr. Sartori makes a trip to Louisville, Ky., for the purpose of selecting his stock of liquors. He buys no whiskies less than ten years old and is particular to get the choicest brands.

Mr. Sartori is a native of Switzerland, where he was a winegrower. He immigrated to California in 1865 and for eight years was engaged in the business of wine selling in Sonoma.

Today Mr. Sartoris has one of the finest, best kept, best stocked places in the city. He belongs to a number of fraternal organizations, being a member of the Elks, a Mason and a Knight of Pythias, and enjoys a well-merited popularity.

LILLY, BOGARDUS & CO.

During the period since the great fire in this city many remarkable mercantile growths have been made. Like the rapid progress of Seattle itself, a number of firms and incorporations have forced their way so far to the front as to attract attention from all points. Particular attention in this connection is directed to Lilly, Bogardus & Co., an incorporated company, which beyond doubt has not only taken a position in the front ranks commercially speaking, but has set an example of progress which has proven of very great benefit to this city. No longer confined to business locally, they reach out all over the West, and their ability to grasp the situation gives this city a prestige for having a live, energetic set of business men. It is corporations and firms like this which enable the government to do much of its transport business from Puget Sound.

Lilly, Bogardus & Co. probably are the most conspicuous examples of Western growth of any concern in this city. Ten years ago they were doing business on a capital so small as to be insignificant; today the volume of their business, in the gross, is exceeded by not more than half a dozen concerns in Seattle. Ten years ago they opened a feed and hay store, having a room fifty feet square; now it takes four buildings, with dimensions as follows, to carry on their trade: One building 120x120, one 60x160, one 60x165, and the other 90x165. The illustration shown in this article gives an excellent idea of the size of these warehouses and of their location and general convenience for shipping. The company employs sixty men; four or five of them are traveling throughout the Northwest selling goods which the company handle. The territory supplied includes Washington, Oregon, British Columbia, Hawaii and the Phil-

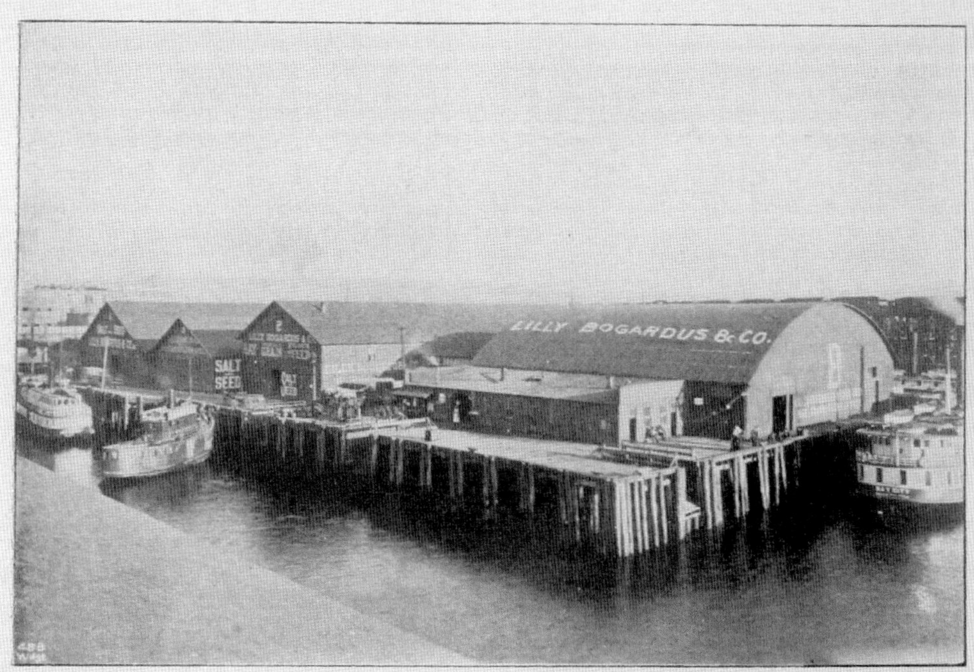

WAREHOUSES OF LILLY, BOGARDUS & CO.

ippines. While the company makes a specialty of hay, grain, flour and feed, they handle very large quantities of cereals, salt, poultry food, and devote much attention to field and garden seeds. In order to properly take care of the seed business, a separate store, as shown in an illustration, is occupied exclusively by this department. So great has this branch of their business become that they now issue a sixty-page illustrated catalogue, devoted almost exclusively to the seed and poultry food business. This store is located at 814 Western Avenue.

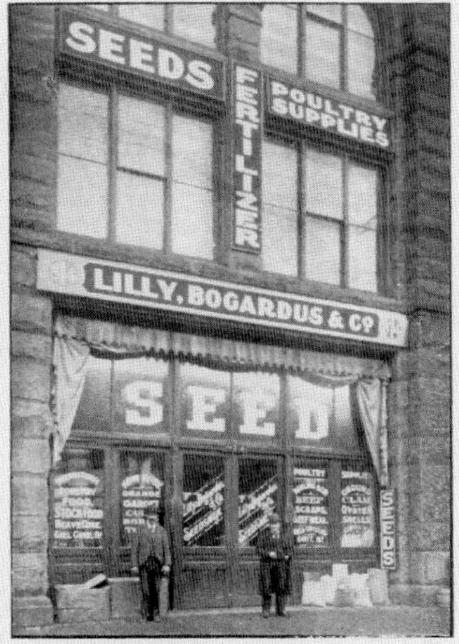

THE SEED DEPARTMENT STORE OF LILLY, BOGARDUS & CO., 814 WESTERN AVENUE.

The company compress all hay into a very small bale for shipment. They were the first to introduce such a method upon the Coast. As a result, they now put 265 pounds of hay in a cylindrical ball eighteen inches in diameter and thirty-six inches long. It has been possible since its introduction to sell Washington hay to Alaska and the Orient and open up a field hitherto unknown. They have a complete feed mill for grinding all their grain products which they sell. They also manufacture poultry foods. Surrounded as they are by splendid dock facilities, they are enabled to load into a vessel of any size. Or, in case of receiving freight from Sound ports or by rail, they are able to unload from either railroad track or from steamboat into their own warehouses. The whole arrangement is most complete. Although they did an extensive business in 1898, last year exceeded it by fully 25 per cent. They are undoubtedly the biggest people in their line on the whole Coast today. C. H. Lilly is president of the company and E. F. Bogardus is manager.

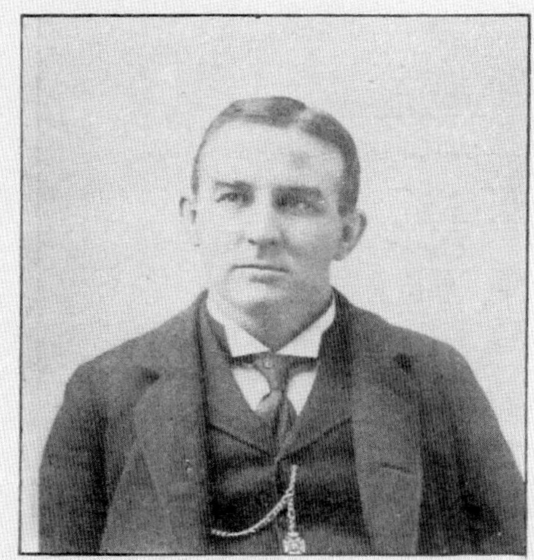

C. H. LILLY.

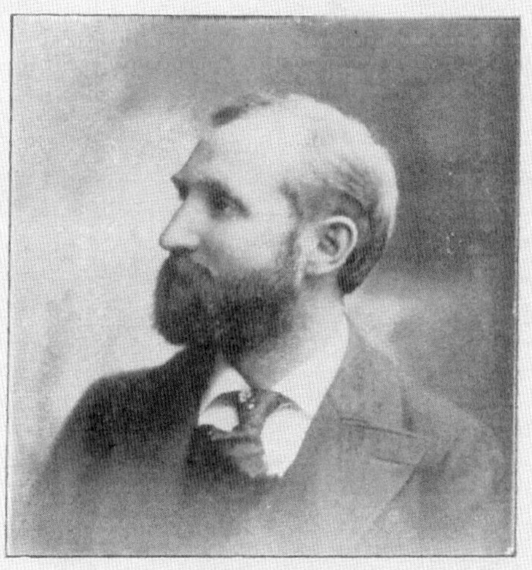

E. F. BOGARDUS.

Mr. Bogardus came to Seattle eleven years ago. For two years he had lived in California, but his home was formerly Champagne County, Illinois, where he was born and raised. He graduated from the State University, and while still young began a small merchandise business with C. H. Lilly, his present partner. When he left the East and removed to California Mr. Lilly kept the store, but latterly, when Mr. Borgardus came to Seattle, he was joined by Mr. Lilly and together they began the business which has since grown to enormous proportions.

C. H. Lilly, the president of the company, has a personality closely interwoven with that of Mr. Borgardus. He was raised in the same county and after completing his education began business with Mr. Borgardus. Both men have been together a good many years now and the success with which they have met in the West is due, beyond question, to their own efforts.

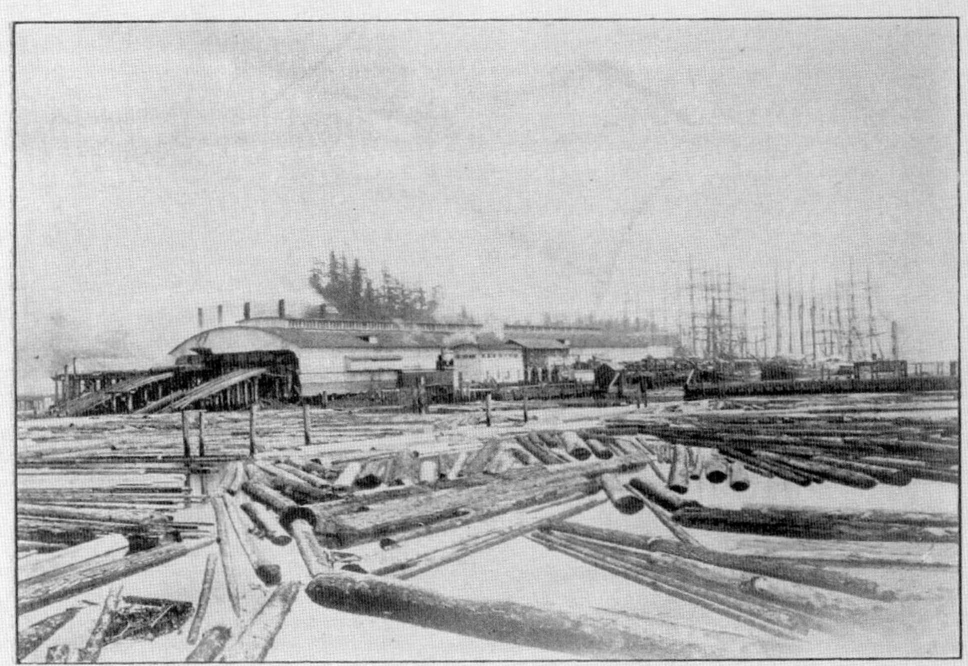

THE SAW MILL AT PORT BLAKELY, ONE OF THE BIG MILLS OF THE WORLD.

ONE OF THE BIG PUGET SOUND MILLS.

The construction of Hoods Canal and the founding of the town of Port Gamble were not contemporaneous events, as new arrivals are sometimes led to believe. The date of completion of the canal is still in controversy. The other event occurred one day in July, 1853, when Capt. W. C. Talbot commenced landing the cargo of the schooner Julius Pringle and started a portion of his crew at work clearing off a mill site and hewing timbers for the mill frame. He was at the head of an expedition sent out by the San Francisco firm of W. C. Talbot & Co. to establish a sawmill and trading post in the new Eldorado of Pacific Coast lumbermen, the Puget Sound country. At that time the firm was composed of Capt. Charles Talbot and A. J. Pope of San Francisco, and Capt. J. P. Keller and Charles Foster of East Machias, Me. A few years later Cyrus Walker, who is the only surviving member of the little band of pioneers at Port Gamble, was admitted to partnership, and still later the company's interests were incorporated under the name of the Puget Mill Company. For thirty-five years Mr. Walker has been manager of the company's interests on Puget Sound, and to him more than to any other man is due the remarkable evolution since 1853.

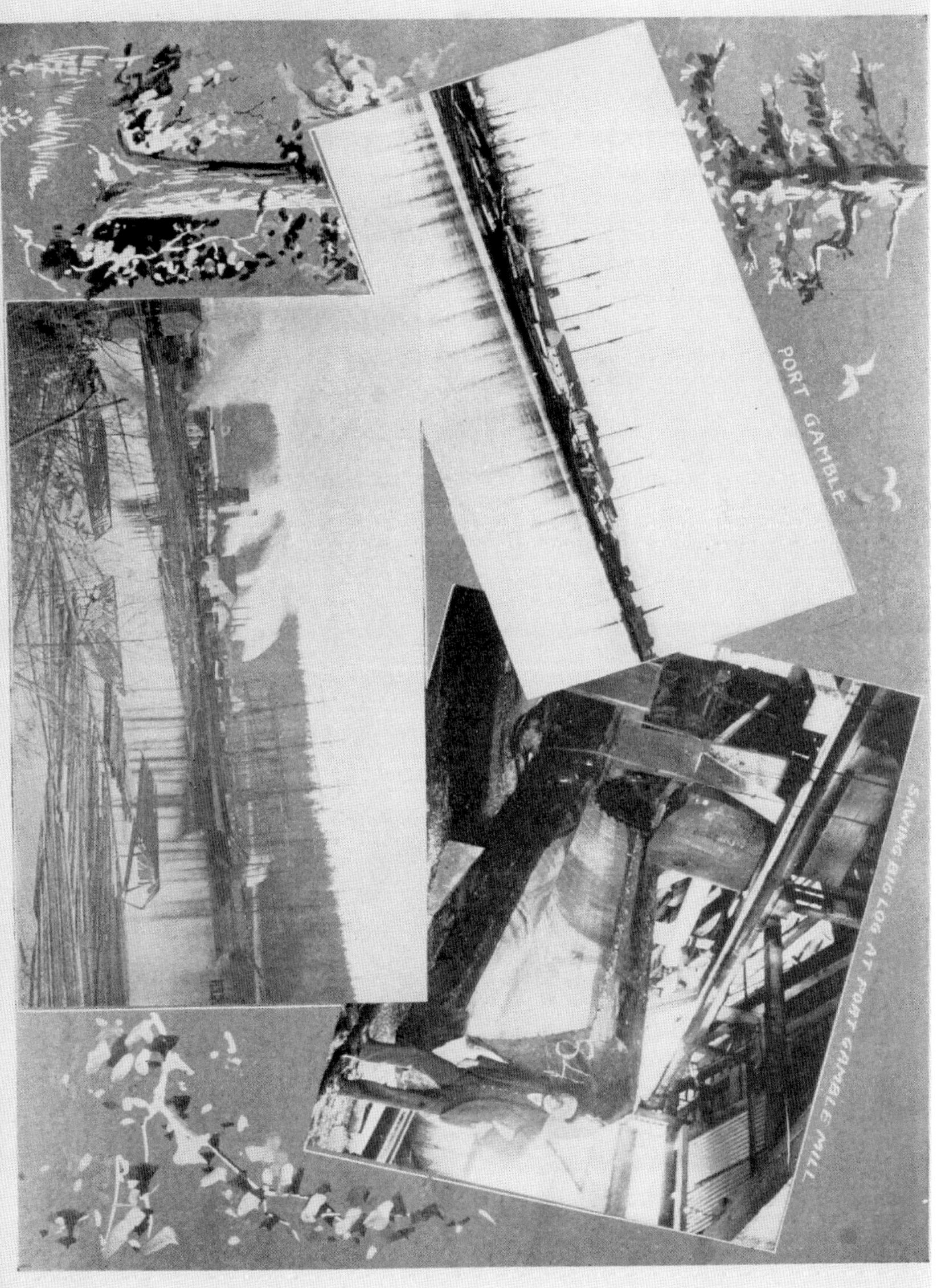
PORT GAMBLE
SAWING BIG LOG AT PORT GAMBLE MILL

The machinery for the mill arrived from Boston on the schooner L. P. Foster, J. P. Keller, master, in September, 1853. Compared with the immense plants that now cover the original site, this mill was a toy. The building was 45x70 feet, with a diminutive engine and boiler, and a single sash saw that would cut 2000 feet of boards a day—some days. The first year's output was 300,000 feet—less than the present aggregate daily output of the company's mills at Port Gamble and Port Ludlow. In 1854 a live gang and an edger were added, increasing the capacity to 15,000 feet daily.

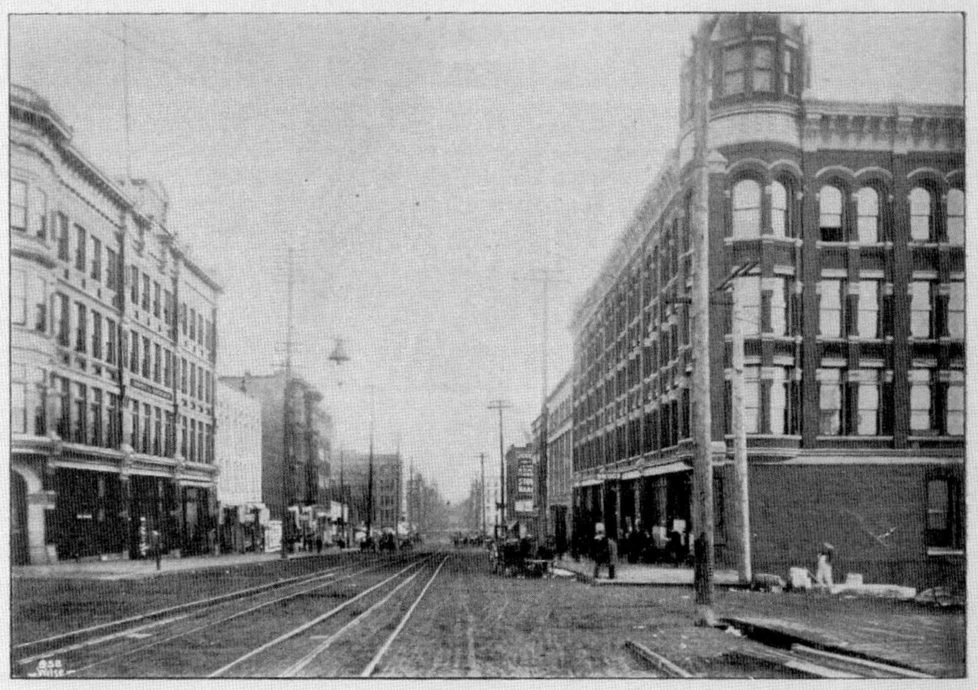

LOOKING DOWN FIRST AVENUE FROM POSTOFFICE.

The identity of the old mill has long since been "lost in the shuffle" of improvements. It has been succeeded by two modern plants adjoining but operated independent of each other. Each is equipped with the latest labor-saving machinery; each has a capacity of 110,000 feet of lumber a ten-hour day, and both give employment to about 300 men. In addition to these two mills the company owns and operates another large mill at Port Ludlow, with a ten-hour daily capacity of 110,000, and employing 150 men. Its mill at Utsalady, on Camano Island, near the mouth of the Skagit River, has not been operated for several years. The three mills cut 100,000,000 feet of lumber during the year 1899; the output at Port Gamble being 62,245,422 feet of rough lumber, 13,349,485 laths and 213,519 feet of pickets. The greater portion of this output went to San Francisco and other California ports, the remainder to Mexico, South and Central America, Hawaiian Islands, China, Japan, Europe and South Africa. The Puget Mill Company's shipments to the Hawaiian Islands alone last year aggregated 33,000,000 feet, or a little more than the total consumption of these islands during 1898.

Next to the Weyerhauser Syndicate, the Puget Mill Company is probably the largest owner of virgin timber in this State. It pays taxes in seventeen counties of Western Washington, and in mills, stores, logging camps and on board its ships gives employment, directly or indirectly, to 5000 men. At Port Gamble alone the company distributes in wages about $18,000 a month, or $175,000 a year. A number of its employes have been on the pay roll for over thirty years.

For the more systematic and economic handling of its business, several sub-corporations have been formed. The mills are operated by the Puget Lumber Company, the stores by the Puget Trading Company, the vessels by the Puget Sound Commercial Company, and the tugs by the Puget Sound Towage Company. The largest ships and steamers can load at its docks, always afloat. With good harbors, good anchorage, big reserve stocks and facilities unsurpassed for filling orders for lumber, spars and piles, the Puget Mill Company caters especially to cargo shipments. The company owns seven vessels and is a shareholder in about fifty more.

Pape & Talbot, San Francisco, Cal., are the agents for the sale of the products of these mills.

Port Gamble was named in honor of Lieut. Gamble of the United States navy, who served in the war of 1812. The town is located on a small bay about six miles above the entrance of Hoods Canal, has a population of about 500, and is a model of neatness, the residence portion being built on a low bluff, while the mills, store, hotel, machine shops, warehouses and lumber piles occupy the spit below. Cozy cottages, surrounded by well-kept lawns, orchards and flower beds; graded and planked streets ornamented with shade trees—these are some of the distinguishing features of the town. Neat lathed and plastered cottages of four to seven rooms are rented to employes with families at from $5 to $10 per month, including water, which is supplied by a gravity system. Bachelors who board at the cook house are taxed $1 per month for the use of comfortable houses that accommodate four men each. The main dining room will seat 194 persons. Separate dining

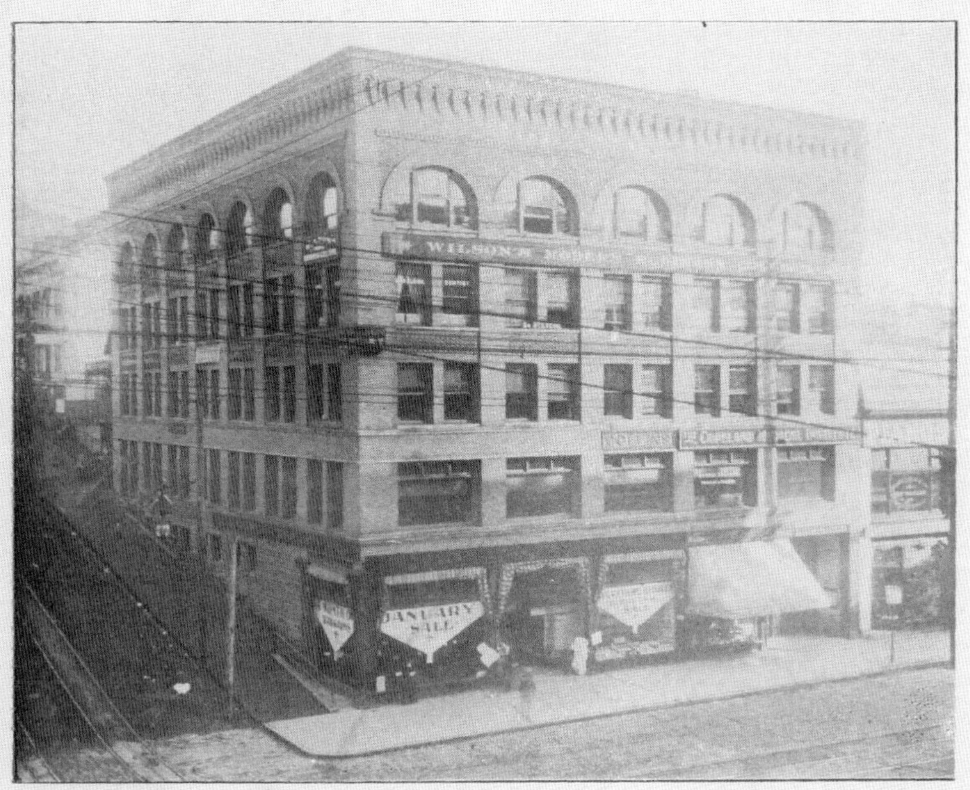

THE COLLINS BLOCK, SECOND AND JAMES. PROPERTY OF JOHN COLLINS.

rooms are provided for the "tyees," clerks and some mechanics who prefer privacy.

The public school has an average attendance of about forty. The little church is free to all denominations, but a Congregational minister is the only one who now holds regular services. An excellent band and orchestra furnish music and entertainment when desired — and sometimes otherwise. Flourishing lodges of F. & A. M., I. O. O. F., K. P., A. O. U. W. and Woodmen of the World hold regular meetings. There is a daily mail service by steamer from Seattle and Port Townsend.

ever made in the State—the famous "Kitsap County Brand;" and last, but not least, a library of 500 volumes for use of employes.

Here there is no regular pay day; here the historical "company store" has no terrors for employes, as they can draw their money when they please and trade where they please. Buying for cash and taking advantage of all discounts, carrying their own freight in their own vessels, the company is able to make the lowest possible prices on everything they manufacture or sell, and to meet competition in a fair way. In its warehouses

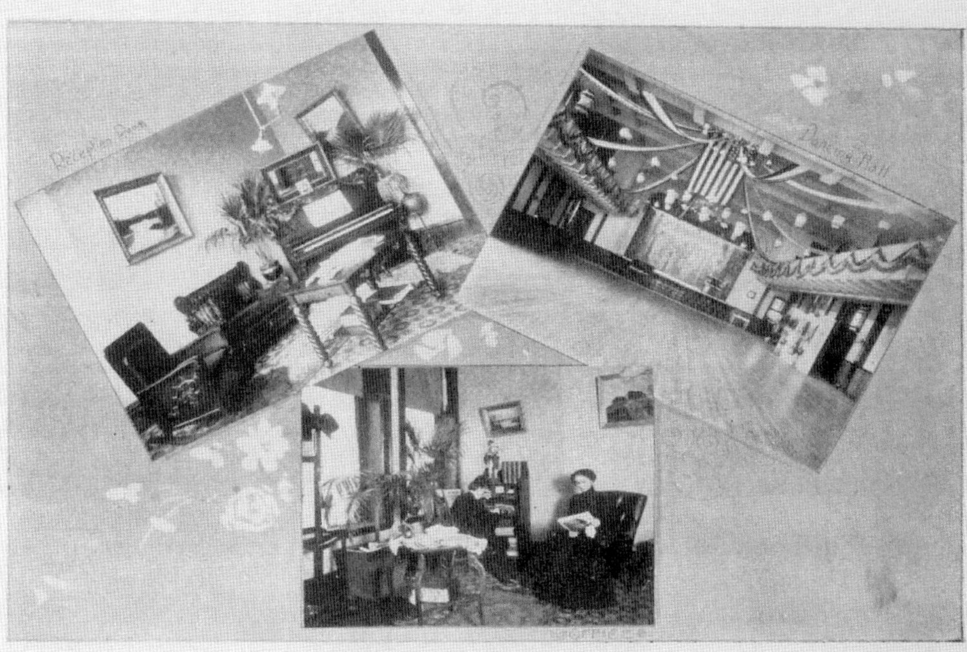

WILSON'S DANCING ACADEMY, RANKE BLOCK ON PIKE STREET.

Space will not permit a detailed description of town and mills, but among those things deserving special mention are the elaborate system of water pipes and automatic sprinklers for protection against fire; a local telephone system, with long distance wire and cable to Port Ludlow; electric plant for lighting mills and town; two immense dry kilns, each holding 80,000 feet of lumber; a planer that handles timbers 14x30 inches in diameter and 120 feet long as easily as it does a piece of 1x2; a feed mill "with a record," it having in the early days ground the first flour

and store the company carries an immense stock of general merchandise. The display in each department is as complete and artistic as can be found anywhere.

WILSON'S ACADEMY.

The Academy of Dancing, Delsarte acting and ballroom and theatrical dancing, which is conducted by Prof. J. H. Wilson in Ranke Hall, corner Fifth Avenue and Pike Street, this city, is one of the most modern schools of this character ever established in the West. Some illustrations which are shown herewith give the reader an idea of the very excellent hall the professor uses and the complete arrangement in the way of dressing rooms, which add to its convenience.

Prof. Wilson has had years of study with America's foremost masters, for which he holds past master's diploma, a guarantee that his patrons will receive the most enlightened education along the lines of physical development, deportment and etiquette. He conducts his school so that his patrons can be accommodated during most any portion of the week. This school is practically the only one in Seattle of its kind and none other can approach it in point of very excellent training which is received. Few institutions can be found in any city where the system taught is more correct or where more pains are taken and where the general results are so high as in the Academy of Prof. Wilson.

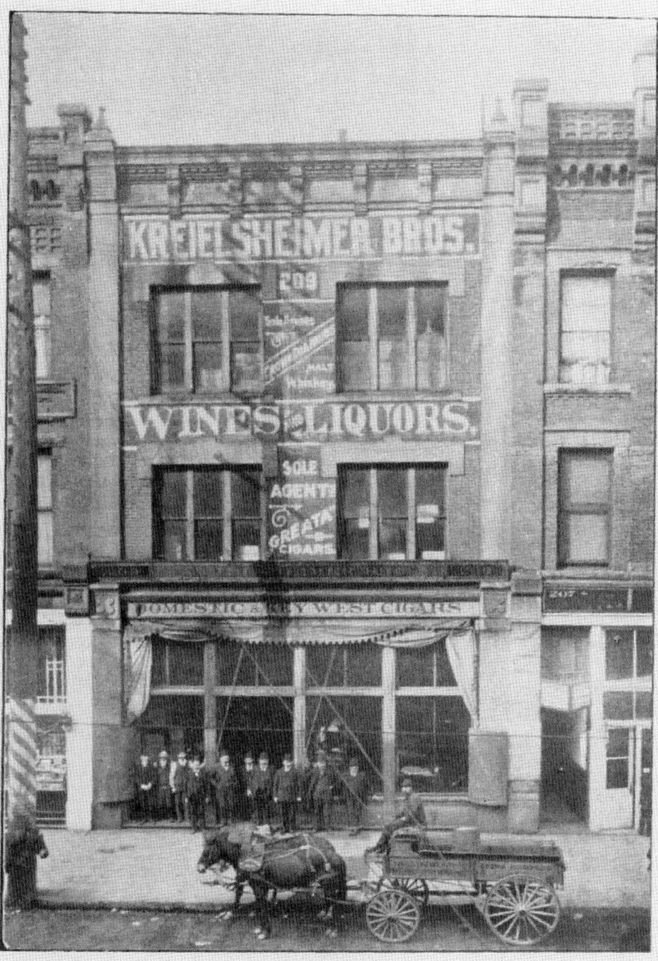

THE WHOLESALE HOUSE OF KREIELSHEIMER BROS.

KREIELSHEIMER BROTHERS.

One of the very heavy wholesale firms doing business in Seattle at this time is Kreielsheimer Brothers, located at 209 First Avenue South. They are engaged in the wholesale liquor and cigar business and have been established here since 1887. This concern has worked up a remarkable business, and includes among its customers the representative retailers throughout Washington, Idaho and Alaska. The arrangement of the offices and the whole establishment is fully equal to any found in the largest cities of America. In addition to the house in Seattle they have offices at 48 and 50 First Street, San Francisco, and at 912-916 Sycamore Street, Cincinnati, Ohio. They make a specialty of a whiskey favorably and widely known as the Crown Diamonds Malt Whiskey, which, owing to its purity, age and quality, is recognized as the leading whiskey of the Northwest.

A very fine picture is herewith reproduced of their house in this city. They occupy the full four floors, shown in the illustration, 30x111 feet in size, and carry a very extensive stock of both imported and domestic wines and liquors, together with a full line of cigars. They employ fourteen men in vious. Judging from present prospects their trade this year will be more extensive than last.

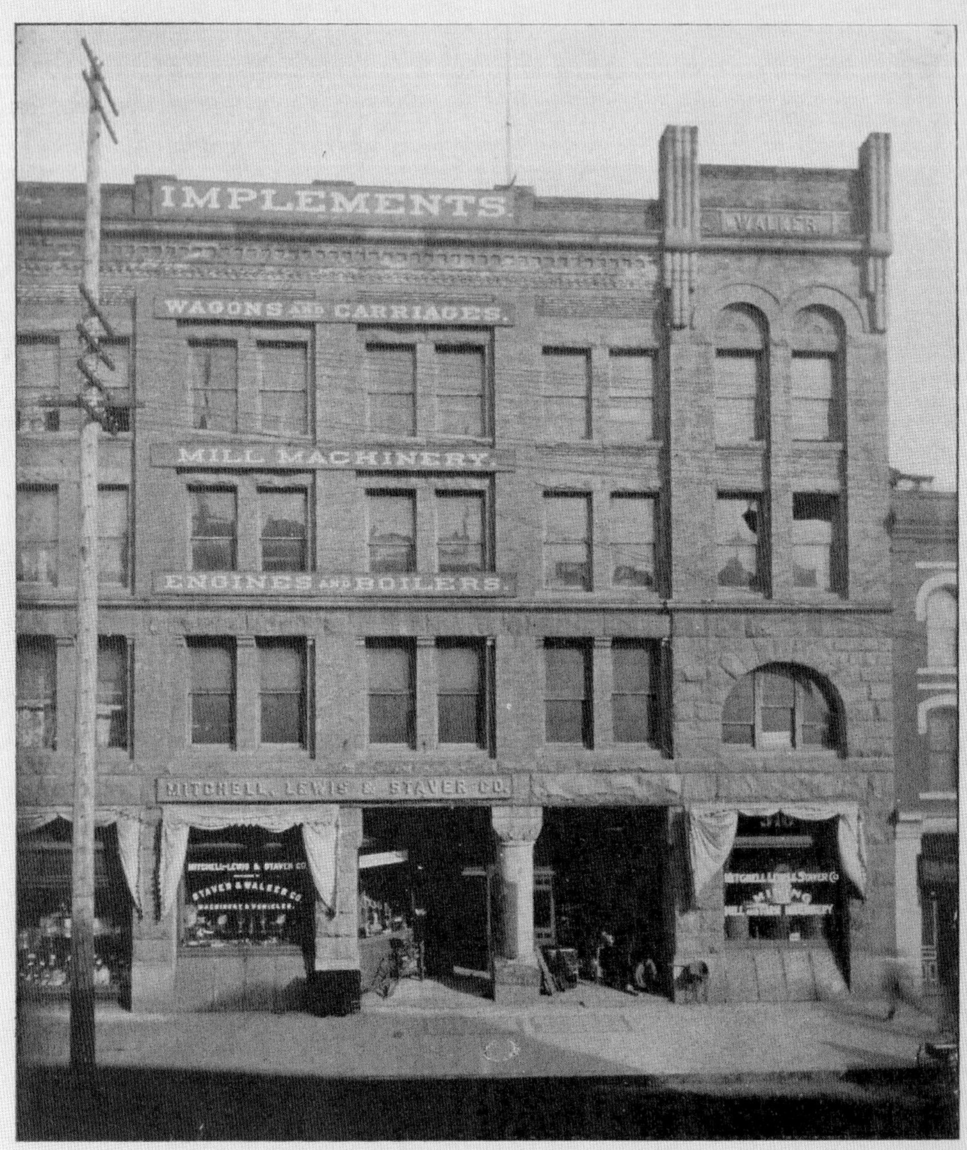

THE STORE OF MITCHELL, LEWIS & STAVER CO.

their store in this city and keep four traveling men upon the road, visiting the trade throughout the region in which they are selling goods.

Their trade for the last year shows a very substantial increase and is fully 25 per cent in excess of the year pre-

ONE OF THE BIG FIRMS.

One of the big firms which has added to the prestige of Seattle as a great big trade center is the firm of Mitchell, Lewis & Staver Company, of which

F. W. Mitchell is the vice-president and general manager. Some very fine interior views of their establishments have been taken and are reproduced herewith. Their location is at 308-310 Occidental Avenue. They occupy a building 60x120 feet with five floors ing, but contiguous to the main store. They have been established here since 1892, and last year the increase in their business was fully 38 per cent over the year previous. They give employment to twenty-five men and keep two men traveling on the road selling goods

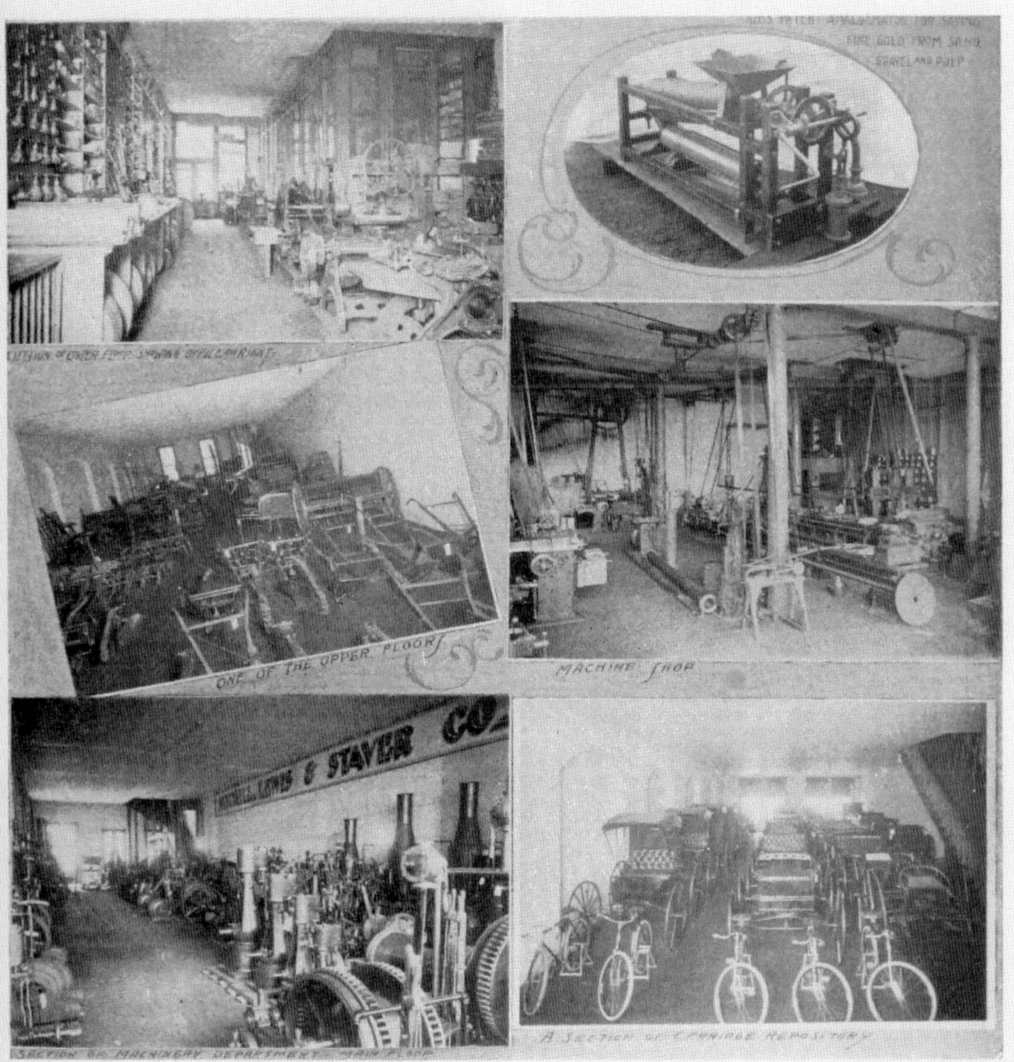

THE ESTABLISHMENT OF MITCHELL, LEWIS & STAVER CO.

and a basement. The character of the goods they handle is principally made up of machinery, consisting of mining, mill and farm utensils, in addition to which they have a very large and complete machine shop in a separate building throughout the State of Washington, British Columbia and all points in Alaska. They make a particular business of dealing in saw mill and shingle mill machinery, boilers, engines and all kinds of mining machinery, air compressors, rock drills, hoists, hoisting engines, ore carts and mining railroads. The company has lately put upon the market some very improved shingle machinery, entirely their own product, and one of these machines at a recent ordinary ten hours' run exceeded the previous cut of shingle mills by nearly 25 per cent, a fact that speaks most highly for a home manufactured product. In addition to their own machine shop in Seattle, a great deal of their manufacturing work is done in the town of Everett, where a large force of men are employed in manufacturing various lines for their trade. In addition to the machinery supplies enumerated, this company handles practically everything in the line of farm utensils, vehicles of all kinds particularly, the latter being made at the great establishment of the company at Racine, Wisconsin, and are among the best products of the kind sold in the West. The company is clearly in the lead so far as size and capacity for handling goods is concerned.

Mitchell, Lewis & Staver also handle the Heiss patent amalgamator, one of the best and most economical machines for saving gold ever invented, and one that wins distinction wherever used.

THE C. SIDNEY SHEPARD CO.

That Seattle is growing more rapidly in a commercial sense than most people realize is evidenced by the fact that some of the largest houses in the United States now have direct representatives in this city. Among the more conspicuous of Eastern houses which have recently recognized Seattle, and one which has branches in most of the leading cities of the United States, is the C. Sidney Shepard Company, which is rated as one of the most extensive manufacturers in the United States, and a company which is known throughout the commercial world. This company has its immense manufacturing plant at Buffalo, New York, and branch houses are located in New York City, Chicago, St. Louis, Kansas City, Denver and Seattle. The product turned out by this company consists of manufactured articles in

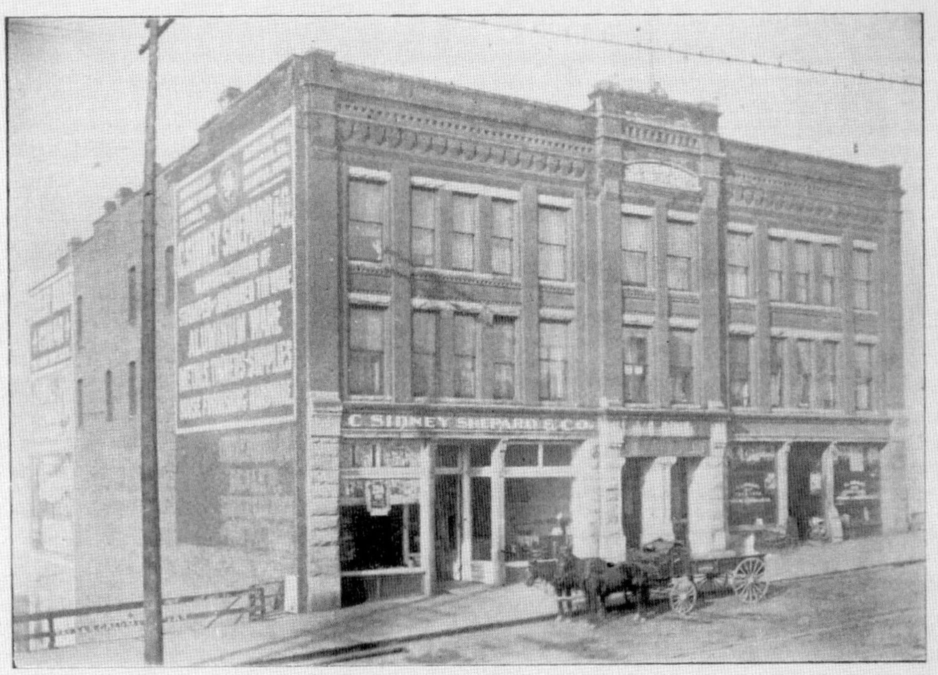

THE WHOLESALE HOUSE OF C. SIDNEY SHEPARD & CO., SEATTLE.

sheet iron, pieced and stamped ware, aluminum and granite ware, sheet metals and tin plates. Probably there is no country in the world but is now using more or less of the products turned out by this great concern, and the fact that a branch store has been established in Seattle, from which all points on the Coast, including the city of San Francisco, are supplied, is naturally affording very considerable prestige to this city. The house here is in charge of Mr. Fred Lee, and his territory covers, as before stated, not only the entire Coast, but reaches the Hawaiian Islands, Australia, China, Japan, Siberia and the Philippines. A very excellent illustrtion is shown herewith of the building occupied in Seattle. It is four stories in height and well adapted to the needs of a company so extensive as this one is; it carries a stock of $150,000 worth of goods, and all shipments are made direct from this city. It is now two years since this store has been opened, and the trade built up has grown to very large proportions. Six men are employed upon the road, and all parts of the Coast are visited at regular intervals, while it requires twelve men in the store to attend to the handling of the big volume of goods which passes in and out. The name of C. Sidney Shepard is a household word throughout the East, and practically throughout the commercial world, and the opening of a big establishment of their own in Seattle is of very great assistance to the people of the West, as it places them in direct touch with one of the greatest manufacturing plants in the country. They are also able from this place to more quickly reach a large and increasing trade with the Orient, which is becoming a very considerable feature.

DAIRYING IS PROFITABLE.

Probably in no department of industry has there been greater progress made than in that made in dairying in Western Washington during the last five or six years. Prior to that time vast quantities of dairy produce were shipped to the Puget Sound cities from California and Eastern states. But about ten years ago the owners of ranch property began turning their attention to the production of butter, eggs and cheese and to improvements in the grade of stock.

The hills and valleys of the Puget Sound basin are admirably adapted to the dairying industry. The absence of cold winters makes it possible for stock to graze in pasture in winter as well as in summer, and the luxuriance with which all kinds of meadow grasses grow guarantees ample food for cows at all seasons of the year.

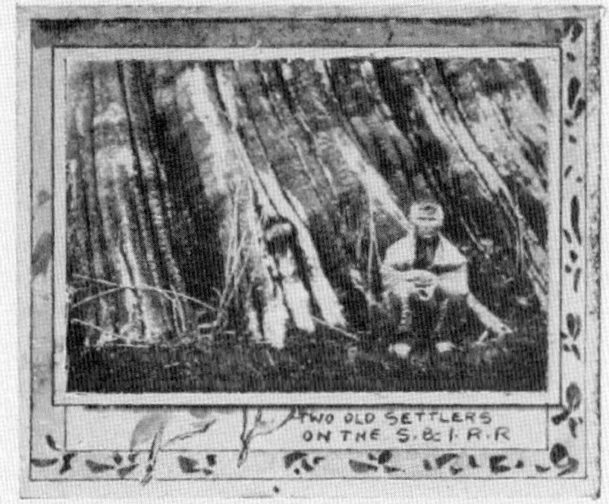

TWO OLD SETTLERS ON THE S. & I. R.R

THE VULCAN IRON WORKS.

The Vulcan Iron Works, which is located in the southern part of the city, or more particularly speaking on Fifth Avenue South and Lane Street, and owns and occupies an entire block of land, is one of the most complete iron-working establishments in the Northwest. Within the past few years the present buildings have been erected and practically every convenience to a well-organized iron manufacturing concern or iron works has been added. The company have been in existence here for twenty-five years, and have now grown to be a very extensive concern, giving employment to from 100 to 125 men the year round. The character of their business is the manufacture of mining machinery of all kinds, logging tools, logging engines, air compressors and all manner of shop work. They also do a very extensive work in manufacturing saw mill machinery, and among recent orders turned out was a very extensive and they have become so popular that no logging camp of any consequence is now complete without one or more

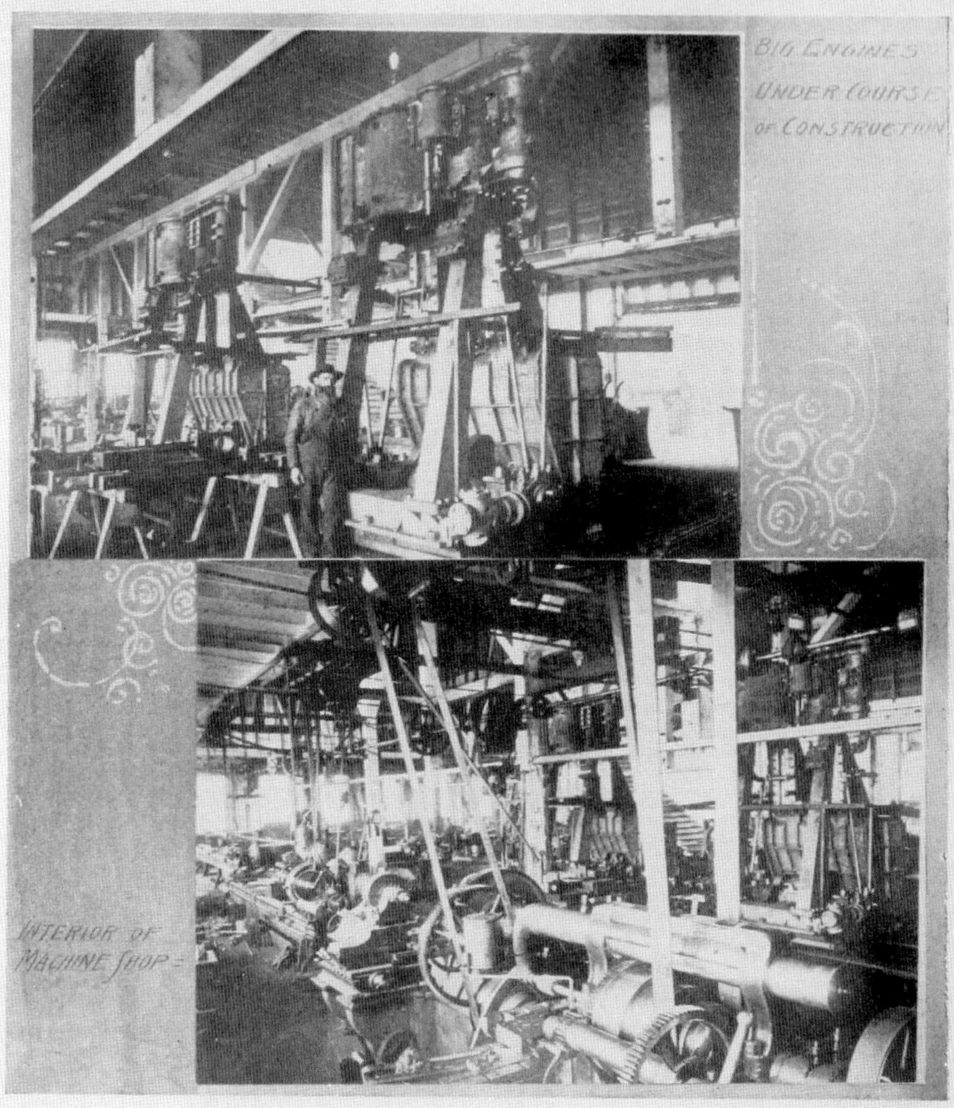

SOME INSIDE VIEWS OF THE VULCAN IRON WORKS.

gang edger for one of the big saw mills. They have also been considerably rushed in filling orders for logging engines—and these engines, by the way, are a marvel in the manner of assisting work in logging camps, of them in order to assist in hauling out logs from the woods, and doing the work which was formerly slowly and tediously performed by six or eight yoke of oxen. The company show a gain of about 20 per cent in volume of business last year over the preceding year. They contemplate doing some additional building alongside of the present ones during the present season in order to give room for their increasing trade. The trade of the Vulcan Iron Works reaches into Oregon as far down the Coast as Coos Bay, all points in Alaska and all over Western Washington. The entire general management and supervision of this big plant is in the hands of Mr. Isaac Hulme, while Mr. H. P. Strickland is the secretary.

THE FEHREN-MARVIN COMPANY.

Fehren-Marvin Company, 230-231 Pioneer Building, Seattle, investment bankers and general brokers, have a well-established business which is attracting the confidence and attention of investors and people interested in real estate and loans. Besides their brokerage and investment business they have most successfully added an architectural and building department, which enables them to handle investments from the standpoint of improving property by building homes and business houses thereon and enables investors to receive a very large revenue from conservative investments made in Seattle realty.

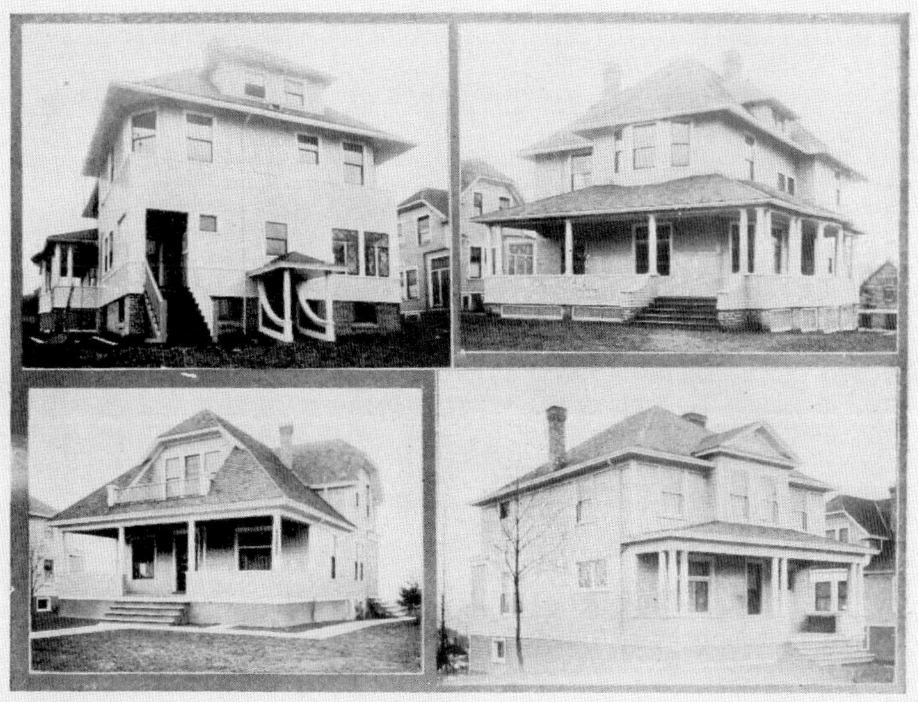

A Pretty Groupe of Residences.
Erected by the Fehren-Marvin Co., showing the excellent character of new homes they have built.

Many of the properties which they have improved for the account of clients are producing a net revenue of from 10 to 15 per cent on the total investment. Fehren-Marvin Company have given especial attention to building artistic residences and in the building of these homes they have introduced architectural features which have not before appeared in Seattle. These improved designs are making this department very popular and largely increase the volume of their business. They also have made a specialty of modern flats and apartment buildings, which at the present time are in great demand in Seattle. A number of illustrations are presented herewith of buildings which have been designed and built by these gentlemen.

Largely through the efforts of this firm the Broadway district and other sections of the city have become very popular as residence districts. Real estate in the sections improved by them has been greatly enhanced in value. This firm has earned the reputation of giving all business entrusted to their care most careful, conservative and reliable attention.

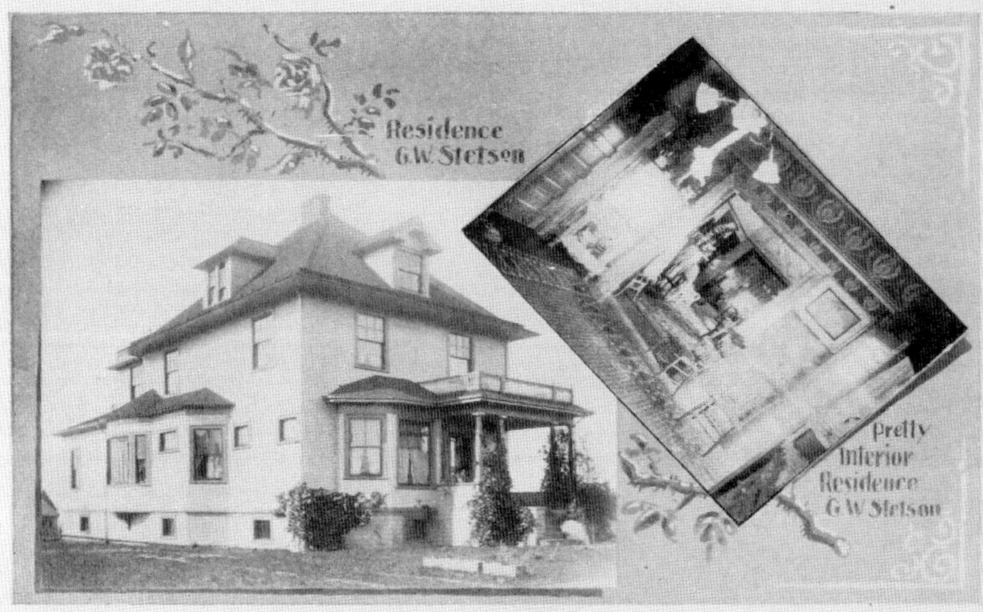

A CHARMING BEACON HILL RESIDENCE.

MANY FINE NEW HOUSES.

The growth of the city for the past twelve months is strikingly illustrated by the value of the building permits issued during the period. More building has been done in the residence districts than in any other part of the city. The structures that have as a rule been erected are on an average more costly and substantially built than those which have heretofore been erected. This is attributed largely to the fact that the greater proportion of the residences which have gone up during the year have been built by persons whose intention it was to occupy them as homes.

KINNEAR ADDITION.

The resident section of this city, popularly known as Queen Anne Hill, is probably the most desirable part of Seattle for homes. Kinnear addition, particularly, is very choice, and all who pay that part of the town a visit are more than charmed with it. George Kinnear, who owned and laid out the ground which has since become so popular, gave the city one of the most handsome public parks within the limits of the city, and no one has really seen Seattle until they have paid a visit to it. Mr. Kinnear has some very desirable residence property still for sale in his addition.

HOTEL ACCOMMODATIONS GOOD.

As might naturally be expected from its business relations and from the vast volume of travel that passes through the city annually, Seattle has an unusually good list of hotels, lodging houses and restaurants. It has been said by careful observers that there are few cities in the world where so large a proportion of the population finds a home in hotels or apartments, and few places where so many business men get their meals in restaurants. There are good reasons for this. With the rapid growth of the city within the last two years all available houses have been taken. In addition to this there has been a vast throng of transient travel, stopping in the city for a few days, only to pass on and make way for another wave of similar proportions. These two years have brought additional recognition of the fact that Seattle is the gateway to Alaska, while at the same time her permanent population has rapidly and steadily increased.

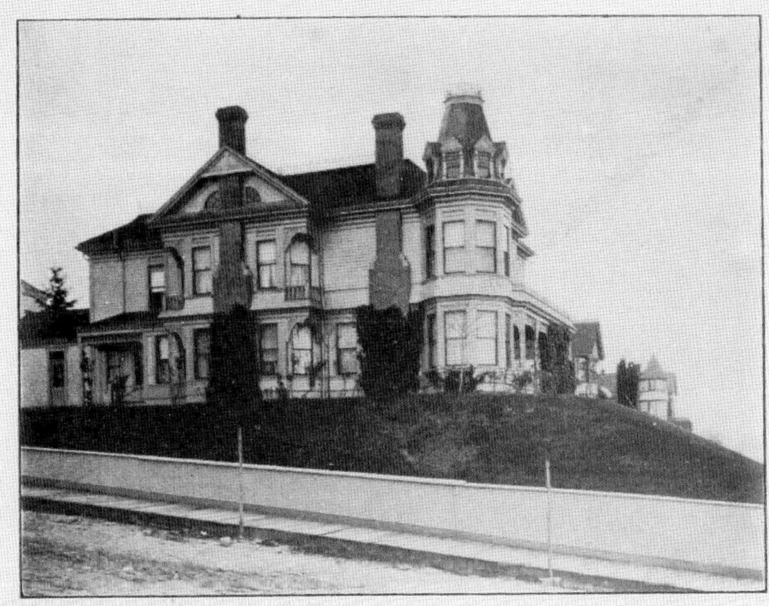

RESIDENCE OF WILLIAM TRIMBLE, 104 ALOHA ST., QUEEN ANNE HILL.

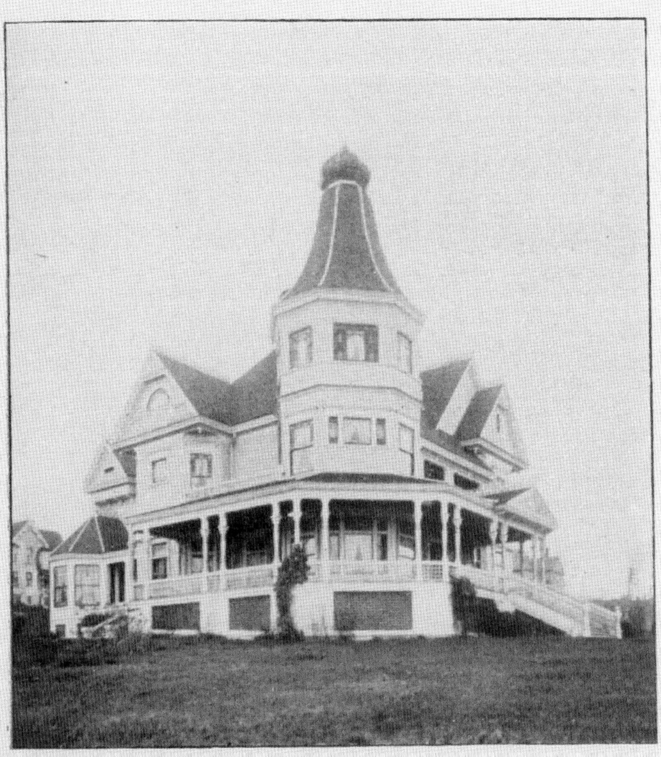

RESIDENCE OF GEORGE KINNEAR, QUEEN ANNE HILL.

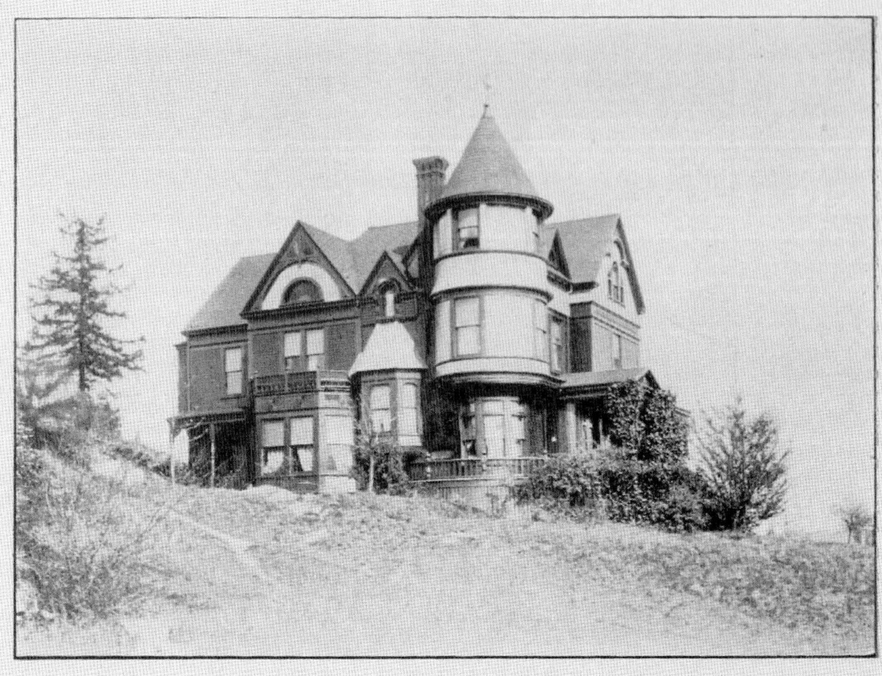

RESIDENCE OF CAPT. W. W. ROBINSON, JR., U. S. A., ALOHA ST., QUEEN ANNE HILL.

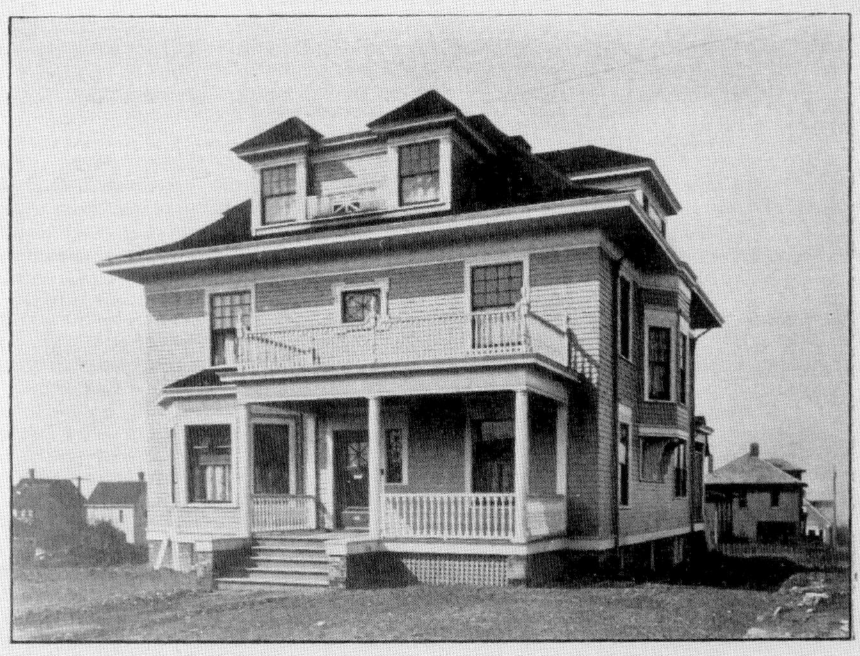

THE NEW RESIDENCE OF WILSON R. GAY, 1733 FIFTEENTH AVENUE.
Lawn and Walks Unfinished.

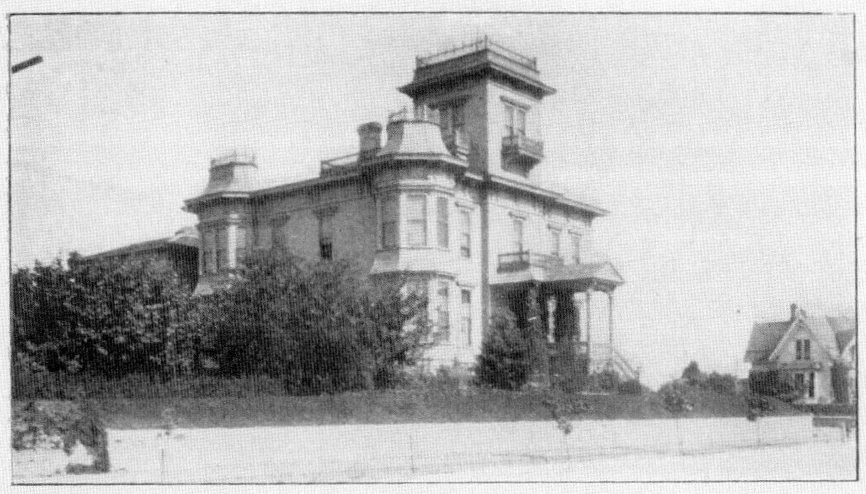

RESIDENCE OF THE LATE GRANVILLE O. HALLER, COLONEL U. S. ARMY, 606 MINOR AVENUE.

THE STATE UNIVERSITY.

The University of Washington is the pride of the whole state, and it does justice to the boasts of the Washingtonians. It is admittedly the most modern college north of Berkeley and west of Ann Arbor. The University has kept pace with the rapid growth of the state and has kept up to the demands of the people. Since its establishment its advance has been constant and steady and every successive state legislature has faced the question of an enlargement of the school of learning.

RESIDENCE OF MORGAN J. CARKEEK, BOREN AVE. AND MADISON ST.

The year just passed has without doubt been the most important in the history of the school. A new departure in the erection of dormitories has been taken by the appropriation of money by the late legislature for that purpose. The buildings, handsome structures of stone and brick, one for young ladies and the other for gentlemen, are now completed and are being furnished. Applications of students for accommodations already more than equal the amount of room, which is estimated to be sufficient for 200 students.

Four hundred and eighty-six young men and ladies are now completing their education at the university. This number is three times that of the students two years ago and the faculty of the institution confidently expect to see one thousand of the youth of Washington attending the lectures of the college two years hence. The members of the faculty now number thirty two and each and every one is exerting his utmost for the benefit of

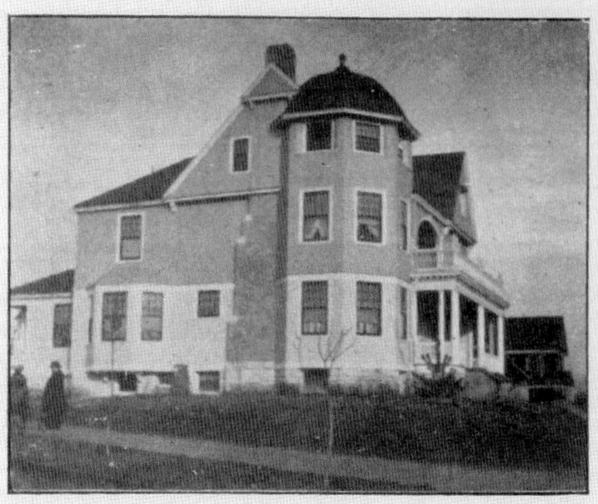

Residence of Geo. M. Stewart.

the school. Much outside work is also being done by the professors, such as lectures and instruction in many of the smaller towns.

MANY RICH MINES NEAR SEATTLE.

Mining in the State of Washington has made wonderful progress in the year just passed. While the eastern and northern portions have received more or less attention from capitalists and mining men for three years past, there are only a limited few of the locations west of the Cascades on which development work, other than as-

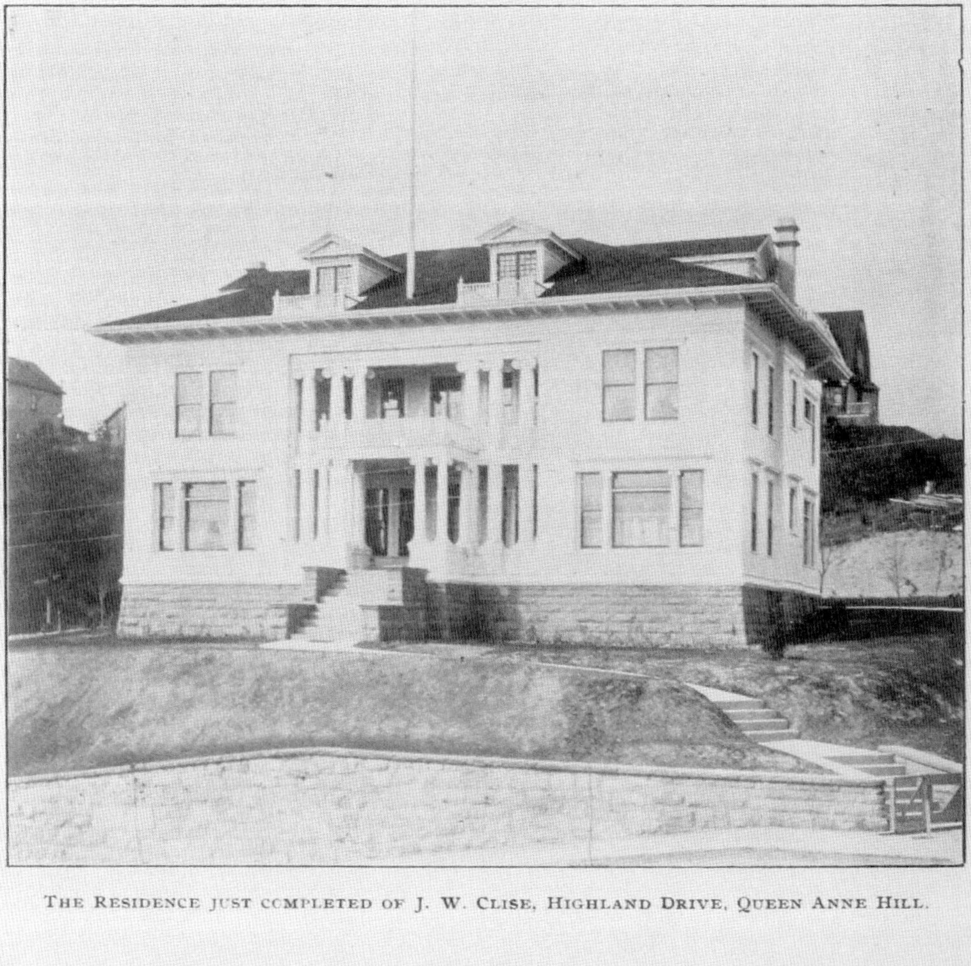

The Residence just completed of J. W. Clise, Highland Drive, Queen Anne Hill.

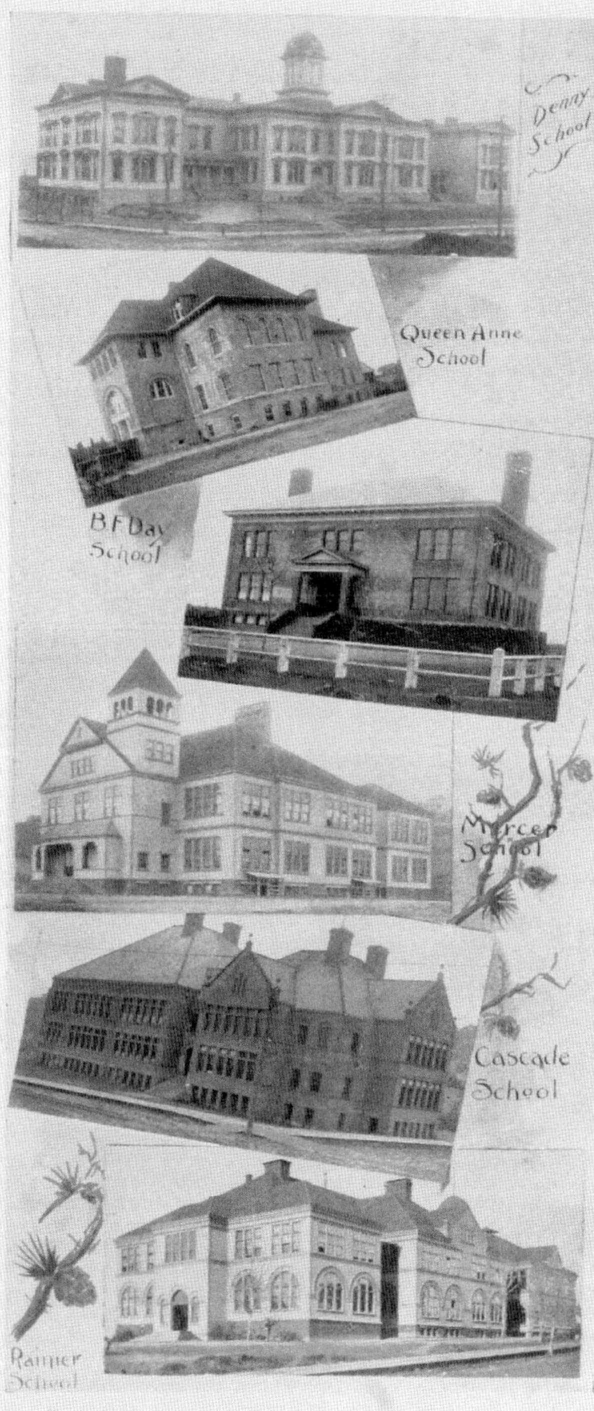

A FEW SCHOOL HOUSES OF SEATTLE.

sessments, dates back for eighteen months. The mining camps of the greatest promise three years ago, Silverton and Monte Cristo, sank into comparative obscurity with the washing away of their only outlet, the E. & M. C. R. R. Contemporaneous with this disasterous event came the Klondike excitement, diverting general attention from everything local. Seattle being the main point of embarkation for the Yukon gold fields, however, brought her suddenly into prominence, and the vast mineral sections naturally tributary to the Sound began to fix the attention of mining men and capitalists in the far East. The result is seen in the increased interest in many of the Eastern money centers in Western Washington mining properties and the development of hundreds of splendid prospects in the past year, many of them being to-day in a position to become paying mines, could their output reach the smelters at a reasonable cost.

The Orcas Island gold mine has reached a stage where success is certain. An aerial tram will be installed in the early spring between the mine and the bay, and shipments to Tacoma or Everett begun as soon as the tram is completed. The rich vein of free-milling ore has proved a true fissure and permanent in extent. The stock was long since withdrawn from the market.

IS STRONG EDUCATIONALLY.

Seattle is fairly covered with magnificent school buildings, that would be a credit to any Eastern city twice her size. Her schools are her pride, and in these, like in all else, the standard is above the average. Not even during the financial stress, which was felt terribly in the Queen City, did the people hesitate to expend money in improving the public school system and making it the best in the Pacific Northwest. Today the educational system of Seattle stands pre-eminently for thoroughness, excellence and the high standard of the various studies taught.

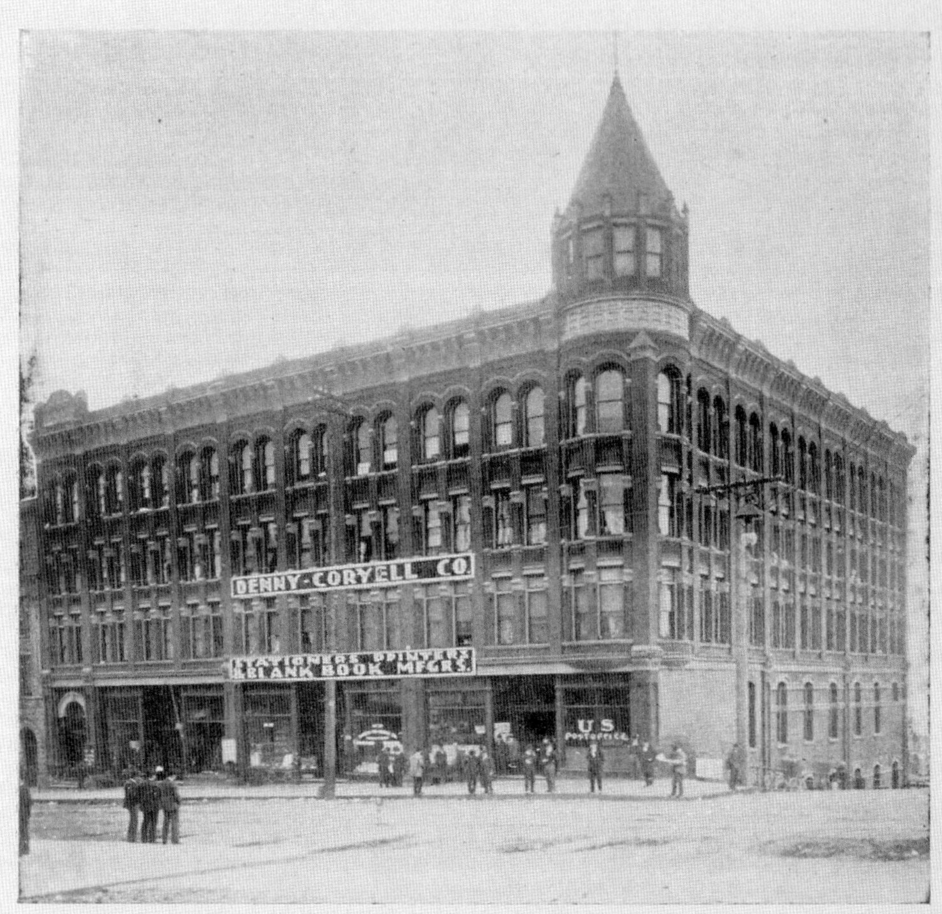

ESTABLISHMENT OF THE DENNY-CORYELL COMPANY.

A BIG PRINTING ESTABLISHMENT.

The Denny Coryell Company is the largest printing and stationery concern in the Northwest. Some illustrations which are shown herewith give an idea of the magnitude of the printing department, and affords also a view of the exterior of the building occupied by this branch of the business. The company has a large stationery store at 716 First Avenue, in which one of the largest and most complete stocks of stationery and office supplies to be found on the Sound is carried. The printing department, of which more particular mention is made, is located at 1221 First Avenue, where it occupies two full floors of the building shown in the illustration. The composing room, business office and branch stationery store occupy the first floor, while the press room and bindery occupy the floor below. The office is complete in every detail, and is well equipped with modern machinery. Recently a new printing press has been added to their press room which now affords the Denny-Coryell Company the best press equipment in the northwest, particularly as the new machine is the largest one ever set up in this state. The company make a specialty of doing very fine work and in printing half tones, such as are to be found in this magazine, cannot be excelled. They employ 33 hands in the establishment at 1221 First Avenue, and in volume of magazine printing, blank books manufactured and the general run of work of all kinds which is produced cannot be excelled by any concern in the west. As a fair sample of the very excellent work this company does, one only need to glance through the various pages of "Seattle and the Orient" to give a comprehensive idea of what good workmanship amounts to.

VIEW OF COMPOSING ROOM OF DENNY-CORYELL COMPANY.

The company is incorporated. Geo. K. Coryell is president, H. O. Hollenbeck is secretary and treasurer, and A. W. Denny general manager. The printing department is under the management of B. C. Smith, a thorough printer and publisher, and one who, by his wide experience, is making his department show a fine record.

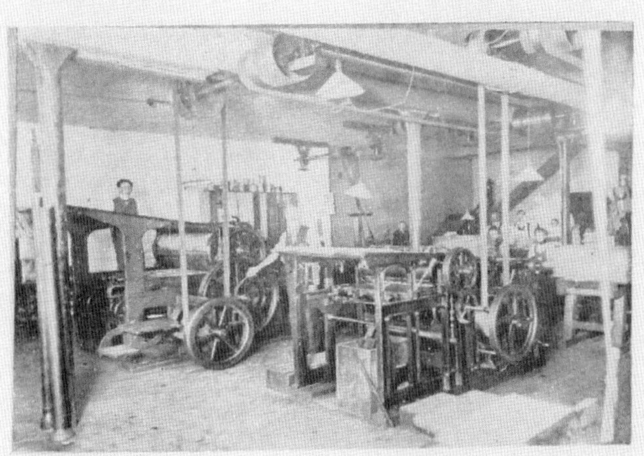

PRESS OF DENNY-CORYELL COMPANY WHICH PRINTED THIS BOOK.

In addition to this very complete printing establishment, in which, not only all kinds of books and magazines, but a fine line of commercial printing is turned out, the company have a very large and extensive bindery. This branch has recently been added to in a very material degree by nearly doubling the room formerly occupied and in otherwise preparing for the rushing trade this company enjoys.

SEATTLE'S NEW WATER SYSTEM.

The contract for supplying Seattle with a large volume of water for domestic purposes is now rapidly progressing and possibly by the end of the present year the new system whereby Cedar River water will be supplied to the residents of this city will be an assured fact. The plans under which the contract has been let calls for the expenditure of very considerable sums of money, and some idea of what is expected, together with the views showing the enormous undertaking, will naturally prove of interest at this time. Every detail of this work has been under the direct personal supervision of City Engineer R. H. Thomson, and

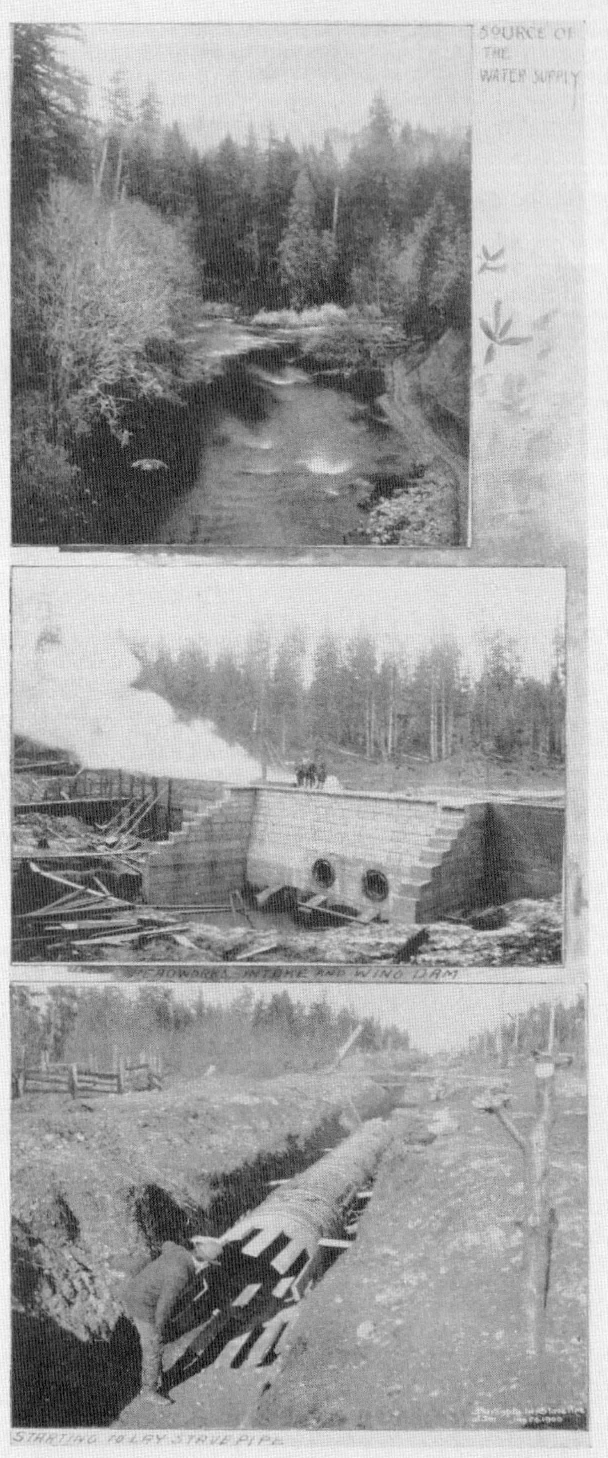

BRINGING CEDAR RIVER WATER TO SEATTLE.
This shows work in hand by Pacific Bridge Company.

he has been called upon to exercise the highest judgment of which his profession is capable. That his judgment has been equal to the requirements is shown in the unqualified admiration expressed by all civil engineers and contractors who have studied the plans and inspected the grounds. The idea of bringing Cedar River water into Seattle is not a new one. It has been recommended a number of times, but not until the past year, or until the contract was let in April, 1899, was the matter far enough advanced to be a reality. One of the pictures which is shown in the article illustrates Cedar River at a short way above where the water is impounded and diverted to the pipes leading to the large reservoirs in this city. The entire Cedar River water shed embraces approximately 210 square miles. The City Engineer indicates that the water which will pass through the intake will average a flow of between 500,000,000 and 600,000,000 gallons per day, or enough to give each inhabitant an average of more than one hundred gallons per day. By a careful regard for the waste of water it is calculated that this supply will do for a population of between 5,000-000 and 6,000,000 people—that is to say, this number could be supplied by the increase of storage reservoirs at various points throughout the water shed drained by Cedar River. The plans which are now being worked out are to supply 25,000,000 gallons from Cedar River direct to the City Park reservoir. The elevation of water at the controlling station at the longest stage will be 520 feet above sea level, and the water in the City Park reservoir will be 420 feet above sea level, thus giving an even one hundred feet in the twenty-eight miles of distance to be traversed by the pipe line. The pipe line itself is a composite of forty-two inches in diameter; and the illustrations which are herewith shown will give an idea of the manner of putting this pipe together, and the way generally that the line is being constructed. Where the head is less than 200 feet the pipe will be constructed of wood, under heads greater than 200 feet of riveted steel. The pictures that are shown show both kinds of material which have been used or contracted for. Laying the pipe, building head works and bringing the water from Cedar River to the city reservoir was let to the Pacific Bridge Company, of which Mr. C. S. Swigart is the resident engineer and manager. The fact that they were able to secure this contract, amounting to something like $900,000, is largely due to the fact that they were enabled to supply a most superior quality of stave wood pipe, on which they have a patent. One of the pictures in this article shows the plant which they have in this city for dipping pipe and for making the staves. The staves are cut from perfectly clear fir boards two inches thick, six inches wide and about twenty-four feet in length. These boards are placed so that the surfaces will be arcs of a circle of forty-two inches diameter, and their edges planed to conform to two radial lines for such a circle. The staves are then bound together just as are the staves of a barrel or tub and banded with steel rods one-half inch in diameter. Where the pressure is light the rods are placed at intervals of twelve inches, and with increasing pressure the distance is decreased until at one extreme point they are but two inches apart. Three sections of the pipe, aggregating six and a half miles long, where the pressure is very great or considered too much for wooden pipe, there has been laid riveted steel pipe forty-two inches in diameter. Across Black River Valley this pipe is seven-eighths of an inch in thickness. All of the

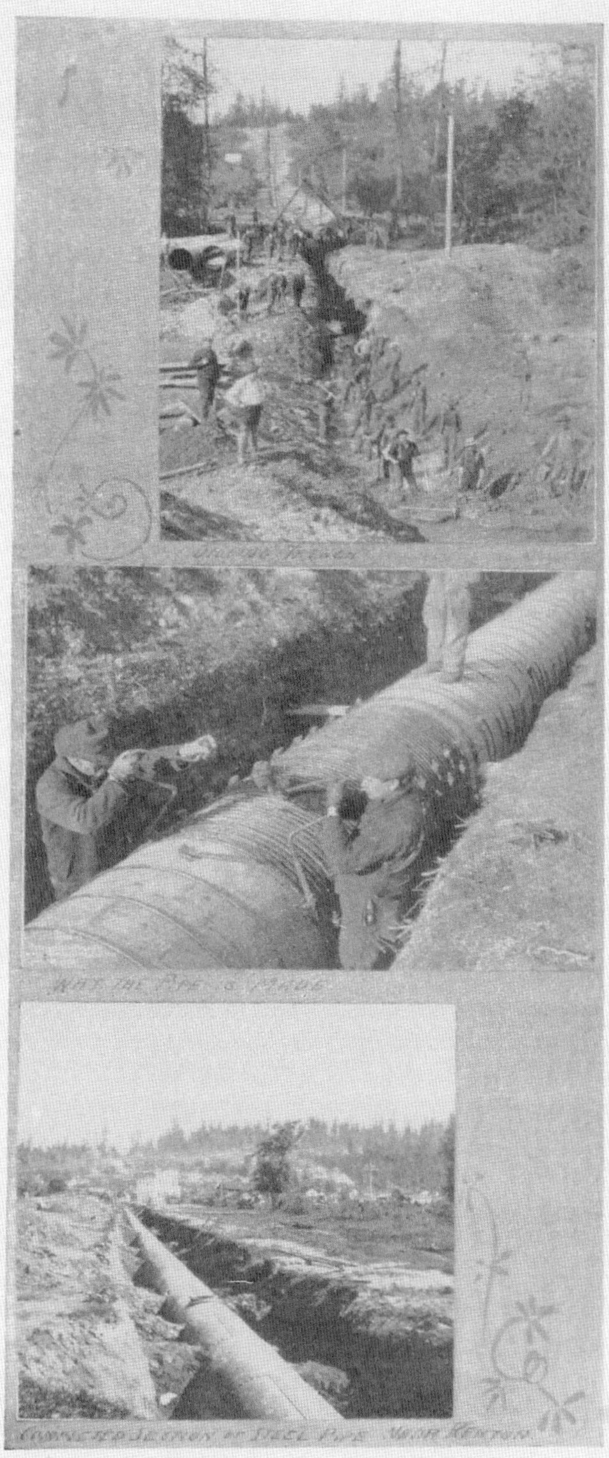

CEDAR RIVER PIPE LINE.

and dipped at the dipping plant referred to by the Pacific Bridge Company, with a coating or composition similar to that used for japanning. The City Park reservoir, into which the pipe line will discharge its great volume of water, will have a capacity of 17,000,000 gallons. It is being constructed to suit the conformation of the ground and is built in the general shape of an egg with the lower end reaching near the southwest corner of the City Park premises. The water will enter the reservoir through a controlling station built of steel and concrete on the south embankment of the reservoir. A low service reservoir is being built just south of Denny Way beginning one-half block east of Broadway. This reservoir will hold about 22,000,000 gallons. In order to reach the highest levels in the city, a pumping station is being erected on Queen Anne Hill in conjunction with a stand pipe. The pumps will be operated entirely by water pressure, the back flow from the City Park to the Nagle reservoir being sufficient to furnish these high points with 3,000,000 gallons a day. The stand pipe which is now being erected will be thirty feet in diameter and sixty feet in height. It is practically a steel tank erected upon a solid concrete foundation, and is high enough to afford water to the highest points in the city.

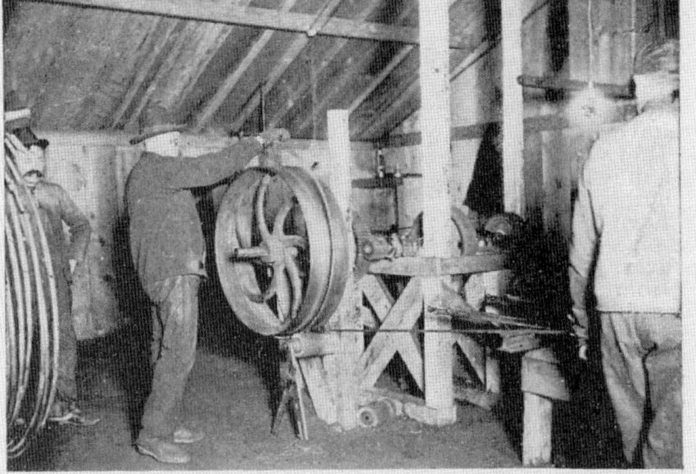

THE SEATTLE PLANT OF PACIFIC BRIDGE CO.
Where Stave Pipe is made and Hoops are Dipped.

The contract for constructing the two reservoirs was let to Smith, Wakefield & David for $315,000. The entire cost of the entire system when finished will be $1,215,000.

THE PACIFIC BRIDGE COMPANY.

The Pacific Bridge Company, who have the big contract for constructing and laying the twenty-four miles of pipe to be used in bringing Cedar River water into Seattle, are employing from 300 to 400 men at the present time, and are losing no opportunity to rush the work in hand with all possible expedition. It is a big contract and one which but few firms are able to undertake. In order to successfully carry this forward a superior quality of stave pipe had to be furnished. This the company had. They owned a patent upon the kind of pipe which was adopted. Besides possessing the pipe they possessed the knowledge of constructing the work, and the city is enabled, in consequence, to get just what they bargained for. The company moved over here in may last from Portland, and opened offices and constructed an auxiliary saw mill and pipe plant in the southern part of the town. In this they employ twenty men. Seventy-five are now laying stave pipe, seventy-five men are at the head works, 125 are on excavation and forty on the steel pipe. Others are employed at various places upon the route. The company is doing some excellent work and making rapid progress with their contract. Their part of the work, as before stated, consists of building the headworks on Cedar River, furnishing and laying the pipe for the system, or, in other words, of delivering the water into the reservoirs in the city.

HON. JOHN COLLINS.

The name of John Collins is identified with the early history of Puget Sound. An independent, courageous man, possessed of keen business sagacity, he has achieved results which number him among the successful business men and financiers of the State of Washington. Mr. Collins was born in Ireland in 1835 and came to America in 1845 with no aid or capital but youth and health to assist him in winning his way in the New World. He lived six years in New York City, and was for six years engaged in the lumber business at Machias, Me., the experience gained there afterward proving of great value. He moved to San Francisco in 1857 and engaged with the Puget Mill Company to work at their mill at Port Gamble, on Puget Sound, where he arrived in September of the same year. He remained ten years in the employ of the mill company, saving enough through prudence and good management to purchase some real estate and also erect a hotel at Port Gamble, a property he still owns. He acquired a two-thirds interest in the Occidental property, and in 1867 he removed to Seattle and assumed management of the business. On the organization of the city government in 1869, Mr. Collins was elected a member of the City Council, and served for three consecutive terms. He was elected Mayor in 1877 and was again elected to the Council in 1881-82. During his term as Councilman he strongly urged the policy of the city ownership of its water works, a policy since adopted. In 1883-84 he was elected a member of the Territorial Legislature. During this session he put through the bill appropriating $6000 for the Territorial University, the largest amount ever given that institution up to that date. He met with great opposition, but carried the measure through by his indomitable will and well-directed efforts. It was the most notable measure of the session.

Mr. Collins' business sagacity has secured for him a large fortune. For many years the Occidental Hotel, owned and managed by him, was the largest and best equipped hotel north of San Francisco. He has been active in the building of railroads, opening up and operation of coal mines, and the establishment of other enterprises. He was one of the incorporators of the Seattle & Walla Walla Railroad, which proved of inestimable value to Seattle, and was one of the organizers of the Seattle Gas Company. He helped in opening up both the Talbot and Cedar River coal mines in 1872 and 1884, respectively. After the great fire of 1889 he at once began rebuilding the Occidental, and, by his example and spirited words, inspired confidence in others. At present Mr. Collins owns the two fine business blocks in the heart of the city, the Occidental and Collins Building, besides valuable realty holdings scattered throughout the city and at Port Gamble and other points. He is a director in the People's Savings Bank and president of the Seattle & Tacoma Electric Railway.

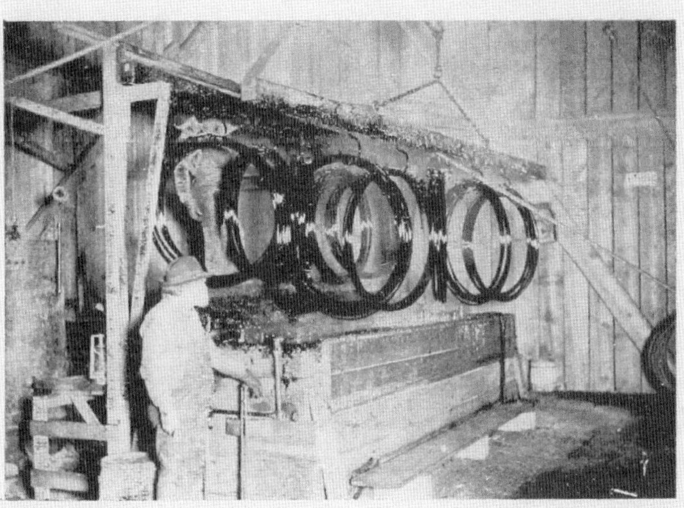

In the Dipping Plant of Pacific Bridge Co.

Mr. Collins is a Democrat and has always been active in the counsels of the party. He was a commissioner in Kitsap County before coming to Seattle, and was one of the fifteen freeholders elected to prepare the new municipal charter under which this city's affairs are at present conducted.

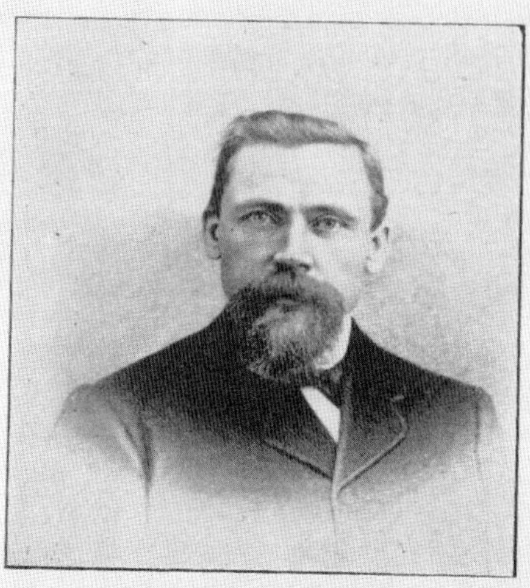

HON. JOHN COLLINS.

Mr. Collins was married in 1851 to Mary Ann McElroy, who died in 1871. In 1878 he was married to Angie B. Jacklin of Seattle. He is counted as one of Seattle's solid men who has always labored assiduously for the city's growth and best welfare.

THE PACIFIC CLIPPER LINE.

The Pacific Clipper Line of steamships and sailing vessels has its headquarters at Seattle, with offices at the southeast corner of First Avenue and Cherry Street. The company was organized in 1898, absorbing the shipping and commission business of E. E. Caine, who had been established for ten years at Seattle.

The illustrations of the Moran Bros.' Co. shipyard show several views of the steamship G. W. Dickinson while the vessel was still in process of construction. The Dickinson was built expressly for the Nome trade for the Pacific Clipper Line by the Moran Bros.' Co. of Seattle, who also have a contract from this company for two large sailing vessels to be used in the Puget Sound-Hawaiian trade.

The Pacific Clipper Line is now operating steamers between Puget Sound and San Francisco and Southeastern Alaska ports.

E. E. Caine, whose portrait appears herewith, has been identified with the shipping and commission business in

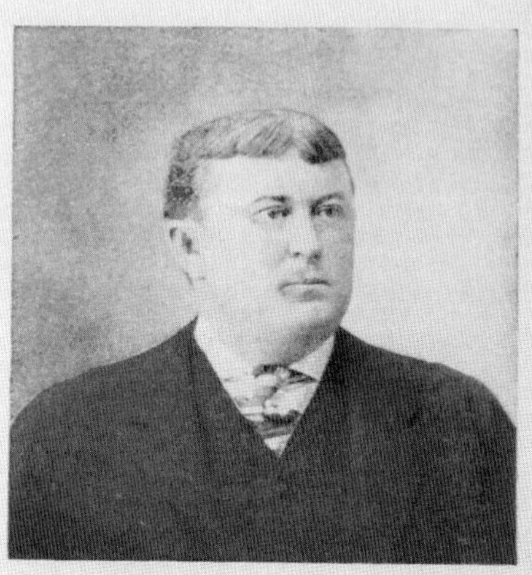

E. E. CAINE.

Seattle for twelve years. Mr. Caine is president of the Pacific Clipper Line and assumes active management of its business. The other officers are: George W. Dickinson of Seattle, vice president; F. P. Meyer of Seattle, secretary and treasurer; M. M. Perl of Seattle, manager, and F. C. West of Seattle, superintendent.

B. BERNARD PELLY.

Hon. B. Bernard Pelly, the British vice-consul in Seattle, has had a residence in this city since 1883, and has held the position which he now has in Her Majesty's service since May, 1889, at the time the position was created. While Mr. Pelly is an English subject and looks after English affairs in Seattle, he has nevertheless become very thoroughly identified with the growth of this city, and is interested in more than one local enterprise here. In addition to being in partnership with J. D. Lowman, under the title of Lowman & Pelly, he is secretary of the Lowman & Hanford Stationery Company and of the Tuck-Hanford Lithographic Company, and he naturally takes a very leading interest in practically all affairs which affect Seattle commercially. The firm of Lowman & Pelly do very much in the handling of estates of various kinds, a great many of which are for non-residents; and they also do considerable in the shape of making loans and investments. Mr. Pelly occupies

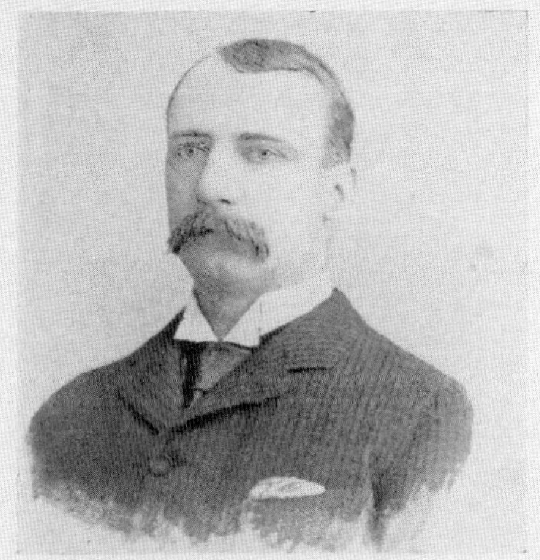

B BERNARD PELLY.

his own residence at 1314 Minor Avenue, and very few persons passing that section of the city can mistake its location because a large Union Jack flying above it makes it quite conspicuous.

HANDLE THEIR OWN WINES.

The wholesale wine and liquor house of Migliavacca & Corgiat, which is located at 109 Main Street, this city, is the only firm which handle their own products. They represent the Migliavacca vineyard of California, and are introducing and putting upon the market some very choice and strictly high grade brands of wines and brandies. Their product has a particularly high value because of its absolute purity. Although established in this city but a little over six months, they now do a very extensive wholesale trade, a trade which extends all over Washington, Idaho and into Alaska. Two men are kept upon the road in their interests. They occupy three floors 40x60 feet and have a very finely appointed establishment. Besides their own wines and brandies they carry a fine stock of liquors and cigars.

PUGET SOUND NATIONAL BANK.

Practically the foremost financial institution in Seattle, and the first one to organize a National Bank, is that of the Puget Sound National, which is located in the Pioneer building at the corner of First Avenue and James Street. Few institutions on the Pacific Coast are stronger financially or can make the same showing of growth that this bank can. It was organized in 1882 by Jacob Furth, who since that period has been at its head continuously. Its directors at the present time consist of Jacob Furth, E. C. Neufelder, James R. Hayden, S. Frauenthal, S. Schwabacher, James S. Goldsmith and L. S. Schwabacher. Since its organization in 1882 up to the present time it has made a steady and continuous growth, and today it occupies beyond the question of a doubt a leading place among the large banks of the Northwest. As forming some idea of the business transacted the following report of its condition at the close of business December 2, 1899, is published:

RESOURCES.

Loans and discounts	$ 573,642.37
U. S. bonds	151,800.00
Other bonds and securities	448,174.35
Furniture and fixtures	2,000.00
Premium on bonds	32,113.85
Due from banks and cash	1,781,947.49
Redemption fund	2,745.00
	$2,992,423.06

LIABILITIES.

Capital stock	$ 300,000.00
Undivided profits	25,691.64
National bank notes	27,050.00
Deposits	2,639,681.42
	$2,992,423.06

Seattle owes considerable to banks of this nature, as with the liberal and progressive spirit which characterizes its management, the ctiy as a whole is very greatly benefited—and it was largely due to institutions of this character that Seattle was enabled to weather the financial storm of the recent depression as well as it did.

Jacob Furth.

Nothing could be more appropriate in speaking about the rapid advancement of Seattle and the substantial character of its financial affairs today than that part of that story be devoted to one who has very materially helped to shape its destinies, both as a city in a great number of enterprises, and also as the presiding genius of one of the largest banking institutions on the Pacific Coast—the one referred to is naturally Jacob Furth, president of the Puget Sound National Bank. He is one of the very few really successful men, a man, as it were, whom the world likes to smile upon because of that success, and to smile more blandly because that success is due entirely to his own unaided efforts, to his own

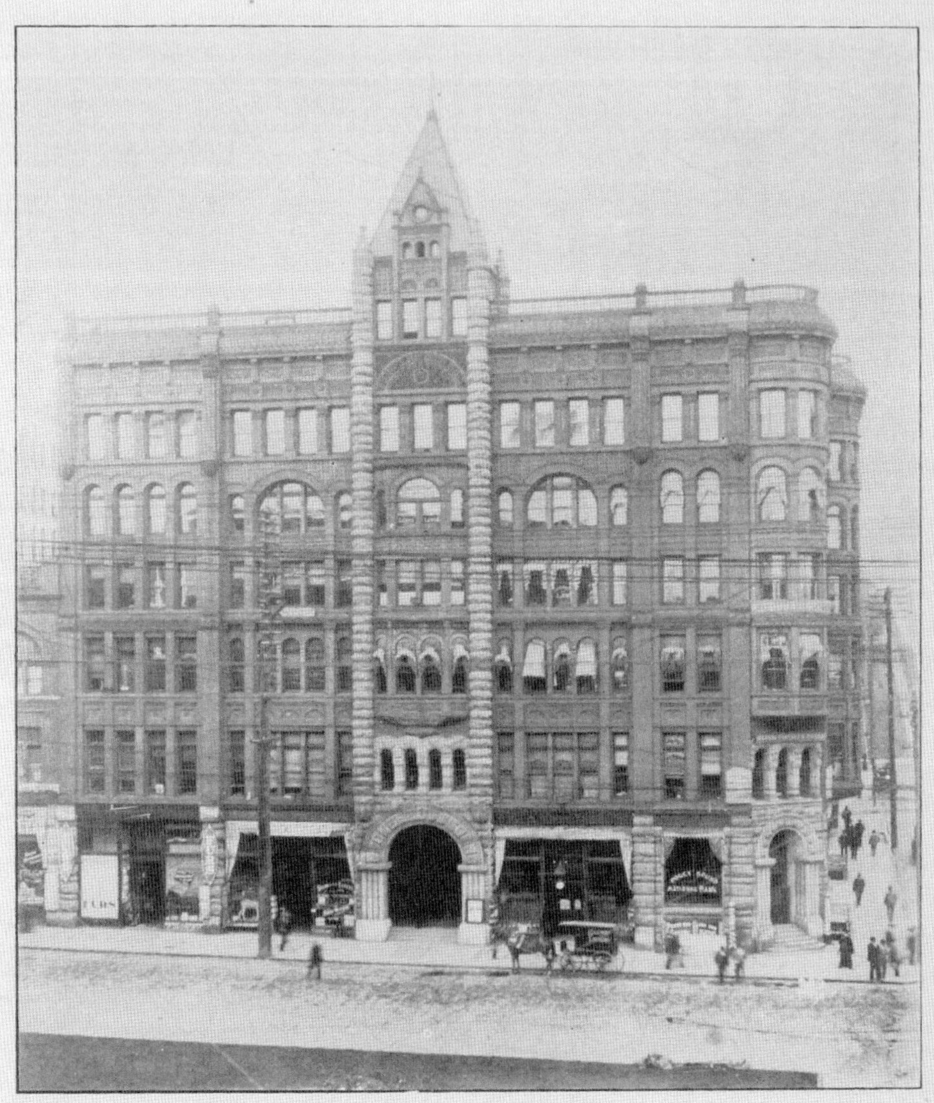

PUGET SOUND NATIONAL BANK.
The Block is called the Pioneer, and is the property of the Yesler Estate, Inc.

force of character, to his own clear, forceful mind, equal to the grasping and unravelling of any skein of financial complexity.

Jacob Furth came to Seattle in 1882 from Colusa County, California, where he had from a very early age been engaged in the mercantile business. Seattle in those days was just beginning to attract attention. He was up here long enough to grasp the situation and to perfect the organization of his present banking enterprise. After the organization he returned to California, but removed here entirely in 1883, since which time his residence has been in Seattle continuously.

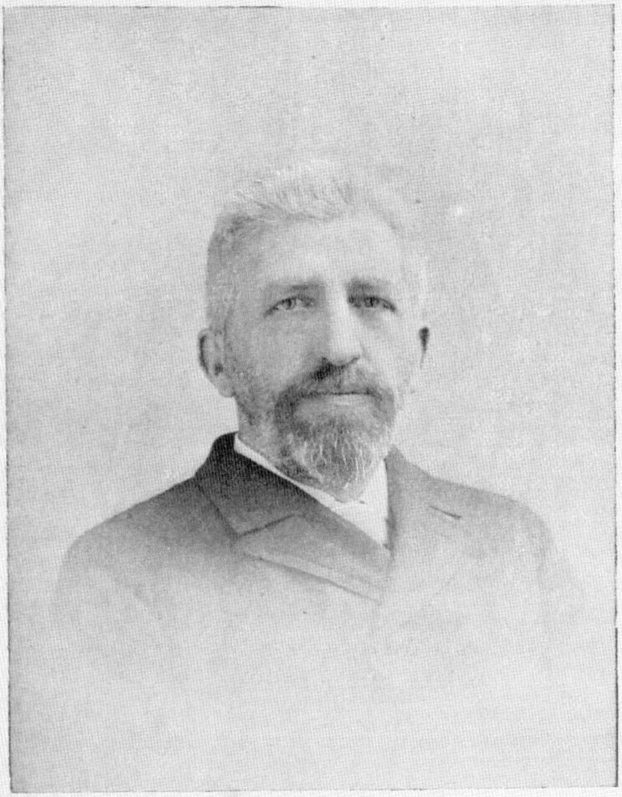

JACOB FURTH.

In 1886 he organized and became president of the First National Bank of Snohomish, a concern of much prominence today in Snohomish County, and of which Mr. Furth is still at the head.

Besides these banking ventures he has become interested in a great many other enterprises, chief of which is the Vulcan Iron Works, the California Land & Stock Company of Eastern Washington and of several of the local lines of street railways. Before the consolidation he was interested in the First Avenue line, in the Madison Street, the Union Trunk and in the Traction Company, and it was largely through his efforts that the plan of reorganization, under a consolidated plan, which has been successfully carried out, that the new system, whereby the separate car lines of this city are assuming superior characteristics, that the project was carried out. It was entirely due to his efforts that the money for the purchase of these lines and for their betterment was secured, and if no other evidence were needed to show his strong executive ability in matters of financial importance, the consummation of this plan would be sufficient to demonstrate it.

Over in Eastern Washington, near the town of Harrington, there is a tract of some 14,000 acres of land, a portion of which is devoted to wheat-raising and other portions to the raising of cattle and horses. This is the property of the California Land & Farming Company, which Mr. Furth organized and of which he is the president. Associated with him in this great undertaking are W. P. Harrington, a banker of Colusa, California, and Dr. Luke Robinson of San Francisco. Their place is under the management of John F. Green. There are now 2000 head of horses and 1500 head of cattle upon the place, and they were the first to take advantage of the great combined harvesters and threshers, which are to be frequently seen in the San Joaquin Valley, to which are attached thirty head of horses, and which not only cut, but thresh and sack the grain while being hauled about the fields. Three of these great combination affairs are in use, and one can form some idea of the magnitude of the farming operations carried on on this big ranch. It is in operations of this kind that Mr. Furth has shown particular force, and it is this force which has easily made him the recognized leader of financial affairs in this section of the West.

R. V. Ankeny.

R. V. Ankeny, who occupies the very important position of cashier in the most important bank in this city, has acquired his knowledge by practical application in all the various branches which go to make up a complex system. He began life in a bank at a

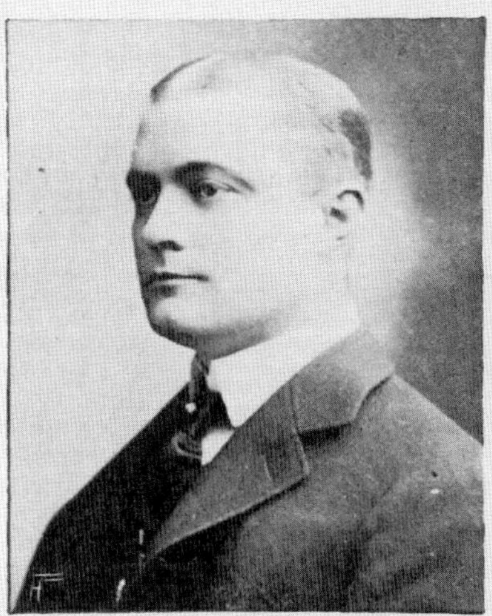

R. V. ANKENY.

very early age, and has step by step gone up the ladder until today he occupies the conspicuous and important position that he does. Mr. Ankeny has been in Seattle since August, 1888, coming direct from Des Moines, Iowa, to take a position in the Puget Sound National Bank as bookkeeper. He was born in Freeport, Illinois, but attended school and graduated in Iowa. As before stated, he accepted a position as bookkeeper upon his arrival here, and successively has filled every position in the bank up to 1894, when he was elected to the position of cashier, a position which he now holds with so much credit to himself and the bank.

In addition to his duties with the Puget Sound National he is the treasurer and interested in the following companies: The Vulcan Iron Works, Alaska-Pacific Express Company, Alaska & Pacific Steamship Company, Bering Sea Development & Improvement Company and the E. G. Rathbone Lighterage Company of Cape Nome. Although a young man, comparatively speaking, there are very few in the West who are exercising a stronger or a wiser influence in financial circles than Mr. Ankeny.

THE BANK OF DEXTER HORTON & COMPANY.

The bank of Dexter Horton & Company, which occupies the first floor of their own magnificent building at the corner of First Avenue South and Washington street, is the oldest bank in Washington, its establishment dating back to 1870. It was founded in that year by Dexter Horton, one of the pioneer settlers of Seattle, and a man named Philips; in 1872 Philips died and his interest was acquired by A. A. Denny. It continued under this ownership as a private banking institution until 1887, when it was incorporated under the laws of the State of Washington. The building which they now occupy was built by them in 1892-3 and occupied in the spring of 1893. It is the only bank in the State, of any consequence, which owns its own block. The illustration which is shown herewith will give an idea of the character of the building, which, by the way, is one of the most handsome in Seattle. Judge John P. Hoyt was the first manager after the reorganization and incorporation, and upon his election to the Supreme Court in 1890, N. H. Latimer, who had had a continuous connection with the bank from 1882, was elected in his stead, a position which he still occupies. The present officers of the bank are: W. M. Ladd, president; R. H. Denny, vice-president; N. H. Latimer, manager; M. W. Peterson, cashier, and C. E. Burnside, assistant cashier. The institution has a capital stock of $200,-000, with a surplus of $100,000, and is one of the great big financial institutions of the Pacific Coast. As indicating its rapid growth and increase of business during the year, it can be stated that on March 1, 1899, its deposits amounted to $1,915,855.54; on

May 31, 1899, the deposits were $1,983,-045.97; July 12, 1899, they had reached $2,210,012.19; on September 7 they had climbed to $2,499,827.90; and on December 2 last they had reached nearly three million dollars, or to be exact, $2,906,569. This is an increase of business that can well be pointed to with pride and a showing which few banks in cities no larger than Seattle can point to. If no other evidence were needed, this remarkable showing of

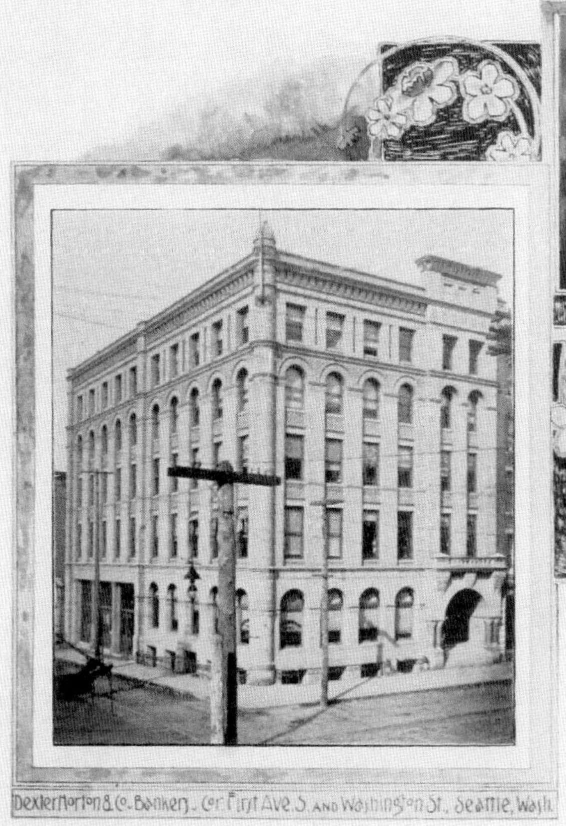

THE BANK OF DEXTER HORTON & CO.

increased deposits would be convincing proof of the high standing this bank has among all circles, commercial and otherwise, on Puget Sound.

N. H. Latimer.

N. H. Latimer, the manager of Dexter Horton & Co., bankers, whose portrait is herewith shown, came to Seattle in 1882 from Illinois. For a year previous to his arrival in Seattle he occupied a position in the First National Bank of Kirkwood, in that State, and three days after his arrival in Seattle was offered and accepted a position as bookkeeper in the bank of which he is now the manager. It was owned in those days by Dexter Horton and A. A. Denny. During the first years with the bank he occupied the positions of bookkeeper, note

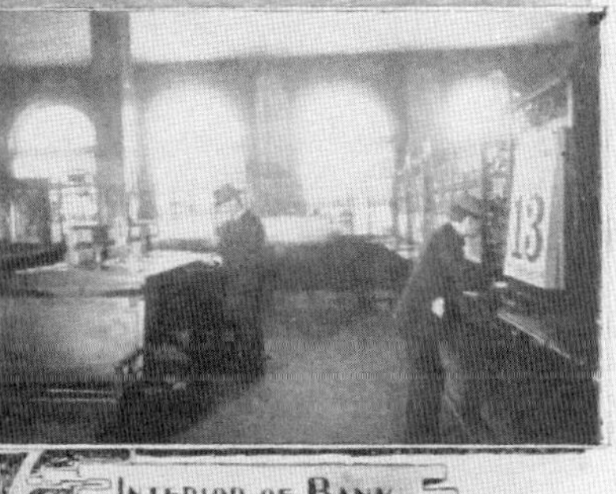

INTERIOR OF BANK

teller, receiving teller, paying teller, and subsequently manager, the latter position having been tendered him in 1890. His long experience with the bank and his wide knowledge of affairs in general on Puget Sound, and particularly in Seattle, make him thoroughly conversant with general bank and financial affairs and fit him more generously for the position he occupies than most men occupying positions of similar trust and responsibility. Mr. Latimer has recently built one of the most handsome residences in this city; it is located on Terry Avenue and Columbia Street, and besides being one of the most elegant homes in this city, commands a view of the surrounding country which cannot be excelled elsewhere in this region of country. He has a family consisting of a wife and four little boys, and the home which he has recently completed is one of most ideal and elegant appointment.

M. W. Peterson.

M. W. Peterson, the present cashier of Dexter Horton & Company, was appointed to this position the latter part of 1899. He has now resided in Seattle for two years. Prior to coming here he was with Ladd & Tilton in Portland for upwards of fifteen years, filling various positions in that big banking institution from bookkeeper to paying teller. Few young men in the West have had a wider range of experience and possess greater knowledge of financial matters than Mr. Peterson, and his selection to the position which he now occupies has been an exceptionally wise one.

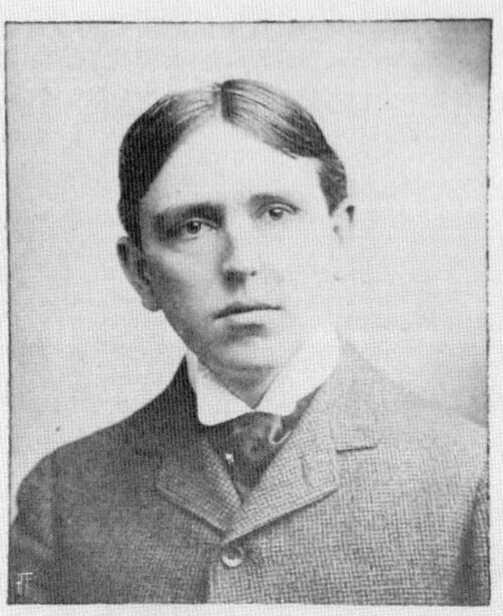

M. W. PETERSON.

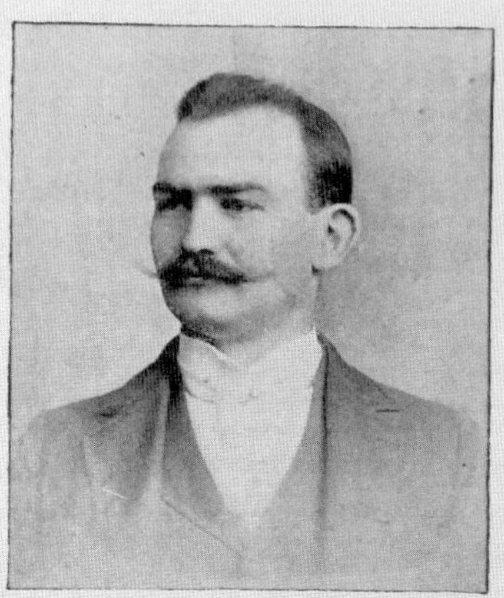

N. H. LATIMER.

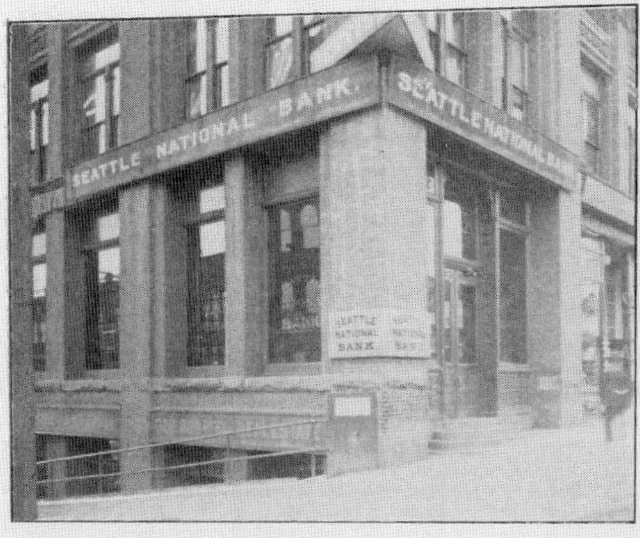

THE SEATTLE NATIONAL BANK.

THE SEATTLE NATIONAL BANK.

The Seattle National Bank, located at the northwest corner of Columbia street and Second avenue, was established in 1890, just after the big Seattle fire, by G. W. Griffith, from Denver, president; W. R. Ballard, of Seattle, vice-president, and Fred Ward, of Seattle, cashier. Two years after the organization of the bank a change took place in the personnel of the management, E. W. Andrews becoming president, John B. Agen vice-president, and S. F. Kelley cashier; the directorate including Messrs. Andrews and Agen, together with J. D. Farrell, Harold Preston, Daniel Kelleher, David Ferguson and T. N. Haller. This official roster still obtains.

The bank does a general commercial business and is a United States depositary. A feature of this institution is that with a capitalization of but $100,000 it has upwards of $1,500,000 deposits. This cannot be said of more than a score of national banks in the United States. The last official statement of this bank, made March 24, 1900, showed loans $568,394.17, U. S. bonds and premium $439,000, warrants, stocks and real estate $119,663.31, cash and exchange $582,961.21. It also showed a surplus of $10,000, undivided profits $3,888.33, circulation $90,000, deposits $1,516,523.95. The capital stock is $100,000.

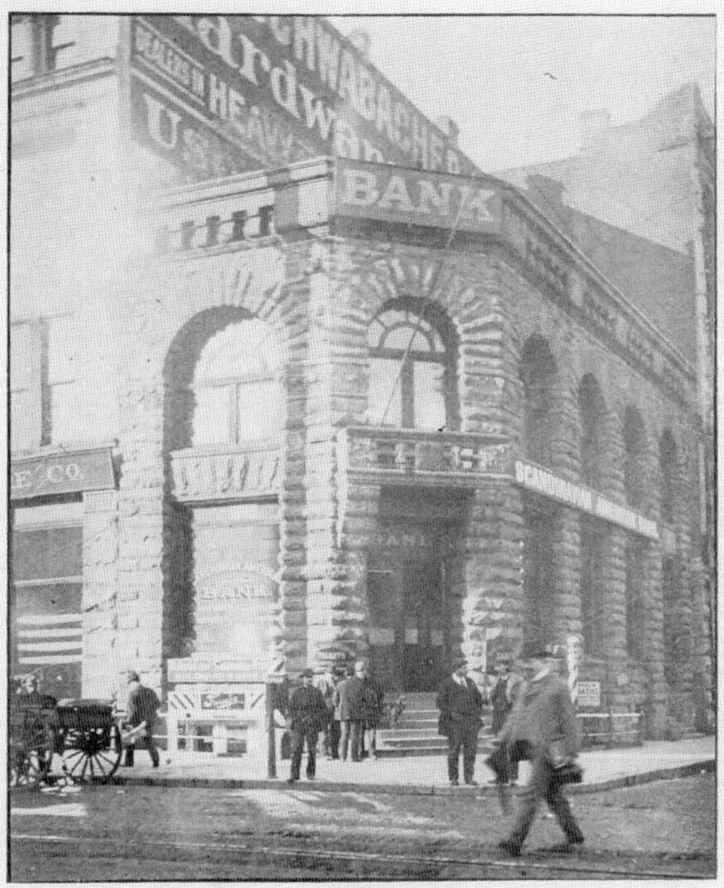

SCANDINAVIAN AMERICAN BANK.
The Building the property of Yesler Estate, Incorporated.

THE SCANDINAVIAN-AMERICAN BANK.

Some illustrations are shown herewith of the Scandivanian-American Bank, one of which presents the exterior appearance and the other gives an interior view, both of which are very excellent likenesses. The bank was first organized in 1892 with a capital of $75,000, and few institutions of a similar character have made the same progress for the same length of time or put themselves on the same substantial basis that this institution has done. It was organized with A. Chilberg as president, W. H. Talbott as cashier, A. Amunds as vice-president, and A. E. Johnson second vice-president. Shortly after its organization Mr. Talbott resigned and moved to Ellensburg, and A. H. Soelberg acted in his stead until he was elected to the position in 1894. As indicating the very remarkable growth of the bank the following statement of deposits is shown:

May 31, 1894	$ 73,539.28
May 31, 1895	117,216.58
May 31, 1896	152,241.16
May 31, 1897	170,594.08
May 31, 1898	421,815.96
Dec. 30, 1899	910,192.56

In the statement which was made on December 30, 1899, the resources are given as follows:

Loans and discounts	$ 476,454.71
Furniture and fixtures	3,000.00
Real estate	36,874.20
Internal revenue stamps	937.08
Capital subject to call	30,000.00
Other resources	3,944.00

County and city warrants........	14,219.18
Cash on hand and due from banks	454,519.02
Or a total of.....................	$1,019,948.19

The liabilities were:

Capital stock	$ 75,000.00
Undivided profits	34,755.63
Deposits	910,192.56

The officers of the bank at the present time are: A. Chilberg, president; E. L. Grondahl, first vice-president; O. O. Searle, second vice-president, and A. H. Soelberg, cashier.

This growth tells a story of one of the most remarkable successes in this most remarkable town. The success has been due to a conservative yet progressive spirit and to a thorough knowledge of financial matters and to the needs of a growing city like Seattle.

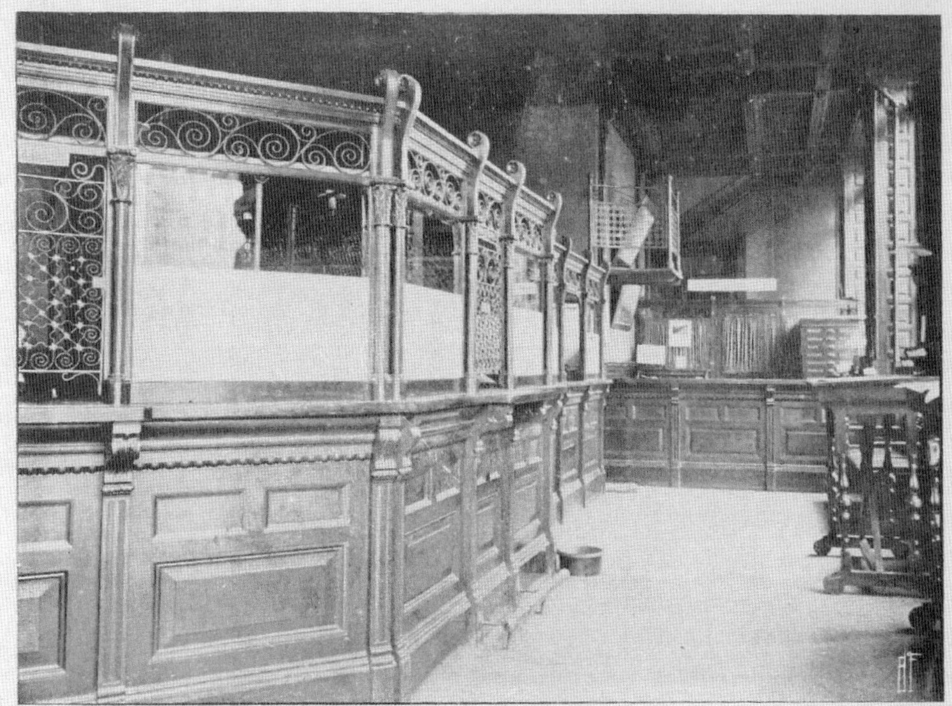

INTERIOR OF THE SCANDINAVIAN-AMERICAN BANK.

A. Chilberg.

A. Chilberg, president of the Scandinavian-American Bank, first came to Seattle in 1875 and engaged in the grocery business and later in the insurance business. He was afterwards made the city passenger agent for the Northern Pacific railroad and served in that capacity for several years, or until he resigned to organize the bank of which he is now the head. When he first came here he was honored by the appointment of Swedish-Norwegian vice-consul, and during the time he was acting as agent for the Northern Pacific he was appointed agent for all the lines of steamships plying between Europe and America, a position which he still holds. In addition to his duties with the bank he devotes considerable time to looking after trans-American passengers. During Mr. Chilberg's long residence in this city he has occupied several positions of trust and importance, among which is that of city treasurer at one time and also the position of councilman. He was a member of the board of education from 1895 to 1898, and of which he was president during the year 1897. He is a man who is very highly regarded by all those who are acquainted with him, and is probably one of the best known men on Puget Sound by reason of his long residence in Seattle.

A. H. Soelberg.

A. H. Soleberg came here from Minneapolis, Minnesota, in the spring of 1892 to take a position in the bank of

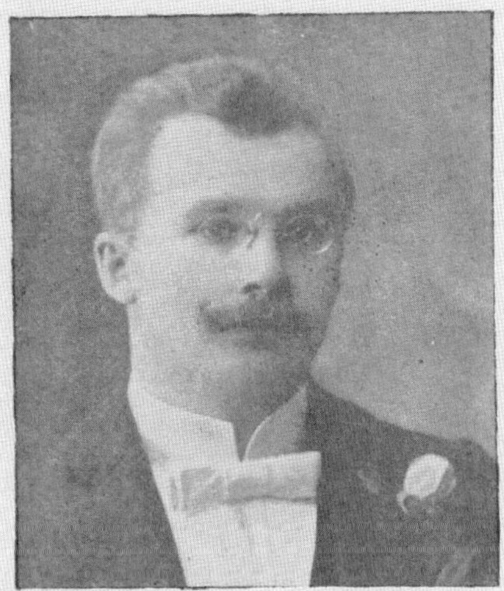

A. H. SOELBERG.

which he is now the cashier. Prior to his removal to Seattle he was engaged in the sash and door business in the Eastern city, and had had a very thorough commercial training. He

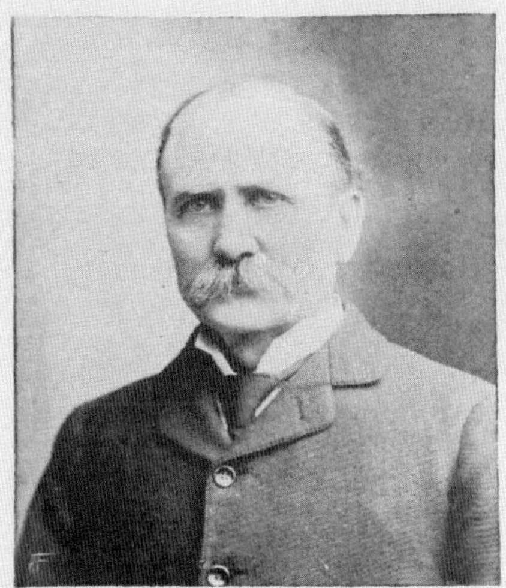

A. CHILBERG.

was born in Norway, where he received a very thorough education, and for several years after his graduation from the schools of his natice country he had an actual training in various business pursuits, so that upon engaging in business in the United States he was exceedingly well equipped to at once begin making progress. The very rapid growth of the institution with which he is so closely allied indicates to a certainty that he has had very much to do with its success. Few young men occupying positions in the commercial world can point to a better record.

E. L. Grondahl.

E. L. Grondahl, who occupies the position of first vice-president in the Scandinavian-American Bank, and who takes a very leading interest in its

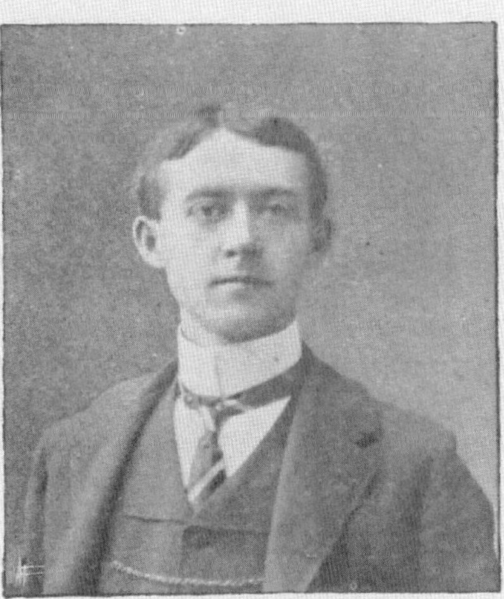

E. L. GRONDAHL.

affairs, was born in Norway and removed with his parents to Red Wing, Minnesota, at a very early age. Although a young man, he has had very large business experience, and prior to removing to this city in June, 1899, he was engaged in the insurance, loan, real estate and law business in Minnesota, and naturally acquired a very sound business training, so that when he accepted a position in the bank in this city, through the purchase of a large block of stock, he was remarkably well equipped for assuming duties of this character. The active management of the bank at present devolves upon both him and Mr. Soelberg.

THE FIRST NATIONAL BANK.

The First National Bank of Seattle was organized in 1882, succeeding to the banking business of George W. Harris & Co., one of the first banking institutions of the city. Numbered in the personnel of the new organization were such well-known and prominent characters as the late Henry L. Yesler, the "Father of Seattle;" Hon. John Leary, Judge J. R. Lewis and the late W. M. Ladd, of the great banking firm of Ladd & Tilton of Portland, Or.

In September, 1898, James D. Hoge, Jr., acquired a controlling interest in the bank by purchase from the Ladds, and was elected to the presidency. The present officers of the bank are: James D. Hoge, Jr., president; Maurice McMicken, vice president; Lester Turner, cashier, and R. F. Parkhurst, assistant cashier.

An official comparative statement is given herewith as illustrative of the rapid growth of the First National during the past five years between 1895 and 1900:

1895.		1900.
$424,000	Deposits	$1,300,000
125,000	Cash due from banks	500,000
500,000	Loans	700,000

Capital stock	$150,000
Surplus and profits	40,000

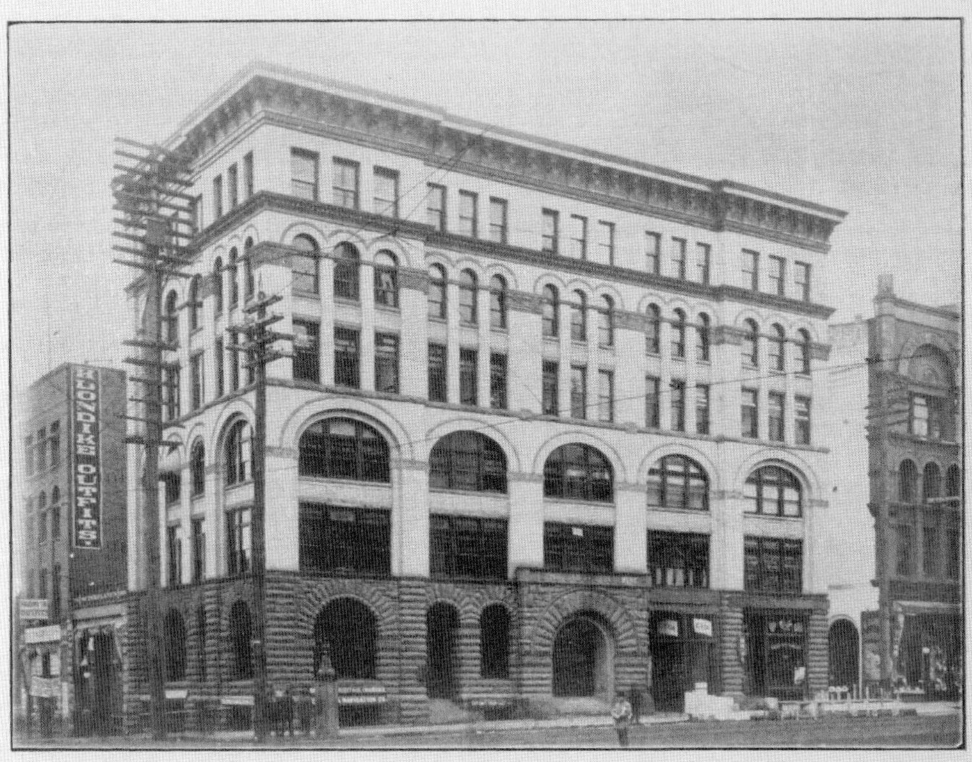

FIRST NATIONAL BANK BUILDING, FIRST AND YESLER.

President James D. Hoge, Jr.

President James D. Hoge, Jr., has lived in Seattle since 1890. He entered the First National Bank as messenger and stenographer nearly ten years ago. After various promotions he finally succeeded to the position of note and collection teller. He remained with the bank four years in all, when he entered the office of the Post-Intelligencer, afterward rising to the position of business manager. On the death

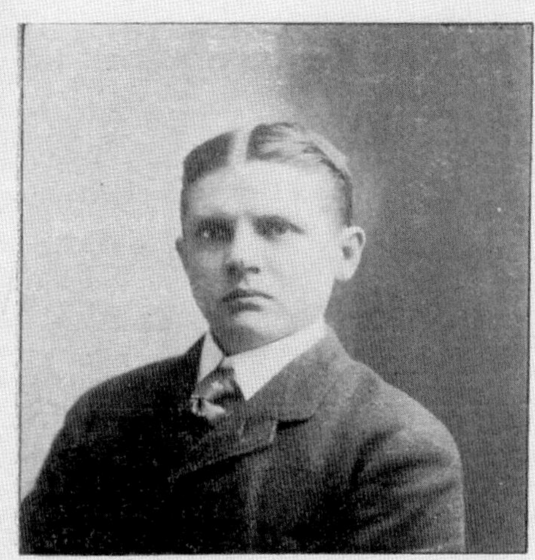

JAMES D. HOGE, JR.

of Hon. Frederic J. Grant, his brother-in-law, the editor, Mr. Hoge became proprietor of the big newspaper. He continued the publication of the Post-Intelligencer until 1897, when he sold out at a large profit.

Finding himself in poor health, Mr. Hoge decided on a trip around the world and devoted some eight months to his travels, devoting considerable time to the banking methods and finances of the various countries—his careful investigations and experiences resulting in most thoroughly equipping him for the responsible position he now occupies, that of president of one of the big financial institutions of the Pacific Coast.

As indicating the bank's growth, it may be well to mention that the deposits, when he assumed control, were about $650,000; now they are practically $1,500,000. Mr. Hoge was born at Zanesville, Ohio, in September, 1871, and hence is the youngest bank president in the United States. He is married and has two children. In addition to being president of the bank, he is also secretary of the Clearing House Association.

The bank's stockholders include such prominent people as L. Murphy, president of the First National Bank of San Francisco; Sol. G. Simpson, the great lumberman; Maurice McMicken, one of the leading attorneys of the city and one of the owners of the Post-Intelligencer; Hon. John H. McGraw, ex-Governor of the State and ex-president

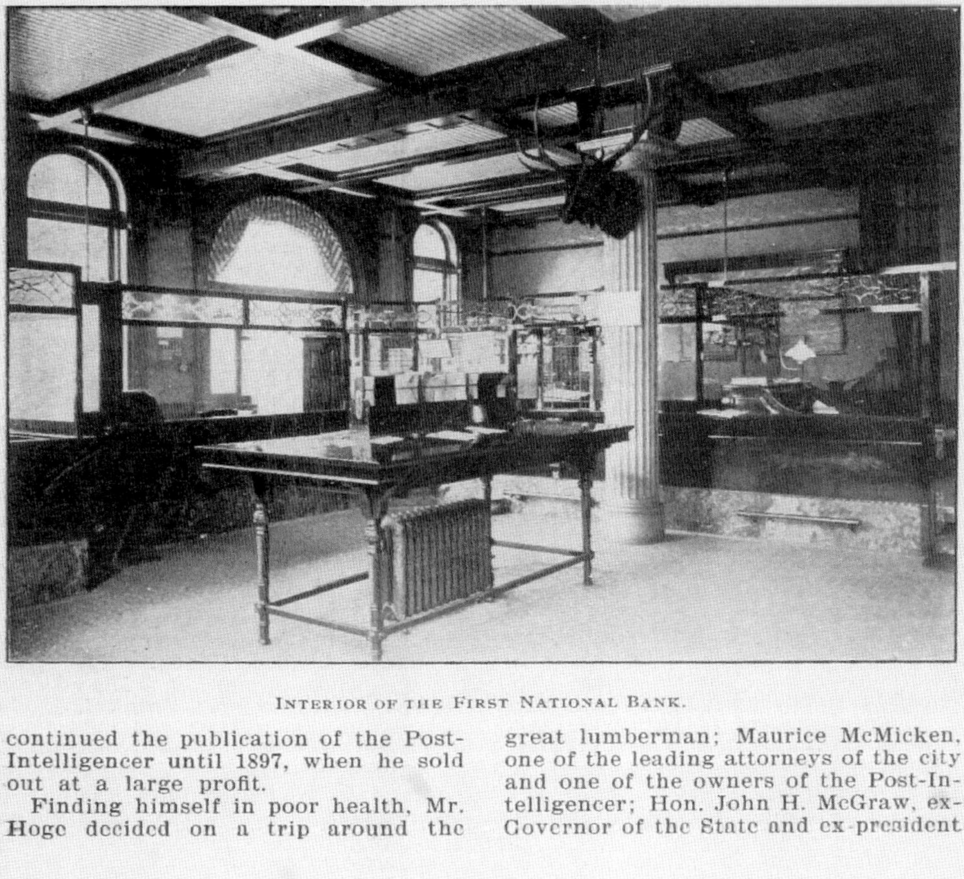

INTERIOR OF THE FIRST NATIONAL BANK.

of the bank, and many others of equal financial strength and prominence.

Cashier Lester Turner.

Lester Turner, cashier of the First National Bank since 1890, is a gentleman of exceptional attainments. He came to Seattle from San Francisco, where he resided for five years. Previous to his residence in San Francisco, Mr. Turner was a successful banker on Wall Street. He is now recognized as one of the ablest bankers in the Pacific Northwest.

The First National Bank is one of the strong concerns of Seattle and the Pacific Coast.

THE NATIONAL BANK OF COMMERCE.

The National Bank of Commerce, which was organized in 1890, is one of the very large financial institutions which give Seattle a high rating in moneyed circles. The statement published on December 2, 1899, shows that it has resources of $1,090,000; capital, surplus and undivided profits, $180,000, and a line of deposits amounting to $1,558,188.80. H. C. Henry is the president, and R. R. Spencer is cashier. The bank occupies premises in the Bailey building, one of the most substantial structures in the city. It is among the most handsomely appointed and conveniently arranged banks in Seattle, as the accompanying interior photographs will show.

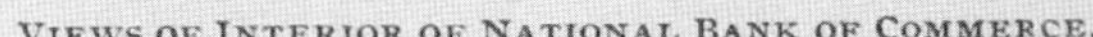

VIEWS OF INTERIOR OF NATIONAL BANK OF COMMERCE.

PEOPLE'S SAVINGS BANK.

One of the best known and safest banking institutions on Puget Sound is the People's Savings Bank, organized in 1889 by James R. Hayden, Jacob Furth, A. A. Denny, W. E. Bailey, Bailey Gatzert, John Collins, John Leary, Otto Ranke and Leigh S. J. Hunt. The first board of trustees were Bailey Gatzert, president; Jacob Furth, vice-president; Arthur A. Denny, second vice-president; James R. Hayden, manager, and Louis Schwabacher, William E. Bailey, John Leary, John Collins and Otto Ranke. The first officers were James R. Hayden, cashier and secretary; Frank I. Blodgett, assistant cashier, and attorneys, Preston, Carr & Preston. The bank was for eight years located in the west end of the Occidental Block, the quarters now occupied by the Hotel Seattle. It has always had the confidence of the people, which confidence was never shaken, not even during the dark days of 1893, when banks were crashing on every hand. The institution recently enlarged its scope to include general commercial banking and a trust company business.

In March of the present year, 1900, the bank changed its location to most elegantly appointed quarters in the Masonic Temple, at the northeast corner of Second Avenue and Pike Street, the building being owned by E. C. Neufelder, president of the institution. The present official roster of the bank is: E. C. Neufelder, president; John Leary, vice presdent; James R. Hayden, cashier; Joseph T. Greenleaf, assistant cashier; directors, E. C. Neufelder, John Leary, R. H. Denny, John Collins and James R. Hayden.

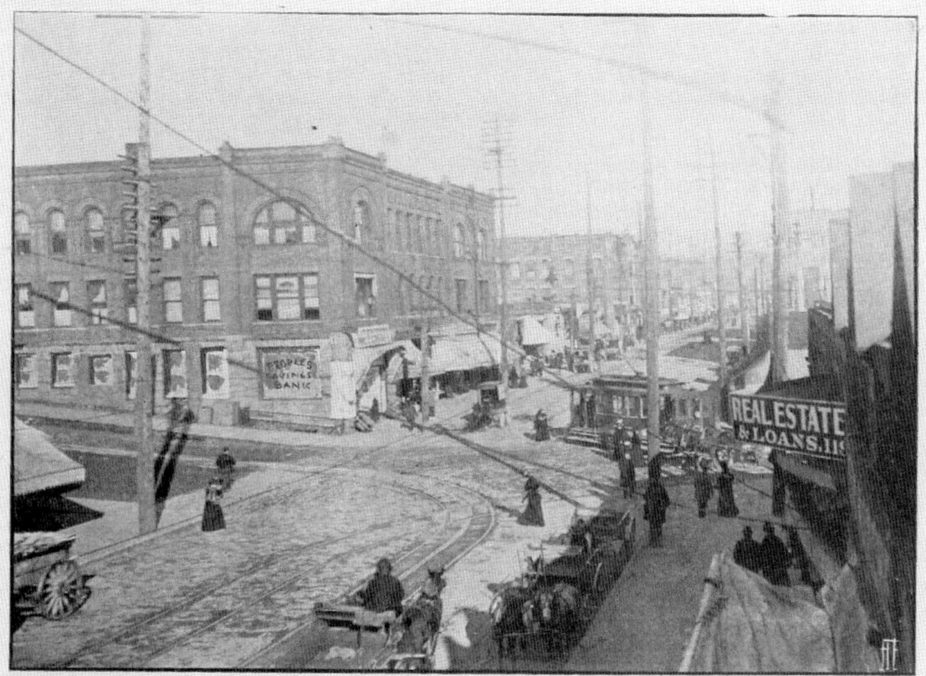

VIEW OF THE NEW HOME OF PEOPLE'S SAVINGS BANK, ON PIKE ST. AND SECOND AVE.

JOHN B. AGEN.

John B. Agen, one of the most popular business men of the city, came to Seattle in 1889, the day following the big fire, from Osage, Iowa. Mr. Agen brought in the first car of butter and eggs received here after the fire, and immediately opened a butter and egg establishment on Seventh and Stewart streets, where he remained until the Colman block was completed on Western avenue and Marion street, the location he still occupies.

Mr. Agen has been in business twenty-three years, and by close application and careful management has built for himself a trade unequaled on the Pacific Coast. He carries on extensive business in British Columbia, Hawaiin Islands and the Orient, besides having branch offices in Alaska and other Sound points.

One of his specialties, and one that has made a great hit, is the putting up of fine creamery butter in oblong square two-pound tin cans, with key opener attached, all under a neat and attractive label. In this manner a great quantity is put up for the Klondike and Nome trade. The label with "J. B. Agen has stood the test," is a guarantee of superior quality.

Mr. Agen's main cold storage and

creamery is at Osage, Iowa, the place that can justly be called the banner butter state in quality and production.

Mr. Agen was among the originators of the creamery butter scheme that has now become so universal, and largely through his efforts people have become educated in butter.

He owns several skimming stations throughout Western Washington, the cream being shipped to the main creamery in Seattle and churned.

Mr. Agen is vice president of the Seattle National Bank, and owns considerable real estate in this city, besides being interested in several sugar plantations in Hawaii.

Mr. Agen is a man of pleasing personality, and one who is generally liked by all who know him, being a member of many of the social clubs of the city.

A picture is shown of his residence on Boylston and

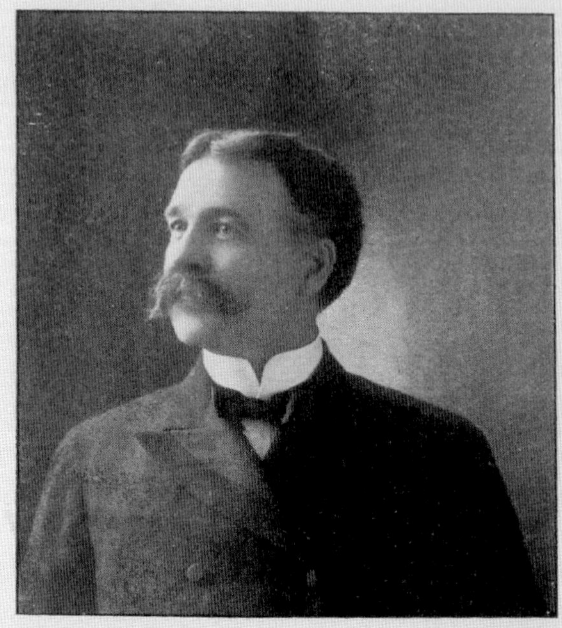

JOHN B. AGEN.

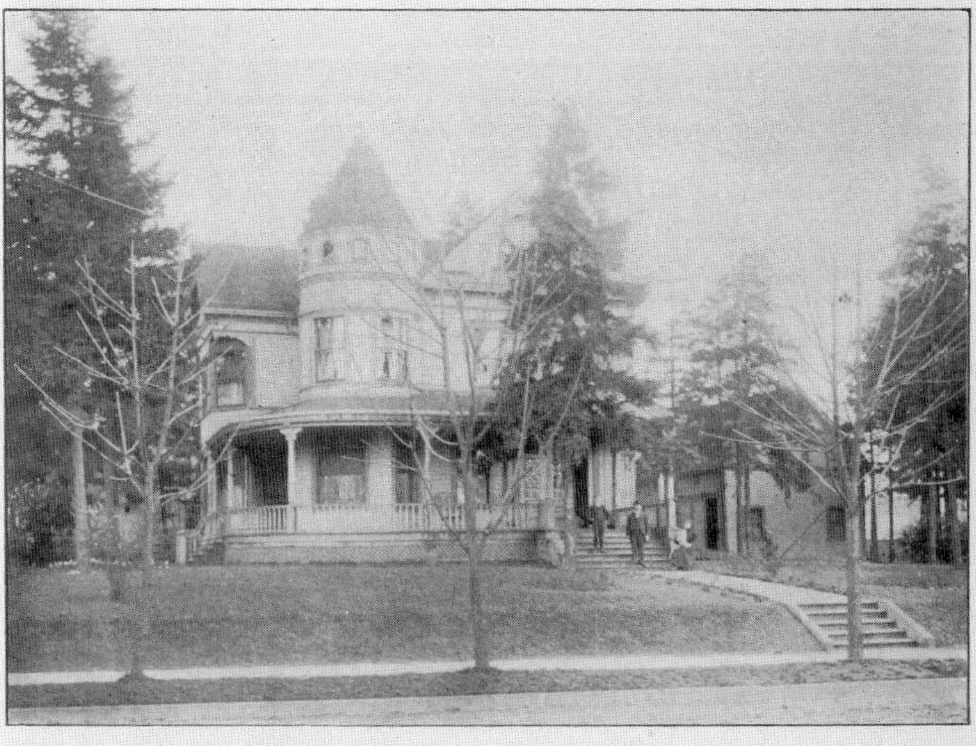

THE RESIDENCE OF JOHN B. AGEN, BOYLSTON AVE. AND SENECA ST.

Seneca avenues, which is considered one of the most attractive homes in the city.

THE BIG MEAT PACKERS.

Among the leading and constantly expanding industries of Puget Sound is the Frye-Bruhn Co. of Seattle, located on the tide flats in the southern part of the city on the line of the Grant Street Electric Railway. The Frye-Bruhn Co. is purely a Seattle institution, owing its inception and growth wholly to Seattle men and Seattle capital. C. H. Frye, president, and Charles Bruhn, secretary and treasurer of the company, were formerly stockmen of Davenport, Ia. Coming to the Coast in 1888, they opened up a retail meat market at the southwest corner of Washington and Commercial (now First Avenue South) Streets. The big fire of 1889 destroyed their place of business, but they immediately opened up in a tent at "the old stand."

In 1893 they branched out into the wholesale trade and incorporated under the present name with officers as given above. They erected a slaughter house fronting on Grant Street bridge, which they ran for four years, when their fast expanding business necessitated the installing of a packing house on a comparatively extensive scale. From almost the very start they consumed all the cattle, sheep and hogs they could procure in Eastern Washington and found a ready market for their output in all parts of the State and in British Columbia and Alaska.

In September of last year (1899) their works were totally destroyed by fire, but with that commendable enterprise so characteristic of Western men, the company immediately erected temporary quarters, which enabled them to partially meet the demands of their enormous patronage, while at the same time they began preparations for the erection of a new plant on greatly enlarged and improved plans. This plant is now finished in all its details and is in operation.

The new plant covers upward of three acres. The main building has a frontage of 110 feet on Grant Street bridge and extends back over the flats 250 feet, being three stories in height. The lower floor is 110x250 feet in dimensions and contains the pickling rooms, space for storing hides and pelts, vats for converting the offal into fertilizers; driers to take care of the blood, bone mills, and the large freezing tank, besides the boiler and engine rooms and ice freezing machinery. The institution is thoroughly modern throughout, being equipped with all the latest machinery and conveniences. It has a daily capacity of 150 cattle, 300 sheep and 500 hogs. The company at present employs 145 men, with a monthly pay roll of $8,500. In the fiscal year ending July, 1899, they slaughtered 8900 cattle, 41,000 sheep and 15,500 hogs. They manufactured during this period 2,400,000 pounds of hams, 1,600,000 pounds of bacon and 1,260,000 pounds of lard, besides 8900 hides, 475,000 pounds of tallow and grease and 685,000 pounds of miscellaneous products. Their sales were $1,500,000. As their business is constantly and rapidly increasing, these figures will augment in proportion.

The plant is complete in every detail, being modeled after the big packing houses of the Middle West, with such changes only as an eye to improvements has suggested. The various processes of converting cattle, hogs and sheep into beef, pork, mutton, etc., and the different by-products are all arranged with a view to economizing time and labor, with a maximum of cleanliness and a minimum of waste. The cattle are killed while standing in a narrow pen by a blow on the head with a steel maul, given by a man on a raised platform. The movement of a lever then sets machinery in motion that opens a door swung on top hinges and tips the platform on which the animal rests, throwing the body into a large room where it is hoisted by the hind feet with a friction hoist, the blood drained, the head cut off and the carcass skinned, dressed and quartered and sent on the way by overhead track and hanging wheel to the chill room, the various processes probably occupying ten minutes and requiring four men. Carcasses are left in the chill room (33 degrees above zero temperature) forty-eight hours, when they are ready for shipment or the market. Where shipped any distance, the meat goes by refrigerator cars, or, if on the water, in refrigerator tanks.

Hogs and sheep are killed with the knife. A boy puts a snaffle on the hind leg of a hog, when the animal is hoisted by machinery, head downward, about fifteen feet, when he is "stuck," and after bleeding a few moments till dead the carcass is dropped into a scalding tank from whence a patent "throw" lifts them onto the scraping ta'ble, where the hair is dextrously removed by an automatic hog scraper, after which it is carried by overhead rail to the "cutter," who dresses the carcass and sends it along to the chill rooms, the whole process not occupying over five minutes.

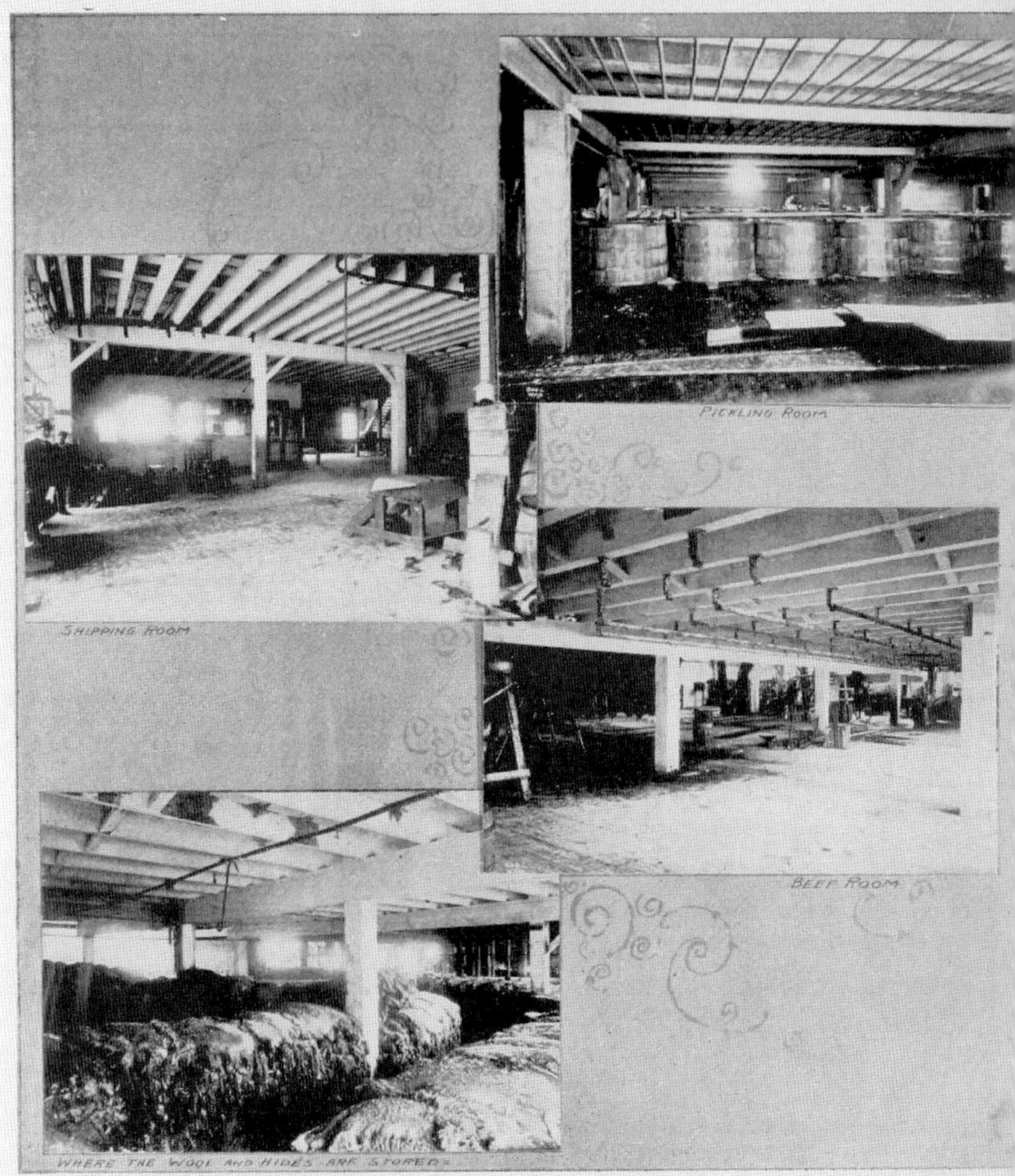

THE NEW PACKING HOUSE OF FRYE-BRUHN CO., SOUTH SEATTLE, THE LARGEST IN THE WEST.

Sheep are strung up after being killed, when they are skinned and dressed and sent along by overhead rail to the chill rooms, the whole work being done by one man to each sheep and requiring about four minutes to complete the operation. All tracks and floors are down grade from the initial point where the animals are slaughtered to the chill rooms to facilitate the moving of the carcasses.

Besides the abattoirs, common to all packing houses, there are chilling rooms, smoke houses, pickling rooms, a sausage department with a monthly capacity of twenty tons, a complete

the shell of the hoofs goes to China and returns to America in various tortoise-shell articles. In fact, nothing is lost, as they say at the works, but "the squeal of the hog."

The company's "F.-B.' brand of pure leaf lard, made in open kettles, has become justly celebrated throughout the Northwest because of its purity and full weight. The demand far exceeds the present capacity of the works. Their "Wild Rose" brand of lard is made from leaf lard and back fat, and is an excellent article.

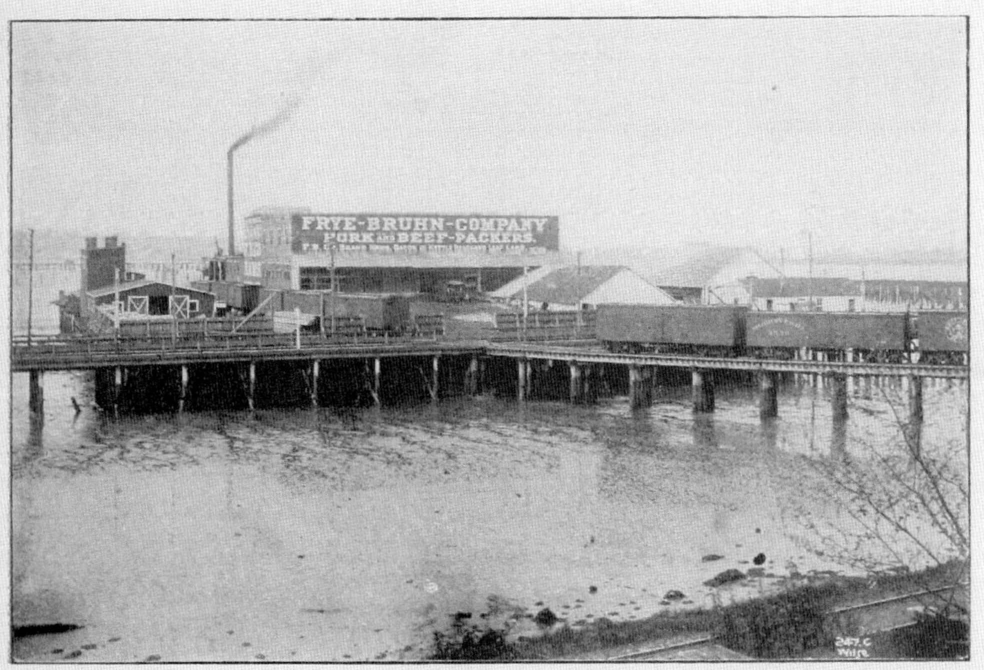

Overlooking Big Packing Plant of Frye-Bruhn Co.

lard refinery, a box-making department, a complete ice manufactory and refrigerator plant and numerous vats and appliances for taking care of the various by-products.

Every part of the slaughtered animal is utilized. Besides the food products the company produces glue stock from the ears and snouts of the animals, neatsfoot oil from the feet of the cattle, bonemeal for chickens and for fertilizing, dried blood for sugar refineries, and fertilizer from the offal. The shin bones of cattle are shipped to Japan, where they are used for knife handles and various other purposes;

The company cure all the hams and bacon that can be furnished them from Eastern Washington, and are obliged, much to their regret, to go outside the State for material to supply the growing demand for their "F.-B" brand of hams and bacon.

The Frye-Bruhn Co. has one of the most complete and modern refrigerator and ice manufacturing plants on the Coast, which enables them to keep the temperature down to the desired point (33 degrees above zero), in their numerous chill rooms, and furnish all the ice necessary in their own immense business, besides supplying fifty tons daily to the trade. The company is fortunate in the possession of an inexhaustible source of the purest water, obtained from a flowing artesian well on the property 1009 feet deep. This water is first distilled by conversion into steam and then condensed in a graduated coil of piping on the roof of the building, after which it is put through skimming, reboiling and filtering processes for the elimination of air and all possible impurities, so that by the time it reaches the freezing pans it is absolutely pure and devoid of any atmospheric trace. The peculiar construction of the plant does not admit of the water again coming in contact with the atmosphere until it is congealed into ice, after having been at first converted into steam. The ice thus produced is clear as French plate and wholly without the objectionable "core," such a common feature in the manufactured product.

The Frye-Bruhn Co.'s products have gained great favor throughout the entire Northwest and bid fair to eventually supersede nearly all importations from the packing houses of the East.

THE MOORE INVESTMENT COMPANY

The work that can be done for the upbuilding of a city by the intelligent, energetic efforts of one firm is exemplified by the results the Moore Investment Company has achieved within eighteen months. It is an inspiration for every man who has pride in the prosperity of Seattle.

After the hard times set in eight years ago, J. A. Moore, the head and front of the company, went to Mexico, developed a mine that turned out to be a bonanza, sold it, and returned to Seattle. He had faith in the city, and backed up his faith by making cash investments in realty. Further, he interested some of his Eastern friends, for whom he bought more than $1,000,000 worth of choice business property now salable at double tne price he paid for it.

By this means he removed bearish influences. The property had been foreclosed. While it remained on the market prices could not enhance and people of means hesitated to invest. But the purchase of these large holdings greatly stimulated the market. Those big deals mark the beginning of Seattle's business and building revival.

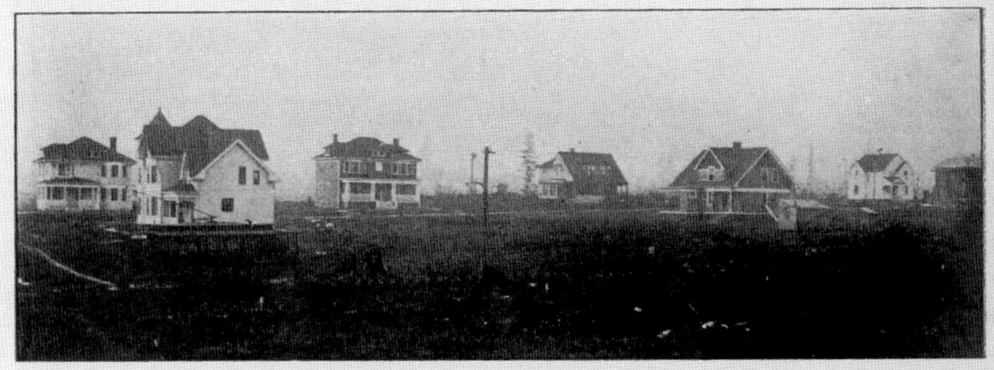

A View on University Heights from Fremont Avenue.
These Magnificent Residences were Constructed by the Moore Investment Co. for Owners.

Early last year Mr. Moore announced his intention of constructing a magnificent apartment house of steel, brick and stone, at a total cost of $150,000. Some scoffed at the project as premature, but before the completion of the foundation applications had been received by the Moore Investment Company far surpassing the capacity of the seven-story building. The company has since started another large block at Second Avenue and Union Street, one of the finest in the city.

But a few days ago Mr. Moore arranged for the construction of another block at Second and Union, to be stone and brick, six stories high, costing $85,000. It will be known as the Whitcomb, and be located diagonally across from the Estabrook. It will be completed and ready for occupancy by early autumn.

All of last summer Mr. Moore advanced money to home builders for the construction of scores or handsome homes on installment payments. That alone was influential in securing several hundred new and desirable families for Seattle. They are now fixtures here and are contributing to the city's growth and prosperity.

One of the Moore Investment Company's enterprises is the opening and improving of University Heights, adjoining the State University. The company graded this fine suburb and put down cement sidewalks at a great expense, and is constructing handsome homes there on easy installments. This is a measure never before undertaken in Seattle. The wisdom of the policy is apparent in the results. More than four-fifths of the lots there are already sold, and homes costing from $1200 to $3000 adorn this educational suburb.

Residence property on University Heights is so much in demand that it is settling up faster than any other part of the city, and values are correspondingly enhancing, and, of course, is sure to be a residence district unsurpassed in point of sightliness, sanitation, nearness to a great educational center, and the association of the cultured, intellectual class of people to reside there.

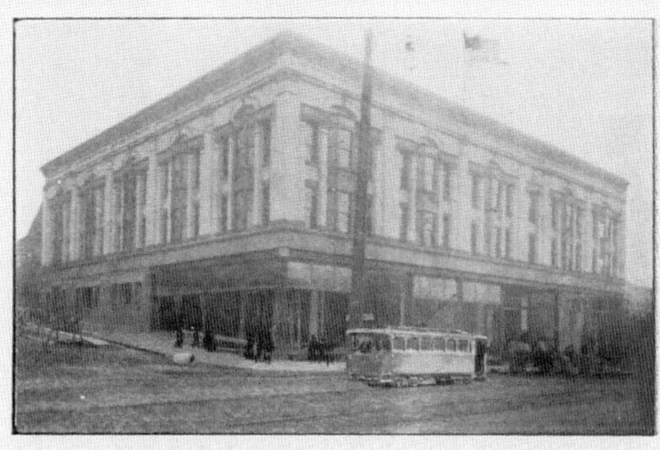

THE EASTABROOK BLOCK.
Second and Union—Constructed by Moore Investment Company.

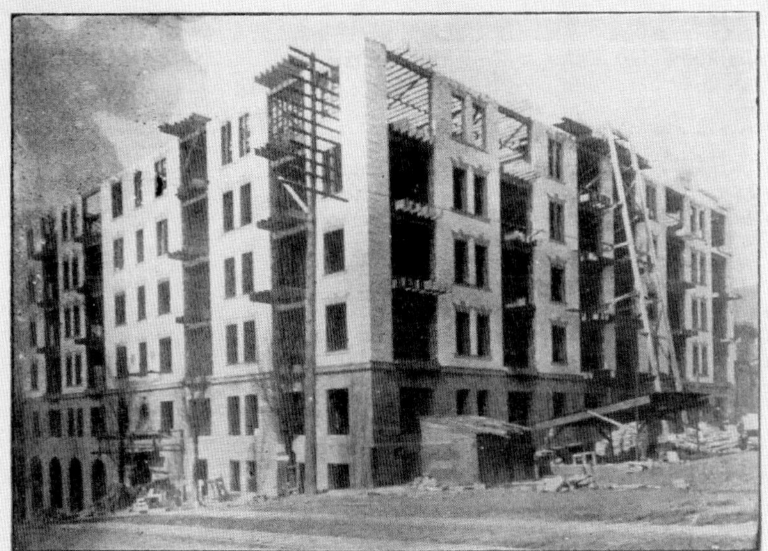

THE LINCOLN APARTMENT HOUSE.
Fourth and Madison—Seven Stories, Stone and White Pressed Brick—Under construction by the Moore Investment Company.

The first of the year Mr. Moore's vast business interests, which include also the development of one of the largest coal mines in the state, has grown to such proportions that he took J. E. Ballaine into the firm. Mr. Ballaine is one of the best known young

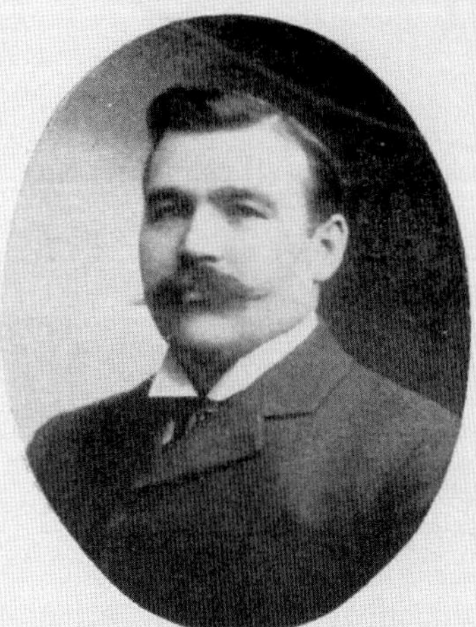

J. A. MOORE.
Head of Moore Investment Co.

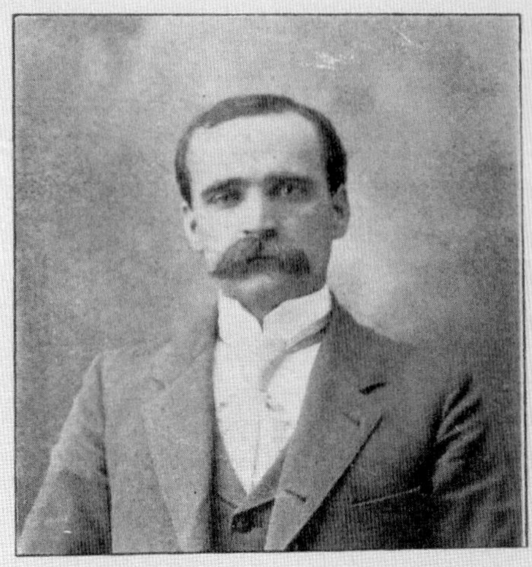

JOHN E. BALLAINE,
Of the Moore Investment Co.

men in the state. He was raised in Whitman County. In his journalistic career he became editor of the southern division of the Associated press, at Washington, D. C., when 25 years of age. He was private secretary to the Governor of Washington and adjutant general of the National Guard, later serving through the Spanish-American-Phillipine war as an officer of the First Washington Regiment.

J. W. GODWIN.

J. W. Godwin, who is the head of the firm of J. W. Godwin & Company, the big wholesale commission firm in this city, has been in Seattle since 1890. When he first moved to this city he organized the commission business under the name of J. W. Godwin & Company and conducted it alone

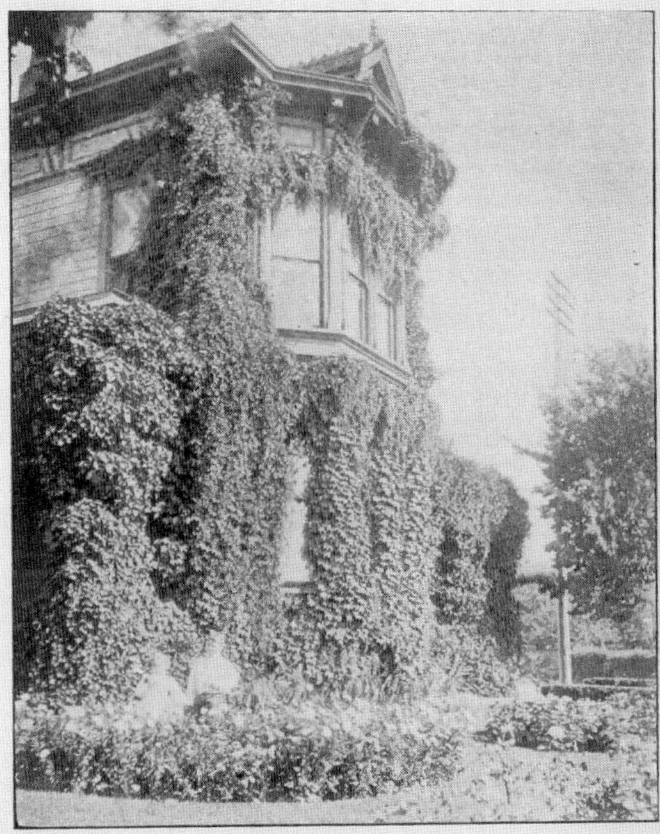

A WINDOW IN THE RESIDENCE OF HON. JOHN COLLINS, MINOR AVE.

til 1894, when it became an incorporated company, at which time he became its president and manager. The store which they occupy is 45x120 feet, and the business conducted is that of a wholesale and retail commission house. They send products into British Columbia and Alaska and all over Western and Eastern Washington, and at the present time are doing a very extensive business.

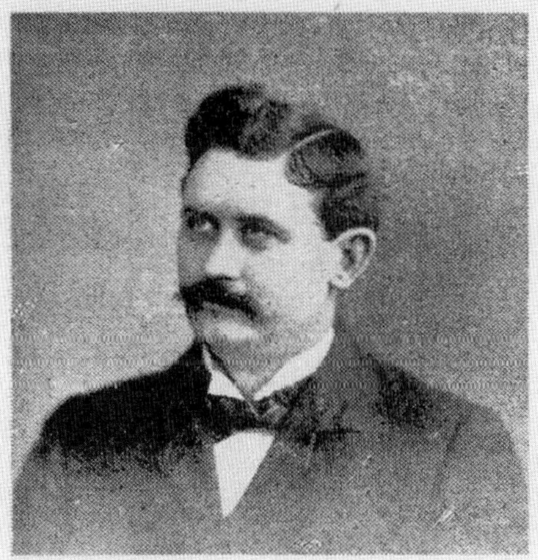

J. W. GODWIN.

One of their heavy products is the importation of bananas, the most of which they receive from Central America. These they distribute in turn throughout the regions of country named. At the present time they employ twelve men in the store in this city and keep one man traveling upon the road. The business for last year has shown a very marked increase over the previous year and is equal to fully 25 per cent gain, and the way that business starts off so far this year there will be a marked increase over last year in the volume of trade.

Mr. Godwin is a native of Virginia and came to Seattle from Philadelphia, in which place he was doing business prior to coming West. Since removing to this city Mr. Godwin has taken a very active interest in all affairs which have a tendency to promote the welfare of the community; and as he has always been closely identified with the Democratic party, his political views since coming here have been eagerly sought for, and it can be said that he is well up in the councils of his party.

In addition to his large commission business, Mr. Godwin is a very extensive dealer in real estate and since coming here has acquired very considerable holdings of some choice tracts.

W. E. McKEE.

W. E. McKee, the proprietor of the Horseshoe, one of the most elaborately fitted up, and considered to be the best conducted saloon on the northwest coast, has resided in Seattle for the past ten years. He was born in Fishkill-on-the-Hudson, in the State of New York, and in addition to living in Cleveland, Ohio, has resided in all the principal cities of the Union, including Des Moines, Iowa, Sioux Falls, Iowa, and Manitou Springs, Colorado. His arrival in Seattle was immediately following the fire, and his first business here was the securing of the privilege to serve refreshments upon the "City of Seattle," which had just been brought around from the East and was plying at that time on the Sound. It was not until 1894, however, that Mr.

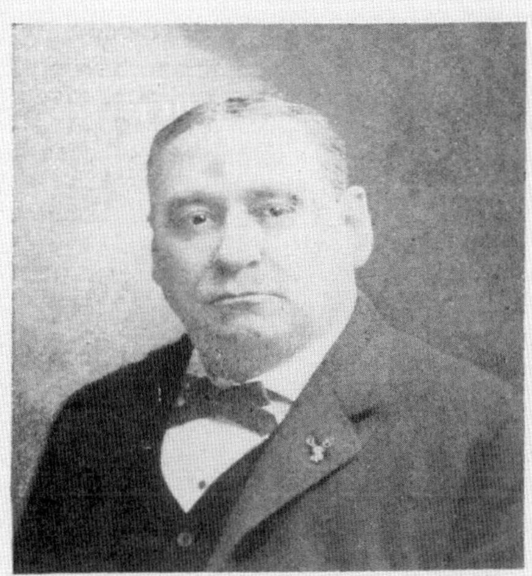

W. E. McKEE.

McKee secured possession of the Horseshoe, and although it had degenerated from the plane upon which it was originated, he soon put it in first-class condition, and today it is recognized as one of the very few places in which gentlemen care to congregate.

He conducts the only public billiard room in the city, and the fact that his house is kept free of objectionable characters, and is run upon thoroughly first-class and legitimate lines, gives it a remarkably high standing in the community. Mr. McKee attributes his success solely to the fact that he employs nothing but strict business principles in all his business dealings. He is an active life member of the Lodge of Elks No. 92, and has been the president of the Rod and Gun Club of this city for the past five years, and was recently re-elected, much against his wishes.

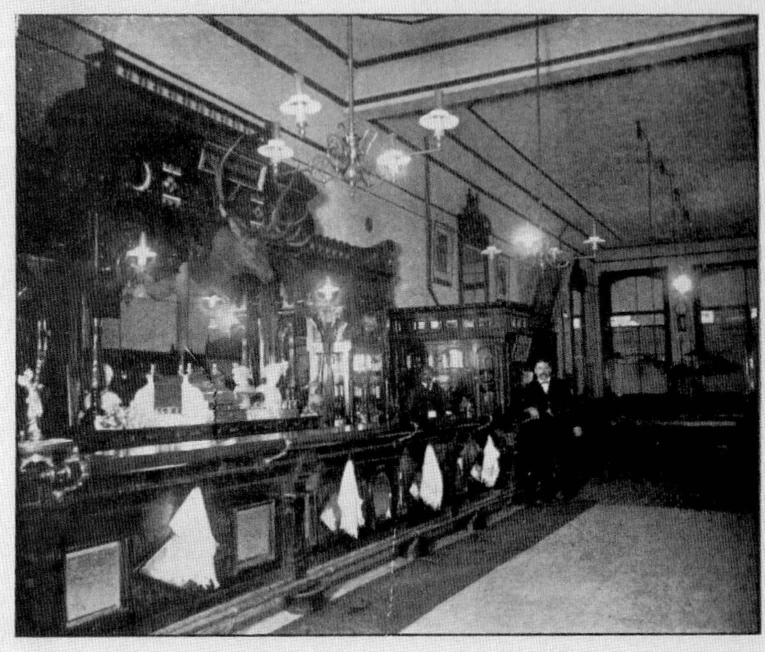

INTERIOR OF THE "HORSESHOE."

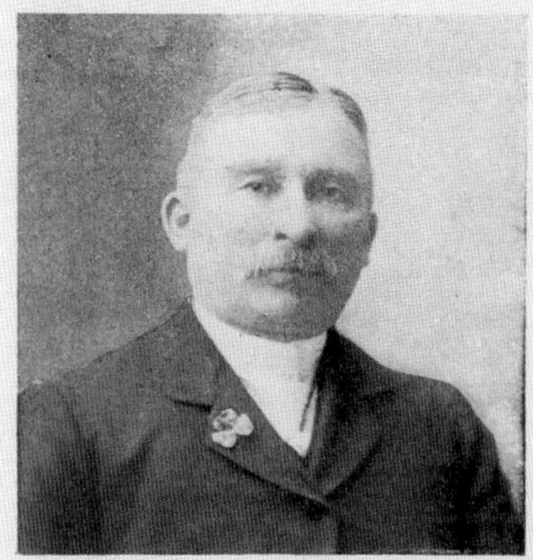

J. P. HOWE.

THE SEATTLE THEATRE.

The Seattle Theatre building, erected in 1892, at the northwest corner of Cherry street and Third avenue, at a cost of $150,000, is a beautiful structure and is strictly a Seattle institution, being a product of Seattle enterprise and Seattle capital. It is fireproof, substantially built and the peer of any first-class theater on the Coast in point of architecture and furnishings. The seating capacity is 1,500. The theater is under the management of J. P. Howe, one of the oldest theater managers west of the Rocky mountains. Mr. Howe's experience covers a quarter of a century, during which long period he has embarked in nothing else, paying all his attention to theatrical business, with no side issues, a record equaled by but a limited few theatrical managers of the present day. Mr. Howe has probably controlled more theaters than any other Pacific coast manager. Between 1884 and 1891 he controlled the North Pacific theatrical situation besides all the first-class theatrical business of Portland, Seattle, Tacoma, Walla Walla, Victoria and a number of smaller cities. During 1894-5 Mr. Howe was lessee and proprietor of the Columbia and Alcazar theaters of San Francisco.

But Mr. Howe's experience has not been limited to the management of theaters, for he has owned and controlled numerous road enterprises, among them being M. Quad's (C. B. Lewis') funny play, "Yakie," which Mr. Howe brought to the Coast in 1880. Aftewards he managed W. E. Sheridan, the great tragedian, in "King Lear," "Louis VII" and a repertoire of Shakespearean plays; in fact, his life has been devoted to theatrical business. The success of the Seattle theater since Mr. Howe assumed its management has been phenomenal and demonstrates the value of experience.

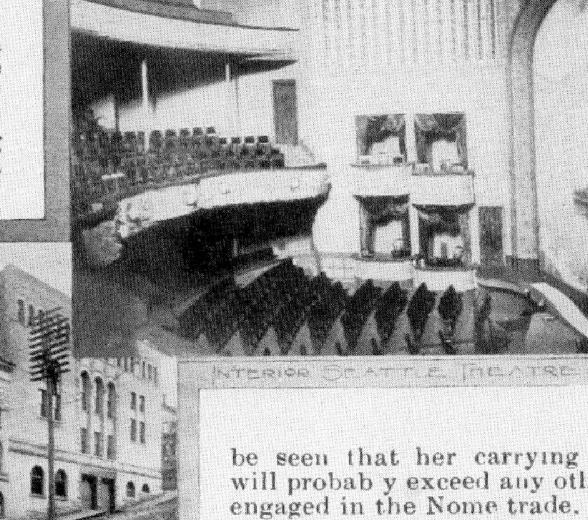

THE SEATTLE THEATRE BUILDING.

FOR THE ALASKA TRADE.

The Washington and Alaska Steamship Company is entering very extensively into the Alaska trade this season. The pressing into service of the steamship Tacoma, recently engaged as a Government transport to the Orient, will add very much to the fine fleet which will ply between this city and Cape Nome. The Tacoma will unquestionably be the finest vessel engaged in this service. She is 330 feet long, 39 feet beam and will carry 500 passengers and 2500 tons of cargo. Her speed is very fast and she is handsomely fitted up with practically every modern convenience. Last year, for the Government, she carried to Manila 860 troops and men. It can thus be seen that her carrying capacity will probably exceed any other vessel engaged in the Nome trade. She will leave here May 25 on her first trip. One of the features about the vessel is the fact that she is fitted with a refrigerator plant in which can be stored fresh meat, and passengers can enjoy this to its fullest extent on the voyage of three thousand miles. The plant has a capacity of fifty tons of ice per day, a very extensive concern. Besides the facilities for keeping cool she has nicely arranged baths and a hospital fitted up in case of any illness aboard. In addition to the steamship Tacoma the company have the steamships Farallon and City of Seattle, both of which ply between this city and points along Lynn Canal. The Farallon has nice accommodations for passengers. She is 158 feet long, 34 feet beam, and will carry sixty first-class passengers and 150 second-class, besides seventy tons of freight. She makes fortnightly trips between here and Skagway. The City

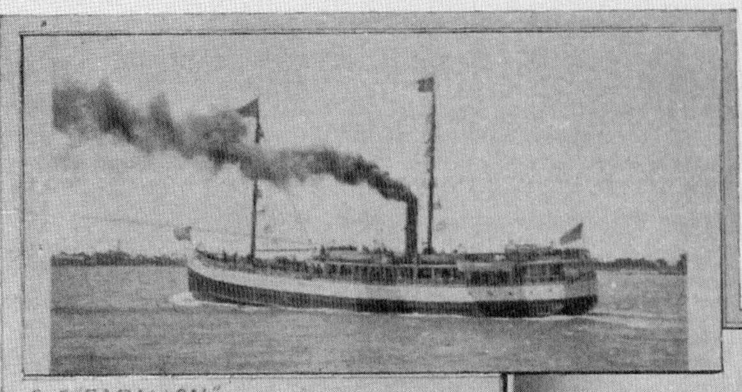

and has accommodations for 600 passengers and 800 tons of freight. She is one of the most successful and popular steamers plying out of Seattle and her owners are exceedingly proud of her. Mr. C. Stewart, manager of the

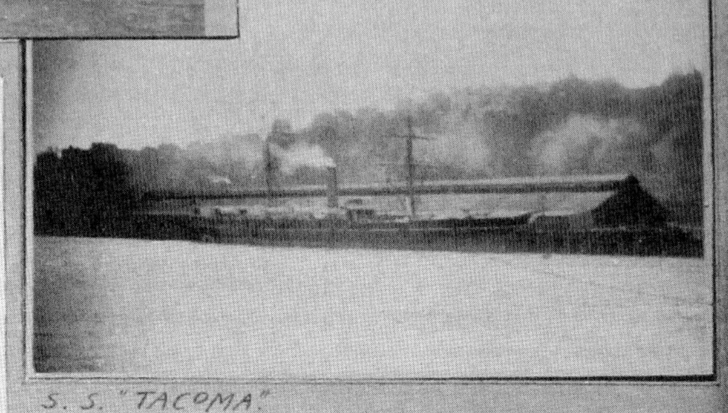

of Seattle (the "Alaskan Flyer"), however, is the favorite of them all. She consumes seven days in making the round trip; although it frequently has been made by her in six and one-half days. She makes three round trips a month from this city, leaving practically every ten days. She is 245 feet long, 38 feet beam,

THESE TWO FINE SHIPS IN ALASK TRADE.

Company, has general offices under the Seattle Hotel.

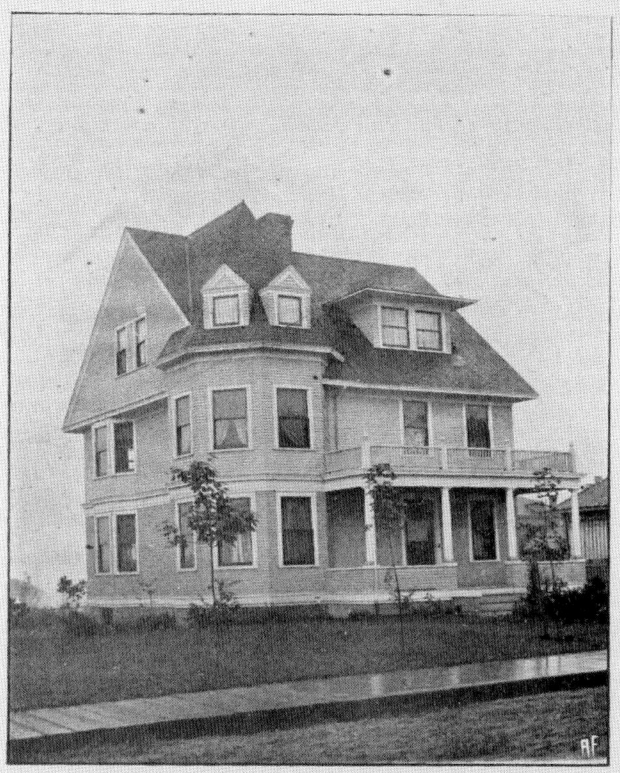

RESIDENCE OF J. E. GALBRAITH, 109 FIFTEENTH AVE. NORTH.

SCHWABACHER HARDWARE COMPANY.

Were it not for the fact that Seattle possesses establishments like the Schwabacher Hardware Company, which is rated as one of the most substantial on the Pacific Coast, Seattle would not now be enjoying the very extensive wholesale trade it does. This company is one of the oldest in the city, the date of their establishment reaching as far back as 1869; and when it is stated that forty-two men find employment in the store and they keep five men upon the road selling goods throughout the State of Washington and Northern Idaho, Montana, British Columbia and into far away Alaska, some idea can be formed of the far-reaching influence of this big firm. In addition to their trade reaching over the territory named, they are also beginning to do business with Hawaii, and in the near future trade relations with Oriental points will probably be established. A very excellent illustration is shown of the exterior of the building occupied, together with an interior view of the salesroom, which is devoted largely to the carrying on of a retail business. The building itself is 60x120 feet, four stories in height, with a basement. An ell 50x100 feet forms a portion and gives an outlet upon Yesler Way, the main entrance being upon First Avenue South. They also have a warehouse upon Railroad Avenue, which is 100x150 feet in size, in which all heavy goods are stored, including heavy hardware, iron and steel and a general assortment of heavy goods The company carries everything in the line, both heavy and shelf hardware, ship chandlery, etc., marine, mill and logging supplies, the value of their stock running up into the thousands of dollars. The personnel of the company is as follows: President, Sigismund Schwabacher; vice-president, James S. Goldsmith; secretary and treasurer, Sigismund Aronson; while George Boole is the general manager. In line with every other wholesale establishment in Seattle, this company shows a very extensive increase for last year over the previous year.

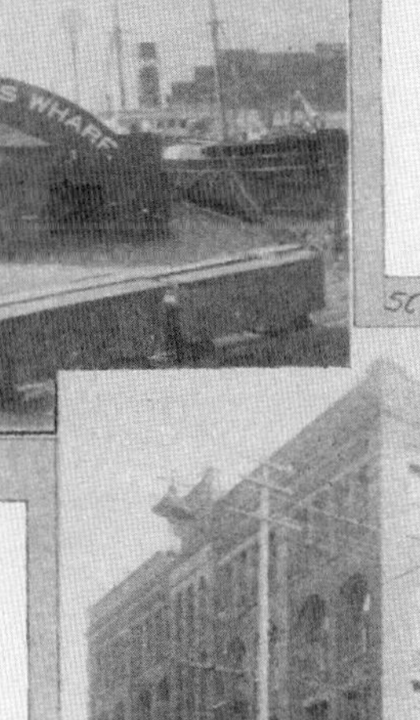

SCHWABACHER'S WHARF

SCHABACHER BROS - WHOLESALE GROCERS

SCHWABACHER BROS., THE BIG GROCERS.

A BIG WHOLESALE GROCERY HOUSE.

When it is stated that Seattle possesses one of the largest wholesale grocery houses on the Pacific Coast it is done without any fear of contradiction. The one referred to is that of Schwabacher Bros. & Co., incorporated, an illustration of whose store is shown herewith. They are located at the corner of Occidental Avenue and Main Street. The building in which they are located is 120x111 feet, four stories high, with a basement, the whole room being devoted to their own purposes as exclusive wholesalers. They give employment in this establishment to sixty people, together with some eight men whom they keep traveling throughout the Northwestern country, comprising Washington, Idaho, Montana and British Columbia, selling goods to the trade. They are the pioneers by many years in supplying the Alaska trade, having agents permanently located in the principal points of Alaska. In addition to everything in the grocery line, they have their own coffee plant, which is second to none on the Pacific Coast, in which they blend and roast and put up under their own brands, the very finest grades of coffee. This comes to them in the crude shape, direct from the plantations, and not through the usual channels which supply the ordinary merchant. Very few larger establishments can be found anywhere in the United States than this one, and the fact of their great size and the influence they exert throughout this region of country gives very great prestige to Seattle as a wholesale center. This firm is large enough to make very considerable inroads in forming trade relations with our neighbors across the Pacific when this trade is more thoroughly worked up. The personnel of the company is as follows: Abraham Schwabacher, president; Jas. S. Goldsmith, vice-president; Sigismund, Aronson, secretary and treasurer. This house was originally established in 1869 by Mr. Bailey Gatzert, who until the time of his death, which occurred in 1893, held the position of president of the company.

PRESIDENT STOCK EXCHANGE.

Anthony Corcoran, President of the Stock Exchange, is one of Seattle's solid, reliable business men; a man of sterling qualities and unimpeachable integrity. Mr. Corcoran has been at the head of the Seattle Stock Exchange since its inception and, owing to his firm stand for legitimate stock transactions and unyielding opposition to "wild-catting" and stock jobbing he has cleared the open field of scores of conscienceless brokers and stock manipulators, compelling them to seek cover, while, at the same time, his management has afforded a free and open trading field for meritorious stocks.

Mr. Corcoran has the courage of his convictions and, whenever convinced that fraudulent deals are incubating, he promptly calls a halt on the perpetrators, be they friend or foe, and the admonition does not pass unheeded, for while President Corcoran is noted for his kindness, generosity and broad charities, he is inflexible in all business requirements, and evil doers quickly learn that underneath the velvet glove is a hand of steel. Seattle can boast of many able business men, but none is more

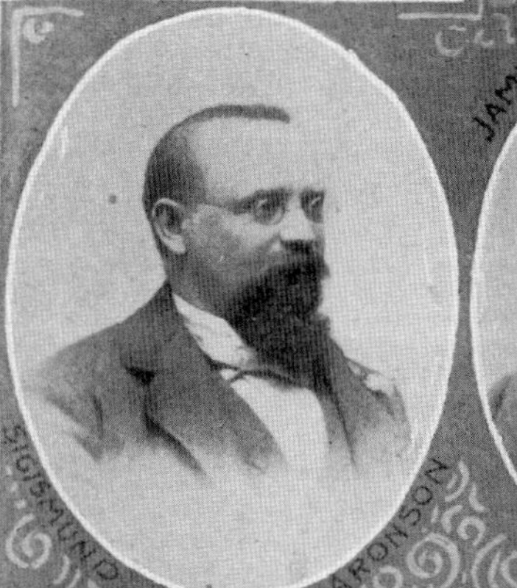

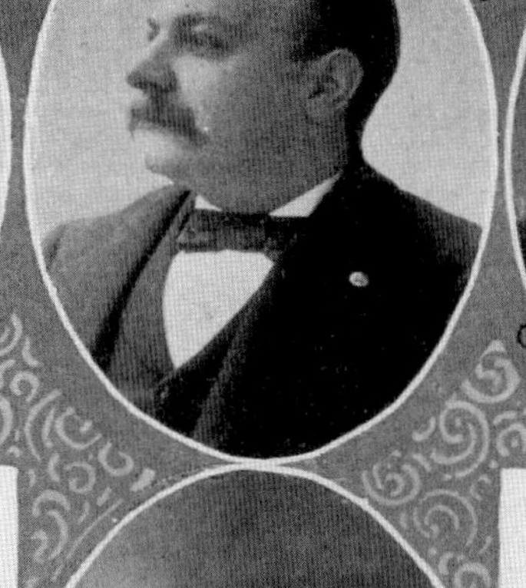

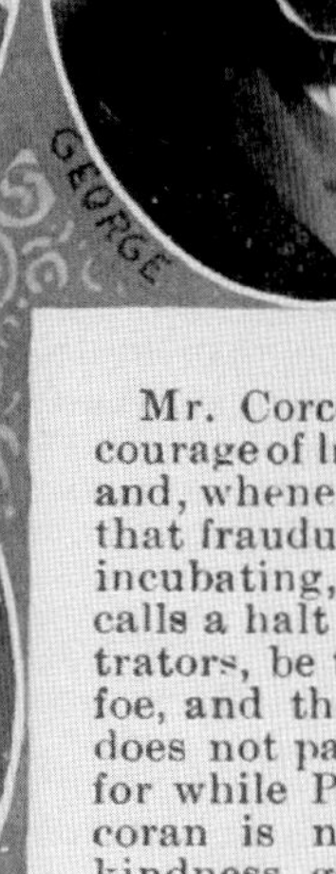

MEMBERS OF THE SCHWABACHER HARDWARE CO. AND SCHWABACHER BROTHERS.

eminently qualified for the position than is Anthony Corcoran as manager of the Stock Exchange.

THE HOTEL BUTLER.

The Hotel Butler, one of the leading and best conducted hotels in the State, and which is owned by Messrs. Hamm & Schmitz, is an institution in which this city points to with no little pride It is thoroughly modern in every way and, although conducted strictly upon the European plan, it has a grill room in connection which rivals anything on the Coast. The block that now forms the hotel was originally built for an office building, but in 1894 the present proprietors converted it into what has since become the most popular hotel in the Northwest. What perhaps is the most interesting part of the Hotel Butler is the strong personality of the two men who have made it what it is today. It was in 1887 that Messrs. Hamm and Schmitz came to this city, the former from the Driard Hotel in Victoria, and the latter from Pomona, Cal. They formed a partnership, and with a combined capital of $500, opened a small coffee house. What they lacked in money they put forth in effort and the general superiority of the coffee they set forth soon compelled them to enlarge. They did this in 1888 by leasing the ground at the corner of Washington and Occidental Avenue, where Clossen & Kelly now have a drug store, and erecting a three-story building, 30x120 in size, in which they opened a bakery and restaurant. The following year, 1889, the fire destroyed the building, but in three days after the great conflagration they were opened for business in a tent in Denny's orchard. Previous to the fire, however, they had bought the property on Pike street where the Snoqualmie Hotel now stands, and almost before the fire had burned itself out they had men at work putting up a building 120x120 feet, three stories in height. This was finished in the fall and opened for business in November. They continued to run this place until 1891, when they sold the property to O'Shea Bros. of Portland for $67,000. Then they took possession of the Arlington, now the Postoffice Block. The

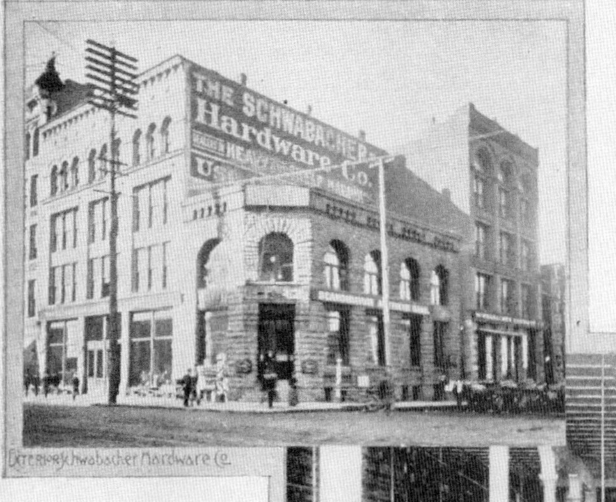

Exterior Schwabacher Hardware Co.

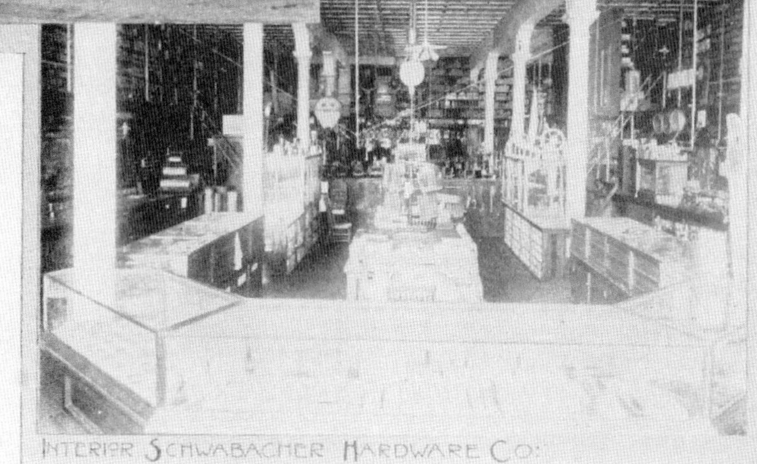

Interior Schwabacher Hardware Co.

THE SCHWABACHER HARDWARE CO.

hard times incident to the panic of 1893 made hotel business very unprofitable, particularly so for a house so far up town. It was during this time that the Seattle Saloon, now the Sutherland, was acquired and which Mr. Hamm managed. In 1894 a deal was finally consummated with Henry H. Schufeldt, of Wisconsin, by which the demands made upon them, and no one works harder or more faithfully than they. Because of this they have reaped a reward which justly entitles them to distinction. No one in Seattle stands higher than the proprietors of the Butler nor have two men in Seattle made a greater success in business than they.

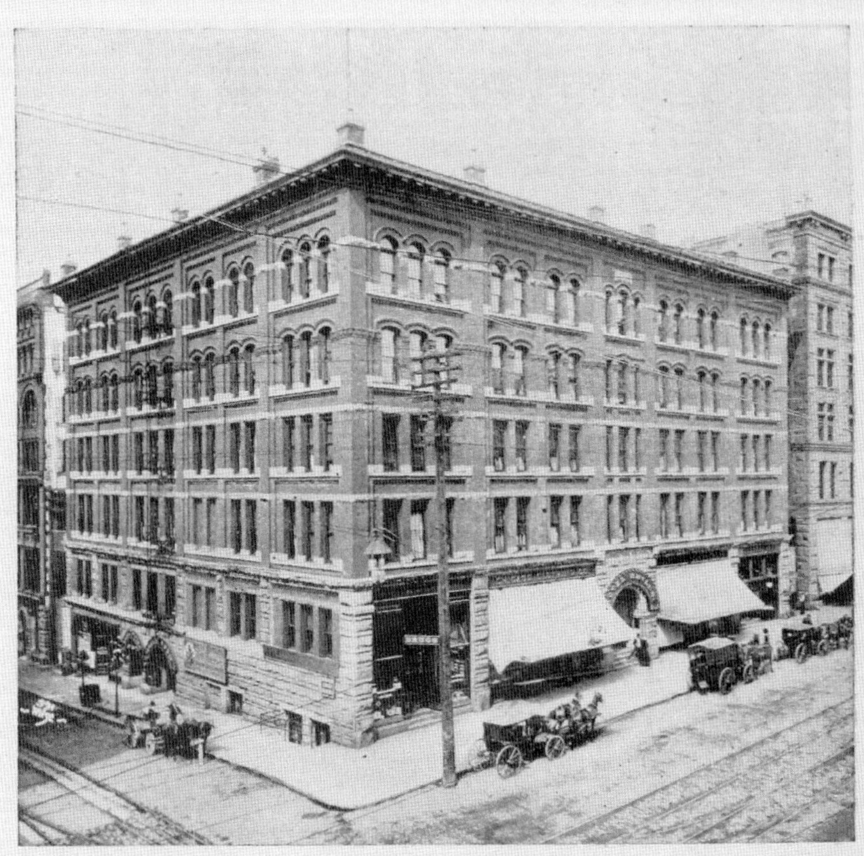

THE HOTEL BUTLER—HAMM & SCHMITZ, PROPRIETORS.

Butler, then an office block, was secured, and the Arlington was given up and both partners threw their whole energies into creating a new hotel, such as they readily saw was soon to be needed. It cost them $50,000 to make the changes required, to say nothing of the money it cost to furnish the house, but when it was finally thrown open to the public it began its popular career and its big business has never abated from that day to this. Both gentlemen are keenly alert to the

The grill room, which is justly celebrated, is supplied with all the best of everything. For instance, the meat used is all Eastern corn-fed stock, and sold as strictly No. 1 quality. This is the reason the meat at the Butler tastes as good as it does. Everything else is in the same proportion.

In addition to the Hotel Butler, Messrs. Hamm & Schmitz own the celebrated Hotel Butler fancy stock farm, located five miles from the city, upon which they have the finest blooded cattle to be found in America. They have a herd of Durhams, Ayrshires and Jerseys. A recent Ayrshire bull was received from the stock farm of J. J. Hill, of the Great Northern, that cost them $800. They also have some Jerseys from the noted ranch of W. W. Sweeney of Oak Harbor. They have 150 acres of fine bottom land, all improved, with good farm houses and all under a high state of cultivation, which makes it the best stock ranch in the West.

Both gentlemen own much valuable real estate in the city. Mr. Schmitz is a director in the First National Bank. He owns his fine home at the corner of Eleventh Avenue and Madison Street, while Mr. Hamm owns the house he occupies at the corner of Terry Avenue and James Street.

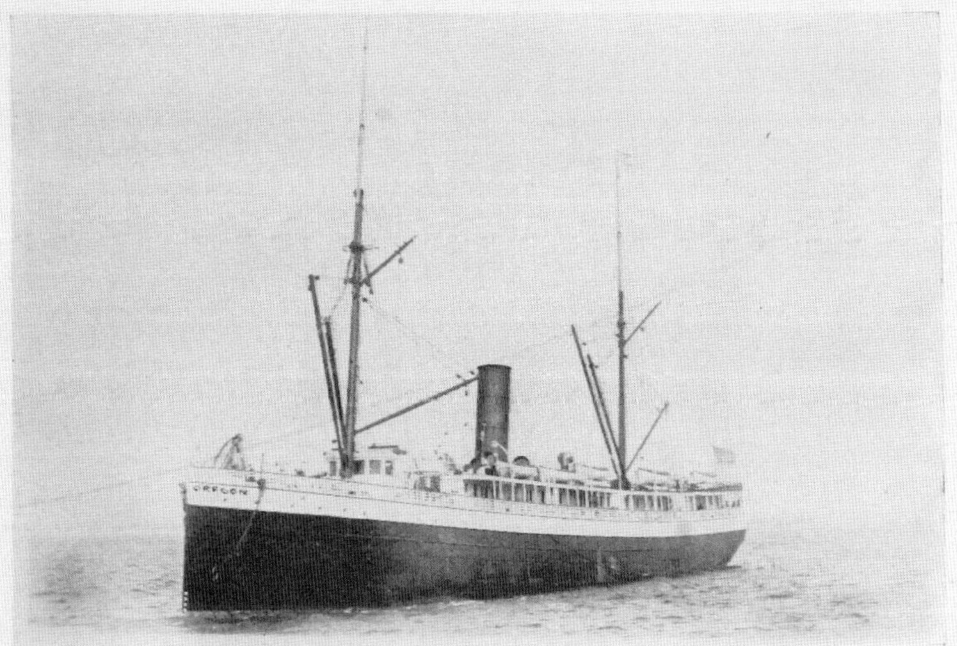

THE STEAMER OREGON.

WILL SAIL IN THE NOME TRADE.

The fine steamship Oregon will soon sail for Cape Nome and take part in the great rush soon to be on for the greatest gold country the West has ever seen. The Oregon will be the finest of the fleet to sail out of Seattle. She has a tonnage of 2500 tons and can accommodate 1000 passengers. She was purchased last fall by S. G. Simpson and associates and at once put in the hands of boiler makers and repairers so that now she is like a new ship. Over $50,000 has been expended in fitting her up especially for the Alaskan trade. F. A. Bell & Company, who will be the general agents of the ship, will also act as agents of the Irrawady, a steamship of 3500 tons, also to go in the Alaska service. In conjunction with these two big ships the steamer Discovery, having passenger accommodations for 100 persons, will be operated as a feeder between St. Michael, Cape Nome and Cape York. The big ships will sail from this city on a regular schedule, the Oregon sailing May 10 and the Irrawady on May 25. Besides these sailing vessels Bell & Company will be agents for the barks Mermaid and Vega and schooners Thos. F. Bayard, all three of which will engage in freighting to Alaska.

A new wharf is just being completed for the use of these vessels, just north of Madison Street. It will be 500 feet long and can accommodate any vessel which comes to this port. A railroad track will be laid along this dock so that freight can be loaded from the cars right into the ships, thus saving shippers both delay and expense in shipping goods to Alaskan points.

THE WHOLESALE DRUG TRADE.

The wholesale drug trade of Seattle practically lies in the hands of the Stewart & Holmes Drug Co. They

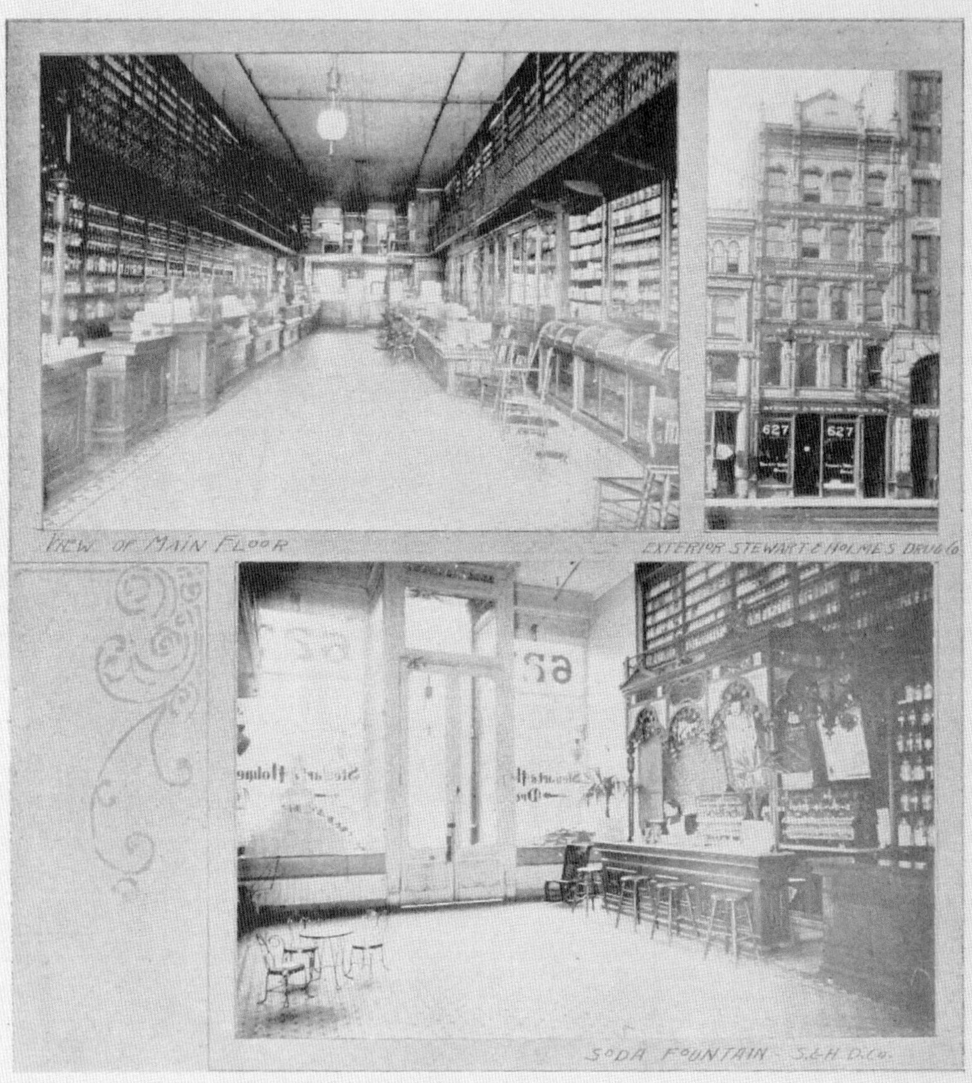

THE WHOLESALE AND RETAIL DRUG HOUSE OF STEWART & HOLMES DRUG CO.

The fleet of vessels which Bell & Company will be general agents for will undoubtedly become popular with people who will have business relations with Alaska.

occupy premises at No. 627 First avenue and utilize the six-story and two basement building 30x110 feet in size. Their establishment dates back to 1882, and shows a history of one continuous rise from that day to this. The volume of their trade at present reaches very enormous proportions, and last year showed an increase of 25 per cent over the previous year. The company, in addition to their wholesale trade, conduct one of the largest retail stores on the first floor of their premises to be found in the Northwest. The goods which are handled comprise every article known to the drug trade. In order to reach the territory in which they do business, four traveling men are employed, and they reach all parts of Washington, Eastern Oregon, Idaho and a portion of British Columbia and well up into Alaska. Forty people are given employment in the various departments of their business in this city. The officers of the company are: A. B. Stewart, president; H. E. Holmes, vice-president, and A. M. Stewart, secretary.

THE NORTHWEST FIXTURE CO.

What is probably the largest electrical supply concern on the Coast has its headquarters in this city. Reference is made to the Northwest Fixture Company, a picture of whose big store is shown in connection with this article. They occupy the entire four stories of the building at 1018 First Avenue and three floors in the Starr building across the street, making a total of 27,000 square feet of floor space utilized for salesroom, storage and manufactory. The company handle everything in the line of electrical machinery, such as elevators, dynamos, motors and electrical supplies in general. These include telephone outfits, electric wire and the thousand and one articles that are used in electrical construction.

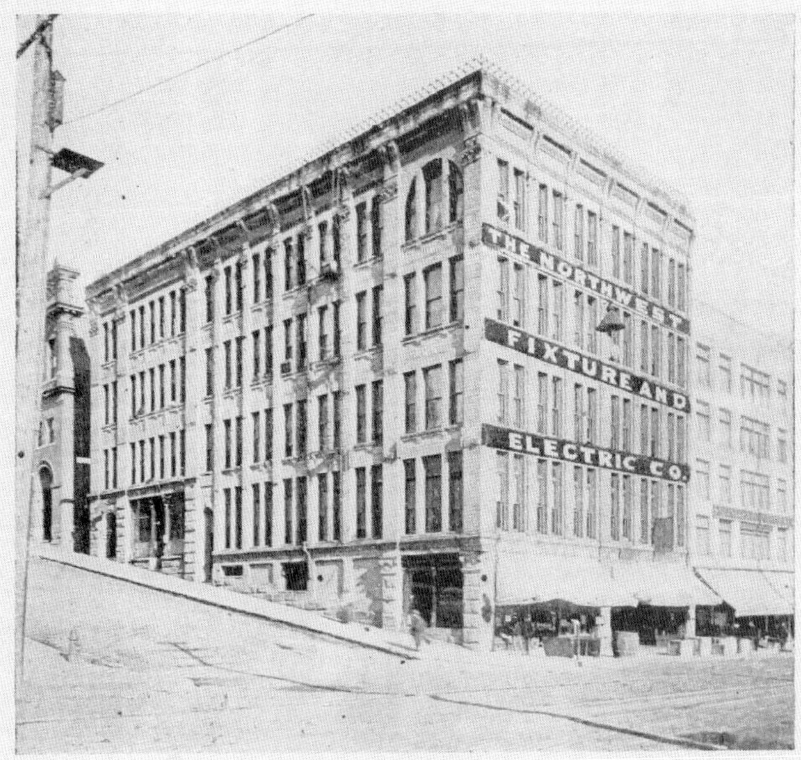

EXTERIOR OF BUILDING OCCUPIED BY THE NORTHWEST FIXTURE CO.

In their factory the company manufacture motors of all kinds, searchlights and many other articles in which electricity takes a prominent part. The company carry everything in the shape of electric and gas fixutres, their stock being the most complete in the Northwest and consists of only the very latest and most elaborate designs such as called for in artistic furnishings. So complete is their stock that it is unnecessary to call upon Eastern houses for goods of this character. They practically supply the entire state in the goods they handle, and their realizing the rapid improvements and necessities of this territory in their particular line of goods, considered it advisable to have an Eastern office to work in conjunction with the home establishment at Seattle and, therefore, while there he opened an office at 26 Cortlandt Street, Havemeyer building, and placed in charge Mr. C. J. Purdy, a man experienced in all lines of electrical works, as well as engines, boilers, etc., used in conjunction with electric lighting plants, and they are now prepared to take up with their Eastern correspondent all matters pertaining to

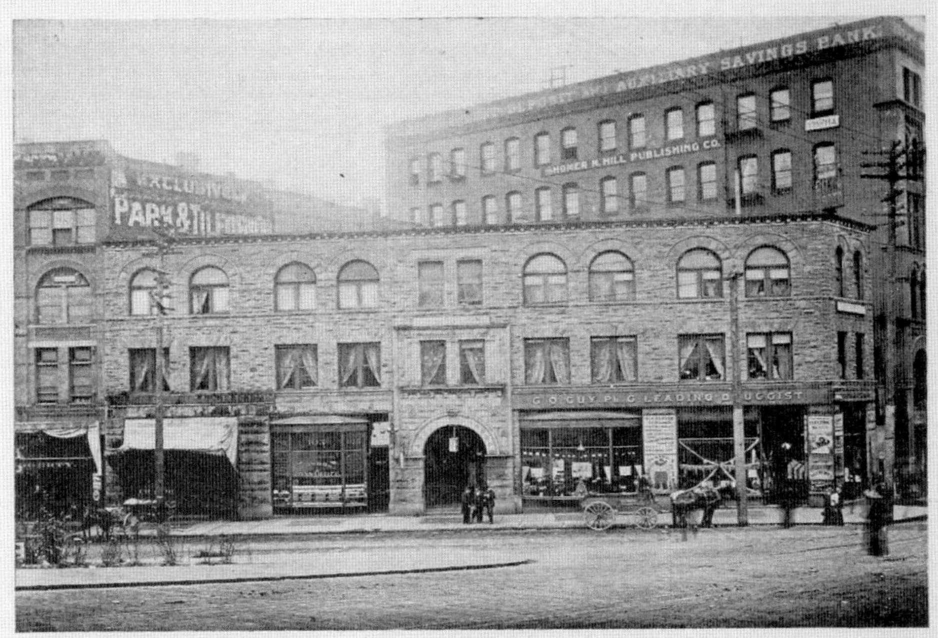

PROPERTY OF YESLER ESTATE, INCORPORATED.
Intersection Yesler Way and Second Avenue.

electrical machinery goes pretty generally over the entire Coast. They do, in this particular, a very extensive business with Alaska and the whole of the Northwest Territory.

Another article which they handle in extensive quantities are grates and mantels. Their stock of this line is very heavy and so varied in assortment as to enable them to furnish practically any design called for.

A. L. Kasson, president and manager of the Northwest Fixture Company, who recently returned from an extended trip throughout the East, and electrical supplies, such as station plants, railroad supplies and all other materials.

In their home office and show rooms, 1018 First Avenue, in addition to the enumerations made above, they carry a full line of incandescent lamps, glass and porcelain insulators, oak pins and brackets, marine and underwriters' wire, sockets, receptacles, continuous battery cells, push buttons, Edison-Lalande batteries, and all kinds of switches, incandescent gas lamps and supplies. All visitors always receive a cordial welcome.

They have recently added to their repair shop many improvements and are prepared to repair or rebuild any kind of electic dynamos, motors and arc lamps, and will send out competent electricians to oversee the construction or installing of electrical machinery or telephone stations.

This being essentially a Seattle enterprise, and as they are carrying a large and complete assortment in their various lines, the people of Seattle and the Northwest Territory cannot do better than to give them a call and get estimates on such work as they may require from time to time.

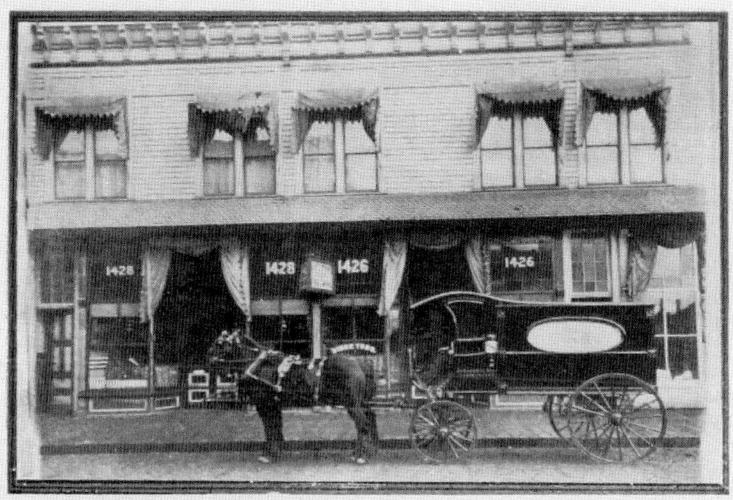

BUTTERWORTH & SONS, UNDERTAKERS.

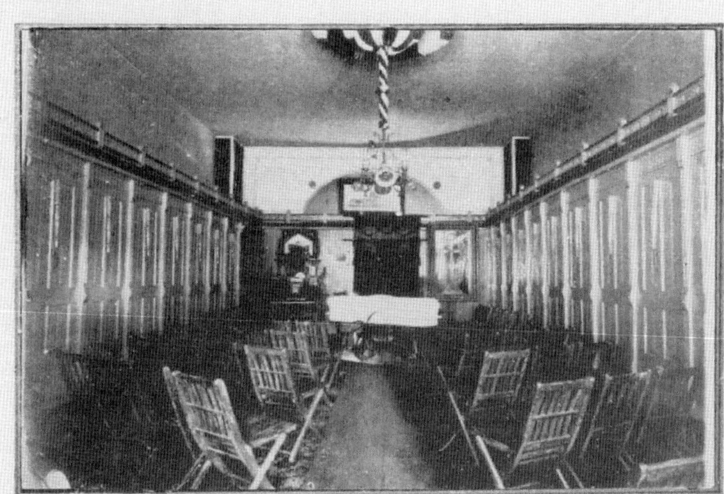

INTERIOR CHAPEL, BUTTERWORTH & SONS, UNDERTAKERS.

E. R. BUTTERWORTH & SONS.

The firm of E. R. Butterworth & Sons (incorporated), undertakers and expert embalmers, doing business at 1426-28 Third avenue, is one of the most reliable institutions of its kind on the Coast. The members of the firm are E. R. Butterworth and his three sons, G. M., Charles N. and Fred R. Butterworth. A valued employe and assistant in the working force is Nathan Anderson.

Mr. Butterworth and his sons have been in the undertaking business in Seattle during the past eight years and have been residents of the state for eighteen years. They come of good old New England stock. Both management and detail of the business is attended to by the working force enumerated. The reputation as skilled embalmers which this company has earned is not excelled by any house in the West. Their expert embalming is performed either at their establishment or at the residence of their patrons, as may be desired. The company leaves nothing undone that can add to the efficiency of their service.

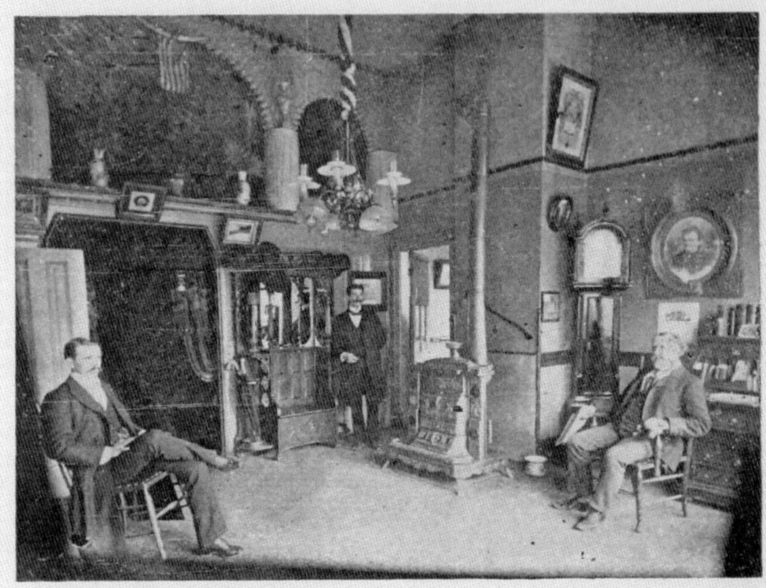

OFFICE OF BUTTERWORTH & SONS, UNDERTAKERS.

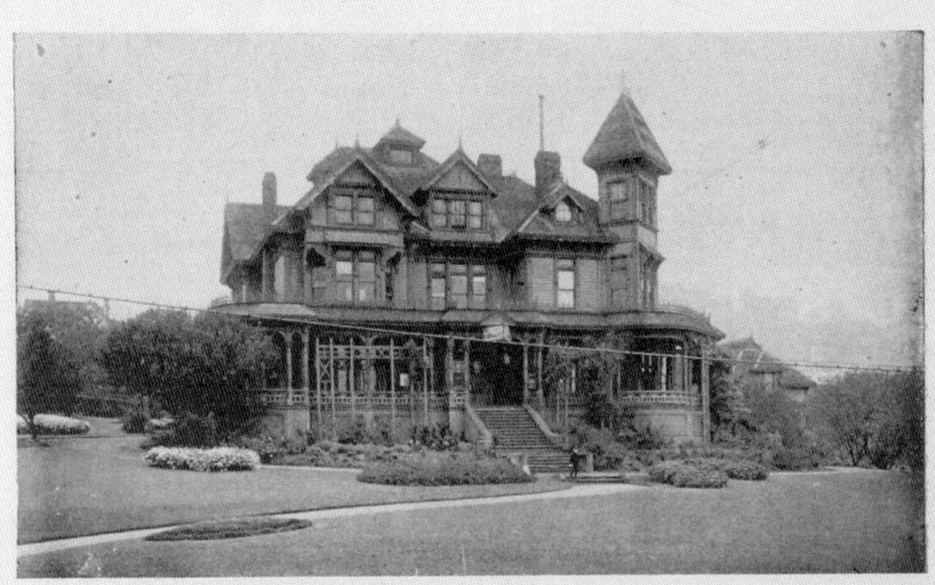

THE PUBLIC LIBRARY BUILDING.
The property belongs to the Yesler Estate, Incorporated,

PROPERTY OF YESLER ESTATE, INCORPORATED.

The Yesler Estate, Incorporated, owns four very conspicuous pieces of Seattle real estate. It comprises the Pioneer Building, the building occupied by the Scandinavian-American Bank, the three-story stone structure at intersection of Yesler and Second avenue and the property which is now used as the Public Library. Illustrations are shown of each of these. The officers of the Yesler Estate, Incorporated, are as follows: G. Poncin, President; Morris McMicken, secretary; Jacob Furth, treasurer, and J. B. McDougal, vice-president. With C. F. Munday, these gentlemen comprise the directors.

SOME WELL KNOWN MEMBERS OF THE LEGAL PROFESSION.

JUDGE THOMAS BURKE.

Judge Thomas Burke of Seattle was born in Clinton County, New York, in 1849. From the time he was 11 years old he cared for himself and provided the means for his own education by farm work between terms of school, and later as a school teacher. He graduated at the Ypsilanti (Michigan) Seminary in 1870 and attended the Ann Arbor University for two years, during which time he also studied law. He was admitted to the bar at Marshall, Mich., in 1874, and filled the office of City Attorney at that place for one year.

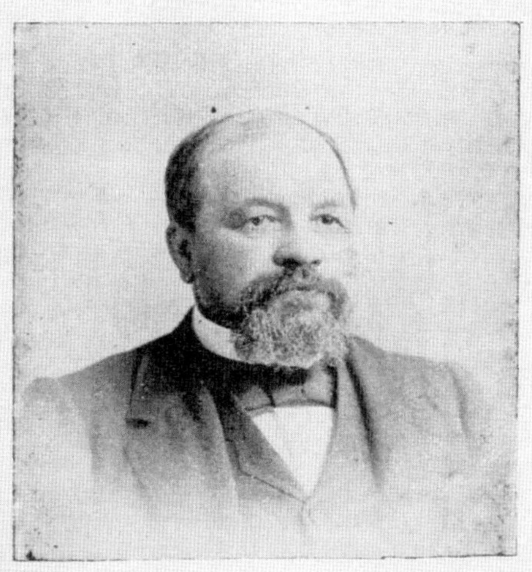

JUDGE THOMAS BURKE.

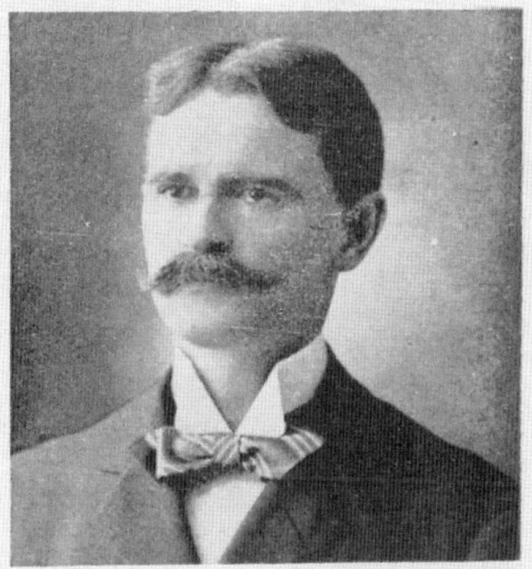

THOMAS F. SHEPHERD.
Of the law firm of Burke, Shepherd & McGilvra

Young Burke came to Seattle in 1875, when it was a struggling city of but 1200 inhabitants, and at once formed a law partnership with Judge John J. McGilvra, then United States District Attorney for the Territory. In 1876 Mr. Burke was elected Probate Judge of King County and reelected in 1878. He was a member of the Territorial Board of Education and chairman of the Board of Education for Seattle. The Judge was a prime mover in the adoption by Seattle of the best and most modern style of school buildings. He was a leader in the Democratic party in King County and the Territory between 1881 and 1883, and was nominated for Congress. Although he received a large complimentary vote and ran far ahead of his ticket, he failed in being elected as he belonged to the minority party.

In 1887 he was one of the chief organizers and promoters of the Seattle, Lake Shore & Eastern Railroad. After 135 miles of the road were built and in operation it was absorbed by the Northern Pacific. Judge Burke remained in the directorate and as attorney for the road till its purchase by the Northern Pacific. He also assisted in the organization of the Seattle & Montana Railroad and worked successfully for the selection by the Great Northern Railroad of Seattle for its Western terminus. He was retained as counsel for the Washington department of the Great Northern Railroad, which position he still fills.

In 1887-88 two chief justices of the Territory died in quick succession and, there being a great plethora of business on the docket, the members of the bar petitioned President Cleveland to appoint Judge Burke to the bench made vacant by death. He was forthwith appointed, but accepted with the express understanding that he might resign when the bulk of the work was completed. His resignation came in 1889, he having served with honor to himself and to the eminent satisfaction of the bar and public.

The Judge has been a constant investor in real estate since settling in Seattle, and has made a number of valuable improvements, the crowning one being the completion, in 1891, of the magnificent seven-story brick and stone structure at the corner of Second Avenue and Marion Street, the Burke Block, costing $260,000.

Judge Burke was married in 1880 to Miss Carrie E. McGilvra, the daughter of his old law partner, Hon. J. J. McGilvra. Throughout his long residence in Seattle the Judge has been an active factor in the city's growth and welfare. He has had a number of law partners—Judge McGilvra, U. M. Raisen and G. Morris Haller. He is now a member of the firm of Burke, Shepard & McGilvra, with offices in the Burke Block.

BALLINGER, RONALD & BATTLE.

The law firm of Ballinger, Ronald & Battle was formed in September, 1897, by R. A. Ballinger, J. T. Ronald and Alfred Battle. They handle a large general practice in both the State and Federal Courts. Each individual member of the firm was distinguished in his profession before the formation of the partnership. Mr. Ronald is an ex-mayor of Seattle, ex-prosecuting attorney of King County and holds an enviable position as a criminal lawyer as well as a general practitioner. Mr. Ballinger has served with credit on the Superior bench in the State, while Mr. Battle has acted as Superior Judge pro tem in a number of very important cases.

The firm ranks among the strongest in the State. Their suite of offices in the Mutual Life Building is not excelled.

Judge R. A. Ballinger.

Judge R. A. Ballinger is a graduate of Williams College, Massachusetts. He afterward lived in Chicago, in which city he studied law and was admitted to the bar. For a while after his admission he practiced law in the State of Illinois, and subsequently moved to Alabama, where he engaged in the practice of his profession. In 1899 he located at Port Townsend, Wn. Here, by reason of his ability and cool discernment of facts, he quickly established a reputation as one of the ablest members of the bar. In 1892 he was elected as Judge of the Superior Court of the State of Washington for Jefferson County, and, by his good judgment, his aptness and his natural grasp of the salient points of the proposition involved, he quickly stepped to the front, became known as one of the ablest and safest judges on the bench of the State. No judge in the State can point to fewer reverses than Judge Ballinger. He was a model judge, and was frequently requested to hold court in different counties of the State. By this means he became widely and favorably known both to the bar and to business men. Declining a renomination in 1896, he transferred his residence in 1897 to Seattle, where he found a broader field for the display of his magnificent talents. He is an indefatigable worker. Notwithstanding the arduous duties imposed by his office and the great research and diligence he brought to bear in arriving at his decisions, he found time during his term to study and thoroughly familiarize himself with the Community Property system—a system prevailing only in the Western States. He is a ready and strong writer. His diction and style of expression is unexcelled, and the dryest subject, under his pen, becomes interesting reading. It was while serving his term as judge that he wrote his work, "Ballinger's Community Property," the only book extant on the subject. It has been reviewed by the ablest minds of the country and has stood the test. He is quoted by all the Supreme Courts of the community property States as extensively as any text book writer since its production. After completing this work, which of itself is a vast undertaking, this tireless student undertook the compilation and annotation of the Statutes of the State of Washington. He compiled what is readily acknowledged by the bench and bar to be one of the best annotated codes in existence. The last Legislature of the State of Washington adopted "Ballinger's Annotated Code and Statutes" as the official code of the State of Washington. After completing this work he was offered by one of the largest law book publishing houses of the country, a large sum of money to write a work on "Federal Procedure," but he declined this flattering offer in order that he might enter upon the practice of his profession. Upon entering actively into this practice, he immediately went to the head and took rank with the ablest and best lawyers of the Northwest; in fact, it is doubtful whether, as a practitioner in the Admiralty and Maritime Courts, he has a superior at the bar. He is yet but in the prime of life, being only 40 years of age. If the past success is a criterion of the future, the prospect for Judge Ballinger is a very promising one.

Alfred Battle.

Alfred Battle was born in Texas, where he studied law and was admitted to the bar. He came to Seattle in 1888. The great fire of 1889 wiped out most of his fine library and office furniture, which was uninsured. Following the fire, the remodeling and regrading of streets in Seattle involved the municipality in endless and heavy litigation and Mr. Battle was employed by the city to assist the Corporation Counsel. One of the first cases of this kind was that brought by the Seattle Gas and Electric Light Company vs. the city to recover $100,000 for damages alleged to have been sustained by reason of the change in street grading. Mr. Battle won this suit for the city. He next won the suit for the city brought by the Oregon Improvement Company involving the right and title to a portion of certain street property. Other cases, including those arising out of the adoption of the Freeholders' Charter, came up in rapid succession, in all of which Mr. Battle took a conspicuous part, and resulted in his becoming the logical candidate for Corporation Counsel in the election following. He did not seek office, but, accepting nomination, he made the race, but notwithstanding he received several hundred more votes than the combined votes of the combined parties (Democrats and Municipal League) nominating him, the entire Republican ticket was elected. During his ten years' practice at the Seattle bar he has been employed in many important suits, among which may be mentioned the notable suit of Dexter Horton & Co. vs. Sayward, involving the Port Madison Mill property; the franchise of the consolidated street railways in Seattle, in which he was employed by the petitioners.

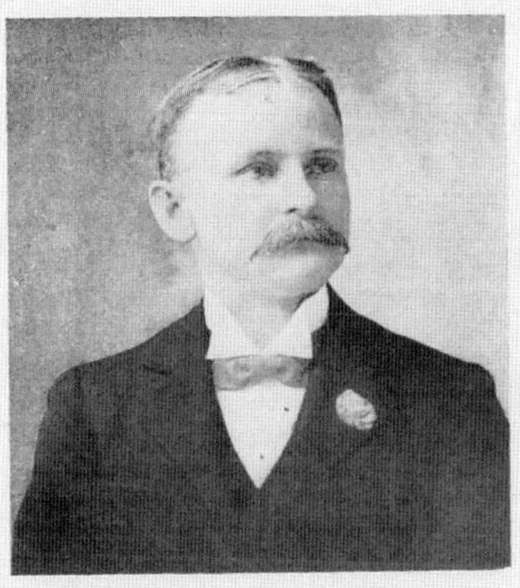

ALFRED BATTLE.

Beginning with the month of February, 1896, Mr. Battle represented possibly four-fifths of the litigated cases and proceedings relative to the Seattle tide lands. Since 1896, in fact, he has made a specialty of the tide land litigation, which, together with corporation and municipal legislation, has constituted the larger part of his practice.

J. T. Ronald.

J. T. Ronald has been a resident of Seattle since 1882, when the city had but about 4000 inhabitants. He came to Washington from California, where he had been engaged in school teaching for seven years, during which period he studied law and was admitted to the bar. Mr. Ronald was born in Missouri and is a typical Missourian, standing six feet three and one-half inches in height, with erect figure and open countenance. When he goes in for a legal scrap it is no "fake," but must be to the finish. He has been engaged in some of the longest and hardest fought cases that have ever been litigated in King County courts.

In 1883 Mr. Ronald was appointed Deputy Prosecuting Attorney for the Third Judicial District of Washington Territory, which comprised all the counties north of Pierce in Puget Sound. It was during this period that he made a record for himself in clearing out vice and crime in various forms. He was in 1884 elected to the office of Prosecuting Attorney for the counties of King, Kitsap and Snohomish, and again re-elected in 1886. He was incumbent of this office during the troublous times attending the "Chinese riots" and murders of Chinamen in King County, Squak Valley. The reform elements of Seattle elected him Mayor of the city in 1892, which office he held with credit for one term. Mr. Ronald was at the state convention of Democrats at Olympia in 1892 nominated for Congress, but refused to accept, as he considered an injustice had been done King County in regard to the Lake Washington Canal. Mr. Ronald is one of the leading members today at the King County bar.

L. C. GILMAN.

L. C. Gilman of the law firm of Preston, Carr & Gilman, with offices in the Pioneer building, occupies a very prominent position among the legal fraternity of this state. Few men have a larger law practice or are more highly regarded than Mr. Gilman. This position has been entirely created by himself since taking up his residence in this city. He moved to Seattle in 1884 from Bangor, Maine. He received his education at the Maine Central Institute. His legal education was received in New York. At the time he arrived in this city there was but little here, save a large amount of energy on the part of those already here to do something. Mr. Gilman was not behind the others in energy, and began to labor as hard as any one for his new home. That it counted goes without saying. As a public-spirited citizen he deserves a full measure of credit and can take no little pride in what has been done by this city during the sixteen years he has lived here. In 1887 he was elected city attorney, a position which he filled with credit to himself. In 1893 he was a member of the legislature from this county and was considered to be one of the most active and valuable members from this county. The present firm of which he is a member was organized in 1897. Mr. Gilman has, in addition to a very general practice, a very heavy amount of business for corporations to look after, and is probably one of the most active members of the bar in this county today.

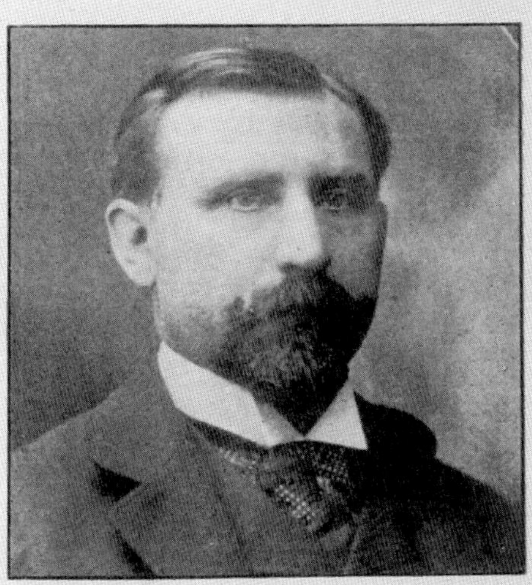

L. C. GILMAN.

S. H. PILES.

S. H. Piles, who is the senior member of the law firm of Piles, Donworth & Howe, who have offices in the Burke block, this city, has lived in Seattle since 1886. He first removed to Puget Sound in 1883 and took up his residence at Snohomish. Mr. Piles is a native of Kentucky, in which State he was admitted to practice law. In 1895 he was appointed general counsel for the Pacific Coast Steamship Company, now called the Pacific Coast Company. Prior to his appointment he was in partnership with J. T. Ronald, one of the distinguished members of the Seattle bar, and in April of last year the

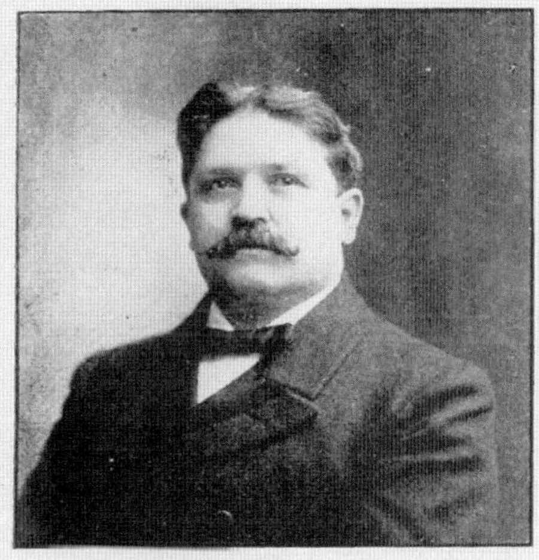

S. H. PILES.

firm of Piles, Donworth & Howe was organized, and one of the strongest legal firms in the State of Washington was thereby perfected. While Mr. Piles himself has never held nor sought office of any kind, he has always been an ardent and active politician, and none stands higher in the councils of the Republican party today than he does. He is a man of very strong personality and has few equals among the strong legal force which constitutes the bar of this State.

JOHN P. FAY.

Hon. John P. Fay occupies an enviable position among the prominent lawyers of the State. As an eloquent public speaker, Mr. Fay has few peers in logic and oratory. While he does a general law business, his practice is principally confined to corporation matters. In the short space of time since coming to Seattle—the spring of 1899—Mr. Fay has built up a large and lucrative law business, and has prospered accordingly. He is a native of the Bay State and was born in 1861. After graduating at Phillips Exeter Academy of New Hampshire, he took a course at Harvard College and later a special law course at the Harvard Law School. He was admitted to the bar in Massachusetts in 1885. Mr. Fay has practiced in the Supreme Courts of the States of Massachusetts, Nevada, Oregon and Washington, as well as in the United States Supreme Court. He was clerk of the Nevada Senate in the winter of 1889.

In politics Mr. Fay was a Republican until the silver question compelled him, in loyalty to his convictions, to join the Fusion forces, where he became a bold and aggressive leader from the very start. In the Legislature following the success of the Fusion forces, Mr. Fay's name was frequently mentioned in connection with the United States Senatorship, although at no time did he place himself on record as a candidate. Later Governor Rogers appointed him a regent of the University of Washington, which position he held until a difference with the executive led to his retirement. Mr. Fay is credited by men of all political creeds with having the courage of his convictions, for had he chosen to remain a member of the

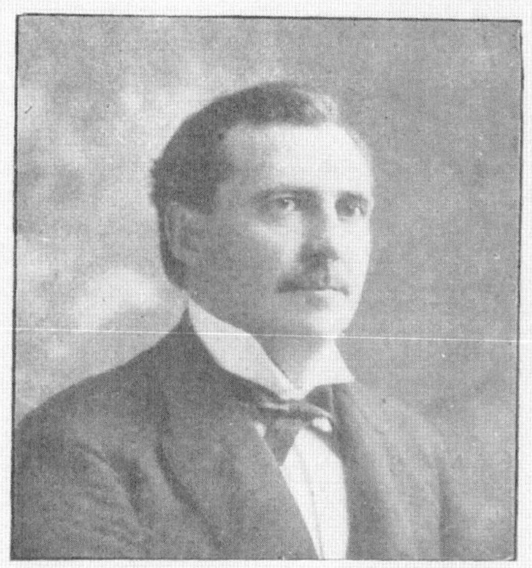

JOHN P. FAY.

dominant party in the Nation and State he could have easily and quickly attained to high political distinction.

JUDGE MILO A. ROOT.

Judge Milo A. Root is one of the best known lawyers in the state. He came to the Territory of Washington in 1883, entering the practice of law at Olympia, where he was subsequently twice elected Probate Judge and twice Prosecuting Attorney. In 1897 he formed a law partnership with ex-Chief Justice Hoyt and located in Seattle. He is now by himself in offices in the New York Block. That his legal career has

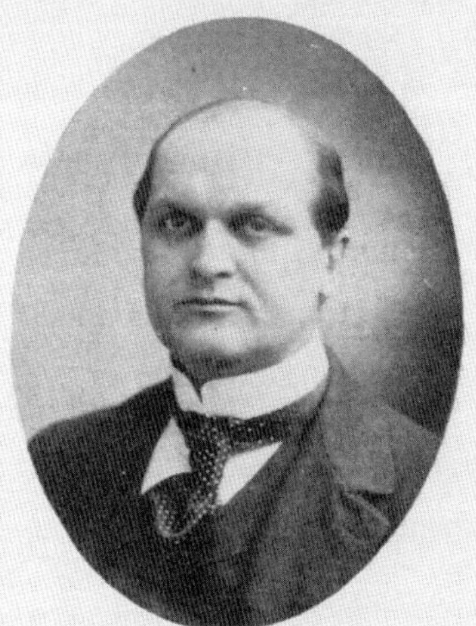

JUDGE MILO A. ROOT.

been a successful one is abundantly evidenced by the court records and published law reports.

Judge Root was born in Bureau County, Ill., Jan. 22, 1863, removing to the State of New York in 1876, where he was educated principally at Albion and Albany. In 1890 he married Miss Anna Lonsdale, a daughter of the late Dr. R. H. Lonsdale, who was one of Washington Territory's earliest pioneers and a friend and official associate of Gen. Isaac Stevens, first Governor of the territory.

Judge Root is a member of several fraternal orders; a Congregationalist in church matters, and a Republican in politics.

JAY C. ALLEN.

Jay C. Allen, who occupies a prominent position with the legal fraternity of Seattle as a member of the law firm of Allen & Allen, with offices in the Dexter Horton Bank building, has probably made as rapid rise and pronounced success for himself as any young man now prominently before the public. He was born July 3, 1869, at the Kentucky Military Institute, near Frankfort, Kentucky, which was founded in 1846 by his grandfather, R. T. P. Allen. When quite young his family moved to Florida. He afterwards attended the Military Institute, from which he graduated in the year 1885, taking the course of bachelor of arts. His standing was second in a class of about forty, and he was the youngest of the number. His grade, however, was a fraction over 9.8 of a possible 10. After his graduation he entered the law office of his father, where he studied law continuously until 1889, when he removed to this city. Shortly after his arrival here he was appointed deputy sheriff for King County by John H. McGraw, the then sheriff, and remained in such position until the expiration of Mr. McGraw's term of office. In 1890 he was admitted to practice law, and at once formed a copartnership with his father, John

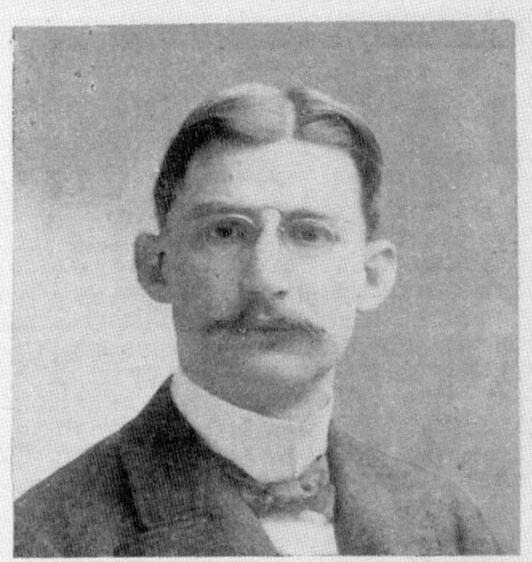

JAY C. ALLEN.

H. Allen, and John Powell, under the firm name of Allen & Powell. In 1897 Mr. Powell retired and the firm continued under the name of Allen & Allen as at present. Mr. Allen is a member of the Superior and Supreme Courts and of the United States Circuit Court, and the District Courts of this State and of the United States Circuit Court of Appeals of the Ninth Circuit. In politics he is a Democrat, and has been quite active in his party's interests since coming to this city. He is a member of the Knights of Pythias, Red Men and Foresters, and is one of the charter members of the Seattle Athletic Club. During February of the present year he was married to Miss Jeanne M. Lynch of this city.

WILMON TUCKER.

Very few of the younger members of the Seattle bar occupy a more conspicuous place than does Wilmon Tucker, who has offices in Dexter Horton & Co.'s Bank Building. His practice is of the very best class and of such a character that it gives him very considerable prestige.

Mr. Tucker was born on a farm in Crawford County, Iowa, June 17th, 1868. He was educated in the public schools of Iowa and in the Normal School at Shenandoah, of the same State. After attending the Normal School for a period of two years, he took up teaching in the public schools for some little time. In 1887 he entered the law office of R. Show Van of Denison, Ia., where he studied for a year. In 1888 he went to Aurora, Neb., and entered the office of E. J. Hainer, one of Nebraska's leading lawyers, and one of her late Congressmen. In 1890 he moved to Seattle and entered the office of John H. Elden, and on December 9th, 1892, was admitted to practice by the courts of this State. He has always had to make his own way and began life for himself at the age of 14, and from that day to this has had to rely entirely upon his own unaided efforts. Since his admission in 1892, he has been actively engaged in practice, and has built up a very lucrative business. Two years ago he formed a partnership with Ivan L. Hyland, late City Attorney of Ballard, a partnership which still exists. Mr. Tucker has been leading counsel in the famous damage case of Taylor vs. City of Ballard, and has conducted a great many other important cases in King County.

He was married on October 14, 1897, to Miss Lilian Snoke, and his residence is on Thirty-fourth Avenue, overlooking the lake. Politically he is a Democrat. He has always been very active in the councils of the party since he became old enough to vote. He attaches more importance to business, however, than to politics, and as a consequence can be found pretty constantly attending to his own affairs.

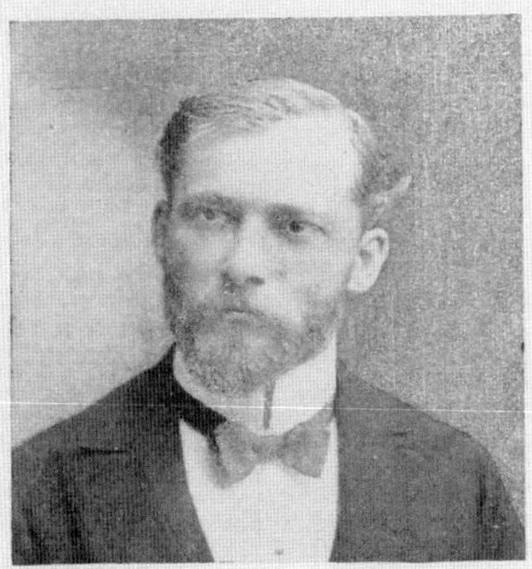

WILMON TUCKER.

JOHN K. BROWN.

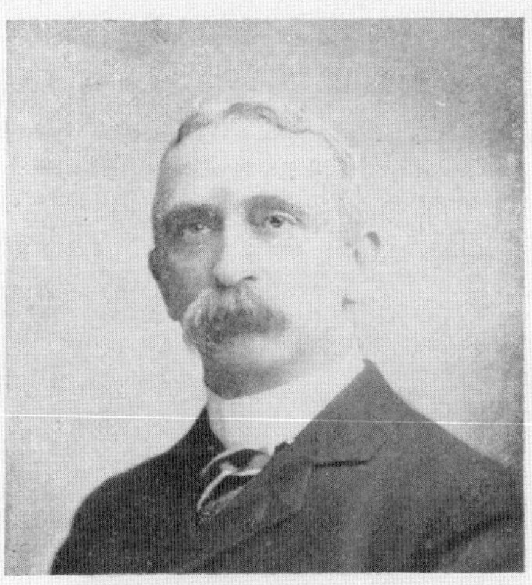

JOHN K. BROWN.

John K. Brown was born December 14th, 1852, at Buffalo, N. Y. He attended private schools in that city until he entered Yale University, where he graduated in 1872. He studied law in Buffalo in the offices of Messrs. Williams & Potter, and was admitted to the bar at the general term of the

Fourth Department of the Supreme Court of the State of New York in October, 1876. He immediately went to Virginia City, Nev., where he resided until 1882. While in Virginia City he was engaged in the practice of his profession and held the offices of Justice of the Peace and Assistant District Attorney. After a short residence in San Francisco he returned to Buffalo, where he remained until October, 1889, when he came to Seattle, where he has since resided and been engaged in the practice of his profession. In March, 1896, he was elected Corporation Counsel of the city and served as such for two years. Among cases of importance in which he has been engaged may be mentioned the litigation resulting from the failure of the Spring Hill Water Company to pay its bonds when its plant was sold to the city; the case of Faulkner against the city of Seattle, in which was finally determined the validity of the ordinance authorizing the construction of the Cedar River water system, and the cases in the Supreme Court of the United States involving the validity of the taxes levied by the city upon shares of national banks.

DANIEL KELLEHER.

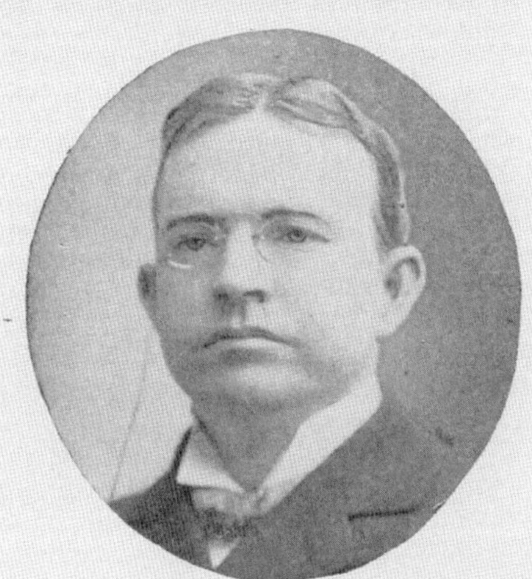

Daniel Kelleher.

Daniel Kelleher, a member of the prominent law firm of Bausman, Kelleher & Emory, was born in Middleboro, Mass., February 5th, 1864, and educated in the public schools of that State. He was prepared at the Bridgewater High School for Harvard College, which latter institution he entered in 1881. After spending four years at Harvard he graduated in the class of 1885. He then went to Syracuse, N. Y., where, as a private tutor, he

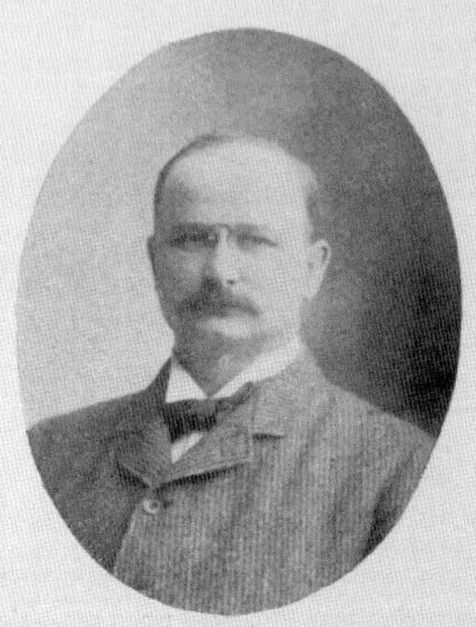

Will H. Parry.

Councilman-at-large and ex-City Comptroller. Mr. Parry is now associated with the large shipbuilding concern of Moran Bros. Co.

prepared boys for Harvard. At Syracuse he was admitted to the bar. In March, 1890, he left Syracuse for Seattle, and in March, 1890, formed a law partnership with G. Meade Emory, a graduate of Cornell University, who came West with him from Syracuse. A year later the firm took in as its senior partner Frederick Bausman, who received his legal education at the Harvard Law School. In the past ten years the firm has been engaged in very active and important business and has conducted much important litigation in the different courts of the State. Mr. Kelleher takes an active interest in political affairs and is a member of many of the prominent social clubs of the city. Though taking a prominent part in the councils of the Democratic party, he is averse to holding political office of any kind. The firm have built for themselves a large and lucrative law practice.

"MORRISON'S."

J. W. Morrison's palace of entertainment, at 621-623 First Avenue, Seattle, has no peer on the Pacific Coast in point of elegance and completeness in appointment and furnishings. No one who has viewed the beautifully frescoed, spacious billiard parlors and magnificent bar will attempt to controvert this statement. "Morrison's" is truly an ideal in high art and beauty of design.

"Jim" Morrison, proprietor of this high-class establishment, made his stake in Alaska, where his wide acquaintance and universal popularity went hand in haud. He has unbounded faith in Seattle and hence has spared neither wealth nor effort in making his place the leading resort for gentlemen in the city, and, for that matter, in any city in the West. A leading fresco artist of Berlin, Germany, has drawn liberally on his genius and skill in decorating the walls, ceiling and vestibule, where may be seen realistic paintings of Puget Sound and Alaska scenery, done in oil, all harmoniously grouped and blended. The six billiard and pool tables are the finest in the city. The bar is a wealth of massive carving in oak and mahogany, French plate mirrors and the latest designs in cut glass. Only the choicest brands of liquors and cigars, served by competent mixologists, are to be found at Morrison's. A splendid feature of the establishment is that no cards, boxes or kindred accessories find a place therein, the aim on the part of the proprietor being to preserve the gilt-edged reputation

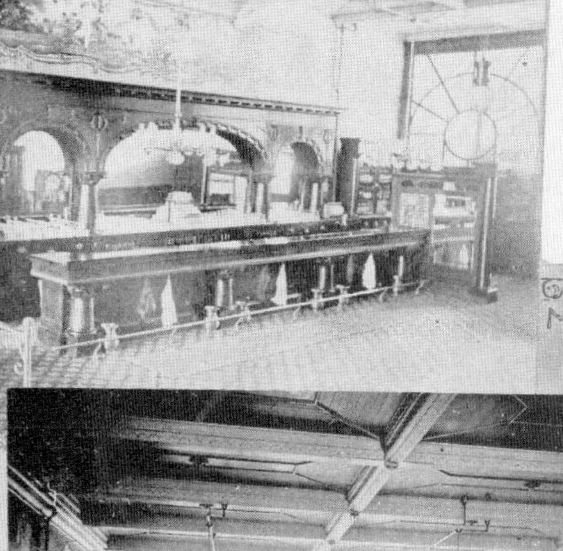

TWO FINE INTERIOR VIEWS OF "MORRISON'S," THE SWELL PLACE OF SEATTLE.

which the establishment has so justly earned. A raised dais along two sides of the billiard parlor on which are rows of elegant oak easy chairs, afford gentlemen an excellent opportunity to watch the tables and players. One must see Morrison's to gain a conception of its many admirable features, as a pen picture must fall far short of doing the subject justice. The accompanying views give but a faint idea of the artistic features of the place.

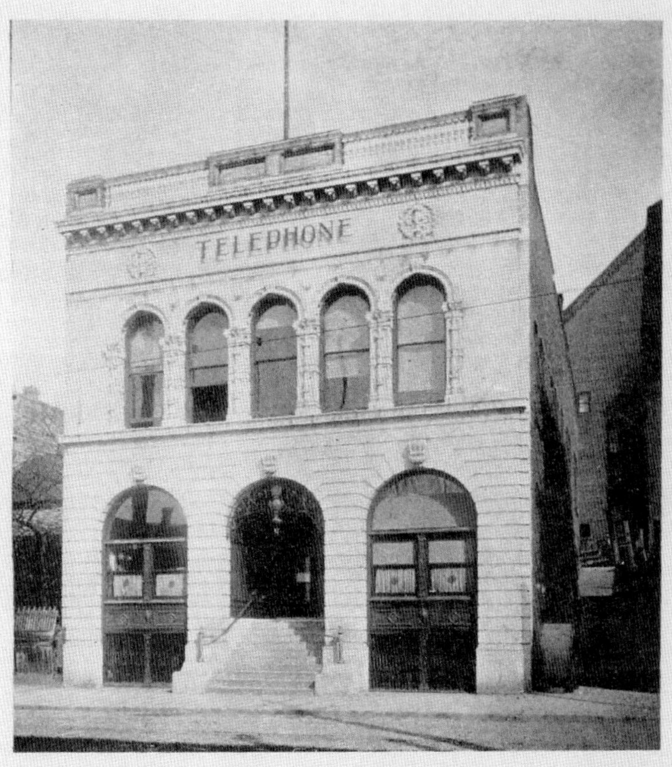

BUILDING OF THE SUNSET TELEPHONE AND TELEGRAPH CO.
Third Avenue, Seattle.

DR. EMIL BORIES.

Emil Bories of Seattle, Wash., son of Herrman and Rosa (Freiman) Bories, grandson of Joachin Bories, was born July 12, 1852, at Auval, Province of Bohemia, Austria. He received his elementary education in the public schools at Sacramento, Cal., and Portland, Or., and in private schools of San Francisco; later he attended the Portland Academy, under Prof. T. M. Gatch, and received the degree of A. M. from the Society of American Literature and Arts, Buffalo, N. Y., in 1891. He commenced the study of medicine in 1875 at McMinnville, Or., under Dr. James T. Augur of that place, and Dr. H. R. Littlefield at Dayton, Wash. He attended four courses of medical lectures, three winter and one summer, at the Bellevue Hospital Medical College, New York City, and at the medical department of the University of Vermont, receiving from the latter institution the degree of M. D. in 1885. He immediately located in practice at Dayton, Wash., remaining there six years, and then removed to Snohomish, Wash.; but the climate, not agreeing with him, he returned after six months to Dayton, and in 1894 removed to Seattle. He served throughout the smallpox epidemics of Columbia County, Wash., in 1880, and along the Northern Pacific Railroad in Montana during its construction in 1881. He is a member of the Inland Empire Medical Society, State Medical Society of Washington, American Medical Association, National Association of Railway Sur-

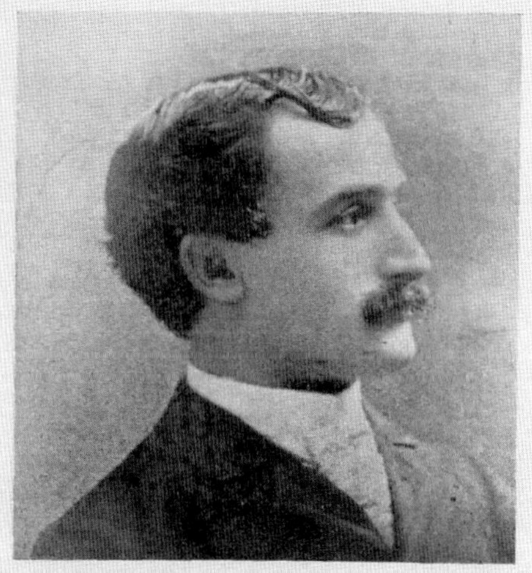

DR. EMIL BORIES.

geons, Pharmaceutical Association of Washington, registered pharmacist State of Washington, Delta Mu Medical Society of Burlington, Vt., and is a medical licentiate of the States of Oregon, Vermont and California. He was resident surgeon of Washington & Columbia River Railway, ex-County Coroner, ex-City Health Officer, lecturer on hygiene, physiology, chemistry and anatomy, Dayton High School, and is medical examiner for several insurance associations and companies. He is a member of the Masonic fraternit, including the higher degrees, Odd Fellows, Knights of Pythias and several other secret societies, and is special correspondent for several literary and current publications of Washington and Oregon. He was a physician for Columbia County, Wash. Dr. Bories is the author of a paper on "Permanganate of Potassium in Rattlesnake Poisoning,'" Medical World, September, 1891; "Cocaine Hydrochlorate in Sea-sickness," Southern California Practitioner, June, 1886; "Apomorphia and Antipyrine in Asthma," Ibid., July, 1888; "Electrolysis in the Treatment of Warts," Philadelphia, October, 1888, and numerous short articles and various formulae which have been published in the medical journals. He has also written a brochure on the impurities of drinking water. In 1891 he invented a stethoscope, intended, with the aid of electricity, to distinguish the sounds of the heart and other important organs more clearly; the instrument is not ready for general use. Dr. Bories married, October 14, 1890, at Baker City, Or., Miss Carrie Gundersheimer of that city. He has one child, a son, Henry Villard Bories. In 1895 he was appointed lecturer on Pharmacognosy, Materia Medica and Toxicology in the Department of Pharmacy, State University, and was appointed in 1897 quarantine officer for the port of Seattle. He is also medical examiner for several fraternal societies.

J. D. LOWMAN.

When J. D. Lowman came to Seattle in 1877 Seattle was rather an insignificant place. His uncle was the

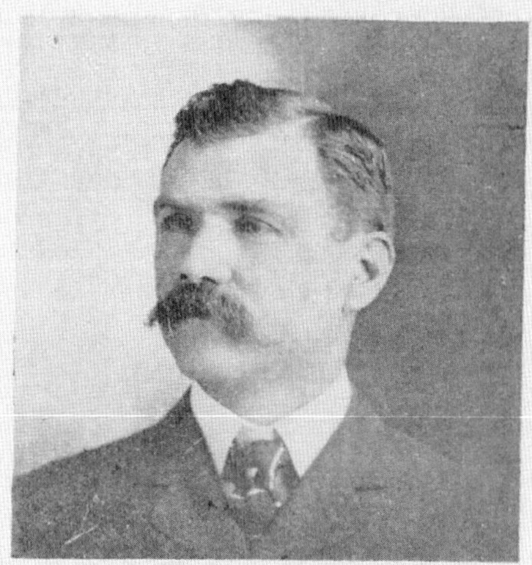

J. D. LOWMAN

late H. L. Yesler, and after Mr. Lowman arrived here he took a position on Yesler's wharf, and looked after that institution for a period of two or three years, in the service of his uncle. At that time Yesler's wharf was practically the only landing place in Seattle, and all ships and all the passengers from points on the Sound, to and from San Francisco, and the East landed at this dock. Subsequently he purchased a half interest in the book and stationery business of Mr. Pumphrey and the firm was changed to Pumphrey & Lowman. After remaining together for two years he purchased Mr. Pumphrey's interest and conducted the business alone for a couple of years. In 1884, at the time Seattle began to grow very vigorously, he organized the Lowman & Hanford Printing and Stationery Company, and still remains at its head. It is now one of the biggest stationery and printing concerns on the Coast. In 1885 he took active charge of H. L. Yesler's business, and was compelled to devote a great deal of time and attention to it, as the affairs were considerably involved. Through his efforts, however, the various interests were straightened out and the business put in a very satisfactory shape. In 1892 he organized the Seattle Theatre Company, and is still at its head as president. He was also one of the owners of the Union Trunk Line Street Railway, which runs up James Street and thence out Broadway to the City Park, South to Beacon Hill and east to Madrona Park, one of the most considerable street car lines in the city. Subsequently he did much towards bringing about a consolidation of the various interests, which have since been consummated. It was he who did much towards carrying the Trunk Line through the depression which followed the panic of 1893, a period when nearly every enterprise here had a precarious existence.

At the present time Mr. Lowman is looking after various large interests of his own, as well as considerable real estate matters which are entrusted to the firm of Lowman & Pelly, and for that purpose keeps an office in conjunction with Mr. Pelly in the Pioneer building.

G. W. STETSON

G. W. Stetson, president of the Stetson-Post Mill Company, has a personal history very closely identified with the growth of Seattle, and one which is more than ordinarily interesting. He came West in 1864 from Waldo County, Penobscot Bay, Maine. He had learned the millwright and bridge building business from his father, with whom he worked up to the time of his leaving home in that year. In following the advice of Horace Greeley, he landed in that year in Portland, Oregon, and his first undertaking was the building of the Ash Street dock for the old O. S. N. Company, and although but 19 years of age, he was given charge of the work and remained there until it was completed. The dock today is one of the considerable institutions which line the Willamette River in the metropolis of Oregon. When this was completed he drifted to Puget Sound, and having a thorough knowledge as a millwright, he secured a position with the Puget Sound Mill Company at Port Gamble, then, as now, owned by Cyrus Walker and Pope & Talbot. At that time mills were few and far between and practically the life which grew

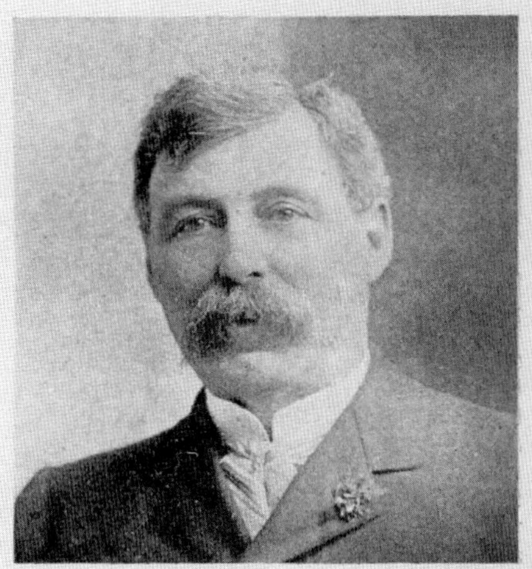

G. W. STETSON.

up about them was all there was to be found on Puget Sound. Mr. Stetson remained with the company eleven years, seven of which he was foreman of the mill. This brought him up to the year 1875, when with the very small capital which he was enabled to save he started a sash and door factory on what is now Yesler Way in this city. After running it a year, or in 1876, the mill was moved into its present location and a general milling business entered into. Its increase and its growth from that day to this has been the growth of the town, and what was then simply a waste of unimproved tide flats has now grown to be some of the most valuable property that lies within the incorporated limits of this city. At the inception of the mill company Mr. Post was taken into partnership, and the entire capital which was used in opening the business was in the neighborhood of $2400. Prior to the admission of the territory as a state the tide flats upon which the mill is now located belonged to the Government, and those having made improvements were naturally accorded the first right to purchase these lands, upon the admission of the state. As they had been at work for a number of years filling in about their mill, they were enabled to purchase the ground which they were occupying and have now nine acres in this tract, all of which has been improved as their business has progressed, until, as before stated, it is among the most valuable real estate within the city. Mr. Stetson occupies a very beautiful home on Beacon Hill, a picture of which is shown herewith. He bought it some five years ago from M. H. Young, since which he has made some considerable improvements in the way of additions, and it is considered one of the most charming homes in that delightful section of the city. It commands a very pretty view of Elliott Bay and practically of the whole water front looking north. Today Mr. Stetson is one of the most substantial men of Seattle, and the small capital with which he started has increased from very inconsiderable proportions until he is rated as one of the very wealthy men of this section. The mill plant which he has built up has kept thoroughly abreast with the times and is considered to be one of the most modern and up to date mills in the country. His success has been due, however, to a thorough knowledge of his business and the closest attention to every detail, and although for a quarter of a century he has hardly missed a day from the usual routine of conducting a large milling enterprise, the fruits of his reward are nevertheless pleasant to contemplate, not only by himself, but by those who are intimately asociated with him, and by the large number of personal friends which he has built up during the period in which he has been in actual business here.

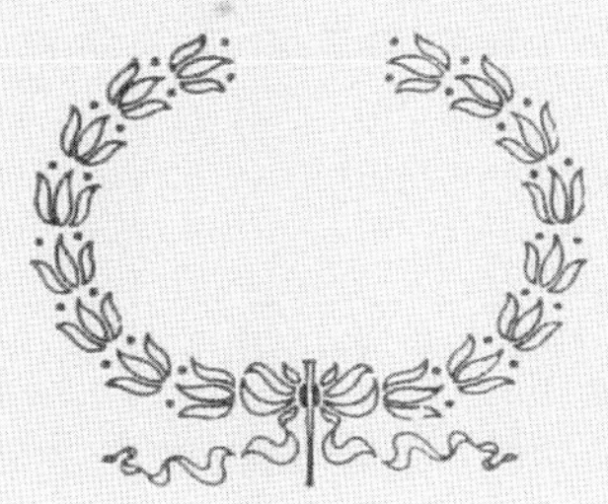

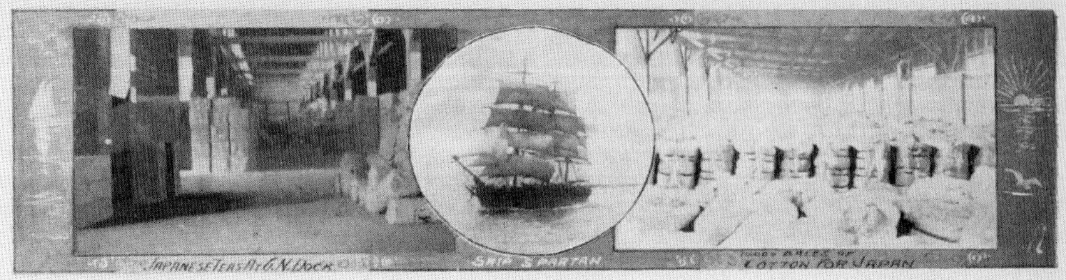

IMPORTS AND EXPORTS IN THE ORIENTAL TRADE AS SEEN AT GREAT NORTHERN DOCKS, THIS CITY.

THE GREAT NORTHERN RAILWAY.

The Great Northern Railway, one of the most extensive railway systems in the world, having a Western terminus at Seattle and an Eastern terminus at Duluth and St. Paul, and, through its allied lines in New York, thus reaching from ocean to ocean, has done more for the settlement of the great West than any other single factor. It was built and operated as a business proposition, and as such is steadily proceeding to aid in developing the great natural resources which are to be found in Washington. Not the least of this vast development lies in the trade yet to be developed with the Orient. The Great Northern was the first to see the possibilities in store for Seattle, its Western terminus, by opening a market in the countries bordering the Pacific, and has steadily pursued a policy which is now developing into very generous proportions. The illustrations at the head of this article will afford an excellent idea of how generous this has already become. In one picture an interior of the Great Northern dock is shown. It shows 10,000 bales of Texas cotton which is waiting to be loaded upon the Oriental liner for consumption by our Western neighbors. In another picture a perfect sea of Oriental merchandise is shown which has just been unloaded from an Oriental liner and which will be consumed in this country. It is thus we have an object lesson in building up trade relations with the people who live just across the water from us. In order to make this trade assume the proportions which rightfully belong to it, the Great Northern is now having built two of the largest vessels ever constructed. They will be big enough to carry the product in a single voyage of the combined capacity of 1,500 cars. With such facilities, and with the possibilities in a country which has upwards of 400,000,000 people, a faint idea can be formed of the future that lies just before Seattle, Puget Sound, and in fact the whole great state of Washington.

Every year there is sent to the Chinese Orient an enormous amount of flour, hardware, manufacturing machinery, salted and canned salmon, condensed milk, structural iron and steel for railroad and other work, cotton, etc. Of these the states of Washington and Oregon supply the flour. Within the last year or two the Chinese people have been brought face to face with the fact that China with its hundreds of millions of people has been outgrowing the ability of its soil to support its people. A commission appointed by the government to solve the problem recognized the advantages of the use of American flour and designated that article as the most suitable food to be added to the Celestial regimen. This has had the effect of increasing the consumption of American flour in the Orient, but where barrels go now, there will be ship loads in the future, for it is only in the large cities that markets for this flour are now found. In the interior American flour is still unknown and it is these markets which the manufacturer must reach. It is here that the millions of people live, that the population is increasing so rapidly, and it is these people, therefore, who must seek the American miller for his flour.

In the state of Washington, tributary to Seatte, Tacoma and Portland, there are nearly seventy mills, with a total daily barrel capacity of about 12,000. Washington is, therefore, easily able to care for the Oriental demand at the present time, and will probably for some time to come. Of the flour mills in Washington, Seattle has four and many directly tributary, and much of this flour is used to fill the Oriental orders. As the demand increases, Seattle must build more mills. She will grow along this line, as she will along every other line, and with shipping facilities—which are sadly lacking at the present time—will become a milling center of more than ordinary importance.

The Great Northern have recently issued a very handsome book under the title of "Greater America," which will be sent free on application to J. W. Blabon, Western Traffic Manager, or to R. C. Stevens, G. N. R. A., at Seattle, Wash.

The Magnificent Train Service.

The trip across America by the Great Northern's "Flyer" from Seattle to St. Paul and Minneapolis, having direct connections with fast trains for Chicago, New York, Boston and all Eastern and Southern points, is a trip of a life time. These trains of the Great Northern are unexcelled for convenience, luxury and speed. The new service just inaugurated is a step considerably in advance of all other transcontinental lines both in the reduction in actual running time and in the very elaborate style which is maintained. Time cards and illustrated information can be secured from all railway and steamship agents, or by writing to J. W. Blabon, or R. C. Stevens, at Seattle.

Furnish Much Information.

The Great Northern, through its General Passenger Agent, is publishing a vast amount of most excellent information in relation to the country traversed by the Great Northern and also about the Orient. Their recent publication, "Greater America," is replete with matter concerning the trade with the Orient and is a most valuable work to possess. It contains the merchant marine of the world, the new colonies of the United States and a lot of other information along the same line. It will be sent free on application to F. I. Whitney, General Passenger and Ticket Agent, St. Paul, Minn., or by J. W. Blabon, of Seattle, Wash.

THE SEATTLE DAILY TIMES.

Nothing could be more apropos in a magazine of this character than a brief reference to the Seattle Daily Times itself, particularly as it has grown to be so much a part of Seattle and Western Washington, and in every sense of the word typifies the character of Western growth and energy. It is unnecessary to go into the early history of the paper save in a brief way. Its early struggles and trials have no part in the period which will be spoken of. Like other concerns, it had its ups and downs. It floundered in an uncertain way, under various managements, until August, 1896, when it passed into the control of the present proprietors, at whose head was Col. Alden J. Blethen, formerly of Minneapolis, Minn., and a man of pronounced newspaper experience. The paper prior to its purchase by Col. Blethen was in no sense a newspaper. Its circulation, as a consequence, was inconsiderable, and its influence next to nothing. The city had a need for a truly representa-

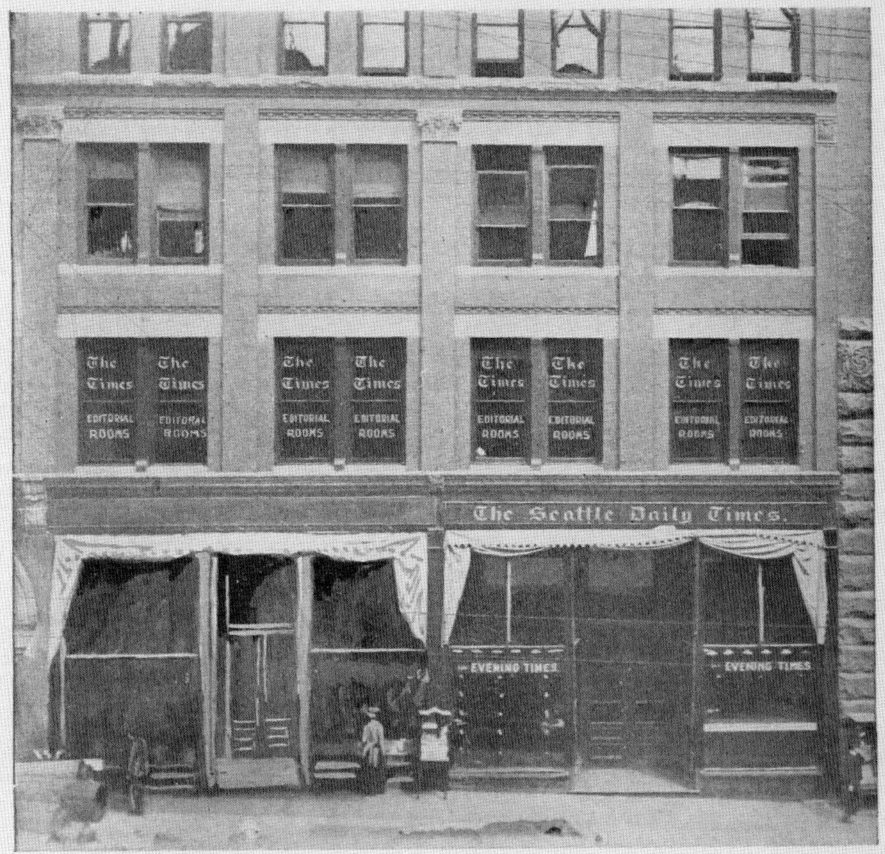

THE SEATTLE DAILY TIMES—EXTERIOR OF THE BUILDING.

tive newspaper, a paper for all the people, and one which, while giving all the news, would be fearless and straightforward in its advocacy of measures in which the general public had an interest. As newspapers are more largely controlled by the great public than any other enterprise extant, their rise or fall indicates most clearly the rating the public gives to them, and hence when the present Seattle Daily Times is held up in comparison to that paper which passed into of Washington. It shows, as nothing else could show, that the people have been given a newspaper in the full sense of the word and that the newspaper has been their friend, that it has stood for all that has been good and fought everything it considered bad. It has been fearless, and it has been vigorous. The man at its head has had the courage of his convictions, and has never been afraid to express them. Coupled with a strong personality has been an intimate knowledge

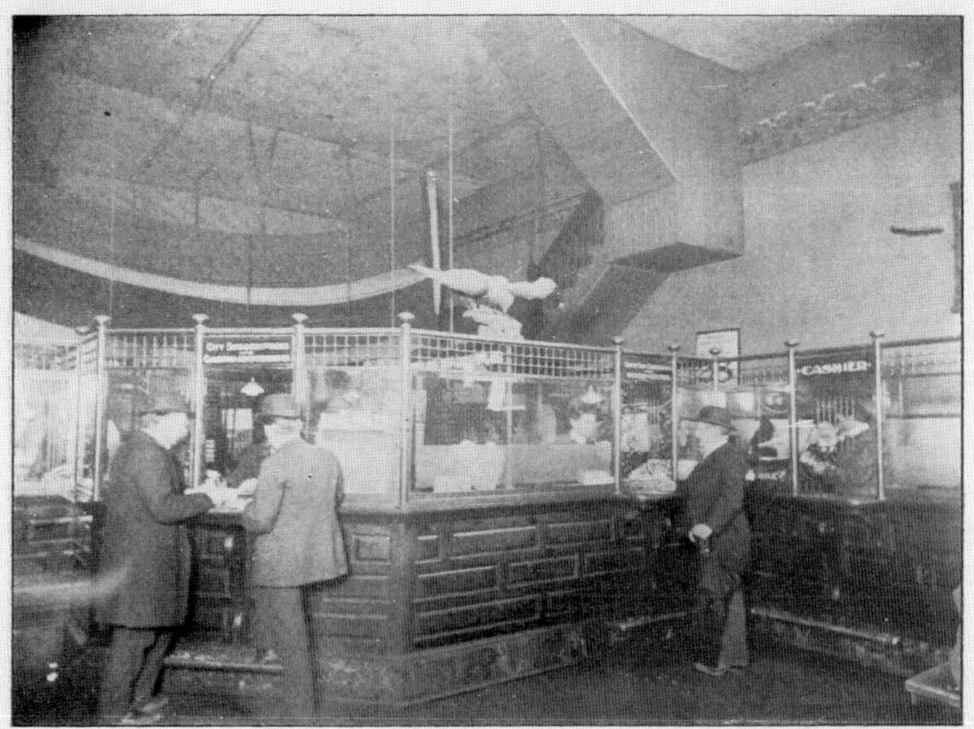

THE SEATTLE DAILY TIMES—BUSINESS OFFICE.

the control of the present owners, in 1896, no better object lesson of the measure of popular favor can be given than to observe first one and then the other. The circulation of The Times in 1896 was but 5,000 copies per day; the circulation of The Times today is 23,000 copies per day. These figures tell a story stronger than columns of type could tell it. It is a mute testimonial of the way The Times has won its way into the hearts of the people living within the great commonwealth of newspaper making. The result is what people see today. It needs no words to tell the story.

The growth of The Times under its present ownership is one of the most conspicuous successes in newspaper publishing which has occurred in the West. It has been one constant climb from August, 1896, to the present. The whole office at first was housed into small quarters on Yesler Way, which would not today be adequate to the room used by the editorial department alone. It was soon found necessary to move, and when the move was made it was to the Boston Block, right into the heart of the city, where the office still remains. The illustrations of the various departments will afford a general idea of how it is arranged, and it will also give the reader some general idea of the magnitude of a plant such as The Times now maintains. There groups, of those in each department are shown. It will be seen that more than 100 persons are thus employed directly producing The Times newspaper, and the expense in salaries alone is very considerable.

As a matter of fact, to publish The Seattle Daily Times requires the expenditure of more than $13,000 every month.

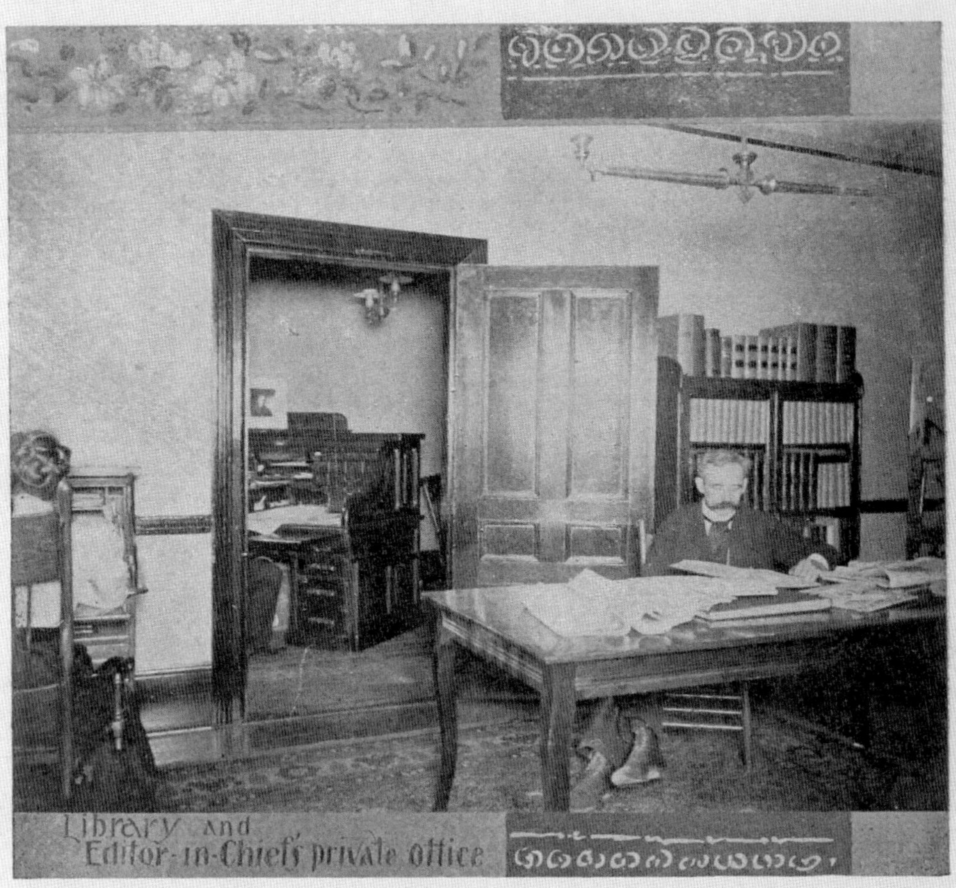

THE SEATTLE DAILY TIMES—LIBRARY AND EDITOR'S PRIVATE OFFICE.

are those, probably, who have but a faint idea of the expense and labor attached to publishing a newspaper such as The Times has grown to be. These illustrations will give them an idea. They include the press room, the stereotype room, the mail room, the composing room, the type-setting machines, the various editorial departments and the business office. Besides these general pictures, portraits, in

The circulation of The Times now extends to all parts of the State, and when the Daily cannot be served to patrons either by agent or through the mail, The Weekly Times makes him a visit fifty-two times a year and serves him with all the news which has previously been printed in the Daily. Thus The Times has grown to be a power in the State, but from the constant growth of its circulation the great public believe in that power and are willing to extend it. They have the conviction that the power of The Times will never be subserved to sinister motives so long as its present owners remain at its head.

The Times has recently added very materially to its equipment and to its general interior arrangement, and today it possesses the most modern newspaper plant in the west. The management prides itself upon the fact that every inch of space is utilized to the best advantage, that the whole space of the office, from the press room to the editorial room, has been laid out with but one central idea—economy of time. In publishing a great afternoon newspaper such as The Times has grown to be, time is everything. Practically speaking there exists but six hours in which the work, under former conditions requiring from twelve to sixteen, is now performed. Therefore in building up the office at The Times every detail in which time could be saved was most carefully observed with the result that few establishments have a more perfect system. This reaches throughout every department.

Recently some additional room was secured on the upper floor of the Boston Block in which a portion of the editorial rooms are located, and an elaborately filled up private office for the editor-in-chief in conjunction with a new appointed library, has been created. These new rooms now afford more adequate quarters, and, as shown in half-tone reproductions, are as fine as any modern newspaper establishment.

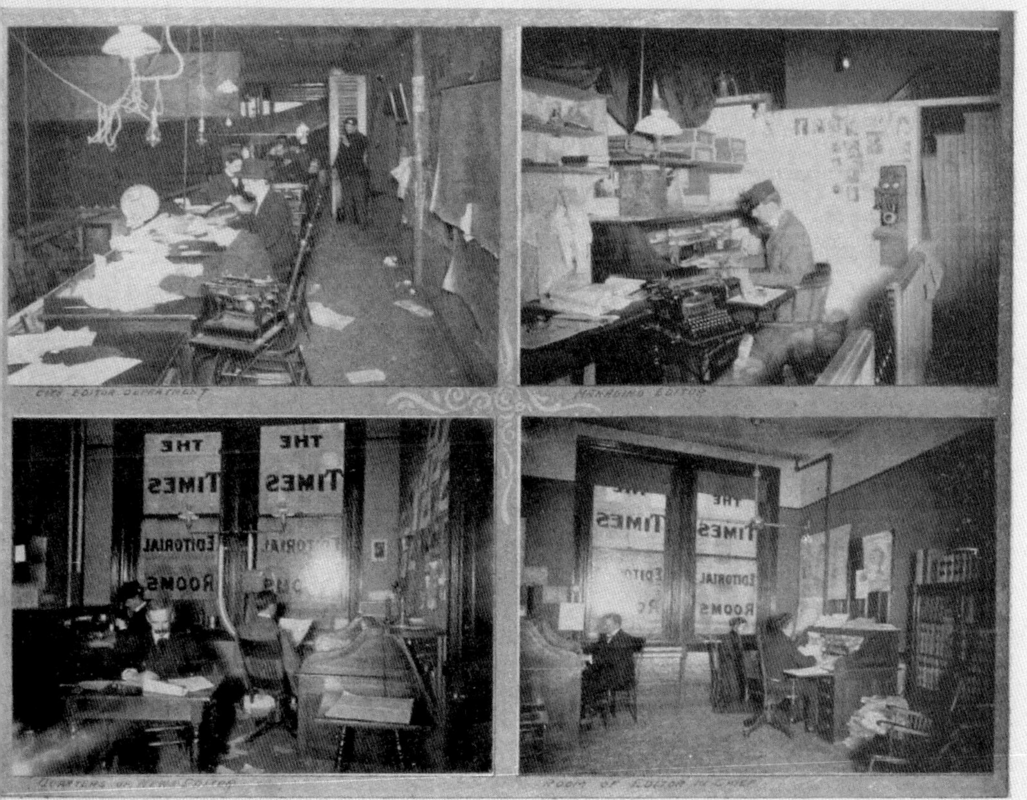

THE SEATTLE DAILY TIMES—EDITORIAL DEPARTMENT.

No single fact demonstrates the strong hold upon the people of the northwest possessed by The Times, so clearly as an analysis of its circulation. There is not a town of any size in any part of

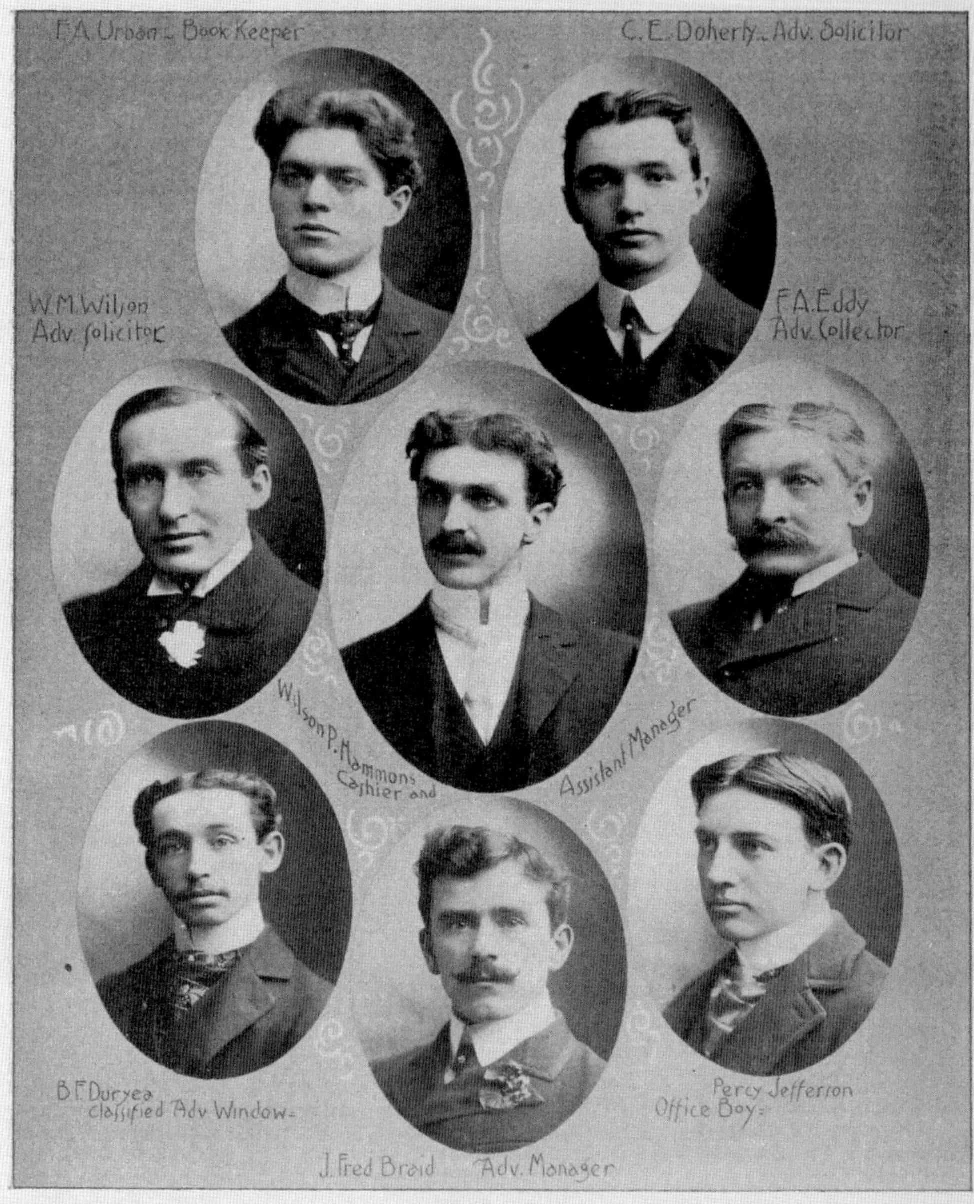

THE SEATTLE DAILY TIMES.

Assistant Manager Hammons and Assistants in Business Department.

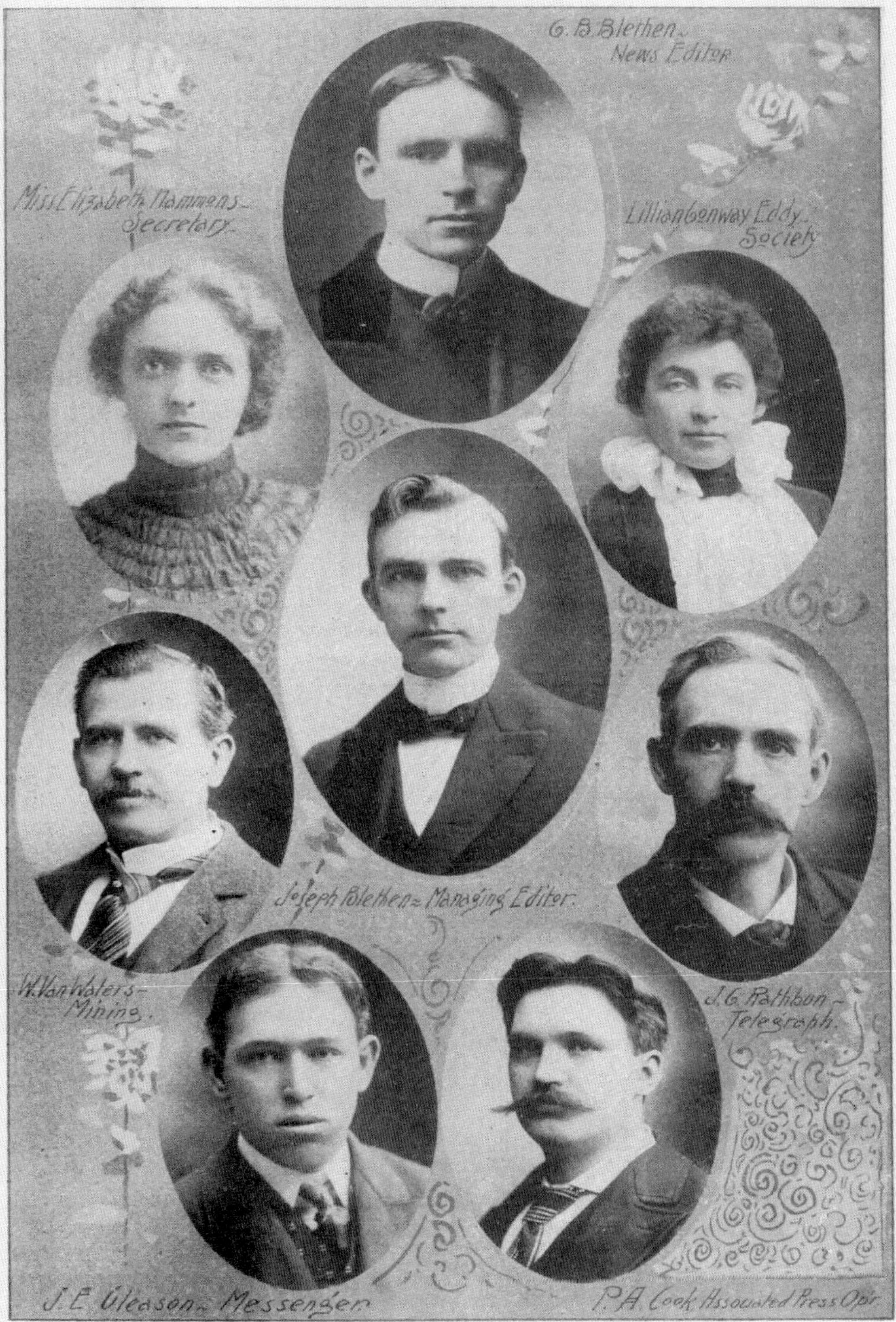

THE SEATTLE DAILY TIMES—MANAGING EDITOR AND STAFF.

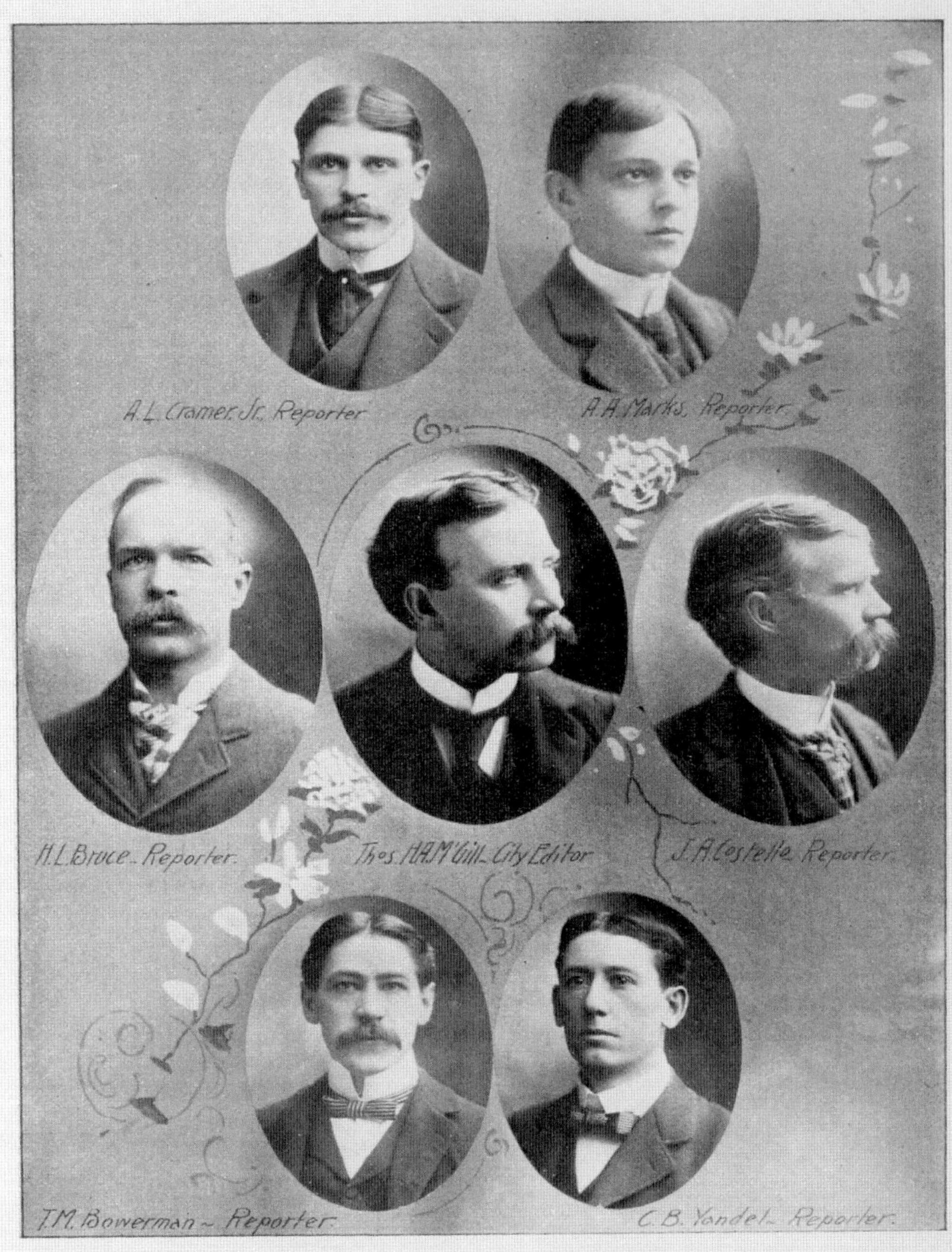

SEATTLE DAILY TIMES—THE CITY EDITOR AND STAFF OF ASSISTANTS.

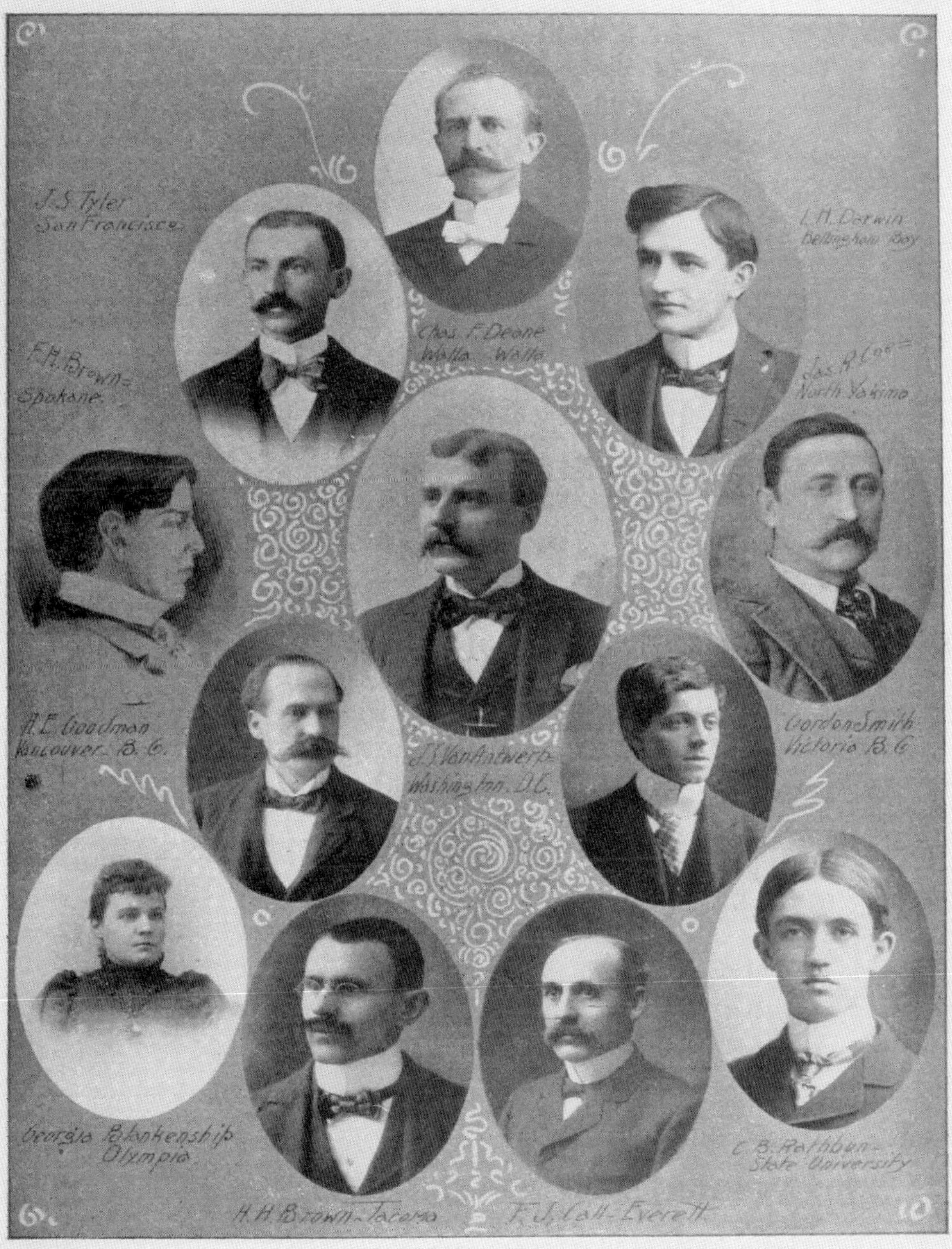

THE SEATTLE DAILY TIMES—STAFF CORRESPONDENTS.

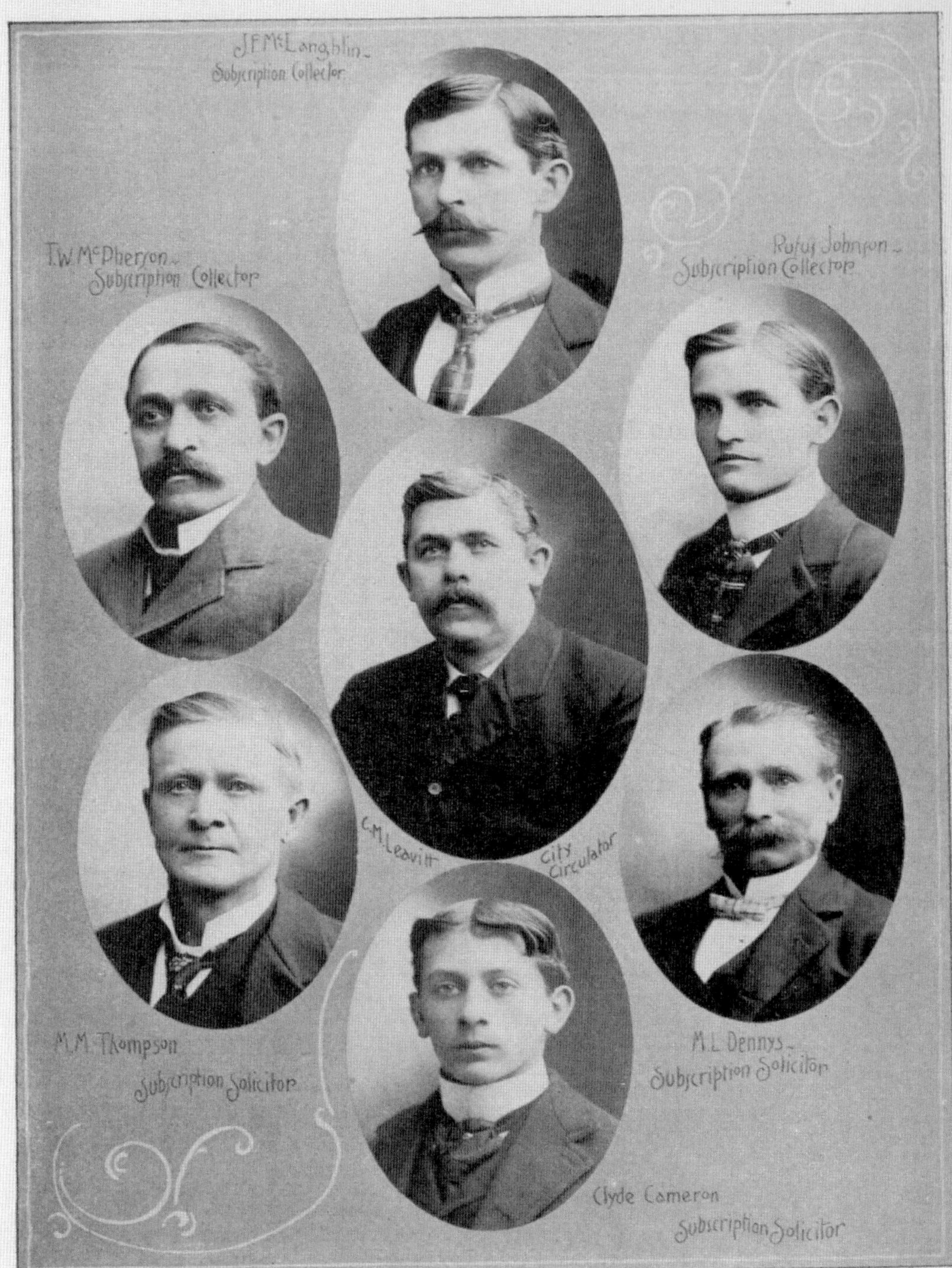

THE SEATTLE DAILY TIMES—THE CITY CIRCULATOR AND ASSISTANTS.

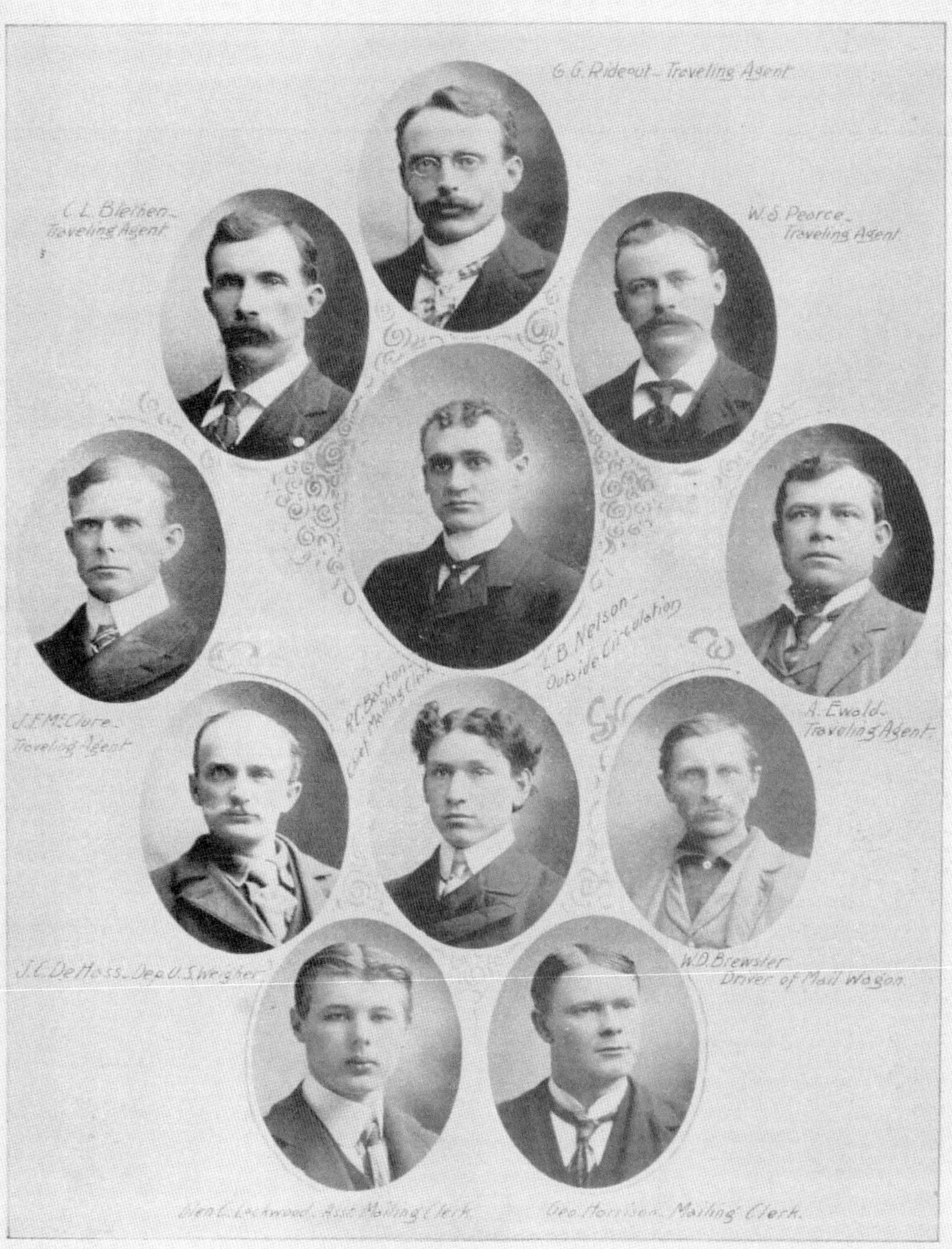

THE SEATTLE DAILY TIMES—THE MEN WHO HANDLE THE OUT-OF-TOWN CIRCULATION.

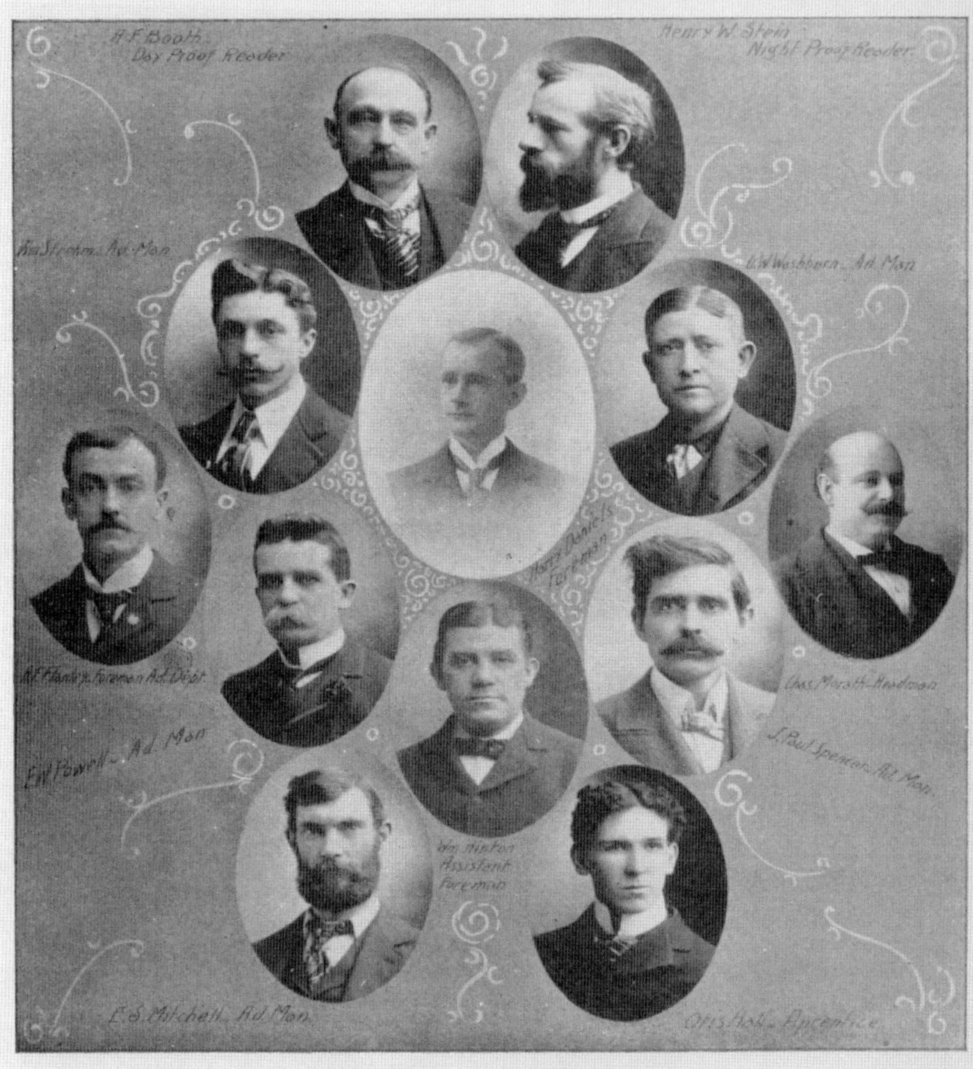

THE SEATTLE DAILY TIMES—THE FOREMAN OF THE COMPOSING ROOM AND ASSISTANTS.

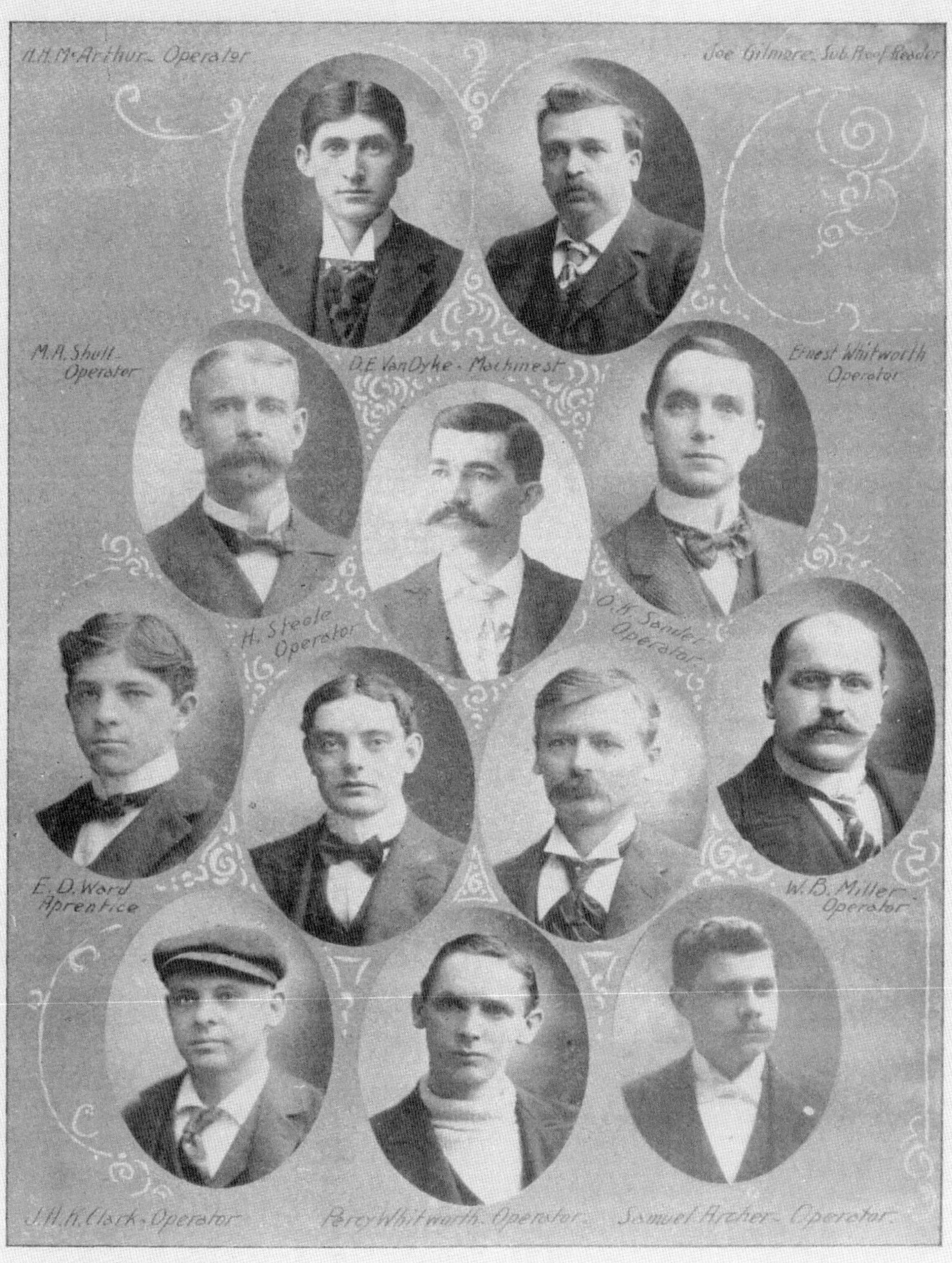

THE SEATTLE DAILY TIMES—THE MEN WHO OPERATE THE LINOTYPE MACHINES.

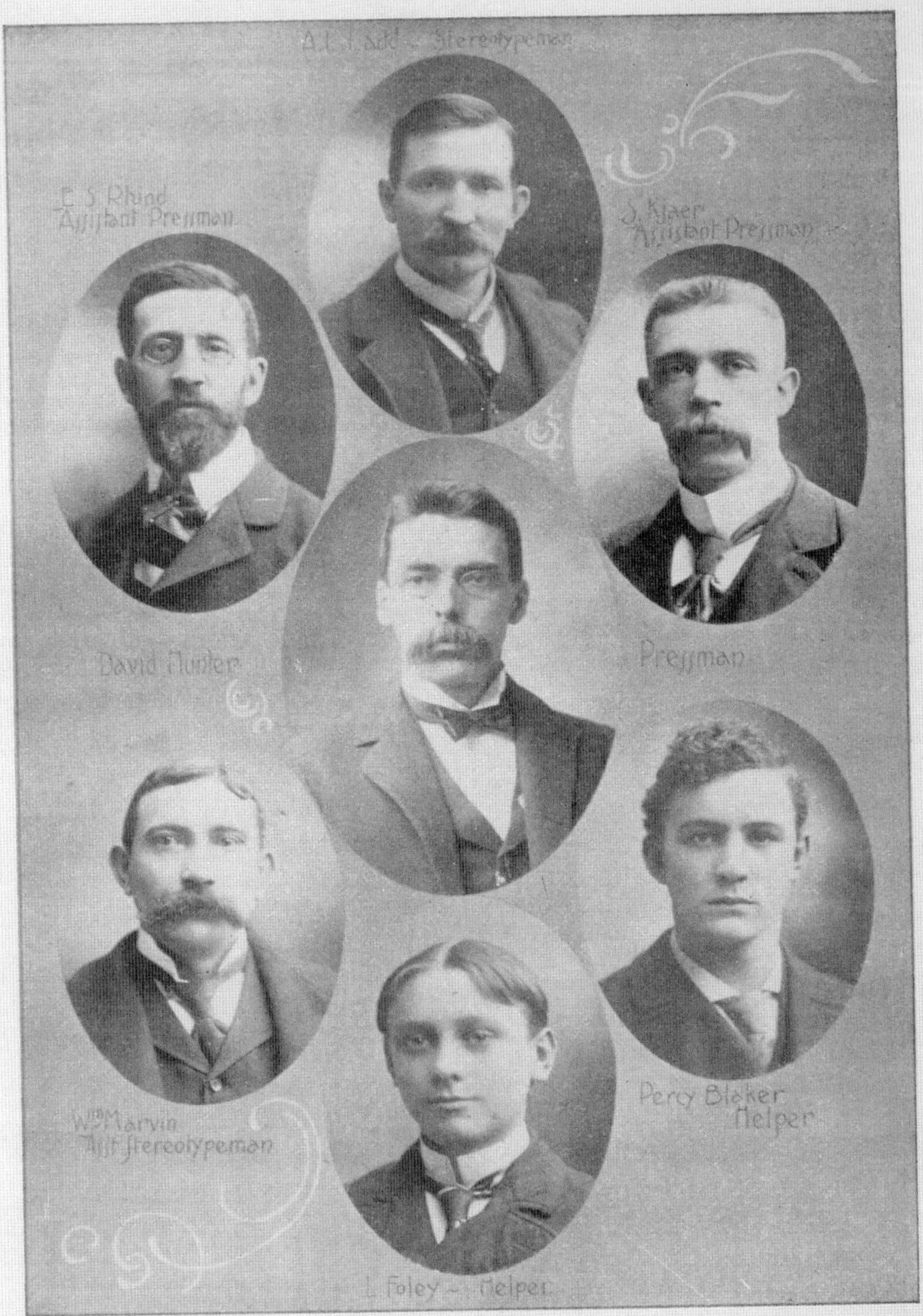

THE SEATTLE DAILY TIMES—THE MEN WHO MAKE THE STEREOTYPE PLATES AND OPERATE THE BIG PRESS

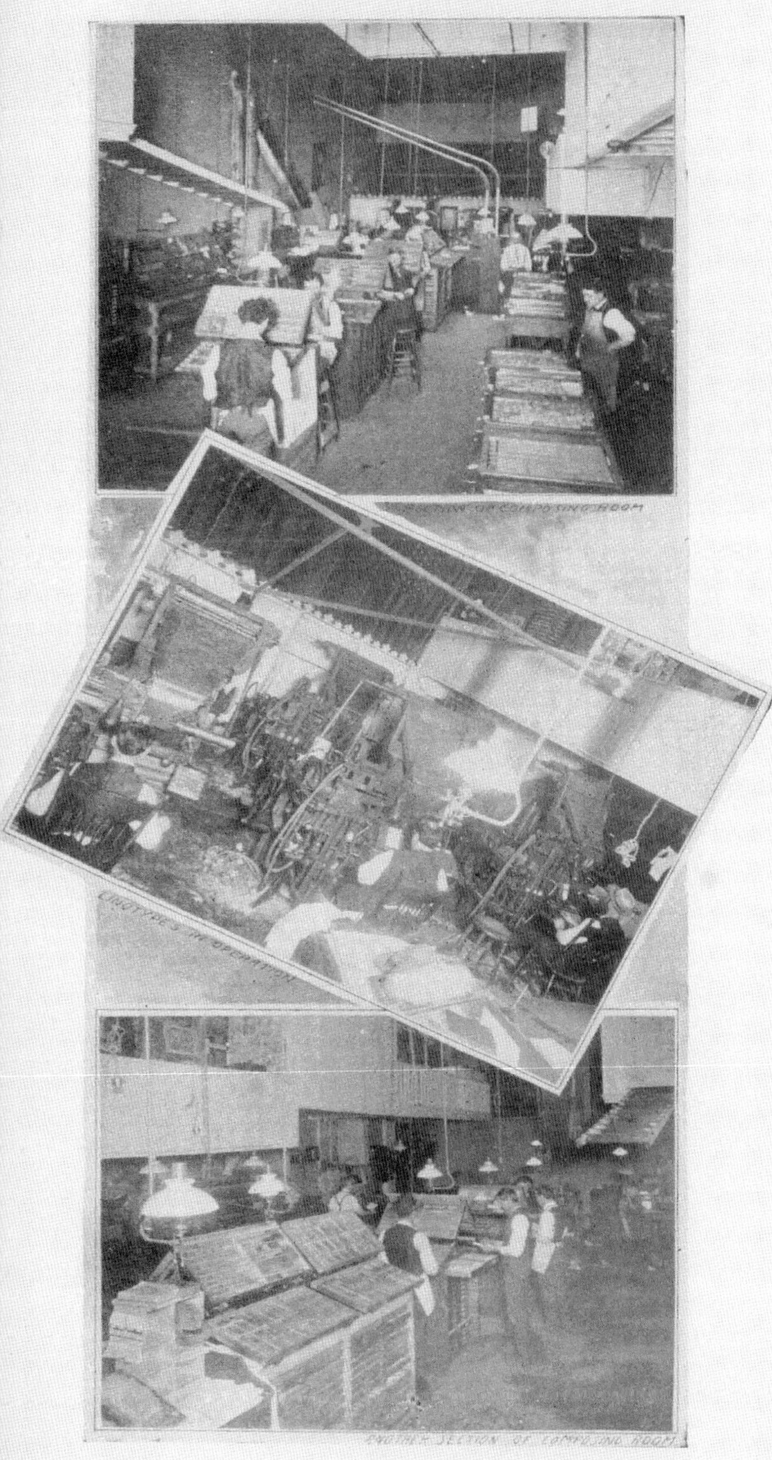

THE SEATTLE DAILY TIMES—VIEWS OF THE COMPOSING ROOM.

this great state where The Times is not delivered by a regular carrier to subscribers the same as in this city, and there is no town even of the most meager importance, or those of the cross-roads order, but have regular readers of The Times, who either receive it through the mails direct or by express or from an agent. No other paper in the northwest, particularly in Washington, has any such circulation. It is therefore, not at all surprising that the paper possesses a wide spreading influence and its advertising space is eagerly purchased at prices considerably in advance of the price paid other papers. It is probably the only paper in the West which has had to refuse the sale of advertising space during the past three months.

It has grown so common with The Times as to no longer create comment for fully three days a week, since the first of January, the sign "no more advertising received for today," has been displayed in the business office by 10:30 in the morning. These are but a few of the numerous indications of the wonderful and steady growth of The Times since it passed into the hands of its present owners. There is one thing which the people of Washington have become convinced of and that is that an afternoon newspaper is the paper of the day and of the future; that it is incomparably superior to the morning paper in every way and is destined to take the lead on the coast from henceforth.

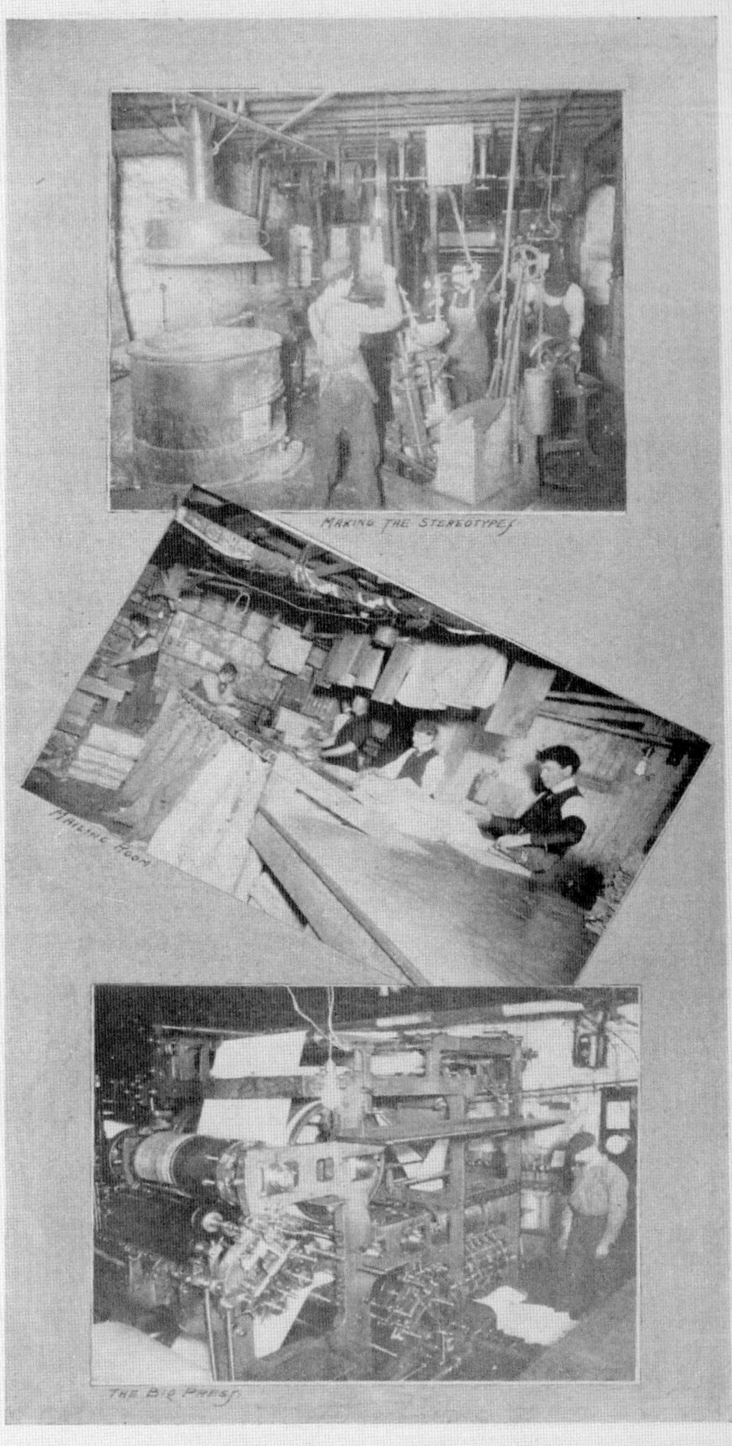

WHERE THE DAILY TIMES IS MADE.

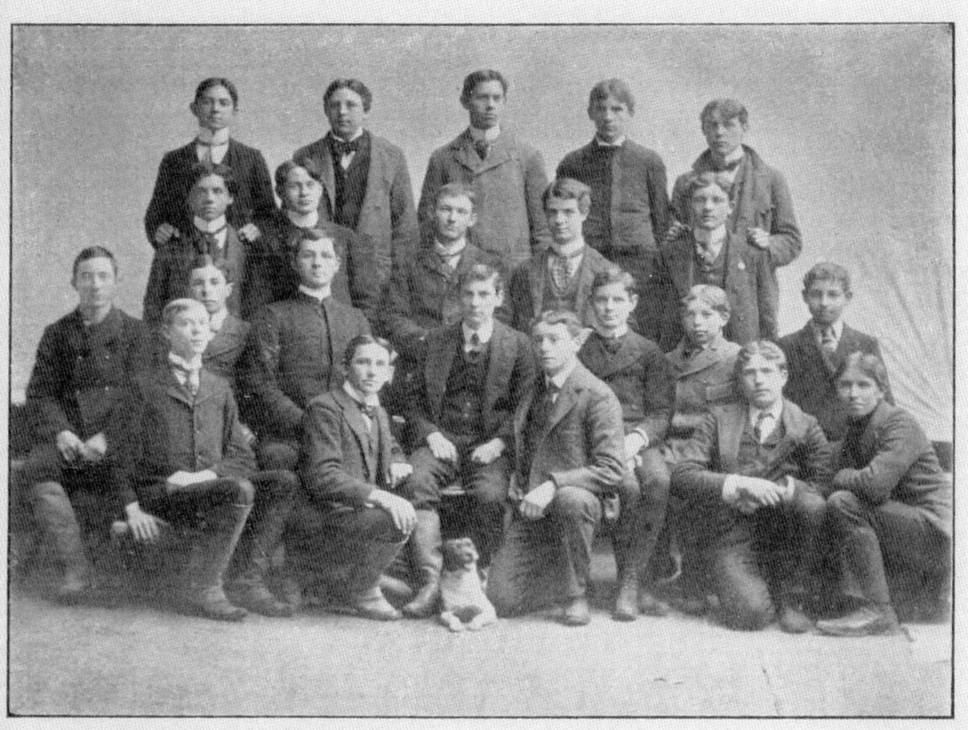

THE SEATTLE DAILY TIMES.
A few of the sixty-five boys who deliver the paper to city subscribers.

INDEX TO CONTENTS.